The Opera of the
Twentieth Century

VISUAL & PERFORMING ARTS

The Opera of the Twentieth Century

A Passionate Art in Transition

WILLIAM SCHOELL

VISUAL & PERFORMING ARTS

McFarland & Company, Inc., Publishers

Jefferson, North Carolina, and London

Library of Congress Cataloguing-in-Publication Data

Schoell, William.
    The opera of the twentieth century : a passionate art in
transition / William Schoell.
        p.   cm.
    Includes bibliographical references, discography, and index.

    ISBN-13: 978-0-7864-2465-8
    ISBN-10: 0-7864-2465-6 (softcover : 50# alkaline paper)

    1. Opera — 20th century.   I. Title.   II. Opera of the 20th
century.
ML1705.S33   2006
782.109'04 — dc22   2006013449

British Library cataloguing data are available

On the cover: Virginia Opera production of *Tosca*; photograph by
Anne M. Peterson, courtesy of Virginia Opera.

Manufactured in the United States of America

McFarland & Company, Inc., Publishers
  Box 611, Jefferson, North Carolina 28640
    www.mcfarlandpub.com

To the memory of my grandfather,
Max Baumann (1873–1922),
who loved the opera

Acknowledgments

I would like to express my thanks to Schirmer (Peggy Monastra) and to Boosey and Hawkes (Jeff Herman and associates) Music Publishers for sending CDs and cassettes of certain operas that have not yet been professionally recorded. And to the Virginia Opera (Stephen J. Baker) for the photograph used on the front cover.

I would also like to thank the staff of the Rodgers and Hammerstein Room of Recorded Sound at the Library of the Performing Arts at Lincoln Center who made it possible for me to listen to some rare recordings that have yet to make it onto CD. And the staffs of the New York Public Library (Jefferson Market) and Westchester Library (Mount Kisco), where I borrowed a great many recordings, librettos, and vocal scores. (I also was able to access many librettos, scores, and recordings at the aforementioned Library of the Performing Arts.)

I queried a number of operatic professionals for their comments on twentieth century operas, and am especially gratified to those few who took the time out to reply: composer Carlisle Floyd; composer William Bolcom; soprano Phyllis Curtin; conductor Richard Bonynge. I have no doubt that both Bolcom and Floyd may want to wring my neck for certain comments I made about their operas, especially Bolcom, but let it be known that I respect anyone who even attempts the difficult task of composing an opera.)

I wish to tender my appreciation to Eve Goodman, who was involved in the early stages of this book, and to the folks at McFarland.

Also thank you to Caroline Schoell; Lawrence Quirk; and Carol and Thomas Altomare. Last, but certainly not least, a special thank you to Barbara McCullough, who has been a friend of mine and my family's for many years, and whose passion for opera is infectious. Barbara has lent me many opera tapes and videos over the years — we have also seen many operas together — and shared many a conversation about the operatic art that has helped inform these pages.

Table of Contents

Introduction

Writing a book about one hundred years of opera is a daunting task.

I could have easily put together a book on the most famous operas of the century and left it at that, but that seemed not only inadequate but unfair. Some of the most memorable operas of the last century aren't performed with any regularity in the world's great opera houses, if they're performed at all, and some of the most famous can be, as heretical as it sounds, rather forgettable. Luckily I have always been interested in the esoteric opera, the little-known gem, the hard-to-find collector's item that will never show up at the Met or elsewhere, so my task was simplified. But I decided to extend my search into a land of operas that even I had never heard, or even — in rare cases — heard of. Then the decision had to be made as to which of these operas — the famous and the not so famous — would be included in this volume. There are some that are simply too well-known, admired, or controversial to be ignored. And then there were those that I felt the public should be made more aware of. (If I excite one reader about an opera that he or she may not have known about but will grow to love, I have accomplished an important part of my goal.)

This book is written with that public in mind, not the critic or musicologist, although even they may find some value in this volume. By and large, musicologists approach opera from a very different direction than the general opera-going public, and they have a perfect right to do so. This explains why some academicians and professional musicians greatly admire certain operas that leave (most of) the public cold. There are those who approach opera on an emotional level, and those who approach it from an intellectual (often pseudo-intellectual) level, and the two groups only on occasion converge. To this writer, opera is one of the most passionate of all art forms, and a coolly intellectual approach (not to be confused necessarily with a scholarly examination) — while not without merit — can sometimes miss the point. In other words, the musicologist, so busy studying and admiring the finer, often mathematical, points and pathways of the score, can miss the forest for the trees. One can analyze to such a point that

1

one no longer hears. This book is always concerned with this question: it may be very clever, revolutionary, precise and brilliant, but — simply put — how does it sound? Therefore I will rarely go into what we might call the infrastructure of the music but rather describe how it will sound to the educated lay person's ear as well as which sections in particular deserve special attention. This should also explain why I devote more pages to certain composers who may not be "fashionable" in the eyes of some members of the musical establishment and fewer pages to more "trendy" — if that is the word — living composers such as Philip Glass. Very few composers get their own chapters, but those that do, deserve them. Sadly, there are those who have a disdain for Puccini, but the fact remains that his operas may be more popular and more performed than any other composer's with the possible exception of Verdi. His output was also prodigious. The work of Pietro Mascagni, next in line as Italy's most important post–Verdi composer, is overdue for serious reevaluation, and his many twentieth century operas are fully covered in this volume. Strauss and Prokofiev get many pages, which is not surprising considering their output — especially vast in the case of Strauss — and importance. I recognize that there are fans of other, more recent composers who will wonder why one or more of their favorites didn't get a whole chapter or more discussion but I hope they will ask themselves, no matter how wonderful these composers are, if their output and importance puts them on the same level as Puccini or Prokofiev.

One thing that must be made clear from the outset is that this is not a book about "modern" opera. It is about operas of the twentieth century — the entire twentieth century. Of course I have included discussion of quite a few modern operas in the book, but I had to be quite selective. There is hardly a local opera company in the United States or abroad that doesn't present "world premieres" of one or two or more brand new operas that are heard and seen by a limited number of people and then are never heard or seen again. Undoubtedly some of these might well be worthwhile pieces, but it is simply impossible in one volume to cover them all or even most of them. Looking at the entire twentieth century — from a global perspective no less — I had no choice but to be choosy.

Composers of the twentieth century worked hard to find their own voice, one that did not simply borrow from the traditions of the romantic composers of the nineteenth century, and they achieved their goal to varying degrees of success: "modern" music — and modern operas — were born. Romanticism may have become terminally ill in the twentieth century, but, as we shall see, it was simply too powerful to ever die completely. Occasionally embers of romanticism still ignite and flare when least expected. The ultimate irony: today, in the twenty-first century, some of the "modern" composers, so enamored of dissonance and so fearful of being emotional to the point of soap opera, sound positively romantic. An even bigger irony: the "modern" composers were often not the first to break away from "old-fashioned" musical conventions. In fact, you'd be surprised who broke the rules long before they did.

In this volume I have decided that a twentieth century opera is one that premiered in the twentieth century, so there will be a discussion of many different composers and many different styles, both romantic and modern and assorted variations. On rare occasions there will be a discussion of an opera composed in the late nineteenth century that was buried away for decades until it resurfaced during the twentieth. (And I have reserved the right to discuss the occasional operetta and Broadway show, for some of our musical treasures are certainly a form of American opera.) I have also included composers whose careers began in the nineteenth century but still came out with a solid body of work in the twentieth. This, of course, includes Puccini, many of whose greatest operas first appeared in the 1900's. Richard Strauss' first opera premiered in the nineteenth century, but all of the rest are legitimate twentieth century works. Of all the major composers (those with a large body of work) discussed in this volume, only Prokofiev's operatic career genuinely began in the twentieth century (his first opera, *Maddalena*, was composed in 1911, although it did not actually premiere until 1979 and then on BBC radio). Add to that short list Benjamin Britten, whose "music dramas" polarized the opera-going public. No other twentieth century composers have been quite so prolific or so successful. (And neither Prokofiev nor Britten has ever been as popular as Puccini.)

This is as good a point as any to mention that I have tried to keep my discussion of operas in roughly chronological order according to the date an opera premiered. The aforementioned *Maddalena*, for instance, is discussed in the chapter that corresponds to when it premiered in the 1970's. If the dates of operas sometimes seem to skip ahead alarmingly for something written with chronological order in mind, it is because I tend to lump the works of a particular composer together unless the premiere of one of the operas is many, many decades distant from most of his other works (as is the case with *Maddalena* and several others).

To some the twentieth century is a wasteland of atonal, tuneless, blathery scores that are vastly inferior to the great "number" operas of Verdi, and the magnificent, infinitely influential canon of Richard Wagner, not to mention the beautiful, intensely theatrical operas of Puccini. A surprising number of twentieth century composers (but not all of them, thank goodness) forgot the very basic tenet that opera was about singing. Too many of them wrote film scores — however wonderful the music — instead of operas. Soaring vocal lines became monotonous, unmelodious "sung-speech." A massive irony of twentieth century opera is that as recording techniques became increasingly sophisticated, opera composers seemed to become less and less interested in writing music that one might want to listen to repeatedly. This book will examine and explain how and why this change came about, and how it affected the very way that many people see this wonderful art form.

But let's remember that (a) Puccini and many of his romantic, tuneful brethren were still operating — rather gloriously — in the twentieth century, and (b) that some of these unfairly excoriated modern operas written by other composers, no matter how "different" they may be, have a genuine and distinct value of their own. In this volume I have tried to separate the musically memorable wheat from the deadly, "too 'clever' for its own good" chaff. The world of twentieth century opera is not a "wasteland," by any means, because — running as it does all the way from Puccini's *Tosca* and Charpentier's *Louise* up to Heggie's *Dead Man Walking* and Corigliano's *The Ghosts of Versailles*— it has something for every taste imaginable.

In the world of opera, as in everything else, let us celebrate diversity! Read on. There'll be operas you love and operas you hate. Things that you yourself might never label "opera" in a million years and operas you're prepared to despise but that may offer you a pleasant surprise or two. And vice versa.

Aren't we just glad we have opera at all!

Long before the twentieth century, in the late 1500's in Florence, aristocrats of the Renaissance created *dramma per musica* (drama through music). Taking classical Greek dramas, they reinvented these great plays by emphasizing the more poetic passages and underlaying them with a few simple chords. As monologues and dialogue scenes began to be sung instead of spoken, gradually recitative came into being. What today we might call incidental theater music soon turned into a part of these theater pieces that was considered every bit as important as the story and words. In this way opera — original plays with singing — was born, although they were still modeled on Greek tragedy.

Jacopo Peri's *Dafne*, written in the final days of the sixteenth century, is considered the first opera, but not a trace of it remains. *Euridice* (1600) by Jacopo Peri and Giulio Caccini, has survived, but it was not as influential as Claudio Monteverdi's *Orfeo* (1607). Monteverdi introduced arias which allowed the audience to hear the characters' inner feelings. The action on stage would stop dead as the singer delivered his or her song. There were choruses and orchestral passages that underlined the action or covered up a change of scene. By the mid–seventeenth century, opera's appeal blossomed from the aristocracy and it had become a popular art form. Operas had originally been presented only in private performances to the very rich, but now there were many opera houses throughout Italy that were open to the public; the very first opera house, Teatro San Cassiano, opened in Venice in 1637. All these centuries later the feeling persists in many people that opera is a performing art that can only be appreciated by the rich, or at least only by Italians, although "common folk" have been enjoying it for over three hundred and fifty years.

With *The Coronation of Poppea* in 1642, Monteverdi abandoned Greek tragedy–style stories and turned to the rich history of his own country. Other composers such as Cesti and Cavalli composed operas in which the dramatic recitative became less important than the aria, which had grown more lyrical. Arias were all the rage, and so was spectacle, at least in court for such special events as royal weddings. Things were still scaled back in the regular opera houses, so there was a kind of class distinction still at work. The term "opera" (which means "work" in Italian) was in popular usage to describe this new type of music and theater by 1650.

By the eighteenth century, the singer was held in even higher regard than before. This was the period of the super-star castrati, such as Farinelli, boys castrated in youth to retain their lovely soprano singing voices. The orchestra and even the story became less important than the singer. Arias were there to showcase the singer's talent, not to help move the story forward nor to illuminate character. Audiences came to see their favorites perform, almost as if in concert. Operas contained little action or movement, and the dramatic element was greatly diminished if not done away with altogether. One of the greatest composers of this period was George Frideric Handel (1685–1759), a German composer whose Italian-language operas premiered in London.

Ironically, it was again a work about Orfeo that changed things, this time German-born Gluck's 1762 opera *Orfeo ed Euridice*. Now there was more action, a narrative structure of sorts, to an opera, and the arias became part of the story as well. The music followed suit, and was tailored to the story and characters, not just the singer. In the late 18th century Wolfgang Amadeus Mozart (1756–1791), another German, became one of the most formidable creative forces in the world of opera. From that moment on Germany would become a leading producer of operas and operatic composers, with German operas looked upon as being more unified and less about pretty singing. France would also produce some fine operatic works, and other countries as well. But throughout the nineteenth century there would be a raging battle between proponents of the Italian style and the German style, culminating in the great Wagner versus Verdi Wars. There would also be skirmishes in Italy between those who preferred opera seria (serious or tragic operas) with those who preferred the newer opera buffa (comic operas).

In the early 1800's came operas composed in what would become known as the "romantic" style, the most famous early example being Carl Maria Von Weber's *Der Freischütz*. Romanticism, a lusher kind of music with perhaps greater expressiveness from an orchestra employing larger forces than before, took hold, not only in Germany, but in Italy, France and elsewhere. In France, German-born Giacomo Meyerbeer wrote a series of French "Grand Opera" spectacles in the early to mid–nineteenth century. The Italians and Germans followed suit.

As the nineteenth century proceeded, *bel canto* (pretty singing) masters such as Rossini, Bellini and Donizetti dominated Italian opera. The stories were much more elaborate, however, more melodramatic (when they weren't farcical, as in many of Rossini's opera buffas), and there was much more action on stage. Giuseppe Verdi came from the tradition of bel canto, but his music added a new degree of intensity. In Germany, Richard Wagner did his own take on opera (or "music drama") and practically reinvented the orchestra. Where other composers used themes, certain musical phrases, to play behind and signify certain characters or ideas, a kind of musical label that didn't alter, Wagner used and, to some, perfected *Leitmotifs* (leading motives), altering the structure of these themes as needed to fit the change in dramatic situations. Both Verdi and Wagner were geniuses, but while the former did not necessarily break any new ground (although he was certainly influential in his way), Wagner changed the way all future composers — and not just in Germany — looked not only at opera but at music in general. During their lifetimes the opera-going public was torn between the two, with most opera fans hating one and loving the other; there was no middleground. Today we can recognize that these two giants left behind a body of work that would be hard for any modern composer to ever surpass.

We'll turn to a literary metaphor to put the these two major nineteenth century composers into perspective. An opera by Verdi is like an accessible, well-written commercial bestseller that a talented author has tailored to popular tastes. An opera by Wagner is like the literary novel that is not for every taste, not as accessible, but is well worth the extra work it takes to understand it.

Meanwhile in France, Russia, and elsewhere, operatic composers were not exactly idle. Such figures as Charles Gounod, Camille Saint-Saëns, Jules Massenet, Pyotr Tchaikovsky, Modest Mussorgsky, and many others were practicing their craft and creating works of lasting importance. In Italy,

Amilcare Ponchielli, who taught both Puccini and Mascagni, developed a style that was quite different from Verdi's. His music was more flowing, slower, less rhythmic, influenced perhaps by the French style of Gounod and others. In Ponchielli, of all Italian composers of the period, the orchestral accompaniment was as important as the vocal line. And the melodies soared at a statelier tempo. Ponchielli would influence many of the Italian composers who came after him. In the works of Puccini and other late 19th century composers the scores would become increasingly symphonic, with longer and longer sections turned over to the orchestra alone.

A major change in opera came about in 1890 with the premiere of Pietro Mascagni's masterpiece *Cavalleria rusticana*, considered the first *verismo* (realism) opera. Although verismo was not a new form of music but was squarely in the romantic tradition, it did have far-reaching consequences. Verismo operas focused not on gods, mythological figures, or kings and queens, but on the average contemporary man and woman and their problems, generally of a sexual, romantic, or violent nature.

Georges Bizet's *Carmen* (1875) is sometimes classified as the first verismo opera, but there are two problems with this theory. Verismo had as much to do with musical style as it did with storyline, and Bizet's style is not in the veristic idiom. Also, can a famous toreador be considered an "average" person? Eventually "verismo" did come to encompass stories about kings and queens as well as characters in period settings, the musical style being more relevant than the subject matter. A cursory examination of verismo will lead the listener to believe that the verismo style is exclusively melodramatic, with nothing but exclamatory vocal writing — and while this is certainly a part of verismo it does not take into account that many verismo operas also have a delicate, tender side to them. Some critics have dismissed the music of *Cavalleria* as being "raw" and "crude" (it eludes these critics that Mascagni, whose music could be quite subtle and sophisticated when called for, was, after all, writing an opera about *peasants*), but this misses the point of verismo entirely. It was supposed to be the stuff of real life, in all its pettiness, sordidness, and emotional intensity. With its sweeping melodies, variety of dances, choruses, brindisi, ballads, and sublime arias, not to mention its famous intermezzo, it's no wonder that *Cavalleria* changed the direction of opera for more than a decade or two.

So successful was *Cavalleria* that the last decade of the nineteenth century and the first decade — or longer — of the twentieth was full of verismo operas composed not only by Italians but by Germans, Russians, and even the French. One example of French verismo (although its musical style was quite different from Italian verismo), Gustave Charpentier's influential *Louise*, ushered in a new era of frankness in 1900. Things would never be the same after that. After the rage for verismo petered out, there were new trends and experiments for composers to explore, some welcomed by the public, some not. There would come a clash of cultures and voices and musical styles — romanticism versus modern, tonalism verses serialism, traditionalism versus experimental — all straining for dominance, each composer struggling to assert himself and convince the public that his new kind of music was what everyone had been waiting for.

The wait is over. Let's explore.

1. Giacomo Puccini, Genius of Melody

Now that we're in the twenty-first century let us hope we can put to rest the tiresome and unwarranted attacks from certain critical quarters on the works of Giacomo Puccini (1858–1924), who has for over a century paid the price for his popularity. To put it plainly and simply, Puccini was a genius. Some critics attack his work as "vulgar" because it lacks subtlety, but while subtlety certainly has its place, it can be vastly over-rated in the opera house, which is, after all, one kind of theater. Verdi and Wagner were not exactly subtle either, but few people would have a problem placing them on a par with Mozart. Puccini was damned by some short-sighted critics because his music was too beautiful; how could it have substance, they wondered, how could it endure in intellectual terms? In music appreciation courses (at least in the United States) Puccini's name and music were never heard, largely because Puccini's work was almost exclusively for the stage; there were no major symphonies or experimental tone poems in his oeuvre. Millions of students grew up thinking "Puccini" was a type of Italian cheese, which is exactly how his detractors would describe him. Besides being beloved by the public, most of his operas are masterpieces and they boast not only surpassing melodic superiority and consummate stage craft, but a deft musical intelligence that is all but absent in sniggering composers whose work betrays not one tenth of Puccini's staggering ability. Frankly, this writer believes that many critics are far more enamored of Puccini than they let on, but are too afraid of seeming old-fashioned, un-hip, or — horrors!— anti-modern to admit it.

Puccini was born in Lucca to a musical family. His own interest in music was cemented by his seeing a performance of Verdi's *Aida* in Pisa when he was eighteen. In Milan at the conservatory he studied with the composer Amilcare Ponchielli, and became acquainted with several musicians, such as Pietro Mascagni and Ruggero Leoncavallo, who were to become his rivals. Puccini became quite close to Ponchielli, whom he found particularly helpful. Another one of his professors was Antonio Buzzini, who had composed an opera named *Turandot* in 1867.[1] After composing *Le villi* and *Edgar*, Puccini had his first real success with *Manon Lescaut*. His first twentieth-century opera was *Tosca*, which premiered in 1900 and takes place in Rome one hundred years earlier. Originally Alberto Franchetti had been going to do a version of *Tosca* but he relinquished the rights to Puccini.[2]

The evil chief of police, Scarpia, lusts for the singer Floria Tosca, and seizes his chance to take her when he arrests her lover, the painter Cavaradossi, for helping a political prisoner escape. Scarpia tells Tosca that she and Cavaradossi will have safe passage out of the country if she sleeps with him, but Tosca, repulsed by his suggestion, stabs him to death instead, after first securing his promise that the firing squad executing Cavaradossi will shoot blanks. When Tosca discovers that Scarpia lied to her and Cavaradossi is not faking his death, she commits suicide.

With this horrifying and tragic opera — two artists destroyed by the venality of one evil and self-absorbed individual — Puccini is generally at the top of his form. While it is not necessarily his best or most beautiful score, it is a very adroit and compelling one. *Tosca* begins with a blaring, brassy, almost dissonant burst of sound that probably sounded like the height of vulgarity to contemporary critics although many modern operas begin in such a fashion (albeit in a less skillful manner). Act one highlights include "Quale occhio al mondo," a soaring duet for Cavaradossi and Tosca in which love and jealousy (and the affectionate indulging of it) take equal measure. Scarpia and Tosca have interlocking arias with his "Tosca divina," in which he uses honeyed words and tones to hide his true putrescence and the sweet words and music behind the gentle bells are ironic contrast to his actual nature; and her "Ed io venivo a lui tutta dogliosa," a "torch song" opera style, as Tosca angrily sings of her alleged betrayal at her lover's hands (all, of course, manipulated by Scarpia). Scarpia's "Va, Tosca" sung to the Te Deum at the end of the act, is a truly magnificent piece which boldly unveils Scarpia's sexual obsession and how the gratification of it matters more to him than anything else. While the number is obviously meant to contrast his evil with the (alleged) goodness of the Cardinal passing by, the mixture of religious and sexual fervor almost makes the piece seem to be celebrating his sensuality and hypocrisy, or at least suggesting that "evil" can run neck in neck with religion. In act two, the entire torture scene, beginning with Scarpia's "Mario Cavaradossi, qual testi momo il Giudice ui aspetta," is excellent, building in suspense and dread, as Scarpia again talks "sweetly" to his object of lust as her lover, unbeknownst to her, is taken to the torture chamber. Here begins a grim ascension to tragedy as Scarpia sings "No; ma il vero," the notes rising with very dramatic tension, this tension not released until Tosca gives Scarpia the location of the escaped prisoner Angelotti and Cavaradossi, learning that Napoleon's forces have defeated the royal troops, sings out "Victoria! c'è un Dio vendicator!/Thou spirit of vengeance awake!" Tosca's "Vissi d'arte," sung as she wonders why this horrible fate has befallen a woman who has only lived for love, God, and Art, is perhaps the first great aria of the twentieth century. Especially when it's interpreted by a superior artist, this piece is almost unbearably poignant. This poignancy continues in the musical interlude as Scarpia writes the safe-conduct for Tosca, the music turning almost joyous as Tosca stabs Scarpia to death with a cry of "Here is Tosca's kiss!" While Scarpia is a truly loathsome human being, one can admire some aspects of his gleeful hedonism.

Caravadossi's act three aria "E lucevan le stelle/when the stars were shining," tries to be like *Andrea Chenier*'s famous act four jail aria and almost succeeds, but is not as beautiful nor as heartbreaking as Giordano's piece. Cavaradossi and Tosca are then given two successive duets which were originally written for *Edgar*; both are memorable if not outstanding. Their third duet, "Sparve il duol," is too brief and too reminiscent of *Manon Lescaut*. However, the martial music behind the firing squad as Tosca sings "Com' e lunga l'attesa" with nervous energy is excellent. The romantic and martial music of act three underline the tragedy, the waste of two lives, by the very fact that their tone is in such contrast to the terrible events that transpire.

Puccini's most famous opera, *Madama Butterfly*, premiered in 1904, but what became known as the original "La Scala" version was not a success, probably because claques formed by jealous rivals did their best to boo at key moments. Puccini revised the opera more than once — there are the so-called Brescia and (definitive) Paris versions — but the differences between each version is not really as pronounced as believed. In each Captain Pinkerton arranges for a marriage to a Japanese girl, Cio Cio San, but doesn't take the relationship as seriously as she does. After Pinkerton returns to sea, the American counsel tries to prepare Cio Cio San for the fact that Pinkerton may never return, unaware that she has given birth to a child. Cio Cio San waits years for Pinkerton to return and complete the happy family but when he does he has an American wife at his side. Pinkerton and his wife importune Cio Cio San to let them have the child to take home with them. Cio Cio San commits suicide just as Pinkerton realizes too late the monstrous way he has treated her.

Musically, *Madama Butterfly* is a high-water mark for Puccini. In act one Pinkerton is given a wonderful duet with the American consul Sharpless ("Dovunque al mondo") in which the American sings about wanderlust and whiskey and states his love 'em and leave 'em, girl-in-every-port credo.

The thoughtful and compassionate Sharpless counsels that "it's an easy creed that makes life enjoyable but saddens the heart." He suggests to Pinkerton that Cio Cio San's "sweet little voice should not utter notes of sorrow." The famous love duet proper begins with Pinkerton's "Viene la sera"; its first sublime stanza is his "Bimba dagli occhi pieni di malia," a beautiful duet of exquisite tenderness within a duet of strong erotic passion, with the music (quite possibly modeled on Wagner's "Liebestod") rising in orgasmic waves. (Puccini is somewhat influenced by Wagner in other sections but never to any great extent.) The original La Scala version of this duet is longer but not as effective; in the revised version that we hear today the blocks of text are broken up into different musical sections. "Un bel di/One fine day" in act two, in which Cio Cio San sings of the day her beloved Pinkerton will return to her, is one of Puccini's loveliest and most poignant arias. One of the most powerful moments in the opera is when Sharpless asks Cio Cio San what she would do if Pinkerton never returned, and she rushes out with her child in her arms so that Sharpless, who had been unaware of the boy's existence, will realize just what is at stake ("E questo? ... e questo?"). The music rises in a crescendo of thunderous emotion, splitting the air like bolts of electrifying lightning as Sharpless is made fully conscious of Cio Cio San's mammoth devotion to Pinkerton and their child. (Some conductors criminally rush through this particular phrase, thereby stripping it of all dramatic value.) "Che tua madre dovra" is another beautiful piece given to Cio Cio San as she wonders what will happen to her and her child; the very dramatic wind up was originally written for La Scala's more intense lyrics, where she sings about death. Some of the major arias in *Butterfly* are so exquisite that you can easily overlook the less dramatic but notable pieces such as the duets between Cio Cio San and the underdeveloped character Suzuki. The humming chorus that bridges acts two and three may seem minor and even monotonous to some listeners, but to most it comes off as very haunting and effective. The splendid intermezzo that opens act three has a marvelous section where the sun comes up (as sailors briefly sing in the background) and birds begin to chirp, an ironic note of hope in a new day that brilliantly contrasts with the tragedy to come. Other highlights include the trio of revelation ("Lo so che alle sue pere") sung by Sharpless, Suzuki, and Pinkerton, as Suzuki realizes that Pinkerton is not really coming back for good, Pinkerton realizes that Cio Cio San did not forget him but indeed "counted all the days and hours," and Sharpless begs Suzuki to help them break the news to Madama Butterfly and cushion the blow. The duet between Pinkerton and Sharpless ("Addio, Fiorito asil") was added to the score after the 1904 premiere. It gives Pinkerton an added opportunity to show remorse and excoriate himself for his callous, unthinking treatment of the Japanese girl. Then there is Cio Cio San's heart-breaking final aria to her son before she commits suicide ("Oame sceso dal truno dell'alto Paradiso"). Although the original version of "Madama But-terfly" has been performed and recorded, the differences between it and the definitive Paris version (aside from the love duet) are minimal. Pinkerton and Kate are really no worse in the original version that in the Paris revi-sion. Kate was just as compassionate in the 1904 version, and Pinkerton — although a callous jackass in the opening of all versions — repents and feels anguish at the end of the original and in the revisions. He does come off a bit as an "ugly American" — but again in all versions. It is in David Belasco's original play that Captain Pinkerton is at his most loathsome.[3]

Although Puccini's next opera, *La fanciulla del West/Girl of the West* (1910) has never achieved the popularity of *La Bohème* or *Butterfly*, it is one of the composer's finest achievements. Also based on a play by David Belasco, it takes place in California during the gold rush. Minnie, the owner of a bar, is beloved by the miners, especially the sheriff, Jack Rance. When a stranger named Dick Johnson shows up at the bar, Minnie has no idea that he is in reality the wanted bandit Ramerrez. When she learns the truth, "Johnson" tells her that circumstances led him into a life of crime, but that he is essentially decent. Johnson is captured, but Minnie begs the miners not to hang him, and the two are allowed to leave together to start a new life. The first major piece in the opera is "che faranno i vecchi miei," one of Puccini's most inspired pieces, a heartbreaking anthem of not only home-sickness and despair, but utter loneliness. It starts out as a song sung by the minstrel Jake; the miners join in, eventually raising money as they sing for the heartsick Larkens to go home to the family he misses so desperately. What's especially interesting about the number is that it is a fine display of tenderness and compassion among men, grizzled miners no less. Then there comes a rhapsodic theme for Minnie as she makes her entrance, separating Rance and Sonora, who are fighting over her. The love theme, some of whose phrases remind many people of the vastly inferior "Music of the Night" from Webber's *Phantom of the Opera*, first appears when Johnson and Minnie dance offstage at the miners' urging; the men gently hum a light, faster version of the tune. It becomes a full-fledged aria when Johnson sings "Quello che tacete." Johnson also sings an arioso to Minnie's theme "No, Minnie, non piangete." Time is severely compressed in act two — every-thing seems to happen so quickly, including Minnie's encounters with John-son, Rance, Johnson's being shot etc.— but it's all quite dramatically viable. When Johnson asks Minnie for a kiss ("Un bacio, un bacio sola!") the music becomes temporarily sinister, forecasting that Minnie is soon about to acquire unpleasant knowledge of the man's background. Minnie does not automatically accept Johnson; in fact, she essentially throws him out of her house once she learns the truth. Only when he is shot does she insist he come back inside. Johnson gives a somewhat specious explanation of his life of crime in the soaring "Una parola sola!" He rationalizes that taking over his father's gang was simply fate. When he swears in act three that he never murdered anyone, a miner counters that if that's the truth "it was only chance that stopped you." Johnson wins over the miners with "Ch'ella mi creda libero e lontano," because he and the men are united by their love of Minnie. Johnson never wants Minnie to know that the men have hanged him; let her think he escaped to a new, better life, he tells them. This scene summons up some fascinating questions. Is he really thinking of Minnie — or what Minnie thinks of him? Or does he realize that Minnie will need the miners when he never returns and she will hate them if she knows the truth? The opera ends with an evocative duet for Minnie and Sonora, the others joining in, as she reminds the miners of all she has done for them and they either agree or argue about whether or not to let Johnson go. The "happy" — or more accurately bittersweet — ending has Minnie and Dick ride off together as all of the lonely miners — not just one of them as in the opening — give in to their despair.

Strangely, the music of *La fanciulla del West* is redolent of even more sensitivity and tenderness than the score for *Butterfly*, possibly because in *La fanciulla* the romance is two-sided. Despite the fine arias and choruses mentioned above, *La fanciulla* isn't really a "number" opera (it is to Puccini what "Falstaff" is to Verdi), one reason why the public has not embraced it as strongly as *Butterfly* and *La Bohème*. Minnie is a gutsy, sad, strong, entirely admirable heroine, one of the most memorable in opera. (Perhaps the most unusual thing about her is that she does not die at the end!) Dick Johnson/ Ramerrez — the thief with a heart of gold, redeemed by the love of a good woman — is rather unreal, but also romantic, appealing and memorable. *La fanciulla del West* is an opera about loneliness and romantic longing, the need for a person who can be all things for you. Minnie needs a man to "take her away from all this," Johnson a "good woman" and her influence, and the miners need and love Minnie as lover figure, mother figure, sister and friend. The opera works wonderfully and is profoundly moving on the level of romantic fantasy. A closer inspection of the libretto could make one wonder why Johnson couldn't have simply rejected the "family business' after he learned the truth about his robber-father's occupation. In real life, of course, men like Johnson with their charm, dash and sex appeal are often irresistible to a certain type of woman and, unfortunately, usually wind up destroying them. It is also interesting that Minnie can forgive Johnson for being a road-agent, as she calls it, but can't forgive his having taken her first kiss; later she is attracted to him for the very same reason. In act three the miners also tell Johnson that they can forgive him for stealing their gold, but not Minnie's heart.

Puccini's *La rondine/The Swallow* premiered in Monte Carlo in 1917. *La rondine*, like *La fanciulla*, is another (even less realistic) romantic fantasy, with both the man and woman seeking one special monogamous love. Young, naive Ruggero comes to Paris and meets Magda at a hot spot, where she conceals the fact that she is kept by Rambaldo, a friend of Ruggero's father. Meanwhile Magda's maid Lisette is having an affair with the unctuous Prunier, who in public harps on his superiority to her. Magda decides to take a chance on finding happiness with that one special love and runs off with Ruggero, but when he talks of marriage and meeting his mother, she realizes a relationship with him will never work, and leaves him heartbroken. Never considered one of Puccini's top operas, *La rondine* has been steadily gaining in popularity over the years because of its tuneful score. The German Karltheatre had originally commissioned a Viennese-style operetta from Puccini, but he counter-proposed a through-sung piece in Italian. (World War One put paid to the plan to premiere the work at the Karltheatre.) Using Viennese operetta as his model, Puccini clearly set out to prove he could write superior (to operetta) music and just as clearly succeeded. The score of *La rondine* positively bathes you in rich buttery romanticism, as if Puccini were determined to overwhelm the listener with one passionate melody after another. The music is superior to the fairly poetic and serviceable libretto which, like the opera, could not be labeled "large-scale." If there's any problem to the music it's that it lacks variety and is occasionally superficial. But those melodies...!

In act one we have Prunier (later Magda's) aria "Chi il bel sogno di Doretta," which sets up the whole conflict of the story. In Prunier's song, the maid Doretta refuses riches from a king because "no gold can buy me happiness." Magda spontaneously contributes the second verse. Doretta is unhappy because a student's kiss awakened passion in her and she longs for its fulfillment. Magda is then give a long aria, interspersed with recitatives ("Ore dolci e divine") in which she thinks back to the happy moment she had with her own student, whom she hasn't seen in years; Ruggero reminds her of this young man from long ago. When Ruggero arrives at Rambaldo's house (he doesn't meet Magda until later) he sings a soaring valentine to the city of Paris, "Parigi." The wonderful music of act two includes a duet for Magda and Ruggero ("No ... restate ... restate") which blossoms into a lilting waltz number with the entire cast joining in. Another rhapsodic duet quickly follows ("Perchè mai cercare di super") as the couple, having just revealed their names, sing of the strong feelings they've awakened in each other. One of Puccini's finest pieces is the subsequent love quartet/brindisi sung by the two couples (Prunier and Magda have arrived at the club) and taken up by the chorus of customers watching them as they powerfully declare their love, the music as full of poignancy and pre-destiny as it is hope, romance and passion. The music of act two is literally intoxicating, creating an atmosphere in which you can believe two strangers can instantly fall in love and personify each other's fantasies, as often happens under the influence of alcohol. As the act comes to a close, a distant voice sings a deceptively up tempo coda ("nella trepida luce d'un mattin"), warning that the dawn will "dispel the enchantment wrought by the moon"—and liquor no doubt. Act three boasts the ravishing final duet "No! Non lasciami solo!" which resonates with regret and anguish as Ruggero sobs and begs a determined Magda not to leave him. In another version of the libretto, Rambaldo shows up in act three to try to tempt Magda back, singing a jaunty little aria about swallows. Ruggero learns of Magda's background in a reply to a letter and rejects her, whereupon she commits suicide. Marta Domingo, who staged this version for Washington Opera, could not see Magda going back to Rambaldo after finding true love at last. Despite its beautiful score, La rondine was a commercial failure for Puccini.

The following year Puccini's trilogy of one acts, Il trittico—one melodrama, one tragedy, one comedy—premiered at the Metropolitan. The first opera, Il tabarro/The Cloak is a compelling work of verismo about a group of Parisians leading lives of the proverbial "quiet desperation." In Giuseppe Adami's poetic libretto, violence is always lurking just below the surface. Michele and his much younger wife Giorgetta (shades of "Pagliacci") live and work on a barge on the Seine. The couple are still mourning the loss of their child, and Giorgetta has sought some comfort in the arms of Luigi, one of her husband's employees, who wants her to run away with him. Michele is suspicious of Giorgetta and determined to discover who her lover is. Catching Luigi on the barge when he comes for a rendezvous with his wife, Michele strangles him to death and hides his body in his cloak. He shows the corpse to Giorgetta who screams in horror. This description of the plot may make Il tabarro sound like a crass shocker, but it is so full of well-realized characters, humanistic touches and that ever-present desperation that clings to every note that it is a prime example of operatic tragedy.

Puccini's fine score is a constant flood of melody. Tugboat whistles add to the haunting spell of loneliness and that certain note of "trouble ahead" cast by the overture. Luigi and others sing a delightful mini-brindisi; Giorgetta and old Tinca dance to a lovely cockeyed waltz; Tinca complains that without drinking and carousing "You'd kill the joy of life!" There's a quote from La Bohème as the song vendor/minstrel sings about the sad story of

"Mimi." In a bit of forecasting Giorgetta at one point sings "the sun is drenched in blood." The first major aria arrives with Luigi's "Hai ben ragione," a powerful anthem of the ultimate hopelessness and futility of life, and more forecasting of his early death. (If there is any problem with this aria is that it expresses the sentiments of a tired, defeated, middle-aged man, not a youth of twenty.) Giorgetta sings a contrasting aria of hope via love and in remembrance of the joys of the past and the confidence that those joys can be recaptured. This aria is reprised shortly afterward and turns into a duet with Luigi; the lovers are back to hopelessness, united in grief, then ecstasy as they think of the past and each other. Although they sing of their mutual hometown, the music reflects their passion for each other, how being together will somehow bring about a better life for both of them. The music is then full of cat-crawling suspense as the lovers surreptitiously discuss their plans. Just as Giorgetta says "If he knew, he would kill us both!" Puccini inserts a big sudden boom like the crack of doom and reprisal. It is during Giorgetta and Michele's informal duet "Perchè, perchè, no m'ami più" that we learn of the death of their baby; the duet climaxes as we learn of how terribly the pair have been affected by it. Michele's "Resta vicino a me!" wherein he asks his wife "why do you drive me from your heart," is a powerful outcry of abandonment and fear, so raw in its emotion that it's almost painful to listen to. When Giorgetta reminds Michele that both of them are older and have changed, Michele insists that he would rather not believe it. Right after this interchange, two young lovers come on to sing a brief romantic ditty in a nice touch of ironical counterpoint. Puccini composed two versions of Michel's climatic aria, "Nulla! Silenzio!" in which he wonders which man is his wife's lover ("your death will end my anguish") and both are equally good. While not as good as its obvious model, *Cavalleria rusticana*, (if only because *Cav* has more variety and therefore richness to its music), *Il tabarro* is still in every way a masterpiece.

The second one-act of the evening, *Suor Angelica*, another of Puccini's great tearjerkers, is pathos par excellence. Sister Angelica has been pressured into a convent by greedy family members after becoming pregnant. She has hoped that they have taken good care of her child, but a callous aunt comes to tell her that the child is dead. Sister Angelica believes that the child would have survived had she been there to care for it. She takes poison, wishing to join her child in heaven, but realizes as she dies that her act of suicide may bring her not only eternal damnation but never-ending separation from the child. She sees a vision of the Virgin Mary with her child, and knows (in her mind at least) that she is forgiven and will join the child in paradise. *Suor Angelica* is full of beautiful music, such as the transcendent, sublime orchestral passages that play as the nuns go off to recreation. We hear the delicate theme of the virgin Mary for the first time as one sister mentions that "the virgin is watching." In her resplendent aria "Senza mamma," Sister Angelica blames her absence for her child's death, her religious delusion the only thing that prevents her anguish from being totally devastating. (In an earlier passage, Sister Angelica remarks of another nun, "If she laments, more severe will be her torments.") Her "La grazia è discesa, dal cielo" is a paean to the Virgin Mary, as the nun is caught "under the spell of a mystic exaltation," which is certainly reflected in Puccini's music. We hear the rhapsodic Virgin Mary theme again as the sister takes the poison. The nuns, who are terrible gossips, tell us all we need to know about Angelica's background. Like the miners in *La fanciulla*, they have compassion for the one among them who suffers so much of homesickness, and pray that the visitor who comes this day will bring her news of her family (a prayer that is answered to the nun's bitter regret). *Sister Angelica*, another story of a decent person destroyed by venal forces, is another small masterpiece from Puccini.

Although not on the level of the first two operas of the evening, *Gianni Schicchi* is possibly the most performed of the trio. Puccini was wise to know that a comedy was certainly needed after the performance of the depressing *Suor Angelica*, and *Gianni Schicchi* is genuinely clever and amusing. In Florence the members of a family are in a dither because their wealthy patriarch, Donati, has left all of his money to the church. Rinuccio gets the idea of asking his girlfriend Lauretta's father, Gianni Schicchi, an old but crafty reprobate, for his advice. As no one knows the patriarch has died, Gianni comes up with the idea of taking his place in the death bed and dictating the new terms of Donati's will. He leaves various heirs certain items, but the bulk of Donati's fortune goes to — Gianni Schicchi! The relatives are outraged but must keep silent, as the penalty for faking a will is rather severe.

Musically, Puccini was only flexing his muscles with *Gianni Schicchi*," which really doesn't call for the kind of dramatic arias he was famous for. Still, No Puccini opera is without its delights and *Gianni Schicchi* is no exception. Rinuccio is given an aria, "Avete torto!" in which he importunes family members to stop being so snobbish about newcomers to Florence (including his future father-in-law, Schicchi), whose fresh blood and intelligence can only make Florence blossom further. Lauretta's "O mio babbino caro," in which she begs her father to intercede so that she can marry Rinuccio, has become one of Puccini's more famous melodies, if for no other reason than its generally baffling use in television commercials. The aria is proof that Puccini can write in a "lighter," simpler style and still come up with a lovely and effective melody. Gianni is given a notable piece ("Addio Firenze") in which he reminds the family what will happen if their deception is discovered — a hand chopped off and exile! On the whole *Il trittico* is an evening at the opera house well-spent.

Puccini's final opera, *Turandot*, premiered after his death in 1926. This was based on a fable of a Chinese princess, Turandot, who asks all potential suitors to answer three riddles. If they cannot do so, they are beheaded. Calaf, the disguised Prince who is the hero of the story, initially hates Turandot — until he gets a look at her and is instantly smitten. Not even the display of the severed head of her last suitor can keep him from attempting to win her hand, to the horror of his father and the faithful girl, Lui, who loves him. Calaf manages to answer the riddles, but, Turandot, a sore loser, wants out of the deal. Calaf allows that if she can discover his true identity before morning he will pay the same price as her other suitors. Turandot goes so far as to have Liu tortured to learn Calaf's name. Still enchanted by the icy princess, Calaf tells her his name just before dawn, but Turandot shocks the court when she tells them "his name is love!" Calaf has finally won the princess' heart.

Even more than *La fanciulla*, *Turandot* is characterized by continuously melodious recitatives, if you can even refer to them as such; everything in the smoothly flowing score is so well integrated that it often seems like a number opera without any recitatives at all. Puccini used certain themes from Chinese songs and developed them in his own Italian style. He does away with an overture or prelude and gets right into the action with the reading of the Mandarin's death decree. The soaring, majestic music of the crowd continues into the "first" encounter between Liu, Calaf, and his father. The chorus sings a haunting song to the moon ("Perchè tarda la luna?"), which adds a strange note of sweetness to the grisly proceedings. This piece ends with the moon/Turandot theme, and blends into the equally haunting Children's Chorus ("La sui monto dell'Est"), suggesting the princess's appearance will bring on the Spring. There is a couplet comprised of Liu's lovely aria of desperation over what Calaf plans to do ("Signore, ascolto!"), and Calaf's response ("Non piangene, Liu!") in which he implores her to continue looking after his father. The entire act is musically rich and builds up to a great dramatic climax with Calaf determined to ring the gong (which will signal his interest in taking the challenge of the three riddles) and everyone else frantically trying to stop him. In act two the music of the minister Pang, Pong, and Ping as they decry their role in the executions, moan over how things have changed since the birth of Turandot, and how they miss their homes and former lives, is quite good, especially their homesick song ("Ha una casa nell' Hunan'), while the fast, rhythmic, exciting, almost bouncy (yet still majestic) music they dance to after they come out of their reverie (that this time Turandot may finally fall in love) is wonderful. In the second scene of act two Turandot sings of her possession by an ancestor who was slain by one of the empire's conquerors ("In questa Reggia"), leading into the gorgeous second half ("Na! Mai nessun m'aura!"), in which she proclaims that "never shall man possess me!" This outstanding piece is matched by the Imperial Hymn sung near the end of the act. Act three's centerpiece is the famous "Nessun dorma"— one of the cornerstones of Great Arias — as Calaf remarks that "no one shall sleep" until the Princess finds out his identity. Lui, who truly bears a selfless (or masochistic) love for Calaf, is given a sweet aria ("Principessa l'amore") in which she tries to explain to Turandot that her love is strong enough to endure any torture. Working from a libretto that he altered slightly, as well as from Puccini's notes, Franco Alfano skillfully completed the love duet for Calaf and Turandot, which is in two parts. The second half simply uses the music of "No! mai nessun...." Puccini himself used several actual Chinese songs for inspiration in other parts of the opera.

Many *Turandot* fans are a bit distressed with the ending of the opera, wishing that the ice princess had gotten her comeuppance instead of a lifetime of supposed happiness with Calaf, although the fact that he tells her his name and is willing to die for her (as Lui was for him) indicates he may not try to dominate Turandot as she fears. You lose all sympathy for Turandot, who understandably does not trust men due to the fate suffered by her ancestor, when she orders Lui, an innocent woman, to be tortured for what she knows. Turandot's aria "Del primo pianto," which is generally cut in performance, supposedly convinces the listener that her change in attitude toward Calaf is sincere, but it may not humanize the woman quite enough. Perhaps the story is above criticism and shouldn't be taken too seriously because it is, after all, a fairy tale.

Despite his great success, Puccini could be deeply distressed by criticism and by the failure of some of his works (such as *La rondine*). There were critics who thought he was lazy, coasting on his popularity by writing operas of limited scope and intellectual interest, that he failed to grow as an artist. One critic, Torrefranca, launched an especially vicious attack on Puccini and claimed "He is not a musician; he does not create art."[4] This was particularly disturbing to Puccini as the attack came during a fallow and depressing period in his life. Although many readers thought Torrefranca was way off the mark, his essay was widely quoted with lip smacking glee by those who were jealous of the composer. In a dark moment even Puccini referred to his music disparagingly as "sugary," which was equally off the mark.

When Richard Strauss once claimed that he had never stayed through to the end of one of Puccini's operas, a friend of his began to wax enthusiastically about the beauty of *La Bohème*, prompting Strauss to say "Ja ja, very beautiful, all melody, all melody." He told another friend. "Everyone thinks I'm hostile to Puccini. It isn't true. But I can't listen to his operas because if I do I can't get the melodies out of my head afterwards. And I can't write Puccinian Strauss."[5]

When Verdi heard Puccini's first opera *Le villi* he found the symphonic element "dominant" and disapproved. Ironically years later Puccini himself would say "People believe symphonic music must rule, and I, on the other hand, believe that this means the end of opera. In Italy, people sang; no more. Crashes, discordant chords, faked expression, diaphanous stuff, opalescent, and lymphatic. All Celtic diseases — true syphilis from across the Alps."[6]

Although Puccini eventually triumphed over all of his detractors and rivals, becoming not only one of the most popular operatic composers from Italy but from the world in general, in his day, like all successful people, he worried about staying on top. He saw each defeat — an opera's failure, too many years without the premiere of a new work, the triumph of another composer's opera — as a sign that he was slipping. One of the most irksome things he had to deal with was the perception that his chief rival, Pietro Mascagni, who'd become famous long before Puccini, was considered by many of their countrymen to be the greater artist.

But Mascagni was to have his own troubles.

2. Pietro Mascagni, Prince of Passion

After Puccini, the most important post–Verdi Italian composer is without doubt Pietro Mascagni (1863–1945). During his lifetime Mascagni was seen as Puccini's chief rival, and his activities, both operatic and personal, fascinated the Italian public every bit as much as Puccini's, if not more so. He burst into the scene with *Cavalleria rusticana* in 1890, which made him instantly famous. Born in Livorno, Mascagni was the son of a baker who saw no future in a musical career. Mascagni entered the conservatory in Milan and, like Puccini, was another pupil of Ponchielli's. He made extra money playing the double-bass and was one of the musicians in the pit for the premiere of his friend Puccini's *Le villi*. He entered the one-act *Cavalleria* in a competition sponsored by the music publishing house of Sonzogno and won first prize. He became as famous and sought after and as fascinating to the public as any modern-day rock star and then some.

While only this first masterpiece has remained in the international repertoire many years after his death, many of Mascagni's subsequent operas were highly successful in their day. These are slowly but surely reasserting themselves as modern-day opera companies both in and out of Italy — delving past the negative and simply inaccurate things that have been written about the composer and his operas for decades — explore how much else this fascinating composer was capable of. Although considered the founder of verismo — and he did two more works that fit squarely within the genre — most of his operas were non-verismo in style. Whereas Puccini was criticized for playing it safe and not growing as an artist (a view not everyone shares, admittedly), Mascagni tried his hand at many different styles and risked failure for his art on a regular basis. By the turn of the century, after having major successes with *L'amico Fritz* (1891), *Iris* (1898) and others, he was considered a figure of massive importance in Italian music. Therefore it was no surprise that his first twentieth century opera, *Le maschere/The Maskers* (1901), with a libretto by Luigi Illica, premiered simultaneously at six theaters (a seventh in Naples was postponed for two days). *Le maschere* was a major experiment for Mascagni; only the production in Rome was successful, however.

The story of *Le maschere* employs the traditional characters of the commedia dell'arte, centering on the love triangle of Rosaura, Florindo, and Captain Spaventa; Rosaura prefers the former but her father favors the latter. Other characters, such as the maid Columbina and the stuttering servant Tartaglia, do their best to help Rosaura and Florindo make their way to the altar. Mascagni decided to write certain numbers in the style of operatic and classical maestros of the past as a homage (although Mascagni's own vivid style informs each piece), and at one point even kind of quotes from his own "Iris" in an act one aria for Columbina. Mascagni introduces each character with lovely individual themes which are later expanded into arias. The overture consists of a delightful, fast section followed by a beautiful slow passage (containing one of Mascagni's loveliest melodies), then a fast string section which occasionally veers into something that may remind listeners of "Flight of the Bumblebee" from Rimsky-Korsakov's *Tsar Sultan*. (*Tsar Sultan* premiered the previous year in Moscow, but it is unlikely that Mascagni had heard it.) Major pieces include: the soaring ensemble of the act one finale, a homage to Ponchielli, a lilting, wistful piece in which nine characters sing at once ("Stretta è la porta"); the wonderful chorus that closes act three ("O Maschera italiana che ispirata"), which is a homage to the Italian mask characters and commedia dell'arte; and the third act duet for Rosaura and Florindo which has a brief, beautiful prelude leading into the main section ("Colma di fiori e incanti") with its sweet, sad, entirely enchanting melody. Rosaura and the Captain are also given a memorable informal duet in act three, as he continues to boast and promise her everything and she ultimately confesses that she loves another ("Signore grande, illustrissimo"), and act two features a very exciting and bouncy "Furlane" dance in which most of the characters take part. Verdi was alleged to have been critical of an act one number in which Tartaglia stutters out a Rossini-type patter song ("Quella è una stra-stra-strada"), pointing out that people lose their stutter when they sing. But are the characters really singing in opera or just the singers on stage? Despite silly moments, *Le maschere* is a charming, amusing, and very tuneful opera — an exercise in neo-classicism twenty years before Stravinsky got around to it — but most of the Italian public was hoping for something different from Mascagni, or perhaps another strong verismo opera.

Mascagni provided the latter in *Amica* (1905) which focuses on a tragic love triangle. Amica's uncle arranges for her to marry Giorgio, who works for him, but she really loves Giorgio's brother, Rinaldo. Not knowing to whom Amica is betrothed, Rinaldo runs off with her to the mountains with Giorgio in hot pursuit. When the two men realize that they are each other's rival, brotherly love overcomes their feelings for Amica. Rinaldo refuses to take her away from his brother, who begs Amica not to go after the departing Rinaldo. But a distraught Amica runs after the man she loves, only to fall to her death as the brothers watch in horror. Mascagni responded to this libretto with a remarkably effective and often overpowering score, brilliantly orchestrated, which some of his critics labeled "Wagnerian." While Mascagni certainly admired the German composer, and some of the effects in *Amica* may well have been inspired by Wagner, the basic style — the sensitivity of its melodies, the exuberance of its choruses — is strictly Mascagni's. *Amica* begins quietly but builds and builds in power until the horrific climax as the composer keeps up a constant tension, a continuous undercurrent of barely restrained violence, and above all else, a steady lyrical force of tremendous passion. While *Amica* is not a number opera as such — the music, all of a piece, flows inexorably toward the horrifying denouement — there are several memorable pieces. These include the haunting overture, with its eerie horns and bells, leading into an attractive *Cavalleria*-like chorus ("Gio spunta rosso il sol") which has its own melodic strength and sorrowful undercurrent. Uncle Camoine welcomes his friends to a party to announce the upcoming marriage in the irresistible "Per quest' oggi." Giorgio expresses his delight at Camoine's decision to unite him with Amica in an exuberant and moving outcry of happiness "Io passar tutti i dì." The crowd celebrates not only the wedding but a love of life itself in the joyous "Beviomo, o Giorgio a te!" Amica, however, only reaffirms her love for Rinaldo in her lyrical piece "Voche mi protegga tu sol," while Rinaldo suggests they run away together in a superb duet with Amica ("Più presso al Ciel"); Rinaldo's arioso "Amica, vieni!" is a splendid, soaring prelude to this duet. The music has an almost martial air to it, signifying their determination to triumph over Camoine's insensitive marital edicts. The act has an incredibly powerful finale as Giorgio realizes that someone has run off with his "beloved." This is followed by a dynamic intermezzo meant to illustrate the tormented emotions of the lovers as they race into the mountains. Although a trifle trite at times the piece is undeniably effective. After confronting his brother and Amica, Giorgio is given an unusual aria in act two ("Orfani e senza pan"), steeped in gloom, in which he remembers how his brother always succored him in his youth and now both love the same woman. Rinaldo and Amica sing another soaring duet ("Amica, son lo che per lui ti parlo") before Amica chases after the man she truly loves ("Vengo a te, Rinaldo"). Mascagni magnificently brings to life the desperation of Amica's final struggles — and the brothers,' especially Giorgio's, emotional response — at the grotesque moment of her death. *Amica* is a true master-piece of verismo.

Isabeau premiered in 1911 and was a major success for Mascagni. In a medieval kingdom the princess Isabeau meets the handsome woodsman Falco, who hopes to find employment in the Royal Court; both are instantly smitten with the other. With the image of Falco in her mind, and to her father's great displeasure, Isabeau rejects all of her suitors. To humble her, King Raimondo orders her to ride nude on horseback through the town; anyone who looks on her will be blinded. Falco thinks the real obscenity would be turning away from Isabeau as if she had something to be ashamed of, and is given a death sentence for watching her. Isabeau tries to intervene to save his life, but he is carried off by an angry crowd and blinded. Making her way to him through the mob, Isabeau is fatally wounded; the two die together as the people realize with dismay what has happened to their beloved princess.

Isabeau is imperfect. Luigi Illica's libretto, inspired by the Lady Godiva legend, has fascinating elements, but Falco and Isabeau are not developed enough for their fate to really grip us (although this problem is surmounted with the right performers in the roles). One interesting supporting character, the King's banished nephew Ethelbert, who comes to court Isabeau with the other knights, is so under-utilized that it's a wonder he was even introduced into the story. Although *Isabeau* may not boast Mascagni's best score, it contains pieces that are among his most memorable compositions. Foremost is Falco's virile aria "Non colombelle," in which he realizes that his gifts of doves are not good enough for the divine Isabeau and calls for a hawk to fly down to them in an exuberant, kick-in-the-face ode to youthful strength and masculine vigor that is a test for any but the most stentorian of tenors. A second remarkable piece is the act two intermezzo which plays during Isabeau's nude ride on horseback; one of Mascagni's most glorious pieces. The sharply ringing bells that begin the piece bring us right into this beautiful, erotic and dreamy interlude, the essence of romance and vibrant awakening passion. It was composed not too long after the married Mascagni had begun an intimate relationship with the much younger Anni Lolli, who sang in the chorus and became his mistress. If ever there were any doubt that the forty-six year old composer had fallen head over heels for the twenty-one year old Lolli, it is that, according to Mascagni biographer Alan Mallach, he gave her an inscribed copy of the sketch of this intermezzo, calling her his "divine inspiration." The intermezzo is as full of caring, love and affection as it is hot sex. However, the massively romantic piece is not music for everyone's taste, certainly not anyone easily embarrassed by displays, even musical ones, of emotion and sensuality.

The opera begins with a sweet, charming chorus ("Sulla fida chinca") singing of Isabeau's routine, the music forecasting her sad fate as well as illuminating her loneliness, as does the Isabeau theme which is heard throughout the opera. In "Questo mio bianco monto," Isabeau explains that her white cloak, which she refuses to shed, is, in a sense, her heavenly armor. In act two Falco is given another outstanding aria ("O popolo di vili!"), as he observes the nude princess, which is as full of erotic force and virility as its act one counterpart. Falco's arias take the "abandonate" quality of "Ciela la mar" from Ponchielli's *La gioconda* to a higher power. Act three highlights include Isabeau's aria "Venne una veccheirella" in which she sings of her guilt over Falco's fate, wishing she hadn't become his patron out of pity. The excellent love duet "I tuoi occhi" leads into the powerful climax wherein both are killed. Also memorable are the chorus that ends act one, and the townsfolks' hymn to Isabeau that begins act two.

Mascagni's next work, the four and a half hour *Parisina* (1913), with a libretto by the great Italian poet, war hero, and lover, Gabriele D'Annunzio, may be his true masterpiece. Usually D'Annunzio's plays were adapted and then set to music, but in this instance the poet worked on an original libretto himself; he and Mascagni worked on the opera together in a villa near Paris. Ugo D'Este, son of Niccolò, tries very hard to despise his stepmother, Parisina, because she displaced his beloved mother, Stella dell'Assassino, in his father's home and affections. Stella urges her son not to have anything to do with her hated rival. But the passion Parisina and Ugo feel for one another overcomes all other feelings, and after he saves her from an attack by corsairs, the two become lovers. When Niccolò discovers this betrayal, he orders their executions. Stella begs her son to denounce Parisina, but he refuses to do so. Stella collapses as Ugo and Parisina are led to the block and death. D'Annunzio's rich, poetic and often perverse dialogue lifts *Parisina* above other stories of this nature. Ugo is a fascinating characterization, confused, petulant, childish, yet somehow heroic, as is his mother, who is almost insane with anger and jealousy. Whatever D'Annunzio fails to tell us about these characters, Mascagni does — and he tells us everything — in his music, which brings them fully to life. Parisina and her husband Nicolo are perhaps not as vividly drawn, but they certainly have their moments. *Parisina* emerges as one of the most intense studies of sexual obsession ever penned; Mascagni responded with the most highly-charged and electrifyingly erotic music of his career.

Although there are fine moments throughout the opera, act two is especially outstanding. Parisina divests herself of her jewels and other accessories as a religious offering in the ravishing aria "Bene morro' d'amore." The sequence when Ugo comes to Parisina's rescue and beats back the corsairs in bloody fashion is set to some of Mascagni's most exciting and dramatic music. One of the opera's most thrilling moments occurs after the battle, when Ugo makes his triumphant entry onto the stage to a magnificent fanfare ("Vittoria! Sia laudata!"). Mascagni follows this with a beautiful duet for Parisina and Ugo ("Vedrete che bene medicarvi sapro") as the former assures the latter that "you shall see that I know how to heal you." Then Parisina is given a splendid piece ("Vedete ecco l'acqua") in which she tells Ugo that she cannot bathe his wounds as she is afraid to touch him, since they have more or less admitted their feelings for one another. This leads into another stunning duet ("Ho combattuto") in which Ugo sings that he thought of only one thing — Parisina — during the battle, goading him on, and she in turn spurs him on in admiration and mounting excitement. Parisina suggests the two of them wander amongst the corpses of the enemy in hopes of finding a man who is barely alive so that she can watch him die as she, the reason for his death, is reflected in his eyes. Controlling herself, Parisina prays to the Virgin to keep her from sinning ("Merce, Maria!"), but as she and Ugo begin to pray in church for freedom from their impure thoughts, their instincts get the better of them and they tear at each other in an all-consuming passion. As the two come together, the music quietly tolls in counterpoint like a prescient death knell. It is all, in a word, exceptional. To some listeners, of course, especially those who have no love for romantic or emotional music, the score of *Parisina* may seem overwrought, vulgar, embarrassingly sexual (embarrassing to them, that is, not Mascagni), and overpoweringly intense; these, of course, are the very same qualities that make the music so vivid and vital to those in tune with Mascagni's emphatic and passionate method.

Mascagni's tearjerker par excellence, *Lodoletta*, premiered in 1917 in Rome. Gioacchino Forzano crafted the libretto from a sentimental and touching story by Ouida, "Two Little Wooden Shoes."[2] Lodoletta is devastated when her foster father, Antonio, is killed in an accident on her birthday. Her neighbor Giannotto loves her and wants to take care of her, but she is more in tune with the exiled Parisian painter, Flammen, who moves in with her so that she won't be alone. This arrangement causes raised eyebrows and nasty talk amongst the town gossips; Gianniotto pleads with her to move out, but Lodoletta has fallen in love with Flammen. Flammen tells her that he feels the same, but fearing that their relationship will only ruin him, she asks him to leave. Both parties are heartsick over their separation, leading Lodoletta to make her way slowly to Paris to find Flammen, who can do little but worry over what has become of her. Lodoletta arrives at his place on New Year's Eve in a snow storm; Flammen comes home to find her frozen body huddled and silent in the snow.

Mascagni never forgets — or lets us forget — that the story of Lodoletta is a heartbreaker, for he composed music, if not always of surpassing beauty, of great delicacy and sensitivity. *Lodoletta* is in no way a verismo opera, and it is devoid of any Wagnerian influence. The music may seem "slight," less impressive, when compared to the impact and dynamism of *Amica* and *Parisina*, but the score is nonetheless full of more than its share of sublime moments. These include the act one Children's Chorus ("Serenata delle fate in onor di Lodoletta"), a serenade of the fairies in honor of Lodoletta; this charming piece has an undercurrent of pathos and even despair that hints of the tragedies to come. (There is also an outstanding children's chorus in act two, "Ah! com' è bella!") Lodoletta's aria "Ah! Cogliete le rame," turns into a soaring ode to springtime. Flammen tries, in child-like terms, to comfort Lodoletta after her foster father's death in the exquisite aria "Sì! E se non piangi più." He is also given an intensely romantic arioso in act two ("E strana la tua voce") in which he realizes that he and Lodoletta are in love and strongly attracted to one another. Flammen's best aria occurs in act three, "Ah! dove aura posato," an outcry of loneliness and despair — over the possible fate of Lodoletta — that has been barely contained and now must break free no matter how unendurable. Lodoletta's final aria ("Flammen, perdonami") as she looks desperately for Flammen and succumbs to the cold, starts with a haunting new melody, then as it proceeds incorporates various themes from earlier scenes into a very long, bravura aria for any soprano. These last two pieces are the two best-known and most frequently performed numbers in the opera. Giannotto is also given an outstanding aria ("Lo vedi, Lodoletta") in act two, another heartfelt piece in which he eloquently expresses his disappointment over losing Lodoletta to Flammen. Mascagni employed some highly unusual orchestrations in *Lodoletta* which sometimes work well and sometimes don't. An example of the former is the Chorus of Dutch Women going to Church in act two ("All'alba di Novembre grigia e mesta.") With its "dissonant" melody and inventive instrumentation of bells, strings and woodwinds, it is one of Mascagni's weirdest — and most interesting — pieces. The act one dirge for Antonio goes on too long but is interesting in its way and builds nicely in intensity. *Lodoletta* will not work for listeners who are unwilling or unable to put themselves into the right mood to accept what some people will see as its corny storyline. Mascagni rightly recognized that the story was one of inexorable tragedy, and just as Forzano's libretto is full of much foreshadowing of grim events, so, too, is Mascagni's score; his focus is always on pulling the listener on the road to that certain tragedy even as he engages and satisfies their compassionate and melancholy instincts. Far from lacking dramatic impetus as some have claimed, *Lodoletta* moves forward with great surety and aplomb. It is a little gem of an opera. The role of Flammen was sung at the Met by no less than Enrico Caruso.

Mascagni's operetta *Sì* premiered in 1919 in Rome. Playboy Luciano will lose his inheritance if he doesn't marry within a month, but fidelity is the last thing on his mind. It is suggested that he ask a Folies Bergere entertainer named Sì to be his bride; she is called "Sì" because she's a girl who never says no (decades before Ado Annie in *Oklahoma*). Luciano agrees that Sì would be perfect, but he never figures on the girl actually falling in love with him. To make matters worse, Luciano falls in love not with Sì but with Vera, the woman he was always supposed to marry. A heartbroken Sì muses on the irony of her falling for the only man she can never have. The ending has an added poignancy because Luciano and Vera aren't very likable, giving all our sympathy to a woman who in other circumstances could have been dismissed as a gold digger. *Sì* is a minor work in the Mascagni canon, but it does have moments of interest. Mascagni ends the first two acts (of three) with lengthy opera-like finales with recitatives and distinct numbers. Highlights include an act one duet between Sì and her male friend Cleo ("Sì! Sì!"), about fallen women and the men who bring about their downfall; and the love duet for Vera and Luciano in act two ("M'amassi tu"), which is certainly ironic considering that Luciano has just married Sì. Act three boasts a lovely "calendar duet" ("Il venot Marzo") with an especially nice refrain in which they take stock of their love affair over the days. The best number in the operetta is the "Duetto del ballo triste/Duet of the Sad Dance" in which Cleo urges Sì to forget her aching heart in a dance.

Il piccolo Marat (1921), set during the French revolution, was one of Mascagni's biggest post–*Cavalleria* successes. A young man, nicknamed "Little Marat" because he wishes to serve Marat, is actually a prince who is hoping to save his imprisoned mother by gaining the trust of her jailers. He got the idea from a fairy tale she once told him about a boy who pretends to befriend an ogre who kidnapped his mother. Now the prince is pretending to help a real-life "Ogre" who is one of the leaders of the revolution, even as he falls in love with the evil man's kind-hearted niece, Mariella, to whom he reveals the truth. With the aid of a carpenter who has been forced to build sabotaged ships to drown prisoners, Little Marat and Mariella manage to escape from the Ogre and free his mother; the four sail away from the horrors of the past and on to a new life. *Il piccolo Marat* is powerful stuff, an imperfect but very exhilarating work with interesting characters and a strong libretto by Giovacchino Forzano and Giovanni Targioni-Tozzetti, co-librettist of *Cavalleria*. As usual, Mascagni's music supplies added depth to the story and characters. While there are moments in the score that are flat or earthbound (some feel these were Mascagni's attempts to be "modern"), the music more often exhibits the composer's lyrical and dramatic inspiration.

There are scenes in *Il piccolo Marat* that stick in the memory due to their theatrical and poignant quality. At the end of act one Little Marat manages to get in to see his mother, and tries to assure her that he will ultimately rescue her. Even as he sings to her, several of the sabotaged boats, full of prisoners who are doomed to drown, set sail. There is a very affecting moment when Little Marat, visibly distraught over what is happening to those prisoners, tries to keep the grim details from his mother. In act two the carpenter tells Mariella, hoping she can intercede on his behalf, of the toll it has taken on him to be forced to witness so many executions. After he tells her that the last straw was seeing a twelve-year-old boy guillotined, she intones "infame ... infame" (infamous) to a musical phrase that sums up her pity, disgust and weariness; we hear this phrase again as she confronts her uncle in act three. The climax of act three as the Prince and the Ogre have a desperate battle as Mariella rushes to save his mother, with the Prince getting shot and the carpenter giving the Ogre a well-deserved whack on the head, are suspenseful and exciting as well as satisfying. The audience's sympathies are fully engaged as they imagine what the lovers are feeling, the prince wondering if his mother and Mariella will get to safety, and Mariella wondering if the man she loves, badly injured, will join them in time or even survive. He does, carried to the getaway boat by the carpenter, for a very moving conclusion that is sentimental in all the right ways.

Touching on so many bases — melodious and modern, grim yet full of honest sentiment — *Il piccolo Marat* struck a chord with the public and was a smashing success for Mascagni. It didn't hurt that much of the music was Mascagni working at a high level. The superb opening of act one goes from a gentle hymn ("Song of the Prisoners," which opens and closes the act) to a thunderous chorus as the people cry out for bread and against the "hoarding" Marats, who, in turn, cry out against their accusers. A constant threat of shattering, barely restrained violence is conveyed by highly attractive chorale music — Mascagni could have taught later composers lessons in how to get across ugliness and yet remain lyrical. Although *Il piccolo Marat* is not a number opera as such, it is more than just music theater (although it could be taken as an excellent example of same) and boasts several memorable pieces, including an exquisite second act duet for Mariella and the Prince ("Avrai nella mia manna la tua mamma"); several powerful arias for Little Marat; and a couple of intense pieces for the Ogre, among others. The beautiful orchestral passages that end the opera are outstanding. Puccini went to see *Il piccolo Marat* and claimed he was not impressed: "Lots of noisy music without any heart!"[3] Puccini was understandably bitter because Mascagni's *Sì*— although frankly not as good — had proved more popular than his *La rondine*. What's worse, *Giornale d'Italia* had declared Mascagni "the noblest creative artist in Italian music." Puccini was in the period between his penultimate and ultimate operas, *Il trittico* and *Turandot* and felt at sea with nothing of his own on the stage. Adding to his fury was the fact that *Il piccolo Marat* was an incontestable hit.

Pinotta, which Mascagni expanded from a cantata he had composed many years before, premiered in 1932 and is perhaps his most delicate score. The music turns this simple and simplistic story of faith in God and in eventual love — a story of two lonely mill workers, Baldo and Pinotta, who realize their feelings for one another are requited — into a work of beauty and poignancy. Act one highlights include the mill owner, Andrea, leading the workers in prayer ("Signore, cui sempre loda"); and the Spinner's Chorus ("Gira, gira"). In act two another spinner's chorus about the irresistibility of love has an irresistible melody to match ("Ormai si sa"). Pinotta sings to the evening star to "stir up a loving heartbeat" in Baldo's "bosom" in "O stella della sera." The climactic love duet ("Quando, Pinotta, guardi la tua stella") is one of Mascagni's most satisfying and heartwarming pieces.

Nerone (1935) was Mascagni's final opera. He had had the idea of composing an opera about Nero since he had read Pietro Cossa's drama about the emperor in 1891, and had started to set it to music before being sidetracked by a novel entitled *Le Vistilia*, which also took place during Roman times. Mascagni ultimately felt the book lacked a certain veracity when it came to things Roman, and after writing some music for the piece, set it permanently aside. Years later, however, some of this music turned up in *Nerone*.

According to Mascagni, he wanted to do an opera about Nero: "to give the people an interpretation of (him) a little less traditional, a little less the tyrant and the puppet; I wanted to depopulate history of its grim figures, to give these again, even with their defects and vices (since this is a heritage of every man and every epoch, a necessary ballast), a prestige, a halo, a significance worthy of ancient Roman grandeur. In short: to substitute living men for old statues carved in series down the centuries."[4]

The Nero of *Nerone* is certainly all too human. A cursory reading of the libretto makes Nero and the other characters seem rather one-dimensional, but with the music (and certainly with the right dramatic tenor in the role), the characters come to life. The libretto was written by Mascagni's old friend, Giovanni Targioni-Tozzetti, whom he affectionately called "Nanni." Nanni was very ill at the time and spent most of his time in bed. Mascagni visited and tried to work with him for about an hour a day; he died shortly after finishing his work on *Nerone*.

The story concentrates on the last days and final hours of Nero's life. Conflict arises when he falls in love with a Greek slave, Egloge, whom he frees, much to the consternation of Atte, another freed slave who has been his lover for some time. At a celebration, Atte gives Egloge poison. Although Nero and Atte now hate each other, the latter helps Nero flee from the usurping forces when he learns he has been declared an enemy of Rome. Atte's heart warms to the man she still loves as they're in hiding, and she urges him to kill himself before he is captured. She stabs herself first to give him courage and inspiration; but a freed slave has to help Nero deal his own fatal blow.

Whatever its historical inaccuracies (although many things remain uncertain about Nero; the latest research suggests he has been unfairly maligned by history), *Nerone* presents a fascinating portrait of the emperor, focusing on his love of art, life, and liquor while refusing to turn a blind eye to his essential cowardliness. This is a Nero who wants to sing (however, badly), paint, sculpt, drink, make love — anything but govern, which he also does badly in any case. Egloge is a naive young woman just awakening to love and the realization of her physical powers, while Atte is the older, insecure, all too cynical, hard-bitten woman out to protect what's hers. She makes no secret of her contempt for Nero, nor — when the time is right — her love for him.

The well-constructed first act consists primarily of skillfully done recitatives with the occasional number, the best of which is an amusing informal duet between Nerone and Atte ("È il maggior dei poeti il nappo pieno!"). In this Nero sings of the glories of the grape, of how everything appears wonderful when one is drunk, as Atte makes sarcastic observations in between the verses of the emperor's unusual brindisi. The beautiful love duet for Nerone and Egloge in act two ("Egloge, o tutta bella") may not be quite top-drawer Mascagni but would probably be considered an outstanding number for many a modern-day opera. The poignant, haunting number for Egloge and chorus which follows ("O Ana diomeme"), in which she prays to Venus to "let me be loved by an equal love," unaware of how little time she has left, is one of Mascagni's most memorable pieces. Egloge and Atte have a confrontation which contains a fine arioso for each, as well as Atte's sinister and quietly powerful piece ("Su te sciagura") in which she threatens to use potions and poison to take care of her rival.

Act three begins with a rousing chorus ("Gloria a Nerone") as Nerone's party reaches the height of drunken merriment and the emperor sings a song to the captive audience. (The tenor who plays Nerone, of course, can not sing as badly as Nerone is supposed to be singing; this must be conveyed through gesture and expression, and the reactions on the celebrants' faces.) Nerone and Egloge have another tender moment as Egloge lies dying from Atte's poison and the emperor tells her he loves her ("Tu soffri, o mio Tesero"). In contrast, Atte is then given a violent and arresting aria ("Perchè m'innamorai d'un uomo tanto") in which she wonders why she ever fell in love with Nero, and tells him that unbeknownst to him she has consistently been looking after him and keeping him safe. As Nerone, Atte, and others flee for their lives, there is a powerful orchestral interlude that marvelously depicts a storm even as it gets across the urgency of Nero's dash to "safety" and an uncertain future. An agitated horn in the background adds to this sense of urgency and panic. For the second half of the final act we're back to the sung recitatives, with the exception of Atte's touching aria ("Ne tu possa mai risvegliarti") in which she realizes how much she still loves Nerone, that she is, in fact, all the fallen emperor has left.

Although the public and critical reaction to *Nerone* when it premiered at La Scala on January 16th, 1935 was not on the level of the almost hysterical reception of *Cavalleria*— which Mascagni sadly noted — the opera was hardly a failure. Mascagni himself conducted *Nerone*, and Aureliano Pertile sang the title role. (Film of Mascagni approaching the podium of La Scala on opening night shows the wariness, aged defeat, and still existing hope etched tellingly and poignantly on the composer's weary face.) Lina Bruna Rasa and Margherita Carosio were Atte and Egloge, respectively. Some reviewers declared the work a "masterpiece." The opera played several cities in Italy, as well as Zurich, but it did not establish itself in the international repertoire.

Some fascists were not pleased with the opera, thinking that Mascagni had created a vulgar caricature of Ancient Rome, and that Nero was hardly the proper figure to celebrate its glories. In the years since the opera premiered, the fiction has been asserted that Mascagni meant the opera to glorify Mussolini's regime, with the dictator being represented by Emperor Nero. Considering that Nero is such a pathetic figure, it is unlikely Mascagni could have meant the work as a tribute; if anything, the opposite. In all likelihood Mascagni was interested in the drama of the story as a framework for his music and had no ulterior political motives. Although Mussolini did not attend opening night, he was anxious for "Nerone" to be a success and may have realized Mascagni did not intend any insult toward his regime nor Italy in general.

Nerone, especially when compared to many works of music theater that came later, is a masterpiece whose charms and strengths grow on those who are in tune with what Mascagni was trying to achieve, and which he succeeded at quite admirably. No *Cavalleria* or *Parisina* perhaps, but not a bad swan song by any objective standard.

But even as Puccini and Mascagni jockeyed for position as top dog in the world of modern Italian opera — a position eventually won posthumously by the former — there was plenty of competition from other Italian composers who would have been only to happy to see one or both of the big two take a tumble and leave the playing field altogether.

3. Sex and Violence:
Italy, 1900–1950

While Puccini and Mascagni battled it out, publicly wished each other success, and made bitchy comments about each other's operas behind their backs, there were many other composers coming out with their own operatic works on a regular basis. Umberto Giordano and Ruggero Leoncavallo were especially prolific, but there were others who had entered the ring. Make no mistake — it took great effort to secure a libretto (snatching it away from a hated rival at the last minute if necessary), complete a score, collect the dream cast that you knew could put your work over, get the right theater and director to champion it, avoid problems with the claques hired by your enemies, and dodge the spears launched by critics who were either jealous, paid off, or simply not in tune with what you were doing. And then, of course, the public was the ultimate judge. If a work particularly dear to a composer failed, as it often did, it was a heartbreak, especially when you consider the effort it took to get an opera mounted — and mounted well — in the first place.

Umberto Giordano (1867–1948) was born in Foggia and studied at the conservatory in Naples. He was inspired by the success of *Cavalleria* to compose his own verismo effort, *Mala Vita* (1892), but it was not a major success. With *Andrea Chenier* (1896), however, a moving, tuneful verismo work set during the French revolution, he crafted a masterpiece that entered the repertory and has never left it. He also had a success with *Fedora* in 1898. It would be easy to describe Giordano's *Siberia* as a knock-off of Franco Alfano's *Risurrezione* were it not for the fact that Giordano's opera premiered at La Scala a year earlier than Alfano's in 1903. There is enough of a plot similarity between both operas to indicate that *Siberia's*" librettist, Lugia Illica, may have been aware of Tolstoy's novel "Resurrection," the basis of Alfano's opera. Some music critics have dismissed *Siberia*," citing the mediocre libretto and making fun of the way Giordano quotes from "The Song of the Volga Boatmen" for some Russian flavor. Of course if a composer is in favor with a particular critic, his "quoting" can be hailed as brilliant; if in disfavor, as meretricious or laughable. Actually Giordano very cleverly and skillfully uses and expands upon the "Volga Boatmen" song in a chorus of prisoners that is one of the most effective pieces in the score.

Instead of a man following his former lover after she is sent to Siberia, as in *Risurrezione*, in Giordano's work, the heroine, the courtesan Stephana, follows her lover Vassili after he is arrested for assaulting a superior officer, the very man who had been keeping Stephana. Joining him in the miserableness of Siberia, Stephana assures Vassili that she truly loves him after he learns of her former profession. The two contrive to escape but Stephana is shot to death after which Vassili collapses over her body. While the story may not convince, Giordano's music certainly does. The score is full of lovely tunes and contains at least two outstanding numbers: Vassili's climactic act two aria "Orride steppe!," in which he describes for Stephana the horrors she will be facing if she comes to Siberia; and Stephana's act three aria "Ascolta! ... il martir," in which she tells how she has been able to face those horrors because of the flowering of their mutual love. Act Three takes place on Easter Sunday. When one character announces that "Christ has risen," Giordano creates a nice theatrical effect with strings, percussion, and chorus. (This is a good example of how early 20th century composers could create throbbing effects which almost sound "electronic" without, of course, using electronic instruments.) This section eases the tension just before the climactic scene when Stephana and Vassily decide to escape, during which Giordano employs light dance music for contrast. Throughout the opera his dramatic hand is sure, enriching a libretto that has its moments but probably did not deserve the consistent melodiousness showered upon it. *Siberia* may be Giordano's best score after *Andrea Chenier*.

Madame Sans-Gêne/Madame Carefree premiered at the Met in 1915 and takes place during the French Revolution, although it is much more light-hearted — and has a much lighter, non-verismo musical style — than *Andrea Chenier* or Mascagni's *Il piccolo Marat*. The story deals with a laundress, Caterina, who winds up a duchess but is seen as déclassé, by snooty court ladies. When Napoleon himself gets stuffy with her she reminds him that she used to do his laundry when he was poor and he still hasn't paid his bill. Caterina and her husband, Lefèbvre, contrive to save the life of a count that they had saved from the enemy years before, and succeed. *Madame Sans-Gêne* is acceptable and modestly entertaining, but the story never quite catches fire and the music, while often very pleasant and adroit, is not that memorable. The best number occurs in act two: Lefèbvre's aria "Questa tua bocca profumata e pura," in which he sings of how Caterina's kisses reawaken thoughts of his youth in Alsace. In an 1919 edition of his famous opera book, Gustave Kobbé, noted that "like most modern composers who do not possess the gift for sustained melody [this is belied by his superior work in *Andrea Chenier* and *Siberia*], Giordano would make up for it by great skill in the handling of his orchestra and constant depiction of the varying phases of the action ... the composer has furnished a musical background, in which the colors are laid on in short, quick, and crisp strokes."

Le cena della beffe/Feast of the Jesters premiered in 1924 at La Scala. Neri and his brother play a joke on Gianetto — throwing him into Arno river and branding him (apparently on his behind)—for daring to love Neri's mistress Ginevra, who is not worth all the fuss but is very sexy. Gianetto successfully conspires to have Neri locked up in an asylum, but Neri gets free and heads to Ginevra's house where he believes she is entertaining Gianetto. Neri breaks in and kills Ginevra and her guest, who turns out not to be Gianetto but Neri's brother Gabriello, who also had a yen for Ginevra. At this realization Neri truly goes mad, and Gianetto, who feels especially guilty at the destruction of three lives because he is unrepentant, is also shattered by the experience. The libretto of *Le cena della beffe*, a fascinating study of hurt feelings, jealousy, and practical jokes carried too far as well as an obvious, blatant mixture of the violent and the sexual, could come off as either a melodrama or black comedy depending entirely on how its presented. There is a certain bizarre lunacy and slightly sadistic cast to the sequence wherein a chained Neri is tormented and nicked with a knife by some of his victims, resulting in a strange, semi-shouted, confusing, but oddly likable octet. Act three boasts a memorable duet between Neri and one of his cast-off lovers, Lisabetta ("Mi chiamo Lisabetta"), but otherwise Giordano's score is second-rate.

Ruggero Leoncavallo (1857–1919) was born in Naples, and also attended the conservatory there. For a brief time he worked on the libretto of Puccini's *Manon Lescaut*, but he and Puccini did not see eye to eye, to put it mildly. Unable to interest a music publisher in backing his own scores, Leoncavallo, like Giordano, hit upon the idea of composing a work similar to *Cavalleria rusticana*— this was *Pagliacci* (1892), which eventually was paired with its model to form the "*Cav and Pag*" double-bill. *Pagliacci*, another masterpiece, was an immediate hit and has never left the repertoire. The bad blood between Leoncavallo and Puccini positively boiled over when both began to work on operatic versions of *La Bohème* at the same time. Leoncavallo claimed that Puccini told him he was going to abandon the subject but in fact only sped ahead so that his version of *La Bohème* premiered over a year earlier than Leoncavallo's. The latter's adaptation, which premiered in 1897, proved a worthwhile and lovely project, and probably would have entered the repertory had it not been for Puccini's more beautiful adaptation.

Leoncavallo's first 20th century opera was *Zaza*, which premiered in 1900, and was quite popular in its day. Zaza is a music hall entertainer who falls for a man, Milio, who turns out to be married. Meeting his child, she realizes that she can not doom the innocent little girl to the kind of childhood that she, Zaza, had, by taking away her father. This may have been a highly clichéd situation even at the turn of the century, but as Milio represents redemption and respectability, a soul-mate and life-reaffirmation, to Zaza, his being married with a child is a tragic development for her, and there is a lot going on under the surface of Leoncavallo's libretto. As well, the composer's sensitive musical skills make some of the trite situations — such as when Zaza first meets Milio's daughter — almost poignant and sentimental in the right way. Sometimes *Zaza* is overstated, almost hokey, like a film melodrama, but there's simply too much pleasant music in it for it to be dismissed. Highlights include Milio's act two ariosos, "Mia Zaza" and "Zaza, Zaza," which are passionate and have lovely melodies; and Cascart's soaring act four aria "Zaza, piccola zingara," in which Zaza's friend tries to convince her that it's ultimately better to give up her married lover. Leoncavallo followed this with several operas that did not establish themselves and have all but vanished.

Leoncavallo's final opera, *Edipo Re*, a one-act treatment of the Oedipus story, premiered a year after his death in 1920 in Chicago; it did not debut in the composer's native country until 1939 when it was broadcast on Radio Audizioni Italiane. Leoncavallo had died before completing the piece; it was finished by G. Pennacchio. *Edipo Re* emerged as a notable, robust work, if a minor one, with a dynamic opening chorus, excellent vocal writing, a major aria for Oedipus, and a sublime love duet whose only disappointing factor is its brevity.

Franco Alfano (1875–1954) is best-known as the composer who completed *Turandot* after Puccini's death, but in his day he was much better-known and far more acclaimed than he is now. Some Alfano admirers point to his 1921 opera *La leggenda di Sakùntala* (whose score Alfano had to painfully reconstruct after it was destroyed during World War Two) as his most artistic and original, but by far his most popular was *Risurrezione* (1904), based on Tolstoy's novel "Resurrection"; *Risurrezione* may well be Alfano's masterpiece. Following the plot of the novel but eschewing most of its philosophizing and dreary religiosity, the bare bones of the libretto at times resemble an especially weepy and convoluted Bette Davis movie: Prince Dimitri has a dalliance with a maid, Katiusha, who winds up pregnant. When he comes back from war, she goes to meet him at a railway station to give him the news, but is heart-broken to see him with another woman, and leaves before telling him. In a development that sounds like something out of "Madame X" instead of Great Russian Literature, Dimitri actually winds up on the jury when Katiusha is put on trial for murder. Dimitri follows the wrongly convicted woman to Siberia in an act of atonement, but — even after the Prince arranges a pardon — she chooses to redeem her life by staying with the political prisoner who needs her and who has helped her rather than go off with the man she has always loved. (This development, while it may sound loopy and masochistic, is actually rather moving and genuine.)

Alfano's excellent, passionate score adds the depth that may be lacking in the libretto. The love duet that ends act one, "Katiusha! ... Cara mi sembra oggi" is rigorously passionate to the nth degree and the whole of act two — the train station sequence — has often been singled out for its dramatic effectiveness and Katiusha's powerful arias "Sì, non è vero?" and "Dio pietoso, fa ch'egli venga alfin." Alfano ends this act with incisive orchestral music that goes straight for the heart. Act three, in which Katiusha awaits a long trek to Siberia from the women's prison, opens with music that is perhaps too lively to get across the utter grimness of the situation. There is, however, an interesting theme as the warden calls out the names of the prisoners, as well as an effective intermezzo. Dimitri is given two outstanding arias "No, Katiusha, non ridere così!" and "Piangi, sì, piangi," and the act ends with an aria for Katiusha ("Sì, son' io!") that is a commingled outcry of hope and despair. Act four's haunting prelude, quivery with expectancy, opens with a lonely horn and builds up to a soaring climax. In between, Simonson, the political prisoner who falls in love with Katiusha, is given the bold, distinctive aria "Quando la vidi." After a sublime final duet "Ed ora, va ... parti," the chorus comes in at the end, layered over a somber, bell-like background effect, and an arresting theme for Katiusha that has played at certain times throughout the opera sounds briefly. Alfano's soaring vocal lines certainly make *Risurrezione* a singer's opera.

Although it may not be the equal of *Risurrezione* for sheer melodic flow and dramatic vitality, Alfano's 1936 opera *Cyrano de Bergerac* was given a brief new life with a production at the Metropolitan Opera during the 2005-2006 season starring Plácido Domingo. The story is the familiar one of Cyrano of the outsized proboscis writing love letters to the beautiful Roxanne on behalf of a young handsome comrade Christian, who looks better than he thinks and talks. (Interestingly, both Cyrano and Christian are tenor roles.) Roxanne falls in love with Christian, not realizing that the words and sentiments in his letters are actually those of the equally smitten Cyrano. The plot becomes a bit ridiculous with Roxanne showing up at the front when the two men go off to war, but recovers with a very moving conclusion: Years after Christian's death, the still-mourning Roxanne finally finds out who loved her best of all and whom she was really in love with all along, but only when it's too late.

Highlights of the opera include Cyrano's act one aria "Je jette avec grâce mon feutre" as he duels with Vincente, during which Alfano's music is as insouciant and insolent as Cyrano and also gets across in musical terms his effortless skill at swordplay. The most beautiful, almost Puccinian, music, of act two is in the second scene, wherein Cyrano, pretending to be Christian, sings of l'amour ("Tous mes appeals d'amour") to Roxanne on the balcony above, from which she becomes so aroused that she eagerly welcomes Christian into her arms and, presumably, bed. Act three contains a gentle love song, accompanied by flute, which Cyrano sings to calm the rattled nerves of the cadets ("Ah! Mais vous ne pensez") and is immediately followed by a contrastingly somber chorus, redolent of weariness and homesickness, for the soldiers. Roxanne's excellent aria "Je lisais, je relisais," in which she rhapsodizes over Christian's letters and begs his forgiveness for at first loving him only for his looks, becomes an informal duet. The opera's finest music is in act four, a seductive recitative for Roxanne and Cyrano (who, dying, has come to tell all), which culminates in a rhapsodic duet and confession scene ("Roxanne, Adieu! Je vais mourir"). Alfano holds nothing back in this touching and masterful sequence. While one can certainly understand Cyrano's need to confess to his beloved, it is also true that he dies leaving her with a lifetime of pain and regret. Those who find the passionate verismo aspects of *Risurrezione* not to their liking may find the more romantic and delicate *Cyrano* more agreeable.

Although he was born and died in Venice, Ermanno Wolf-Ferrari (1876–1948) spent so much time in Munich and other German-speaking areas that he is often considered a German composer. Adding to the confusion is the fact that his operas were at first more successful in Germany than in Italy. His greatest success, *I gioielli della Madonna*, however, was in the Italian verismo tradition. Although his first opera *La camargo* premiered in 1896, Wolf-Ferrari's best-known operas are 20th century works. The first of these is *I quattro rusteghi/The School for Fathers*, which premiered in Munich in 1906. Here Wolf-Ferrari was working in a similar vein to Mascagni when the latter did *Le maschere*; a Rossini-like comedy with some "modern" touches. The storyline pits stuffy old husbands and fathers who stick to outdated tradition and long for the days when women did as they were told against these same more open-minded, tolerant wives whose wisdom, of course, brings happiness to all in the end. Lunardo wants his daughter Lucieta to marry a friend's son, Filipeto, even though the two have never met or even seen one another — and Lunardo insists that that remain the case until their wedding day. Filipeto dresses in drag at one point just so he can get a look at his future bride. Luckily Lucieta has been clued in to the deception and the two — once Filipeto has been unmasked — feel an immediate attraction. This whole business outrages Lunardo who wants to call off the wedding, but Felice, another talkative wife who butts into everyone's business, convinces him otherwise. The highlights of the opera include Lunardi's aria in which he maintains that he must be obeyed in all things; Filipeto's aria ("Lucieta xe un bel nome") in which the young man wonders if the girl he is to wed will be as pretty as her name; and the wonderful ensemble pieces that end both act one and act two. There's also a notable trio in Act one in which Lucieta and her step-mother react with dismay to Lunardo's news of the arranged marriage. Beginning with the delicate, tuneful introduction, *I quattro rusteghi* is a lyrical and charming work that in its day gained much favor in first Germany, then Italy, before slowly making its way to the states where it was less successful. Despite its pleasures, the score is much less inventive than Mascagni's for *Le maschere*.

Wolf-Ferrari's *Il segreto di Susanna* (Susanna's Secret) premiered in Munich, where it was sung in German, in 1909, and reached the Metropolitan three years later. This amusing, pleasant trifle has to do with the Count Gil, who suspects his wife Susanna of being unfaithful. After a number of arguments and reconciliations, it turns out that Susanna's big secret which she has been keeping from the count is not that she has taken a lover but that she's taken up smoking. The Count is overjoyed and the two share a puff as they delight in the joyous end of their misunderstanding. The one-act opera combines Italian lyricism with Germanic orchestral effects. Although there is a pretty duet for the couple ("Il dolce idillio") as they reaffirm their love at the midway point of the opera, and both count and countess are given nice arias to sing, the most passionate music, "O gioia, la nube leggera," is reserved for Susanna's love aria — to her cigarette.

I gioiella della Madonna/Jewels of the Madonna premiered in Berlin in 1911. Having failed to win much popularity in Italy, Wolf-Ferrari decided to compose a work that was clearly modeled on *Cavalleria rusticana* and just as clearly influenced by the music of Pietro Mascagni. Just as the action of *Cavalleria* takes place on Easter Sunday in Sicily, the story of *Madonna* unfolds on the Feast Day of the Madonna in Naples. The opera represented a complete change in style for the composer; he may have had cynical motives for doing so but the ironic result was Wolf-Ferrari's one unqualified masterpiece. Gennaro is in love with the girl who has been raised as his sister, Maliella, who in turn loves Rafaele, the charismatic leader of a gang of bandits. To prove that he is her only worthy lover, Gennaro steals the jewels from the statue of the Madonna and presents them to her, whereupon they make love. Even Rafaele is appalled at the crime and rejects Maliella, who has adorned herself with the jewels. She commits suicide, as does Gennaro at the base of the statue.

The opera begins with an explosion of sounds, color, energy and melody as we see and hear a variety of men, women, children, lovers, fruit sellers, clowns, flirters, drinkers, and musicians in little mini-dramas that bring the Festival day to vivid life; a brilliant opening full of poignancy and expectancy. The act one highlights include Gennaro's heart-breaking aria "Madonna, con sospiri," in which he preys for the Madonna to relieve him of his "hopeless passion" for Maliella; his mother Carmela's aria ("Oh la spina che mai") in which she tells Gennaro how and why she found and adopted Maliella (which expands into a duet for the two); and Rafaele's "In nuvola bianca," as he compares Maliella to the Madonna as a child's chorus sings behind him, Maliella joining in for a duet, and then a booming chorus of bells and drums erupting in another explosion of sound to end the act.

In act two the music for Gennaro's outburst of love for Maliella is not as passionate as the music for Maliella and Rafaele (who declare their lust for each other) because the latter couple's feelings are mutual. Gennaro's aria "No, la Madonna" is a lovely piece that becomes a fine duet with Maliella as she becomes totally absorbed in the jewels which he's stolen. She transfigures religious ecstasy into sexual ecstasy, and winds up willingly making love to Gennaro as she sings "I am yours, Rafaele!" in an intensely erotic sequence (if not on the level of *Parisina*). Act three boasts a wonderful chorus of Comorristi (a criminal secret society which is the Neapolitan version of the Mafia) as they kiss the pretty Stella to the protest of the other girls ("Compagni evviva"), culminating in a salute to Rafaele as he enters their domain. The dance music that follows is described in the libretto as "a regular orgy in the Apache style" but the music does not reflect this, as if Wolf-Ferrari were too afraid to let himself go and compose something that might be seen by the musically priggish as "vulgar." Also notable are a Mascagni-like intermezzo at the start of act two, and the intermezzo that opens the third act. A variation of a lusty chorus sung by Rafaele and his men ("Aprila bella") it's a colorful and delightful piece that is a nice contrast to the grim events about to unfold. The opera has a very moving wind up with Gennaro's suicide as he again sings an exquisite prayer to the Madonna. This scene is modeled on Mascagni's "Addio Mama" from *Cavalleria*, with Gennaro saying good-bye to his mother, although, unlike Turridu's mother, she is not actually present.

Gennaro is a sympathetic figure to some extent, but like most single-minded unrequited lovers he doesn't necessarily care about the needs or desires of the object of his affections. The libretto by Zangarini and Golisciani is very good, although some characterizations and details could have been richer. *Madonna* is unusual for Italian operas of this period (and operas in general) in that the baritone role (Rafaele) is larger and more dynamic than the tenor's.

Although Wolf-Ferrari apparently had no more success with *Madonna* in Italy than with his earlier operas (although *Madonna* was applauded everywhere else and became his most popular opera) it must have made some impression on the Italians; his next opera, *Sly*, with a libretto by Giovacchino Forzano, premiered not in Germany but at La Scala in 1927. The opera takes the character of Christopher Sly from Shakespeare's "The Taming of the Shrew," and makes him the butt of a cruel practical joke by an obnoxious earl. Kidnapped from a tavern while drunk by the earl, Sly wakes up in the latter's castle, where the servants have all been instructed to pretend he is lord of the manor, and the earl's mistress, Dolly, his wife. Sly is told that he has just recovered from a prolonged loss of memory. By the time Sly is made aware of the hoax, reminded that he is a penniless debtor, Dolly has genuinely fallen in love with him, but he commits suicide. Sly is more realistic than Dolly in that he realizes the idea of their having a life together, which she suggests just before she discovers that he's slashed his wrists, is ludicrous. Dolly is an underwritten character and she falls in love with Sly too easily. Pity, yes. Attraction, yes. But love? Even taking into account that the opera is a type of romantic fantasy, it's still a bit much. *Sly* is similar to *Tiefland* (see chapter 7) in that it's the hero and not the heroine who dreams of a romantic figure whom he eventually meets.

The opening of the first act is colorful and full of activity, if not as frenetic as the opening of *Madonna*, with a tavern full of card players and cheaters, drunks annoying chess players, the hostess hollering at drunks, a hullabaloo over the theft of several wine bottles etc. all scored with equal color by Wolf-Ferrari. The entrance of Dolly, an attractive, apparently wealthy and definitely out-of-her-element woman, into the tavern is handled with dramatic aplomb. Sly sings an aria ("Un orso in musoliera innamorato") called the "bear song," which forecasts his unhappy fate. A bear falls for a cat whose coat and hue remind him of the she-bear he loves. When the cat, not knowing bear language, fails to respond, the bear eats her. Sly mistakes himself for something else and is also consumed. Sly's subsequent aria "Ma bevi! bevi!," in which he drunkenly reveals his disappointment in life and utter loneliness ("I'd give my life just to hear the voice of a wife or child who'd say to me 'Good morning, Sly'"), tells us all we need to know of the poor man's past. The splendid act two love duet ("È la vita!"), in which Sly gives full vent to his romantic passion, and Dolly (unwillingly and guiltily playing him) realizes that she does care for the man, incorporates a "dream" theme first heard when the earl unfolds his plan to make Sly think he's living in a wonderful dream. A nice touch has the earl knocking Sly out of the dream state by pretending to be the sheriff knocking on the tavern door. Sly's long climactic aria in act three ("Eppure ... era commossa") which carries him from one emotion to another, hope, anger at what was done to him, despair, finally suicide, is quite fine in spots but never quite as musically vivid as one would hope. It is dramatically effective, however, and provides a moving wind up to the opera.

Francesco Cilea (1866–1950) was born in Palmi and attended the conservatory in Naples; years later he became the director of the institute. His opera *L'arlesiana* (1897) was popular in its day, but he only had a lasting success with *Adriana Lecouvreur*. This work premiered in 1902, and, until recently, has remained popular ever since. The story details the struggle between the (real life) actress Adriana Lecouvreur and the Princess de Bouillon over a handsome soldier named Maurizio who is really the pretender to the Polish throne. The two women really work themselves up into a lather over this guy, letting loose with bitchy ripostes in act three: the princess suggests that Adriana recite a soliloquy from "Ariadne Abandoned"; Adriana responds with a passage about an adulterous wife and even points directly at the princess to make her point. In act four the princess gets her revenge by sending Adriana poisoned flowers, which kill her to Maurizio's despair. The opera is typical of many others of its type in that serious matters of warfare are treated almost indifferently, taking a back seat to the romantic complications of soldiers. (Cilea also made many cuts to the score, which affected Arturo Colautti's libretto.)

Cilea is in full command of his musical powers with *Adriana*. While he does "repeat" some of the music, as some critics have charged, which is true of many composers, it is generally only specific themes that are reprised; in fact Cilea's melodic invention never flags. In act one Cilea employs the unusual device of having one chorus start a sentence and another group of singers finish the sentence, this being repeated throughout the number. There is nothing deep or startlingly new about *Adriana*. It is just an extremely entertaining opera that boasts an especially tuneful and often beautiful score, and great opportunities for strong singers to show off their technique. In act one these include Adriana's aria "Io son l'umile ancella del Genio creator," in which she responds to flattering praise by stating that she is only a vessel for artistic expression; and Maurizio's gorgeous piece comparing Adriana to mother, home and country, compliments which even she finds "high-flown"; this is reprised as a duet. In act two the Princess describes the sweet agony of waiting for her lover to arrive ("everything is suspended between doubt and desire") in "Acerba volutte." She and Maurizio have an effective informal duet as she realizes that Maurizio loves another ("Che mai diceste"). Maurizio begs the princess to be kind and tells her he'll always cherish her help and friendship ("L'anima ho stanca"). As good as these pieces are Cilea really takes off with the ravishing love duet between Maurizio and Adriana at the end of the act ("Tu sei la mia vittoria"). The ballet music of act three does not begin auspiciously, but gets much better as three Goddesses (Hera, Athena, and Aphrodite) show up to demand the Golden Apple of Hesperides meant for "the most beautiful of all," with the music matching the nobility of Hera, savagery of Athena, etc. The opening music of act four is saturated with a sense of doom, evoking a feeling of the clock ticking away for Adriana; this same music is used for her aria "Poveri fiori." Adriana and Michonnet (who also loves the actress) have a touching duet ("Bambina, non ti cruccior") in which both sing of how you must go on despite the agony of unrequited love. Adriana and Maurizio are given another beautiful love duet as they declare their devotion to one another ("No, la mia fronte"). This is an especially moving number and the opera itself concludes on a poignant note with Adriana's untimely demise. *Adriana* is truly the kind of opera they just don't make anymore.

Another Italian opera of the period that was once very popular until recent times was Italo Montemezzi's *L'amor dei tre re/The Love of Three Kings*, which premiered at La Scala in 1913. Montemezzi (1875–1952) was born near Verona, and he, too, was influenced to a certain extent by *Cavalleria*. In his opera, Italy of the tenth century has been invaded by barbarians. One of the spoils of war is the lovely Fiora, who looked forward to marriage to Prince Avito but instead was forced to wed Manfredo, the son of blind King Archibaldo. While Manfredo is off fighting, Fiora and Avito have a secret rendezvous, prompting Archibaldo to strangle his daughter-in-law. Hoping to ensnare her lover, the King puts poison on Fiora's lips, assuming Avito will sneak into the crypt for one last kiss. He does so — and dies — but so does Manfredo, whose corpse Archibaldo also discovers. Sam Benelli's libretto, based on his play, is interesting but the characters are stick figures at best. There are some critics who see *L'amore dei tre re* as being more elegant and superior to the verismo operas of the period (or at least an example of "higher-class" verismo), but they ignore certain inescapable realities about the work. Yes, Montemezzi's score is exciting and attractive, unusually orchestrated, with smooth tones and distinctive harmonies, it exudes a rushing urgency, but it is also very derivative (a potpourri of Wagner, Puccini, and other composers), and has limited melodic inspiration. Motives aside, Montemezzi has a tendency to recycle the same few ideas without the variation that would make them less repetitive. Today we have a great many composers who are actually better at orchestrating than they are at composing; Montemezzi could be one of the first. This is not to say that Montemezzi can not craft some very expressive and sensitive moments, such as in act two when Manfredo (in a recitative) asks his wife for something of hers that he can hold "close to my heart when I am away" ("Oh Fiora, dammi alcuna cosa tua che mi possa tenere presso al cuore, mentre sarò lontano"). Montemezzi sets this to an absolutely exquisite phrase, and there are others. Also, while *L'amore* is not a number opera as such, there are some memorable pieces. These include Archibaldo's stirring first act aria ("Italia! Italia! è tutto il mio ricordo") in which he narrates the tale of how as a young soldier he and his comrades came upon Italy, fell in love, conquered her, and will never leave her; Manfredo's heartfelt aria in act two ("Suonata è l'ora della partenza"), in which with raw intensity he bears his heart and soul to Fiora, needing her to care for him as he rushes back into lonely battle; and the beautiful ensemble piece in act three as the mourners surround Fiora's tomb ("Fiora, Fiora, non dai tu la risposta?"). The act two love duet for Avito and Fiora is rather Wagnerian and undeniably ravishing. Montemezzi simply recycles this material for Avito's and Manfredo's final arias over the corpse of the woman they loved. Manfredo, in particular, should not be singing to the music used to illustrate the passion between his wife and another man.

Franco Leoni (1864–1949), another pupil of Ponchielli's, had much less success than Puccini or Mascagni, although he did compose one opera that remained in the repertoire for a limited time: *L'oracolo/The Oracle*, which premiered at Covent Garden in 1905 and finally reached the Metropolitan ten years later. Leoni had moved to London after finding little encouragement in his native country, and his earliest operas had English texts (*L'oracolo* has an Italian text). He did a few operas after *L'oracolo*, including a version of *Francesca da Rimini* (1913) but these did not catch on. *L'oracolo*, which is only borderline verismo, has been mislabeled as a kind of "horror" or "Grand Guignol" opera because the main murder weapon is a hatchet and the characters are Chinese — the story takes place in San Francisco's Chinatown — bringing forth visions of the evil Dr. Fu Manchu in minds that are more comfortable with stereotypes. The excellent opera is actually a moving tragedy. Chim-Fen, owner of an opium den, wants to marry Ah-Joe, the daughter of the merchant Hu-Tsin, but she only has eyes for San-Lui. During the procession of the dragon when everyone is distracted, Chim-Fen kidnaps Hu-Tsin's baby son Hu-Chi, hoping that his father will offer Ah-Joe's hand in marriage to whomever finds his boy. But San-Lui discovers the child before Chim-Fen can return him, so Chim-Fen murders the man with a hatchet. Ah-Joe is driven literally insane with grief over the death of her lover. San-Lui's father, the distinguished doctor Win-Shee, finds the little boy and returns him to Hu-Tsin. Quietly speaking to

Chim-Fen, who feigns indignation over San-Lui's murder, as they sit on a bench, Win-Shee first stabs, then strangles, the horrible man who murdered his son. A policeman walking by thinks the two men, one of whom is dead, are engrossed in conversation. When he turns the corner, the body drops to the ground. San-Lui is dead, Ah-Joe is insane, and a good and decent man has been driven to murder.

Leoni's score is consistently lovely and colorful, reminiscent of Puccini if only because of its continual strain of lyricism. Consisting of one melody after another with hardly any recitatives, it builds in intensity to a satisfying conclusion. The opera begins and ends with the crowing of a cock. Win-Shee and Chim-Fen sing a duet ("Pensa prima all'uomo lussurioso") in which the latter asks for advice and in reply the doctor actually sums up his character and warns him about the consequences of his behavior. This piece has an added power and poignancy when Win-Shee reprises it as he holds the corpse of the man who murdered his son at the end of the opera. During the procession, there is an attractive, sinister chorus ("Il drago! Il drago!") as the crowd calls for a dragon to "rise from the waves" to protect them even as an atrocity, the kidnapping of the small boy, takes place behind their backs. Win-Shee is given a haunting aria, a foreshadowing of tragedy, that swells into a melancholy chorus ("Vedo sei placide lune"). The centerpiece of the opera is a love duet which begins as Ah-Joe's ode to the sun and dawn — sort of an "it's great to be young, alive, (and sexy)" aria — which culminates in a chorus that repeats the beautiful theme ("Bianca luce silente"). Despite an excellent recording conducted by Richard Bonynge and with Joan Sutherland and Ryland Davies as the lovers, the opera is hardly ever revived, and should be. "All of us involved in it found it highly dramatic and touching," wrote Joan Sutherland in her memoirs. "The reviews talked of the indebtedness of the work to Puccini, some with quotes like 'Poor man's Puccini?' and re-quoting Henry Krehbiel's assessment in 1915 of it as 'Puccini and water.' However, they had to admit it was 'a powerful and interesting work.'"[1]

Riccardo Zandonai (1883–1944) was a pupil of Mascagni, and although Zandonai developed his own (perhaps grimmer) style, the influence of his teacher is readily apparent. Among his several operas, the one lasting success was *Francesca da Rimini* (1914), although its popularity has faded. The last major production of the work was at the Metropolitan in the 1980's. Although the libretto was by Tito Ricordi, it was based on a play by Gabriele D'Annunzio, and, as usual, has an emphasis on forbidden love and twisted passions. Mascagni's *Parisina*, which premiered the year before, was a more monumental piece (it is said that Zandonai, perhaps out of jealousy, and because the works had similar plots, did not like it), but *Francesca* is also in its way a masterwork. Lovely Francesca has been promised to the brutal Gianciotto of the barbaric Malatesta family. To make the idea more palatable to her, she is tricked into believing that the more poetic-looking Paolo, Gianciotto's brother, is the man she is to wed. Francesca and the real Gianciotto are married, but Francesca and the handsome, sensitive Paolo can't fight the feelings that they have for one another. Aided by the third Malatesta brother, Malatestino, Gianciotto catches his wife and Paolo together and kills them.

The total effect of the opera is very strong, featuring music that is consistently absorbing with its gloomy undertones beneath the essentially lyrical structure. Even the romantic music has an almost violent underpinning, a tone of constant simmering menace. There are few set pieces or major melodies in the opera, but it seems to work without them for much of the music is splendid, such as during the "silent" love scene in act one. The effect of this purely orchestral sequence, when Francesca hands Paolo a rose and the two fall in love, is so marvelous, the music so beautiful, that they actually don't need to sing a note. Act four features a brief but vivid, ravishing duet ("Vieni, vieni, Francesca") that is a burst of untrammeled passion cruelly cut short by their sudden and violent deaths. Music for Francesca and her husband is also quite good, imbued with a kind of romantic hopelessness, while the battle music in act two is rousing and effective. The bit in act four with the brothers carrying about and playing with the severed head of an enemy — a symbol of the utter bestiality of the well-named Maletestas (two out of three at least) — is an inspired touch. Act three, when Paolo first comes to Francesca's chamber, is superb throughout, especially Paolo's aria "Perché volete voi," in which he tells of how miserable he's been and how obsessed he is by thoughts of the sister-in-law he loves. Of more manageable length than *Parisina*, and with a similar plot, *Francesca* will undoubtedly continue to be revived while Mascagni's opera — at least in its full length — languishes.

Ottorino Respighi (1879–1936), born in Bologna, is better-known internationally for his tone poems than for his many operas, which nowadays are rarely performed. His *Belfagor* premiered at La Scala in 1923. In this the title character, a devil, has heard once too often a doomed soul lament that his wife was responsible for his fall from grace, so he decides to see if this is true by getting married himself. Through subterfuge Belfagor manages to wed a girl named Candida in place of her lover Baldo, but Candida, still faithful to Baldo, will not sleep with Belfagor, who falls in love with her. Aided by her mother, Candida manages to escape from the devil and is reunited with her one true love; the devil is stymied. Resphigi's score is a notable one, especially the somber prologue, the shimmering love music throughout the opera, and the final duet in which Baldo, stirred up by the devil in disguise, wonders if Candida has truly been faithful to him. Baldo is convinced of her fidelity when the church bells start pealing all at once.

Respighi's best-known opera *La fiamma/The Flame* premiered in 1934. The plot deals with a woman, Silvana, who falls in love with her stepson, Donello, and uses the magic powers — or la fiamma — she inherited from her mother to bewitch him into loving her back. Silvana's husband Basilio is literally shocked to death when he finds his wife and son together, and Silvana is convicted and sentenced to death for killing her husband and ensorceling his son. The libretto has its fascinating elements, although one might wish that the characters, especially the lovers Silvana and Donello, were better developed and that another quarter to half an hour had been added to the running time. Heavily influenced by Mascagni, Respighi sets the libretto to music with a sure hand, employing lyrical and well-orchestrated recitatives with some memorable arioso and chorale numbers, as well as many wonderful bits of color and melody. The sophisticated, elegant music always fits perfectly to the dialogue, actions and emotions of the characters. Act one has no outstanding arias, although Silvana's "No Monica, really," in which she explains to her handmaidens how oppressed and unhappy she feels in the palace, and Donello's "Dear scenes of my childhood," in which he sings to Silvana of how well he remembers the home he grew up in and its surroundings, come close, as does the climatic chorus of the mob as witch Agnes (who tells Silvana of her mother's abilities) is led away to be burned at the stake.

In act two Respighi writes insinuatingly amusing music for the opening sequence when Donello teases the handmaidens about their virginity or lack of same. (This has to do with an idol of Aphrodite that allegedly tears the clothing off women who are not chaste.) The music at the end of the act, as Silvana uses her dormant powers to ensnare Donello, and calls him to her for a passionate kiss, positively vibrates with urgent, rising, unrestrained eroticism. Silvana is also given a genuinely melodious aria ("Ah, ah, disaster"), which becomes a duet with her husband Basilio, as she reacts with horror to the news about her mother and Basilio tries to console her.

Act three's centerpiece is a superb love duet ("That magical moment") between Silvana and Donello which perfectly captures the sensual flavor of their night trysts and Silvana's total abandonment to long-delayed, forbidden passion. This is swiftly followed by another beautiful duet ("Ah, let me die now") during which Donello keeps stirring as if from a dream, awakening momentarily not from a spell, but out of guilt over betraying his father. Out of context the music leading up to Silvana's trial scene may sound like cheap strains from a biblical movie, but it adds tension and creates suspense over what will happen to the anti-heroine. The choir's "Praise be to God the Son," a musical depiction of the battle of Christianity vs. the pagan forces represented by the witch Silvana, may be too beatific for all tastes, but is rather magnificent. The third act also has a few pieces that may be effective in one regard, but are otherwise mediocre or simply blah. Overall, however, *La fiamma* is an impressive work.

When Pietro Mascagni first entertained thoughts of doing an opera on Nero, Arrigo Boito, one of Verdi's greatest librettists and the composer of *Mefistofele* (1868), was already working on his own opera on Nero, but Mascagni scoffed at the notion that he would finish it before his own version was complete. He knew that Boito was, to put it mildly, a slow worker. Although Mascagni was unaware of this at the time, Verdi was urging Boito on to finish his version of *Nerone*.

Boito never did finish *Nerone*, only the second opera of his lifetime (it was completed by Antonio Smareglia, Vincenzo Tommasini, and Arturo Toscanini), yet, ironically, it premiered in 1924, beating out Mascagni's *Nerone* by eleven years, mostly because Mascagni had gotten sidetracked by other projects. Boito's version, although a noteworthy opera (and certainly a curiosity) in its own right, finishes second to Mascagni's, although it does have its own fascinating aspects. As in Mascagni's opera, Nero fancies himself an artist, singer and composer, as he did in real life. Apparently Nero has murdered his own mother and told the senate that she was plotting against him, and once discovered, took her own life. (This is more or less inspired by actual events.) In addition to the misadventures of Nero, Boito's libretto creates a conflict between the forces of pagan evil in the guise of the priest Simon Magus, and Christian goodness in the form of somewhat Christ-like Phanuel. There's also a vestal virgin named Rubria (good) and a wild camp follower, like something out of D'Annunzio, named Asteria (bad), who has a perverse hero worship for Nero. In her act one aria ("Vo' seguirlo"), as she sings that "horror attracts me like a lover, the only ecstasy I know is in wild and violent dreams" she seems to be lost in sadomasochistic fantasies. "Love which does not kill is not love," she adds. Simon Magus is given an excellent piece ("S'avanza una gran nube") in which he sings to Phanuel of the "temple that will have dominion over the earth" and offers him money for his "magic." The music for the climax and finale of act one is excellent, including the processional chorus ("Apollo torna") and the chorus in which Nero is welcomed like a young God ("Ave, Nerone"). In act two Simon Magus urges Nero to stare into a mirror and strike a shield to dispel any phantoms he may see ("Ecco il magico specchio"); sinister, rhythmic background chords help put this aria over. Asteria urges Nero, who has condemned her to death, not to throw her into a snake pit, as she is a snake charmer and their poison will not kill her ("Invan me danni!"). She reaffirms her adoration of him and his destructive ways and assures him she'll pursue him until death. Nero sees her as a wretched "incubus" (or succubus). There are two more acts which contain some nice pieces but nothing especially outstanding. Despite many compelling moments and striking music, Boito's *Nerone* doesn't quite jell, and the emperor himself, strictly a one-note villain without any nuances as in Mascagni's version, seems to get lost at times amidst all the other characters. Boito's *Nerone* is less likely to be revived than Mascagni's.

Puccini, always with one eye on what his various rivals were up to, was determined to attend a rehearsal of the opera, which was being conducted by Toscanini at La scala. Toscanini spotted Puccini where he was hiding, and ordered him out of the theater. Puccini was still determined to hear "the famous *Nerone*, in which I believe very little," and figured a composer of his stature would have no trouble getting into the dress rehearsal. He was wrong. Toscanini had heard of Puccini's negative comments about *Nerone*, which he, Toscanini, had personally worked on, and was in no mood for Puccini's sniggering. Puccini was again told he had to leave the theater upon the direct orders of Toscanini himself. Puccini was mortified.[2] *Nerone*'s premiere was a success (although the opera itself ultimately was not), which further rankled the hurt Puccini. Puccini did not live long enough to see Mascagni's version.

Meanwhile in Spain, there was a similar interest in sex and violence, as the verismo style began to insinuate itself into the national musical theater known as zarzuela.

4. The Passion of Zarzuela: Spain, South America, Cuba, 1900–1950

While few Spanish composers were seen as being at the forefront of operatic output in the twentieth century — certainly not as compared to Italian and German composers — they were not exactly idle, either. A great many Spanish composers contributed to the national musical theater of Zarzuela. Zarzuela is a form of musical entertainment that has been popular in Spain and other Spanish-speaking countries for centuries. There were baroque zarzuelas in the mid seventeenth to eighteenth centuries but these were replaced in popularity in the mid-nineteenth century by romantic zarzuelas, of which there are two types: género chico zarzuelas are short works geared toward a more popular audience; género grande zarzuelas are longer, two to three act works with much more operatic content. Most zarzuelas are combinations of opera or operetta and musical theater, although some are full-scale operas without any spoken dialogue or musical comedy style numbers. By the twentieth century the popularity of zarzuelas was not as great as it had been, but there were still many romantic zarzuelas up until the 1950's.

Among the major composers of the genre were Jacinto Guerrero (1875–1951); Francisco Alonso (1887–1948); Pablo Sorozábal (1897–1988); Federico Moreno Torroba (1891–1982); and Amadeo Vives (1871–1932). Guerrero's zarzuelas include *Los gavilanes*, from which comes the lilting "Mi aldea"; *La rosa del azafrán*, which boasts the fetching can-can like "Canción del Sembrador"; and *El huésped del sevillano*, which features the soaring aria "Raquel." Alonso composed such works as *Coplas de Ronda*, from which comes the pleasant if standard "Serenata," and *La parranda*, whose best-known number is "Canto al Murcia." Pablo Sorozábal composed *La des manoja de rosas* and *La tabernera del puerto* (1936) — which has been called "the last great zarzuela"[1] — from which comes the memorable and dramatic aria "No peude ser." Torroba's *Maravilla* (1941) smacks as much of the music hall as it does the opera house, featuring such teasy and catchy numbers as "Amor, vida de mi vida." His better-known *Luisa Fernanda* (1932), which has long spoken dialogue sequences, deals with a triangle between the title character and two men named Javier and Vidal. Most of the music is very pleasant and tuneful, even infectious, and there is at least one outstanding number, when Luisa's act three arioso ("Cállate, corazón!") becomes a duet with Javier. The "happy" but downbeat ending has Vidal nobly giving Luisa to her true lover Javier, who did not exactly treat the woman very well to begin with.

Amadeo Vives began by writing serious operas in the late nineteenth century, but he found zarzuelas more lucrative and composed literally dozens of them. His most famous is *Doña Francisquita* (1923). Francisquita loves Fernando, who supposedly loves the snippy actress Aurora. Fernando's father, Don Matias, also loves and wants to marry Francisquita, to the amazement of the girl's mother, who thinks Don Matias wants to marry her. To make Fernando jealous, Francisquita pretends she is interested in his father. A number of amusing situations develop from this basic premise, which could have been easily resolved if Francisquita at some point only admitted she loves Fernando, who is clearly only using Aurora to make Francisquita jealous. A ridiculous scene in act two has Cardona, a friend of Fernando's, dressing up in drag supposedly so that he can sneak up on women, and somehow make love to them, but of course it's only the men who make passes. (A more sophisticated piece would probably make something out of that.) The problem with mounting *Doña Francisquita* as an opera is that there are many more spoken dialogue sequences than musical ones, but at least the music is charming. Act one boasts a wonderful Chorus of the Wedding Party, and there is a fine duet in act two between Aurora and Fernando in which she declares love and he denies it. Interestingly, the act two duet between the true lovers Francisquita and Fernando, while itself lovely, is not quite as good.

Another prolific composer of zarzuelas was Rafael Millán (1893–1938), who generally worked in collaboration with A. López Monís. One of their most memorable creations was *El pájaro azul* (circa 1920's) which, like many zarzuelas, is a combination of music hall songs, Gilbert and Sullivan pastiches, and genuinely operatic duets and arias. Among the highlights of the work are the sweeping ensemble "Yo fui él que la besó" which leads into the act one finale, and the outstanding duet "La luz de la luna," which is the centerpiece of act two. There is another memorable aria in act one, but the whole zarzuela is full of good tunes of varying degrees of intensity.

The most famous of all zarzuelas — thanks largely to its being championed by Plácido Domingo — is Manuel Penella's *El gato montés/The Wild-cat* (1916), a prime example of género grande. Soleá was once the lover of the man now known as El Gato Montés, who committed manslaughter and had to go into hiding. In the meantime, the abandoned Soleá has fallen for the bullfighter Rafael, whose family has taken her under her wing. "Gato" reappears to lay claim to Soleá and tells Rafael that if he survives his upcoming bullfight, he will still have to deal with him. Rattled by this threat, Rafael rallies his courage but succumbs in the arena and is killed. Soleá dies of a broken heart, and as Gato mourns her the authorities close in on him.

Penella's music, clearly influenced at times by both Puccini and Mascagni, simply flows along with great adeptness and dramatic tension. Basically *El gato montes* is a work of verismo, although the music is perhaps lighter than that of the Italian veristi. Act two works up a great deal of suspense over what will happen to Rafael in the bullring, and is very dramatically handled by Penella. The wonderful bullfighting theme (later adopted as the official bullfighting anthem in Madrid) that plays when Rafael is in the ring, captures the spectacular aspects, although hardly the ugliness, of the sport. Soleá has a lilting aria in act one, "Juntô dende chavaliyô," as she explains the lifelong devotion of El Gato Montés, and there is a delightful chorus in act one ("Claro q'e si!") as the crowd expresses its jubilation at the return of their hometown hero Rafael, the great matador. Arguably the greatest number in "El Gato Montés" is Rafael's powerful act two aria, "Señó, q'e no me forte er ualó," in which he prays that his courage not fail him before he enters the bullring for the final time.

Although the characters could have been developed much more (and if we knew the exact circumstances of Gato's manslaughter we might have had more sympathy for him), they are not necessarily unrealistic. For instance, Gato is typical of a certain criminal type who never takes responsibility for the misery he causes, especially, in this case, for Soleá, whom he supposedly adores... He is so self-absorbed that at the end of the opera he assumes Soleá has died out of love for him instead of Rafael. With a twisted love triangle that has fascinating aspects and music that is first-rate if not quite spectacular, *El gato montés* is one zarzuela that will probably have a long shelf-life.

José María Usandizaga was another zarzuela composer who was influenced by the Italian verismo movement in such operas as *Las golondrinas* (1914), but others were swept up in the success of *La viuda alegre* in Madrid circa 1910. This was actually Franz Lehar's 1905 operetta *The Merry Widow*, which was so popular in translation that many Spanish composers fell all over themselves trying to emulate it. Other zarzuela works eschewed Vienna for other locales: Pablo Luna's *Molinos de viento/The Windmills* (1910) was set in Holland, and Jose Serrano's *La Canción del olvido/The Song of Forget-fulness* (1916) took place in Naples. Luna also had a success with *El niño judío* in 1918. Jesus Guridi's *El caserio/The Little Farm* was an enduring work that premiered in 1926.

According to Steven Blier, "Zarzuelas don't seem to have the wit and irony we associate with Offenbach or Gilbert and Sullivan. The plot devices are typically: (1) men passing themselves off as illegitimate sons of nobility, (2) people romantically obsessed with someone from a different social class or age group, (3) smuggling and (4) bloodletting caused by romantic jealousy."[2]

Not every Spanish composer during this period became famous because of their zarzuelas. Manuel de Falla (1876–1946) and Enrique Granados (1867–1916) both wrote zarzuelas, but their best-known works—*La vida breve/Life Is Short* and *Goyescas* respectively—are considered legitimate operas. Both of these works, as indeed was true of many zarzuelas, were influenced by the success and style of *Cavalleria rusticana*. But whereas *Goyescas* is a first-rate verismo-style classic, *La vida breve* is just a third-rate imitation of *Cavalleria* without Mascagni's melodic inspiration and dramatic intensity. While there aren't as many recordings of *La vida breve* as there are of *Cavalleria*, there are at least a dozen versions on CD, yet there aren't many recordings of the far superior *Goyescas*. This is probably because Falla's music is held in high regard in certain musical circles, although his *La vida breve* is rarely mentioned nor perceptively analyzed by these same critics. In his estimable *Lives of the Great Composers,* Harold C. Schonberg writes: "Falla's output is small, but everything he composed is jewel-like in its workmanship.... Falla was not only far above any Spanish composer of his day; he was the only Spanish composer of the day who rose above mediocrity." Music critics, of course, look at a composer's total output, not just his operas, and may not even be sincere fans of opera. A hard cold look at *La vida breve*, which premiered in Nice (in a French version) in 1913, suggests that despite its being a verismo opera, there is little to recommended it to fans of verismo or anyone else for that matter. It has some nice moments, of course, but it's as if it were the verismo opera that only people who really don't like verismo opera can appreciate. *La vida breve* is perhaps more a folk opera than anything else, for it lacks the sustained tension and dramatic thrust of true verismo.

The by-the-numbers plot deals with a young woman, Salud, who drops dead after she confronts her lover, Paco, who, true to rumor, is about to marry another. The two-part love duet for Salud and Paco in act one is pleasant but second-rate, but there is a delicate, mournful theme for Salud that plays now and then throughout the opera and is excellent. The music for the flamenco dancing is perhaps the most arresting feature of the opera but it is usually improvised by the musicians. Salud's act one aria, "Hasta las canciones," in which she sings of a heartbroken bird fluttering to earth and dying, sets up the ending, in which she seems to will herself to die; the aria itself is minor. But the opera ends just as the confrontation between Salud and Paco might have become interesting. The intermezzo that plays between acts one and two is no match for Mascagni's in *Cavalleria*. Accomplished craftsmanship is all well and good, but in an operatic work it can not stand alone, and is no substitute for memorable arias and theatrical panache.

Granados' *Goyescas* also has a very basic story — a flirtation between a bullfighter, Paquiro, and a beautiful woman, Rosario, in Madrid leads to tragedy — but the music is so well-done and expressive that it easily overcomes all of the flaws and shortcomings of its limited libretto. The opera began life as a series of piano pieces (also called *Goyescas*) inspired by the paintings of Goya, whose work Granados much admired. Granados reworked the music into a full-length opera for the Paris Opera, but it never played Paris due to World War One. Instead it premiered at the Metropolitan Opera in New York in 1916 (it took Falla's *La vida breve* another ten years to reach the Met). Granados and his wife sailed to New York for the opening, which was the crowning — and final — moment of the forty-nine-year-old composer's career. On the return voyage, the ship was torpedoed by a German U-boat. Granados dived in after his wife when she fell out of a lifeboat and both of them drowned, leaving behind six children back in Spain.

In the ironic opening of *Goyescas*, celebrants are tossing around "peleles," straw figures meant to represent "tiresome or unwanted" lovers. Rosario feels this way about her boyfriend Fernando (hence her flirtation with Paquiro) at first, but comes to realize how much he means to her when he has been "discarded" by a knife thrust from Paquiro, giving the opera a circular feeling and a moment of closure. *Goyescas* could be dismissed as just another *Cavalleria* clone were it not for Granados' above average, evocative score, which is as technically polished as anything by Falla but also richly orchestrated and layered with unusual rhythms and timbres. There is a winning duet between Fernando and Rosario in act one ("Temiendo entre sonrojos") which becomes a brief quartet with Paquiro and Pepa. Scene nine of act three has melodious recitatives for Fernando and Rosario which swell into a beautiful and exciting love duet ("No sabes que es amor...!"), while Rosario's music in scene ten, as she clutches dying Fernando and sings over his corpse, manages to be moving — thanks to Granados — despite the one-dimensional quality of the characters.

While Granados' *Goyescas* is far more deserving of revival and recording than Falla's *La vida breve*, the latter composer did other works that are of interest. For instance Falla's short 1923 opera *El retablo de Maese Pedro/ Master Peter's Puppet Show* is so different from *La vida breve* that you can scarcely believe they have the same composer. This short work was commissioned by the Princess Edmond de Polignac, who also commissioned works from such composers as Stravinsky for performance in her private parlor. The opera begins with a pastiche of far eastern type music, then there is a notable orchestral piece ("La sinfonia de Maese Pedro") as patrons at an inn take their seats in preparation for the puppet show they are about to witness. The puppet story deals with the rescue of an Emperor's daughter, Melisendra, by the heroic Gayferos. A boy soprano intones (mostly tunelessly) what the audience is about to see in the puppet show, which is then enacted to background music of a vaguely Elizabethan nature. In the audience is one Don Quixote, who jumps up in irritation whenever the boy "embroiders" the narration or is inaccurate. As the puppet "villains" chase after the escaping lovers, Don Quixote jumps up on the stage and slashes at them, destroying the puppets and ruining the show in the process. Don Q. gets the most lyrical music in the piece: the arioso "Oh, Dulcinea," and the aria, celebrating knight errantry, "Oh vos otros." The music for *El Retablo* is slight, but lovely and delicate at times, and the total effect of the opera is quite charming.

In other Spanish-speaking nations across the ocean, other musicians continued the tradition of zarzuelas, opera, and musical theater. Cuban composer Gonzala Roig came out with the zarzuela *Cecelia Valdes* in 1932. The story takes place in the 1830's and concerns a mulatto, Cecelia Valdes, who has fallen in love with a white man, the wealthy student Leonardo. There are other complications besides the obvious ones. Leonardo may dally with Cecelia, but he intends to wed the more "appropriate" Isabel. A black musician named Pimiento is madly in love with Cecelia and savagely jealous of Leonardo. It then turns out that Leonardo, who has impregnated Cecelia, is her own half-brother! Pimiento crashes Leonardo's wedding to Isabel and murders him. The plot may be sheer verismo, but the music is, typical of the zarzuela, a smattering of styles that don't always fit the grim, disturbing storyline. A traditional overture leads into a kind of bouncy "calypso"-like number with somber undertones ("Delores") that is hardly typical of the 1830's. Still, there is a strangely haunting aspect to the piece. The song Cecelia sings about herself is forgettable — although Steven Blier describes it as "an irresistible medley of Cuban dance tunes — habanera, pachanga, huapango — part Carmen Miranda, part Victoria De Los Angeles" [3] — but there is an "old-fashioned" lilting operatic duet, heavy on the strings, that smacks of no one so much as Victor Herbert. Cecelia's final, tormented aria is underlaid with a "calypso" beat but again it makes for an effective touch.

Heitor Villa-Lobos (1887–1959) was born in Rio de Janeiro, Brazil, where he began as a self-educated street musician who worked his way up to opera composer only to have the production of his first opera, *Femina* (1908) canceled because the company, for which he played in the orchestra, couldn't pay its debts. *Izaht*, a highly colorful piece about gypsies, the underworld, and the high-born intermingling in Paris, premiered in Rio in 1940. His opera *Yerma*, which premiered in Santa Fe in 1971, was a verismo-style work that wasn't mounted until after his death.

In the late 1940s the theatrical entrepreneurs who had been responsible for *Kismet*, Robert Wright and George Forrest, got the idea of creating another hodgepodge musical, only this time it would be from the work of a living composer. The two men were surprised that Villa-Lobos was willing to participate, but as his operas weren't exactly being presented at the Met, the composer undoubtedly thought that this would be one way for his music to reach a wider audience — and in New York City at that. Villa-Lobos wrote some new material for the score, and used other pieces from his operas or from discarded sketches. Forrest and Wright wrote the lyrics and came up with the basic concept.

The result was the operatic–Broadway hybrid *Magdalena (A Musical Adventure)* (1947), which takes place in Colombia on the Magdalena river in 1912. The book was an odd affair of a woman named Maria who is in love with a bus driver, Pedro, who, unlike Maria, has no use for religion. The General who owns the emerald mines has a sexy girlfriend named Teresa who comes to Colombia to be with him, but when he decides he wants to marry Maria, Teresa feeds him such a tremendous banquet that he drops dead. There's a strike at the mines by Muzo Indians who are mistreated by the General's hirelings, Pedro's pagan friends steal a statue of the Madonna, which he returns, reuniting him with Maria, making for a happy, if simple-minded conclusion. Pedro is perfectly willing to love Maria as she is, but she's unable to accept that he has not converted to Christianity as she has. Well, at least there's the music. *Magdalena* has an extremely classy score for Broadway, written by a genuinely operatic composer who — unlike regular Broadway composers — really knows how to orchestrate his music, and did. The score boasts such memorable pieces as the beautiful and majestic "River Song"; the highly-attractive "emerald" duet sung by Maria and Pedro about the gem they found together as children; and "The Forbidden Orchid," a passionate duet for the same couple. The sleepy ballad "Magdalena" as a character known as the "old one" sings about the river is cleverly combined with the "Broken Pianolita" dance as youths keep kicking an old player piano each time it breaks down until it starts to play again. The greatest number bar none is "Food for Thought," Madame Teresa's incredibly sexy, suggestive and vibrant dance number as she sings of "life, love and food" in a saucy but "classical" tango uplifted and much enlivened by Villa-Lobos' orchestration.

While the Italian composers were obsessed with sex and violence — and not just on the opera stage — and the Spanish produced their zarzuelas and other works, the French — not entirely immune to the influence of verismo — were pursuing their own paths. From France would come more than one opera that would revolutionize the entire operatic industry.

5. Elegance and Romance: France, 1900–1950

There were many new and experimental types of operas being done in France throughout the twentieth century, but in at least the first half of the century, the more traditional types of operas had not yet disappeared. Who was more traditional than the great and prolific Jules Massenet? Although many of his best and most famous operas were behind him — *Herodiade* (1881), *Manon* (1884), *Le Cid* (1885), *Werther* (1887) and *Thais* (1894) — Jules Massenet was still a force to reckon with in the twentieth century and he continued to have many successes. The first of these was *Cendrillon*, his take on the Cinderella story.

Cendrillon was actually composed in 1895, and had its premiere in mid–1899 at the Opéra-Comique, but as it was written for the centennial it can be considered Massenet's first twentieth century opera. *Cendrillon* adds a living father, Pandolfe, for the girl along with the bossy "wicked" stepmother. At least as memorable as Rossini's *La cenerentola*, Massenet's version is romantic and amusing in equal measure. Highlights include the lovely opening piece of lute, violin and flute that opens act two and plays throughout the recitative that follows. The three musicians are playing this very simple, elegant, and infectious piece for the prince's amusement, but it fails to lighten his somber mood. Also memorable is the duet for Cinderella and the Prince that ends the act ("Eh bien ... laisse te main dans la mienne pressé") in which they declare their mutual love — just as midnight arrives. Their beautiful act three duet ("Tu me l'as dit ce nom") is in the best romantic Massenet tradition. On the debit side is the fact that the pleasant but unremarkable ballet music in act two seems to go on forever. Cendrillon's recitative-aria "Seule, je partirai, mon père," in which she decides to go into the woods alone to die, never quite develops a strong enough melody to become the major aria it should have been. But there's more than enough good music in *Cendrillon* to make it a notable addition to Massenet's oeuvre.

Massenet's *Sapho* first premiered at the Opéra-Comique in 1897, but Massenet came out with a revised version of this opera in 1909, adding a new act (four). This is another entry in the sensitive-country-lad-in-love-with-an-"experienced"-city-woman category. *Sapho* is actually Fanny, a beautiful artist's model who has been around; Jean is the provincial young farm boy with whom she becomes involved. Massenet's scoring is typical, nothing inventive or innovative in orchestration or effects, nothing special at all, but while *Sapho* is not a masterpiece like *Manon* or Verdi's *La traviata*, there are too many lovely things in the score for it to be spurned. These include Fanny's heartfelt plea in act five (the original act four) for Jean to reaffirm his love for her as she does her love for him, "Pendant un an je fus la femme," which is full of a *Manon*-like lyrical heartache. Also in this act is a wonderful duet between Jean and his mother ("Et mon coeur pour le tien") as they reaffirm their love for, and understanding of, each other. (In the new act four added by Massenet, Jean confronts Fanny after learning about her past and the two break up, causing Fanny to run after him in act five.) Massenet gives all of the principals notable arias: Jean, shy and afraid that the women at a party will laugh at him if he tries to dance, sings a gentle aria about his Provence ("Ah! qu'il est loin mon pays") in act one; his mother, Divonne, sings a song of farewell and maternal devotion ("Petit, voicí ta lampe") as she passes by the lamp with which she watched over her beloved son when he was a child (act two); and Fanny has a fairly powerful moment in act three telling off the men who dared to tell young Jean about her notorious past as the model "Sapho" ("Mon bonheur vous a fait"). Of course Jean has a lady friend back home, Irene, and she gets to remind him in act five that after all the years he can still come to her with his problems as she would go to him ("Si j'avais un jour quelque"). However, Fanny's aria "Ce que j'appel le beau," in which she responds to Jean's comments about the uplifting value of art and replies that a love between two people that lifts them above petty concerns is even greater, is marred by its similarity to a piece by Tchaikovsky; this is the main love theme, unfortunately. The love duet in act three is merely mediocre.

Le Jongleur de Notre-Dame (1902), about a juggler who joins a monastery and finds faith and redemption before he dies, has many admirers — Massenet himself was convinced it was to be his masterpiece — but he composed at least two other great operas in the twentieth century, *Chérubin* and *Thérèse*. *Chérubin*, which premiered in Monte Carlo in 1905, is one of Massenet's most delightful stage works. *Chérubin* is in a sense a sequel to Mozart's *Le nozze di Figaro* and follows the romantic exploits of the seventeen-year-old Cherubino. The opera presents the amorous youth as an officer involved with several ladies, including a Spanish singer, his attractive tutor, and the count's ward, Nina. Once Chérubin himself is hurt by being forgotten by a one-night-stand (of sorts), he understands what women feel and opts for a mature mutual love (over mere sexual adventuring) with Nina. *Chérubin* boasts a very effective, consistently pleasing and lyrical score with an amusing, bawdy, yet tender libretto. Despite the lack of many outstanding "numbers," everything just comes together in *Chérubin* and it works beautifully.

The opera begins with a wonderful, tuneful overture that has just the right amount of energy and sense of fun. Act one boasts Nina's aria, "Lorsque vous n'aurez rien a faire," in which she recites the intensely romantic lyrics of Chérubin's love poem to one of Massenet's loveliest and most delicate musical confections. In act two, Chérubin manages to effortlessly seduce the Spanish dancer L'Ensolleillad by coming on all teary, virginal and pathetic in the aria/duet "Où importe demain et tout l'avenir!" In act three, L'Ensolleillad hails the "love that dies in one night" ("Vive amour qui rêve") in a beautiful piece with a haunting flute and guitar background. This and the act three duet for Nina and Chérubin ("Aimer, sentir, souffrir..."), in which they declare their mutual love, are the finest pieces in the opera. The first soprano to play Chérubin was Mary Garden.

Thérèse, which had its first performance in Monte Carlo in 1907, is considered Massenet's second "verismo" opera after *La Navarraise,* which had the same librettist, Jules Claretie. During the French revolution, Thérèse is married to the older Andre Thorel, to whom she feels great affection and gratitude but no particular passion. That is reserved for her former lover, Armand, the Marquis de Clerval, who had to flee France after leaving his estate in the good hands of his friend Thorel. Now he has entered the country in secret and wants Thérèse to run away with him. Thérèse has agreed to do just that, until she finds out that her husband has been arrested and sees him being led off to the guillotine in the street below. She shouts out to the crowd, sealing her doom, then runs down to join her husband in death.

Massenet does a masterful job of scoring *Thérèse.* His music recreates the tension, horror, and sheer suspense of the period and the opera's situations. Pulling the listener back in time, it expertly creates a highly compelling mood and the exciting prelude grabs you from the first. All of the main characters are given expressive arias exploring their innermost feelings, and the music for the fifth scene in act one is particularly memorable. This is the sequence wherein Thérèse and Armand are reunited and contains two ariosos for the latter: "Le Passe," in which Armand explains that Thérèse is his most sacred memory of the past; and "Oublier! T'oublier!," in which he recalls dancing a minuet (which plays in the background) with Thérèse at the ball at Versailles. Act two contains a beautiful trio for the principals, "Adieu, maintenant," in which they bid each other — and their secret hopes — farewell. Of special note is Thérèse's aria, "Ah! Viens, partons!" in which she agrees to run off with Armand. In addition to these and other lyrical flights, Massenet's scoring adeptly punctuates dramatic moments such as when the orchestra unleashes a burst of sound as a background to Armand's anger when he discovers revolutionary posters plastered all over his childhood home and former property.

Armand, who wants to run off with his friend's wife, would be a loathsome character were it not for two things: Andre and Thérèse were lovers before she married Thorel, and Armand does not seem to be aware that Thorel has been arrested (in any case he says nothing about it). Thérèse does not want Armand to look out of the window because she's afraid if he learns of Thorel's fate he won't go (the lovers have arranged a rendezvous for later on) and will also die. The ending of *Thérèse* would be particularly unsettling if the heroine, who is only twenty, makes her sacrifice only out of a sense of wifely duty, but there are indications that she dies for love. In her first aria, "Oui, ta femme rest seule," she expresses her fear of the future, that one day Thorel will not return to her side. It is possible that Thérèse at first decides to join Thorel out of duty, but once she spots him in the crowd, it is love, her complete unwillingness to let this fine man die alone, that motivates her actions. While the libretto may not underline this, it is tacit, adding a poignant undertone to an action that would otherwise seem masochistic or even demented.

Massenet's *Don Quichotte/Don Quixote* premiered in Monte Carlo in 1910, and was the last of his operas to remain fairly popular over the years. In this Dulcinea (or Dulcinée) is not a low class kitchen slut and whore (Aldanza) transformed into a lovely virgin (Dulcinea) by Quixote's imagination and chivalry, but a combination, more along the lines of the eternally amused, much admired Sapho in his earlier opera. Highlights of the score include Don Quichotte's love song to Dulcinea, "Quand apparaissent les étoiles," which becomes a duet with her after Don Q's brief sword fight with another suitor, Juan; Sancho's moving aria in defense of his master, "Ça, vous commetiez tous un acte épouvantable"; and the Entr'acte between acts four and five, virtually a cello solo hinting at the grim ending to come. One of Massenet's loveliest pieces, it is sung by Dulcinea at the end of act five. *Don Quichotte* could be labeled as pleasant but minor Massenet, but it has too many lovely things in it to be dismissed, and on the whole the opera works beautifully on an emotional level. Yet there's nothing in it quite as beautiful as Mitch Leigh's "Dulcinea" from *Man of La Mancha* (more of which later). Massenet fashioned the title role for Russian bass Chaliapin, who sang it in Monte Carlo, where Lucy Arbell was his leading lady. Apparently Massenet hoped to make Arbell his own leading lady, of sorts, as he became quite taken with her charms — at first. Afterward he found her rather difficult.

Massenet's final opera was *Cléopâtre*, which premiered in Monte Carlo in 1914, two years after his death. In this our gal Cleo is depicted as an anything-for-a-thrill slut, but she does genuinely fall in love with Mark Antony at the end, and the opera certainly gets across Mark Antony's utter obsession with Cleopatra. *Cléopâtre* is not especially moving, however, because neither character is exactly likable. While the music never has Puccinian beauty, Wagnerian power, nor Mascagnian intensity, it is often quite lovely and effective, making *Cléopâtre* work perfectly well as a melodious stage spectacle. An interesting bit in act two, scene two has Cleopatra turned on by a sexy male dancer named Adamos; so jealous is her freed slave/lover Spakos, that he attacks the youth. The folks in the tavern turn on him and Cleopatra (who is in disguise) until she calms the crowd by revealing who she really is. In a disappointing aria ("C'est bien! Je croyais tout connaître") she thanks the crowd for giving her a new thrill: fear! Not so disappointing is Cleo's act three aria in which she offers her slaves a kiss if they drink a cup full of poison ("J'ai versé, le poison"), which is sensual and deceptively "romantic." There is a beautiful duet for Cleo and Antony in act four ("C'est l'heure la plus douce") about the loveliest hour of all being the hour when they are reunited. Also memorable is Cleopatra's final aria "Grands Dieux," when a sudden terror overtakes her sacrifice with the asp: "I cannot die — I who was all love, all joy — I who was Cleopatra. My eyes grow dim...." There were critics who found *Cléopâtre* too similar to Massenet's *Thaïs* (1894). According to Massenet biography James Harding, *Cléopâtre*'s "melodic line follows, with almost the same intervals, the sinuous pattern of the courtesan's vocalizing" and dubbed it, strangely, "sub–Debussy pastiche."

Massenet's light may have dimmed and eventually gone out in the early years of the twentieth century, but he still left behind a solid body of memorable works that are alive with romance and musical poetry. (His other twentieth century works are *Ariane* (1906), *Bacchus* (1909), *Roma* (1912), *Panurge* (1913), and *Amadis* (1922); of these, only *Amadis* and *Roma* have been recorded as of this writing.)

As Massenet was composing his final operas, there were other French composers who were determined to change the way the French public — and the world — saw opera. A year after *Cendrillon* made its debut, Massenet's pupil Gustave Charpentier (1860–1956) came out with *Louise*, and two years after that Claude Debussy (1862–1918) offered his *Pelléas et*

Mélisande. The two operas were both highly influential to varying degrees, but they could not be more unalike. Charpentier's masterpiece, despite some "fantastic" elements in act three, is decidedly naturalistic, and a prime example of French verismo (although its style is very different from the Italian type). The opera made quite an impression on Leoš Janáček — who admired it greatly, at least at first, and studied it carefully — and other composers, and with its frank treatment of "free love" among the young helped open the doors to increasingly sophisticated librettos dealing with all manner of licentiousness. Looking at this intensely romantic opera today, it may be hard to imagine that once upon a time it was considered rather scandalous.

Louise lives with her loving father and stern mother in a suburb of Paris, and is in love with the poet Julian. The parents object to the relationship because Julian is a bohemian with little money. Julian importunes Louise to move in with him in Montmarte, but the mother comes to get her back, citing her husband's illness — his broken heart over Louise's desertion — as the reason why she must return. Once home, Louise realizes that her father will not accept that she is no longer a little girl, and runs off again to Julien and the lights and romance of Paris as her father shakes his fist and cries "Ah! Paris!" It is a powerful, bittersweet conclusion.

Louise's mother is ridiculously priggish towards Louise's relatively innocent flirtation with Julian. Yet she compares the poet to her tired, hardworking husband, and understandably sees the former as a loafer. Louise's father simply says to Louise, "If we are prudent toward those who notice you, it is (because) having arrived at the end of the road that you begin, we know all the miseries of it." It is clear that Louise's parents have respect but no great love for one another, and Mother is deeply disappointed with her life. She feels that "free love" is "only a way to slide out of marriage," even though her own marriage is no picnic. She is physically abusive with Louise, yet shows ultimate love for the girl when she tries to prevent the father from hurting her and throwing her out of the house. (There are possible hints of the father's incestuous feelings for Louise, which may explain the mother's love/hate attitude toward her daughter, but it is not clear if this was Charpentier's intention.)

Charpentier wrote the libretto as well as the score, and managed the great feat of not only exploring the points of view of the major characters — all of whom are three-dimensional and utterly alive — but of minor ones in assorted vignettes and ariosos through which their hopes and sorrows and resentments are made vividly clear. (A minor character named Gertrude is given the touching, telling line: "For the kiss of a young lover, without regret I'd give the remainder of life.") The prelude to act two captures the sights, sounds and smells of Montmarte at dawn with its colorful orchestration.

Although clearly influenced by Wagner, Charpentier developed his own style which is redolent of Paris and the young, and his music at times exudes an exquisite tenderness.

Act three is saturated with music of a momentous gorgeousness, detailing as it does the growing love and passion between Louise and Julien, and indeed their passionate love affair with the city of Paris and all that it represents. There is the beautiful prelude, comprised of several recurring themes, that encapsulates the idyllic happiness of the couple in their love nest in Montmarte. Louise's rapture-of-love aria "Depuis le jour," is arguably the finest in the opera and has become a famous concert number, but it is equaled by other beautiful pieces, such as Julien's aria "De Paris tout en fête" which turns into a duet and a glorious tribute to Louise and the city of Paris. This leads into one glorious number after another: the duet and chorus where the celebrants sing "let us be free according to our conscience"; the chorus of Bohemians' "Jour d'allégresse," which is a hymn of the triumph of their art and philosophy over their poverty; the Father of Fool's aria "O jolie!," during which he crowns Louise the Muse of Montmarte; and the Chorus of the Apotheose, a superb number in which most of the people on stage sing in homage to Louise while others simply comment on the action. Some mothers sing that Louise has forgotten that "her parents are worried"; some cynically comment that "it'll be the worse for her"; while a group of urchins note of the excitement that "It's better than at the opera!"

Charpentier wrote some especially interesting music for the father, Pierre, who is introduced in act one to a "heavy," somber theme of sheer aging weariness tempered with his affection for his daughter. We hear this theme again in act three after Louise's mother appears with a dramatic flourish to interrupt the festivities; the grim music paces the mother as she slowly approaches Louise to tell her of Pierre's illness. Pierre is given a lot of material in act four. In his aria "Après vingt jours de paresse," he sings about the hardships of life, of being tossed aside by the young (especially your own children) ("[they] wait that death shall come to deliver them from those who would die for them.") Initially his aria "Voir nature une enfant," in which he sings of watching his child grow, protecting her, loving her, only to have her taken away, is the most moving in the opera, but the father almost seems demented in his reluctance to accept that Louise is grown up. This is underlined in his subsequent lullaby "Reste ... repose-toi...," which makes it clear that part of the problem is that he is unable to accept his own age and mortality and hopelessness. It is also true that Pierre doesn't want to see his daughter ruined by a wastrel and have the life of poverty he sees as her future. And, of course, Julien will not marry her.

Jules Massenet admired *Louise*—"you are an admirable artist and my heart was filled with happiness on hearing the cheers of the whole audience," he wrote Charpentier — and was genuinely overjoyed with Charpentier's and other pupils' success. For his part, Charpentier was grateful that Massenet had never forced his own style on his students but let them develop in their own way. "I owe an enormous amount to Massenet because he made me understand music, and, above all, love it," he said.[1]

If *Louise* was the most romantic of operas (despite the blunt anti-sentimentalism of the scenes with the parents), Charpentier's sequel, *Julian*, was one of the most anti-romantic, this in spite of the fact that its fantastic, almost surrealistic quality is in direct contrast to the naturalism of *Louise*. Charpentier took some of the music from a short piece called *La Vie du Poéte*, and the full-length opera premiered in 1913. The prologue has Julien and Louise living together in Rome. Julien is preoccupied with his dreams and hopes, and as he sleeps Louise feels duty-bound to support those dreams. (It is possible that the rest of the opera consists of Julien's actual dreams.) Julien genuinely wants to make the world a better place and ease mankind's suffering and may be seen by some as a Christ figure, although it is by no means conclusive that this was how Charpentier wanted him to be perceived. The four acts take the poet through various life stages and are named for them: Enthusiasm (act one); Doubt (act two); Impotence (act three); and Intoxication (act four). In each act, Julien encounters a woman who is a different aspect of Louise.

In act one Julien is full of youthful idealism, ardor and optimism, and the music is gloriously *Louise*-like. He knows that many poets, seekers of truth and beauty, fail miserably, but he is certain that he will succeed. In act two, a disillusioned Julien, whose idealism has apparently been sorely tested, has wondered onto a farm where he meets a peasant's daughter — also named Louise — who wants to help him forget his (somehow) "lost" love; apparently Louise has either died or left him. Julien rejects the peasant girl, sensing that a relationship with her will only intensify his grief. In act three, Julien now feels despair over his wasted efforts, and tries not to join the chorus of "Hapless Poets" who have given in to a feeling of utter hopelessness. God seems uncaring to him, and he curses the heavens. His grandmother, another aspect of Louise, tries to console him. In the final act, an older, dissipated Julien encounters a grisette, possibly a prostitute, who also reminds him of Louise. They dally, she laughs at him, and Julien drops dead at her feet, probably of cirrhosis of the liver. Is this Julien's true fate, or only his fear of his future? Charpentier had lived in miserable poverty during the years in between the composition of *Louise* (the early to mid 1890's) and its premiere and knew all too well the consequences of failure. In the thirteen years since the major success of *Louise*, it is possible that

Charpentier was disillusioned by his own failure to bring out a work of equal importance (*Julien* was not successful). Despite its flights of fancy *Julien* charts the stark disappointments of most men's lives from youth to middle age with an almost chilling accuracy. Enrico Caruso sang the role at the Met.

Claude Debussy (1862–1918) was born near Paris and for much of his early life had planned on a career as a concert pianist, studying piano for years at the conservatory. When that didn't work out as intended, Debussy turned to composition instead. He did few operas: *Rodrigue et Chiméne* (composed in the late 1880's to 1890's) and *La Chute de la maison Usher/Fall of the House of Usher* from Poe (composed from 1908 until 1917) were never completed by Debussy and never performed as full-fledged operatic pieces. In between Debussy composed the work that made him famous in operatic circles, *Pelléas et Mélisande* (1902). In a French variation of literaturoper, Debussy simply set the play by Maurice Maeterlinck to music (shortening it in the process).

Pelléas is the brother of Golaud, a widower who has met his second wife, the mysterious Mélisande, in the forest where both have lost their way. Golaud's wife and brother become friends, but eventually something more develops between the two. As Pelléas has been ordered to travel by his father, he meets with his beloved sister-in-law for one last time outside the castle walls. After they kiss, Golaud runs Pelléas through with his sword. Mélisande gives birth and dies with Golaud still uncertain as to how far her affair with his brother had gone. The story is fascinating and suspenseful as well as intriguing (we never do learn the full facts of Mélisande's past, for instance) and the music of *Pelléas* is delicate and attractive if never energetic or passionate in the Italian manner. (The plot recalls Mascagni's *Parisina* in certain details but of course Mascagni's music is full of much more full-blooded eroticism, melody and intensity.) There are really no set arias, although there are moments that come close. Rather, *Pelléas et Mélisande* is "music theater" elevated to high art, and to some ears is vastly superior to the later works of Benjamin Britten (who also composed "music theater" pieces) and Alban Berg's *Wozzeck*, another kind of atonal music theater. It may be said that Debussy's score is more full of melodiousness than actual melody (aside from a few moments), but the music enriches the slightly-drawn characters and provocative situations.

The evocative introduction to act one perfectly encapsulates the whole haunting quality of the opera. There is a lovely passage in act two when Golaud sings "Et puis l'été," and the music fills briefly with light and warmth. Debussy creates a magical effect in scene three of act two as the title duo enter the cave to allegedly search for her missing wedding ring and the music creates a sense of mystery and awe, reflecting the fear and wonder felt by the couple. The beautiful introduction to scene two of act three hints strongly of the heartbreak and tragedy to come. The music throughout scene one of act three keeps threatening to turn into a love duet between Pelléas and Mélisande but never quite gets there, although Pelléas' "Je les nove, hé le noue aux" is almost an actual aria. With the music that bridges scenes two and three of act four, Debussy kicks into high gear, composing music that is full of (muted) passion, lyricism and decided beauty. Scene four has the longest sustained lyricism in the opera, but again the music, although it certainly swells after the couple declare their love for one another, never quite becomes a love duet. Pelléas' "On dirait que" is the closest thing to an aria in the opera. The opera's most intense and dramatic music occurs in act five as Golaud asks Mélisande if she loved Pelléas (a dramatic underline to this "forbidden love" as opposed to an aria or melody) and, perhaps, the most full-bodied melody in the opera is for Grandfather Arkel's arioso "Attention ... Attention." The opera has a moving conclusion as Mélisande dies of a broken heart, Golaud still isn't sure if she loved him or his brother, and their little baby girl faces her own heartbreak.

The influence of *Pelléas* can not be underestimated, both on French composers such as Fauré, and composers of other countries, such as Britten. As the century progressed, the "number" opera would take a lamented, and perhaps lamentable, back seat to operas that consisted of fascinating stories and highly effective background music, but few high-class arias of melodic distinction. In private Debussy had a low opinion of Massenet, who wrote just such operas, but in the magazine *Revue Blanche* he commented that Massenet occupied a special position because the public loved his music, although he noted that "such a gift is not indispensable, particularly in art," adding that "have you ever heard it said of young milliners that they hummed [Bach's] the 'Passion according to Saint Matthew?' I don't think so, yet everyone knows they wake up singing *Manon* or *Werther* in the morning. Let us make no mistake about it, this sort of delightful reputation is secretly envied by more than one of those great purists who have to rely on the somewhat laboured respect of cliques to revive their spirits."[2]

Richard Strauss never thought much of *Pelléas et Mélisande*, asking "Is it always like this? Nothing more? There's nothing, no music. The harmonics are very subtle, there are good orchestral effects, it's in very good taste, but that's nothing at all. I consider it no more than Maeterlinck's drama, by itself, without music."[3] Surprisingly, Puccini had a somewhat higher opinion of it, thinking Debussy's opera had "extraordinary harmonic qualities and diaphonous sensations in the instrumentation. It is truly interesting, in spite of its somber color, as monotonous as a Franciscan's habit. The subject is interesting."[4]

Paul Dukas (1865–1935) is best known as the composer of *L'Apprenti sorcier/The Sorceror's Apprentice*, but he also composed a notable opera entitled *Ariane et Barbe-Bleue* (1907), which covers the same territory as Béla Bartók's *Bluebeard's Castle* but beat it out by eleven years. Unusual and intriguing in story and settings, it deals with Bluebeard and his new wife, Ariadne, who unlocks the forbidden seventh door and frees her husband's former wives, all of whom have been locked in the cellar of the castle. The masochistic women worry that the angry peasants will kill Bluebeard, even after he's kept them all prisoner in horrible conditions for many years. If the opera has a moral it is that some people, even given opportunities to extract themselves from their miserable situations, will simply resign themselves to fate and make no attempt at escape. The women of *Ariane et Barbe-Bleue* are like certain modern-day variations who become pathetically attached to the very men who consistently torment them. As for Bluebeard, he is given virtually nothing to sing and is hardly ever on stage, although his negative influence certainly permeates the story.

At times Dukas' music is reminiscent of Debussy's *Pelléas et Mélisande*, and is often much too languid (if not as much as *Pelléas*) and even uninspired, but there are more memorable moments, such as the wonderful dark theme that runs through the overture and the opera itself. The opening is decidedly bizarre, but effective, presenting a chorus of townsfolk outraged to see a new bride arriving at the castle of reprobate Bluebeard. The powerful song of the wives calling to Ariane "Les cinq filles d'orlamonde" (which was inspired by a folk song of that title) provides a strong ending for act one. There are lyrical recitatives, and Ariane is given a number of nice arias, such as "O mes clairs diamants!" which she sings in praise of the diamonds behind one door; and "Mais toi-méme," with which she tells the imprisoned wives that life and sunshine await them above. The opera was a favorite of the German composer Erich Wolfgang Korngold.

Gabriel Fauré (1845–1924) was sixty-two when he encountered Lucinne Bréval, a Wagnerian soprano, at Monte Carlo in February 1907. She told him that a young playwright named René Fauchois had written a libretto based on the *Odyssey* expressly for her, but it needed to be set to music; wasn't it time for him to try composing an opera? (Fauré had already come out with a mammoth and unwieldy tragédie lyrique entitled *Prométhée* in 1900 which employed much spoken declamation along with music.) Fauré found the subject matter sympathetic, and after meeting with Fauchois and making suggestions, decided to compose the score. He decided to employ Wagnerian leitmotivs (there are very brief passages in the opera when the music sounds Wagnerian), but otherwise his music would be delicate enough to allow the singing — which Fauré felt was of primary importance — to come through. He was very influenced as well by Debussy's *Pelléas et Mélisande.*"

Although Raoul Gunsbourg, the director of the Théâtre de Monte Carlo, had offered to mount the work, the finished score did not meet with his approval. It is a question as to which Gunsbourg objected to more: Fauré's music, or the fact that mounting the opera, called *Pénélope*, might crowd out performances of his own opera, *Venise*, which he was championing at the time. Gunsbourg was not above using his Theatre to promote his own product, which he felt was superior to everything else he was being offered. Then Breval for one reason or another had withdrawn (a Wagnerian soprano was not really the best choice to sing Penelope), necessitating the hiring of another singer, who had to be paid off when Breval again offered her services. There were three performances in March of 1913, but Faure found these rushed and unsatisfactory. The *Journal de Monaco* found Breval to be less passionate than she was "grand." "I feel as if I have produced a work that is deadly boring, dull and lifeless," Fauré wrote to his wife. (Fauré was being unduly harsh in his assessment, although *Pénélope* can seem very "deliberately-paced," particularly if a conductor prefers a slower tempo.) A pupil of Fauré's, Charles Koechlin, wrote that "despite so many successful effects, I fail to find in the orchestration ... of *Pénélope* that same simplicity, grandeur, perfect mastery and charm as in the composition itself." Fauré admitted that the criticism was "justified."

Pénélope[5] opened in Paris at the Théâtre des Champs-Elysées on May 10, 1913 — Breval repeated the role — and was a triumph, but the work failed to enter the international repertoire; it eventually was mounted at the Opéra-Comique (1919), and at the Paris Opera (1943), where the wartime atmosphere gave the opera an added resonance. Fernand Pécoud, a young music student and composer, orchestrated small sections of the opera, and it was later re-orchestrated or "corrected" for the Paris opera staging by an impresario named Inghelbercht, but these corrections were later thrown out. It is now thought that Inghelbercht was trying to incorporate into the work the more modern musical principles of the period, but his revisions did not prove to be improvements. Ironically, Fauré's old piano teacher, Camille Saint-Saëns, found the opera in its original form to be "modernistic." In March 1913 he wrote "I make a superhuman effort to get used to *Pénélope*. But I cannot attain that state of mind that would enable one to refrain from ever concentrating on any one key, or to encounter, unmoved, consecutive fifths and sevenths, and chords that vainly await a resolution that never comes.... Fauré has leapt straight to the head of the 'youngsters' with enormous superiority over them. It was a very able move on his part. But what an example for the students to see their master constantly break the rules we teach them!" Fauré felt, as did many other operatic composers of this period, that the old style opera consisting of "numbers"— arias, following duets, following choruses, and so on — was forever a thing of the past.

As the heroine of the opera turns aside every suitor in her persistent belief that Ulysses will one day return to her, *Pénélope* emerges as a story of enduring love. Highlights include the evocative prelude with which Fauré pulls in the listener with great skill; Penelope's powerful aria "Ulysse! Fier époux" just before Ulysses enters the scene disguised as a beggar; and Eumée's arioso "Sur l'épaule" as Ulysses has a sweet interchange with a shepherd boy. The scene in act two when Ulysses reveals himself to the other shepherds makes full use of his exciting trumpet theme. In act three Fauré adeptly builds suspense over the coming confrontation between Ulysses and Penelope's many suitors; and the exquisite finale of the opera is almost overpoweringly beautiful and moving as Penelope and Ulysses sing of their love for one another and heap grateful praise on Lord Zeus. Throughout the opera Fauré displays his ability to use the orchestra to increase dramatic tension. While the through-composed score may never draw universal admiration, it has too many fine things in it to ignore. Aaron Copland thought that *Pénélope* was "one of the best operas written since Wagner."[6]

André Messager (1853–1929) is most famous for *Véronique*, which premiered in 1898, but he composed quite a number of operas and operettas during his lifetime. One of his most memorable works, the delightfully amoral and charming light romantic opera *Fortunio*, premiered in 1907. Jacqueline is married to an old man (André) who is more like a father than a husband, but is nevertheless possessive and jealous. Jacqueline begins an affair with the virile soldier Clavaroche. When Andre beings to get suspicious, Clavaroche importunes Jacqueline to sidle up to a sensitive clerk in Andre's office, young Fortunio. Fortunio will be a decoy, an innocent dupe: Andre will focus on Fortunio's obvious crush on Jacqueline and be less inclined to ponder his wife and Clavaroche. Still suspicious, Andre plans to trap his wife's lover and kill him; Clavaroche wants poor Fortunio to fall into the trap and die in his place. By this time, however, Jacqueline and Fortunio have genuinely fallen in love, and she sends a message to him hoping to save him. She is astonished to learn that Fortunio is willing to die for her. André's trap fails, Clavaroche is summarily dismissed, and Fortunio hides in Jacqueline's bedroom as an unsuspecting André goes merrily off to bed!

The music of *Fortunio* is consistently melodious and the titular hero, a melancholy and sensitive youth, is given several memorable arias. In act one he gets a tender piece ("Oh! non! La vie que tu mènes") in which he sings of how he hopes one day to find his soul mate. "It is doubtless I shall die the very day I meet her," he says, "without uttering a word." In act two, he waxes poetic about how he's losing all sense of his peaceful childhood and home ("J'aimais la vieille maison"). In act three there is his love song ("Si vous croyez que ja vais dire") which he sings at Jacqueline's request but which actually reflects his feelings of unrequited love for her. Even better is his actual unrequited love aria, "Une angoisse exquise et martelle." Act three also has an intensely lyrical exchange between Jacqueline and Fortunio who declare their love for one another in an informal romantic duet ("Depuis ce jourlà"), culminating in another beautiful aria for Fortunio, "Elle m'aime!" (She loves me!). Messager saved the best for last however, with Fortunio's act four aria "Au coeur! au coeur!" when he mistakenly thinks Jacqueline doesn't love him; this turns into a formal duet with Jacqueline.

Massenet's pupil, Henri Rabaud (1873–1949), was born and died in Paris. When he was twenty-one years old, he won the Premier Grand Prix de Rome, and went on to compose several symphonies, operas, and a nocturne based on the legend of Faust. His best-known opera, *Marouf, savetier du Caire/Marouf, the Cobbler of Cairo* premiered at the Opéra-Comique in Paris in 1914. Marouf is married to an impossible and evil woman who berates him mercilessly and even lies so that he is beaten by the police. Marouf leaves home with a group of sailors, is shipwrecked, and found unconscious on the shore by a childhood friend named Ali. Ali has Marouf disguise himself as a wealthy merchant, so impressing the sultan that he wants Marouf to marry his daughter, fully expecting Marouf to deliver a caravan of treasures. As the princess turns out to be unexpectedly beautiful, Marouf considers himself unworthy of her, but she falls for him and defends him against the suspicions of the vizier. Marouf confesses to the princess that he has no caravan or even a penny and she urges him to flee for his life; she will accompany him disguised as a boy. The two encounter a poor, kindly Fellah who turns out to be a genie; the genie turns the treasure he guards into Marouf's caravan. The caravan arrives just as the sultan is about to have Marouf executed. All ends happily, Marouf's wife back home conveniently forgotten.

All told *Marouf* is a pleasant and amusing evening's entertainment with attractive music is that is redolent of the far east and its colorful settings. The many arias are lyrical and pretty if not especially memorable. The best music occurs in act five, when the poor Fellah transforms into a genie ("Que parles-tu de mort!") and explains that he guards a wonderful treasure. The music here is very somber and dramatic, then full of suspense and excitement as a host of dwarves load the treasure into the caravan, making for a splendid wind-up.

Maurice Ravel came out with *L'Enfant et les sortilèges/The Bewitched Child* in 1925. A bratty little boy learns not to be destructive and hurt little animals when he is shown the consequences of his actions. Attacked by a pack of animals, he selflessly helps a squirrel that has been inadvertently injured by the mob, and thus wins over the crowd of forest creatures, who call for the child's mother to help him. With this scenario, Ravel illustrates how a child grows up to develop a conscience and feelings towards other beings besides himself. This very charming, even touching, and overall excellent fantasy opera-ballet has music that at its least is pleasant and sincere, and at its best, very memorable and well-done. The highlights include the chorus of shepherds and sherpherdesses ("A dieu, pastourelles!"); the child's arioso ("Toi, le coeur de la rose") about the lovely storybook princess whom he has helped destroy; and especially the squirrel's arioso ("Oui, c'était pour mes beaux yeux!"), in which the little creature tells the boy that his eyes, once trapped and haunted while he was caged, now reflect only freedom. The bizarre "musical duet of mewings" of the black cat and white cat blends into the music of the garden in the moonlight, full of animals, and then into the somber arioso of the tree ("Celle que tu fis") which was wounded with a knife by the boy the day before; the other trees join in until the dragonfly ("Où es-tu?") wonders where her friend, whom the boy trapped and pinned, might be. *L'Enfant et les sortilèges* is truly a magical experience. Prokofiev admired Ravel's "complete mastery of stunning orchestration" but was dismayed by what he felt were "whole slices of colorless, watery, out-dated, unnecessary material" which he deemed "impressionistic."[7]

Darius Milhaud (1892–1974) studied at the Paris conservatory and became one of Les Six, a clique of composers whose works were considered subversive by some critics of the day. He composed several operas, none of which gained a firm foothold in major opera houses. *Les Malheurs d'Orphée/Misfortunes of Orpheus* premiered in 1925. This half hour opera boasts fine orchestrations and not so memorable melodies. Milhaud gives Orphée and Eurydice an unconventional — and unexceptional — love duet ("Moi! bien aimée!") at the end of the first act, and act two contains Orpheus' lamentation that he can heal everyone but the one he loves the most ("O querisseur sans espoir"). The animals in the story are given two choruses: in the first they lament Eurydice's illness, and in the second her death. *Les Malheurs d'Orphée* is a pleasant but minor work with a very abrupt conclusion. Some might find the music a bit reminiscent of Stravinsky.

Arthur Honegger (1892–1955) was another member of Les Six. Employing a libretto by Jean Cocteau, Honegger's *Antigone* (1927) tells the tragic story in three acts and eleven scenes comprising a total of forty-five minutes. Honegger is perhaps a better orchestrator than composer, although the orchestra in this piece is used more to create effects than "music." The choruses in scenes two and three are distinctly minor, although the chorus in scene nine ("Toi, couronne de mille noms") is the liveliest number in the opera. (Indeed, its percussion background almost makes it sound like a kitschy Broadway number from the sixties.) Scene seven contains a nominal aria in contralto Coryphée's "Amour qui saisit les uns," with its compelling horn background the best of a weak field. The music is briefly lyrical and even striking at the end of scene seven and in much of scene eight, but always quite minor. The story of Antigone deserves a great opera, and Honegger's *Antigone* is not it. Although the work does have a certain dramatic thrust to it, it is strictly theater with background music, often garish film music, in fact, underscoring the action. Separated from whatever visual spectacle there may be on stage, *Antigone* is a bore.

Ernest Bloch was born in Geneva in 1880, grew up in Switzerland, and died in Portland, Oregon, as a United States citizen in 1959. He traveled to Paris where he met Debussy and came under his influence. His best-known work and only completed opera is *Macbeth*, which premiered at the Opéra-Comique in Paris in 1910. Bloch's version did not and never will erase from anyone's mind Verdi's great adaptation of the Shakespeare play, but Bloch's *Macbeth* is certainly not without merit. Bloch is perhaps better at atmosphere and orchestration than he is at vocal writing (or at least melody), but occasionally even this can be strong and dramatic. There is effective music when Macbeth sees the spectre, and the powerful wind up to act two contains a memorable informal duet for Macbeth and his wife ("O Macbeth! Macbeth!") and an aria for the title character ("Ah! Non! Non!") which is essentially a continuation of the former. The choral writing that wraps up the opera is exciting and first-rate, and there are some wonderful orchestral passages in the opera's interludes. But it is unlikely that even frequent revival of the work would ever put it on the same plateau as Verdi's masterpiece in the minds of the public.

The Italians and the Spanish had their hot-blooded pieces shot through with erotic mayhem, the French had their epics of more tasteful delicacy, and the Germans...

The Germans had Richard Strauss.

6. Wagner's Heir: Richard Strauss

Richard Georg Strauss ((1864–1949) was born in Munich, Bavaria, the son of a horn player and a beer heiress, and his early years were immersed in music. He began composing when he was very young, and his first symphony — his father played in the orchestra — debuted when he was only sixteen. He was told to look to the future of music, which was Wagner. He became a conductor of note even as his tone poems and other orchestral works were garnering him fame. He was thirty when his first opera, *Guntram* (1894) reached the stage. His output for both concert hall and opera house became prodigious.

Much that is untrue and unfair has been circulated about Strauss. He was seen as a self-centered money grubber when he actually fought for copyright laws and royalty rates that would benefit all composers, not just himself. He rightly saw no reason why any artist should starve, an attitude for which he was wrongly excoriated. He was described as cold and aloof when it was simply that he was not "hale and hearty" and took a while to warm up to strangers. Perhaps the most odious canard about Strauss is that he was sympathetic to the Nazis or was even a Nazi himself. In truth, Strauss felt that Hitler and the Nazis had destroyed Germany and brought on the destruction of the great opera houses of his country. As for the Jewish question, Strauss' daughter-in-law and beloved grandsons were Jewish and he constantly feared for their safety. Strauss' collaboration with the Jewish librettist Stefan Zweig after the death of long-time partner Hugo von Hofmansthal only ended because the Nazi's demanded it. Strauss was no Nazi and never joined the Nazi party.

If his advanced years alone were not sufficient cause for not leaving Germany during World War Two, the fact remains that the Nazis wouldn't have let him go. Although the Nazis distrusted Strauss for good reason, he was seen by them as a national treasure. If Strauss had managed to get out of the country, there was always the danger of reprisals against his son and daughter-in-law and their children. Not only Strauss, but his son Franz was slandered unfairly as a supporter of the Nazis.

Strauss' second opera — and his first twentieth century offering — was *Feuersnot/Fire Famine*, which premiered in 1901 in Dresden. A sorcerer's apprentice named Kunrad lets the children of 12th century Munich literally tear his house apart so that they can have wood for their midsummer bonfires. When he bestows a kiss on a young maiden, Diemut, without her permission, she decides to humiliate him in retaliation. She lowers a large basket from her balcony, invites him to ascend to her side, but leaves him stranded halfway up for the amusement of the crowds. He casts a spell that extinguishes all the fires in the town and vows that no fire will ever be rekindled until Diemut acknowledges her love for him. When she does so — a fire of love is apparently burning within her — the fires are relit in spectacular fashion (depending on the budget of the opera house). *Feuersnot* is definitely Strauss "Lite"; the music is perfectly pleasant for the most part but unspectacular. At first you're reminded more of Humperdinck than Strauss because of the gentle opening sequences with all those children. The score contains a lively waltz, a pretty aria for Diemut, and a rather nice duet, but the opera's most glorious music is in the long orchestral piece at the end of the opera which signifies the igniting of the fires of love and the reigniting of the fires of Munich. This leads into the brief duet and chorus that closes the opera. *Feuersnot* was meant by Strauss as a tweaking and rebuke of the city of Munich, where his first opera, *Guntram* ((1894), was a failure. Kunrad, the apprentice, was meant to be Strauss himself, while the unseen (but not entirely unheard) sorcerer was, of course, Wagner.

Salome, taken from the play by Oscar Wilde, premiered in Dresden in 1905 and was an immediate success with the public if not with critics. John the Baptist (Jokanaan) has been imprisoned by Herod. Herod's stepdaughter Salome, toys and flirts with Jokanaan but is ignored by him to her fury. When Herod, who lusts for her, says he will give her anything she desires if she will only honor him with a dance ("The Dance of the Seven Veils"), she demands the head of John the Baptist. Herod tries to dissuade her to no avail, and the head is delivered to her. When she kisses the head with a certain gross passion (Jokanaan had refused to kiss her previously), Herod is so outraged that he orders his men to crush Salome with their shields. With this opera, Strauss got to have his cake and eat it too: the powerful and dramatic score manages to be both "modern" and romantic at the same time, a style he would later use with equal success for *Elektra*. There is an excellent theme for Jokanaan that runs throughout the piece, and a number of effective arias for him to sing as well. Much of the orchestral music is memorable, such as the orchestral interlude between scenes three and four, and the highly dramatic flourish, heavy on percussion, that occurs as the severed head is carried up from the cistern inside which Jokanaan had been imprisoned. "The Dance of the Seven Veils" suits its purpose (wisely a dancer is often substituted for the soprano for this sequence), but is not an especially great piece of music. The quintet of arguing Jews ("Das kann nicht sein") is more interesting, but the best thing in *Salome* is the long, masterful aria ("Ah, du wolltest mich nicht deinen Mund küssen lassen, Jochanaan!") that Salome sings mockingly yet passionately to John's severed head, rhapsodizing again about the whiteness of his skin, blackness of his hair etc. and confidently asserting that had he only looked upon her he would have loved her and that "the mystery of love is greater than the mystery of death." Finally there is the chilling juxtaposition of Salome's final romantic arioso suddenly switching into Herod's enraged order to the guards to kill her that instant. *Salome* boasts a perfect synthesis of words and music, Strauss' compositions a perfect complement to Wilde's quite sick and utterly fascinating text. John the Baptist is so unremittingly sanctimonious and sexist that you long for him to be beheaded. "I will not allow him to raise the dead," rants Herod. "It would be terrible if the dead came back!" Strauss himself, who was never a fan of religion or religionists (and has undoubtedly taken the heat for that), stated "You know, Jochanaan is an imbecile. I have no sympathy at all for that type of man.... I tried to compose the good Jochanaan more or less as a clown...."[1] Benjamin Britten, who could never have composed a piece of quite such power, thought that *Salome* was "a great and epoch-making work."[2] Puccini described *Salome* as "the most extraordinary thing, terrible cacophony, there are some very beautiful things in the orchestra, but in the end it wears you out."[3] Strauss' biographer Michael Kennedy writes that "*Salome*, for the first time in the history of opera, explored the mental pathology of the characters, much of this being achieved by the 105-strong orchestra which, like a stream of consciousness, tells us what is in the characters' hearts and minds before they know it themselves."

Strauss' next work, *Elektra* (1909) is another powerhouse. This marked the first time Strauss worked with his most frequent collaborator, Hugh von Hofmannsthal. Elektra wanders about in a rage waiting for the opportunity to strike back at the mother, Clytemnestra, who murdered her father, Agamemnon, with the help of her lover, Aegisthus. Elektra's sister Chrysothemis does not want to help her murder their mother, but her brother, Orestes, whom she feared dead, shows up and assists her in her bloody deed after a joyous reunion. Overcome with emotion, Elektra literally dances herself to death at the conclusion. *Elektra* (1909) is virtually a symphonic opera, with interesting orchestrations and background music that help carry one through some blathery vocal stretches (such as the confrontation between Elektra and Clytemnestra) although there are also some very effective vocal lines. The opera opens with a burst of the main three note theme. In Elektra's aria "Ageamemnon! Agamemnon!" she sings with an almost incestuous passion of her dead father and how she wishes to "do honor of his tomb." This piece introduces the magnificent Agamemnon theme, the beautiful Elektra theme, and (in a more subdued manner) the savage climactic dance music. Chrysothemis proclaims that Elektra's hatred prevents her from having a normal life and children; "better death than mere existence!, she cries ("Du bist es, die mit Eisenklammern"). Strauss crafts menacing music to usher Clytemnestra on stage, and provides a wonderful background to the scene when she receives news of Orest's (alleged) death and she and her companions cackle with triumph and glee; Orest theme is introduced in this section. The sequence wherein Elektra tries to convince her sister to help her murder her mother and Aegisthus crackles with tension and is vaguely lyrical. This section contains arias for Elektra which contain a more traditional Straussian lyricism (without being that melodious): "Wie stark du bist!" and "Von jetzt an will ich deine Schwester sein." In the first Elektra tells her sister how strong and robust — and hence capable of murder — she is; in the second she describes how she hopes to help her prepare for her future husband and care for her baby and so on. The sequence when Elektra and Orest discover each other at first features excellent dirge-like music, then develops a strong lyrical strain and boasts the outstanding aria "Orest! Orest! Orest!" in which Elektra gives in to her supreme joy that her beloved brother is alive. This beautiful piece, so sensitive and haunting, is a tender and touching testament to the bond of love and support that exists between siblings — did Strauss ever compose anything quite as lovely as this? The scene also contains the arioso "Der ist selig," in which Elektra express her pleasure that action will at last be taken against her mother. The climax features Elektra's aria "Ob ich nicht höre?" and her duet with Chrysothemis "Wir sind bei den Göttern"; both are stunners. Then the aforementioned savage dance music bursts into full expressiveness and Elektra falls dead at the moment of her greatest triumph. For maximum impact the music of the climax must be played at just the right tempo and with the proper dramatic emphasis — especially those final tense soundings of the three note theme that begins the opera. The exclamatory, intense, erotic music of *Elektra* makes it sound at times like German verismo, although its subject matter hardly concerns "ordinary" people.

Strauss' next opera, *Der Rosenkavalier* (1911), became his most popular and the one he supposedly wanted to be remembered by, although in many ways it's a step backward from *Elektra* and certainly doesn't have that opera's raw passion or impact. But Strauss had every right to take an abrupt turn and showcase his versatility with something more traditionally romantic. In Vienna the thirty-two-year-old Princess Werdenberg, known as the Marschallin (wife of the Field Marshal) is having an affair with the seventeen-year-old Count Octavian while her husband is out of town. When her lecherous cousin Baron Ochs suddenly arrives, Octavian disguises himself as the maid Mariandel, with whom Ochs flirts. The baron is engaged to the lovely Sophie, and needs a young man to enact a tradition in which a nobleman bears a rose to another man's intended as a symbolic token of her fiancé's esteem. The Marschallin suggests that Octavian do the deed. Presenting Sophie with the rose, Octavian falls in love at first sight and vice versa. Ochs and Octavian come to blows, then Octavian again dons a dress in a plot to remove Sophie from the baron's slimy clutches. The Marschallin good-naturedly accepts that youth calls to youth and makes no fuss as she leaves the lovers Octavian and Sophie alone together.

In act one Strauss includes, as he would often do, an "affectionate parody" of an Italian tenor aria ("Di rigori armato il seno") which is almost as good as the real thing, and probably a stand-out in the score for those listeners who prefer Italian music over German. In the Marschallin's aria "Die Zeit, die ist ein sonderbar Ding," she expresses her fears about growing older and the inevitable end of Octavian's love for her. "We do not heed [time], time has no meaning, but there comes a moment when time is all we feel," she sings. This leads into an informal duet that never quite develops an actual strong melody. After Octavian is moved to tears, fearing that the Marschallin wants to end their relationship, she wisely comments: "Ah, now I am the one who must console him, for the day, be it soon, be it late, when he will leave me." Another stand-out in the score is the beautiful second act duet in two parts between Octavian and Sophie as he hands her the rose and each is instantly smitten ("Mir ist die Ehre, widerfahren"). Even better is the second part of this piece ("Dahin muss ich zurück") in which they sing in counterpoint; the trumpet solo in the background is an added plus. Then there is the famous act three trio ("Hab' mir's gelobt"), immediately followed by a nice duet for Octavian and Sophie ("Spür' nur dich"). Although the trio (for Sophie, Octavian, and the Marschallin) does have a certain beauty and poignancy and is just a bit goose-bumpy, it is wrong to consider it, as many do, Strauss' most memorable composition. While it is certainly the best thing in *Der Rosenkavalier* it is frankly not that great compared to the wonderful pieces in many of his other operas.

Despite its popularity, there are problems with *Der Rosenkavalier*. Although it doesn't seem to bother most fans of the opera, it must be suggested that a nearly fatal flaw is in making the young lover Octavian a "trouser" role sung by a soprano. Octavian may dress up as a girl, but on stage it is simply a woman doffing her male drag and dressing up as — a woman. A man wearing a dress might be hilarious — and *Der Rosenkavalier* is a comedy, after all — but there's nothing particularly funny about a woman dressed as a woman. Another problem, libretto-wise, is that the characters are all one-dimensional. And while there are many nice things in the opera, *Der Rosenkavalier* is overlong and not as musically rich as it needs to be to support the length. Despite some "delicate" moments in the score, the music is also rather heavy considering the light libretto and subject matter. Strauss received some criticism because the opera incorporates waltzes in a story that takes place eighty years before the waltz was introduced in Vienna, but this is a mere quibble compared to the other problems. It is entirely possible that some of *Der Rosenkavalier*'s devotees are simply not familiar with the composer's other, far superior works. While the opera, especially in the character of Baron Ochs, bears some resemblance to Verdi's *Falstaff*, it is really not in the same league.

Ariadne auf Naxos originally premiered in 1912, but the revised version of 1916 is the one most frequently performed. The story is simple and irresistible: the wealthiest man in Vienna has scheduled two major entertainments for his guests, an opera and a performance by a troupe of commedia dell'arte players (the prologue). But the host is so afraid that the performances won't end in time for the fireworks display that he demands both comedy and opera be put on at one and the same time (the opera). In the opera-within-an-opera Ariadne pines for Theseus, who dumped her on the island of Naxos, but the handsome God Bacchus appears and with one look Ariadne is convinced that it is much better to love another than to be dead. Underneath the burlesque and humor and exaggerated characters of the prologue (act one), there's a depth and poignancy to Hugo von Hofmannsthal's libretto. The best piece in the prologue is the composer's aria "Seien wir wiedergut!" in which he passionately sings that music is the holiest of all the arts. Act two — the opera/comedy itself— has many lovely things in it, but Strauss really outdoes himself in the romantic music for Ariadne's encounter with Bacchus. Every instrument in the orchestra seems to be playing (actually Strauss achieved great effects with a comparatively small orchestra) as Bacchus and Ariadne meet face to face. The scene culminates in a masterful, almost unbearably beautiful and deeply moving duet — truly music of the Gods — "sind wir schon da" in which Ariadne chooses life with Bacchus over death. The duet moves us, as does the opera itself, because it resonates with something magical, outsized, larger than ourselves, straining for the unattainable yet coming ever so close to reaching it. There is no use in denying that *Ariadne auf Naxos* has aspects both silly and absurd, but

Strauss' music makes it surprisingly powerful. In the revised version Strauss wisely does not bring back the commedia dell'arte characters at the end except for an amusing bit with Zerbinetto.

Die Frau ohne Schatten/The Woman without a Shadow premiered in 1919 in Vienna. An empress is actually the daughter of the spirit master Keikobad, who tells her that unless she casts a shadow within a short time her husband, the emperor, will be turned to stone and she must re-enter the spirit kingdom. Aided by a sinister nurse, the empress contrives to get the shadow (the ability to give birth) of a discontented earth woman, the wife of Barak. But given an opportunity to simply take the shadow the empress refuses to do so no matter what the cost, knowing it will leave Barak's wife barren. As the empress has finally developed human compassion, Keikobad restores the emperor to his normal state, and both she and Barak's wife look forward to having a family. The "woman without a shadow," of course, is a woman without a child. While the basic premise of the opera is dated and even wildly sexist, it works if taken on its own terms and in the context of its less-enlightened times. It can be moving even to those who are not in tune with its message, because all of us were once children and all of us, presumably, had mothers. Despite serious flaws, including over-length, problems in pacing, an awkward and stilted libretto by Hofmannsthal, the opera contains some of Strauss' most beautiful music. This includes the orchestral passages as the nurse and the empress make their way to the "normal" Earth, as well as the music relating to the fantasy that the disguised nurse summons up for Barak's wife (it is interesting that she is never given a name), and some of the ensembles that accompany it, although the slave girls' music is banal. There is the haunting chorus of watchmen ("Ihr Gatten in den Häusen") in which they praise the family lifestyle, matrimony and children, with Barak's weary comments in counterpoint (his wife has split their bed in half with the nurse's help and refuses to sleep with him). The second scene of act two consists entirely of the emperor's long aria ("Falke, Falke") in which he follows a falcon to where his wife is staying and discovers she has been consorting with humans to his dismay and anger. The dissonant "cries" of the falcon contrast with the romantic violins in a pretty and dramatic number. Act three contains several outstanding pieces, such as the duet between Barak and his wife ("Schweigt doch") wherein she regrets what has happened and sings how much she misses him, with him joining in to also express his regrets. In "Aus unsern Taten steigt" the empress rejects her nurse's admonitions and expresses admiration for humanity. There is a very powerful musical response to the empress' coming across her husband turned into unmoving stone. The final ensemble, started by Barak with the emperor, the empress, and their unborn children joining in is absolutely sublime and deeply moving. Whatever its politically incorrect aspects, *Die Frau ohne Schatten* is much too musically impressive to discard.

In *Intermezzo* (1924)Strauss took real-life events and fashioned them into an opera about a composer, Robert, whose wife, Christine, mistakenly believes he is having an affair even as she draws closer to a baron who hopes his attentions to the wife will lead to a positive introduction to her husband — and his patronage as well as hers. Strauss' marriage to his wife Pauline, a former soprano, was complex and happy. Pauline was decidedly prickly, but also loving and faithful. She was understandably upset, if not furious (her maid Anna was also upset), by her characterization as being rather thick-headed, childish and bitchy, but it's an affectionate portrait all the same; Strauss allows himself to be depicted as being a bit dull. It all seems generally good-natured, with the real life events only used as a starting off point for a piece that is both amusing and touching. *Intermezzo* emerges as a tribute to the friendship of a long marriage, to the very idea that husband and wife can be — and should be — best friends.

Like *Elektra*, although it's a very different from it, *Intermezzo* is the type of opera that Verdi was always afraid would develop in time in that the orchestra plays a more important part than the voice. *Intermezzo* is very much like literaturoper, with generally short, quick lines of dialogue set to music. Some of the recitatives are unexceptional, but more often they are lyrical and adept with the occasional melodious arioso. Highlights include Christine's very lovely piece ("Ein hübscher Mensch") which gets across her growing infatuation with the baron without her ever having to say it. In act two the beautiful interlude between scenes three and four gets across the idea of Robert and his conductor Stroh rushing to tell Christine the truth about "Mitzi" Mayer, and the frantic emotions involved. Strauss ends the opera on a gorgeous high note in the final scene as husband and wife reconcile and declare mutual devotion, oddly beginning with a comparatively sympathetic discussion of the baron ("Er ist sicher kein Gauner") culminating in a beautiful finale and informal duet ("Du bist mein Schoner").

It may be that the two people who most liked *Die ägyptische Helena* (Helen in Egypt) when it premiered in 1928 were Strauss and his librettist Hugo von Hofmannsthal, and it may be that that is still the case, as the opera has not grown in popularity over the years. It isn't the music — not top-drawer Strauss by any means, but quite good at times — but the convoluted and rather tedious libretto about a sorceress, Aithra, working her wiles on Menelas (or Menelaus) and Helen at the end of the Trojan war. Menelas wants to kill Helen for her betrayal of him with Paris; Instead, after many an interference via spells and magical potions, the two are reconciled. Hofmannsthal's' whole idea for the opera was to explain how the reconciliation of Menelas and Helen came about, but his explanation is long-winded and often undramatic as well. Some critics have bizarrely labeled this as Strauss' "bel canto" opera, but the music is as wonderfully intense as ever, presenting Strauss in his usual booming, Wagnerian mode. What most comes across beneath the lyrical passion of the score is an almost palpable anger. There are times when the music seems so absorbent and energized that it can leave a listener positively drained, not uncommon for Strauss.

There are a number of fine arias for the principals, and a boy, later killed, named Da-ud, but the duets for Helena and Menelas are especially noteworthy. "Bei jener Nacht" has the two remembering their night of undying love, and the outstanding final duet, "Gewogene Lüfte," is proceeded by a tremendous force of sound as a pair of gloriously caparisoned horses are brought onto the stage for the twosome to mount. Strauss gives Helena an excellent introduction in act one, where her dramatic entrance is followed by a quietly shimmering melody of elves. Menelas' act two aria "Ewig erwählt," in which he declares he will never again be parted from Helena, becomes a trio with Helena and Aithra joining in. The beginning and ending of the opera reveal the highs and lows of von Hofmannsthal's art. The business in act one in which a slave repeats everything that has been said by a magical singing seashell is quite dull, but the climactic scene of *Die ägyptische Helena* is a bristling, impressive chain of suddenly changing and contrasting moments: the lyrical trio; soldiers bursting forth from backstage in a menacing mode (over the death of Da-ud); the child of Helena and Menelas arriving on horseback leading to a new serenity, all handled beautifully by Strauss on the musical end. What has probably prevented a successful revival of *Die ägyptische Helena* is the simple fact that with so many operas to choose from, Strauss fans will invariably look to something even better. Or something more along the lines of *Der Rosenkavalier*.

For instance, *Arabella*, which premiered in 1932, concerns a family in Vienna who find themselves in straitened circumstances. Count Waldner and his wife have two daughters, the besieged-by-admirers Arabella, and Zdenka, who poses as a boy because it would be too costly to bring her out in Viennese society. Arabella is loved by the officer Matteo, who in turn is loved by Zdenka, who secretly pens the love letters he receives from *Arabella*. Waldner hopes to interest his wealthy old friend Mandryka in Arabella, but it is Mandryka's similarly named nephew who answers the summons and falls in love. A misunderstanding results when Zdenka contrives to have a romantic encounter with Matteo; Mandryka — and Matteo — thinks he's had an assignation with Arabella. But everything is cleared up, Zdenka reveals her true femininity to the startled (and relieved) Matteo, and romance triumphs for two happy couples: Arabella and Mandryka; and Zdenka and Matteo. The most intriguing aspect of von Hofmannsthal's libretto is the business with Zdenka luring Matteo to her room (with a note supposedly written by Arabella) and making love to him in the dark, leaving him to believe he's had sex with her sister.

In act one the lyrical recitatives lead into a sublime duet between Arabella and Zdenka (who is a touching figure), "Aber der Richtigel," in which Arabella explains that her fickleness and inevitable disinterest in a suitor will disappear when the right man comes along. Her sister sings that she only wants her to be happy with a worthy suitor. The music has a strange underlying poignancy to it. Act two features lovely music during the exchange between Arabella and Mandryka, which slowly builds in passion as Arabella becomes as smitten with Mandryka as he is with her, culminating in the tender duet "Und du wirst mein Gebieter sein." Despite some other pleasant music, Strauss seems to be treading water in this act — as well, except for Arabella and Mandryka meeting little else happens — making act two somewhat unsatisfying. Strauss employs horns and strings to interesting effect in the dissonant, brassy overture to act three, which has some stirring music between Arabella and Matteo, who mistakenly believes he has just had a night of passion with the woman. The opera concludes with Arabella's lovely "Das war sehr gut," in which she tells Mandryka that she has changed her mind and is prpared to be his forever. *Arabella* is a charming, if unspectacular work in the Strauss canon.

Die schweigsame Frau/The Silent Woman premiered in 1935. This is an amusing, good-natured, and even moving comedy with a libretto by Stefan Zweig and first-rate music from Strauss. Morosus, a wealthy retired admiral, has an acute sensitivity to noise. When it is suggested to him that he marry, he wonders where on earth he could find a woman who could keep silent. At first Morosus is delighted to be reunited with his wandering nephew Henry, but is horrified to discover that he heads an opera troupe and that his wife Aminta is prima donna; Henry is cut out of the will. When Morosus orders his barber to find him a silent woman, the barber comes up with an idea. Morosus winds up "marrying" a disguised Aminta, who plays it quiet and deferential at first but then turns into a screeching shrike. Henry promises his uncle that he will find a way to get him divorced from "Timidia," and brings in other members of his troupe for a phony divorce hearing in which Morosus is told he is stuck with the shrew. But then Henry and Aminta reveal the hoax. Morosus is so relieved that he responds goodnaturedly to the trick that's been played upon him, calls for a party, and

Henry is back in the will. The first act highlights include an aria for Morosus in which he proclaims that "a silent woman is to be found only in church-yards"; the duet for Henry and Aminta in which they confirm their love and their loyalty to their troupe; and two delightful ensembles, the second of which occurs as the Barber hatches his plan to save Henry's inheritance. In act two the sequence wherein several potential brides (all members of the opera troupe) are presented to Morosus has especially fine music, including an informal duet for Morosus and Aminta. The music for Morosus' aria (which becomes a duet with Aminta) "So stumm, mein Kind," as he chooses the disguised Aminta for a bride, gets across Morosus' essentially kind nature, which Aminta responds to, becoming ashamed of her part in the hoax. There's also an excellent formal duet for Morosus and Aminta as they prepare for the wedding, and another duet for Aminta and Henry that is quite lovely in its romantic simplicity. Strauss' music adds sublime pathos to Morosus final aria in act three, "Wie schön ist doch die Musik," after the hoax has been exposed.

 Friedenstag/Peace Day (1938) is a one-act epic about the Thirty Years' War of 1648. The hungry and desperate inhabitants of a besieged city beg their commandant to surrender, but he refuses to disobey his orders to fight to the last. He would rather blow up the fortress than allow it to be over-run by the enemy. He urges his wife Maria to leave, but she tells him that she would rather die than go on alone without him. Just as the fuse is about to be lit, a delegation from the other side shows up seeking reconciliation. The wary commandant nearly comes to blows with his opposite number, but Maria intercedes and peace is finally declared to the jubilation of every-one. *Friedenstag* presents a fascinating situation and intelligently explores the opposing points of view of the people: fighting to the last gasp versus surrendering to live and prosper. The main flaw with Joseph Gregor's libretto is that it needs to be longer and the characters better developed. Originally a love triangle involving the commandant and his wife was to be part of the plot; it should have been included. Although *Friedenstag* may not be one of his masterpieces, Strauss is nevertheless in fine form in this opera. Near the beginning of *Friedenstag* a young lad sings an Italian love song ("La rosa, ch' è un bel fiore") which is interspersed with German recitative between a corporal and a private, his gentle song effectively contrasted with the ugli-ness of war, the boredom of the watch. etc. reminding the soldiers of the love and simple pleasures they're missing. This is another example of Strauss' propensity of having Italian tenor arias in his operas. The private's "Nie war ich Kämpfer, nie ein Held" is a memorable piece in which he admits that he hates fighting and wasn't cut out for it, but will not leave the side of his commandant, who is "a great soldier," in spite of it. There is a beautiful duet between the Commandant and Maria ("Mich stärkte die Sonne") as he expresses a soldier's view of the nobility of war and loyalty to your country and sovereign, and she curses war and sees her and her husband's deaths as victory over it. Earlier Maria is given an especially fine aria in "Nein, nicht Todes Nebel," expressing her fears over what may transpire in this seemingly never-ending battle. The climactic chorus beginning with Maria's "Glocken! Glocken!" (The Bells! The Bells!) is a sublime and powerful evocation of heartfelt joy after experiencing literally decades of despair. The opera's final chorus, "Wagt es zu denken" is a beatific piece of spiritual and religious excitation.

Daphne premiered in 1938. Daphne, the nature-loving daughter of the shepherd Peneios, is loved by her childhood friend Leukippos. As Daphne feels no sexual passion for anyone, her maids tell Leukippos that he would be better off disguising himself as a woman. During the rites of the Dionysian feast, Apollo, who is also in disguise, arrives and falls for Daphne; he unmasks the femininely dressed Leukippos and an argument ensues in which Apollo kills his rival. Daphne is so heartbroken that Apollo realizes he has no chance with her and asks Zeus to intercede. Daphne's greatest wish is realized as she is transformed into a laurel tree, becoming one with nature. While the libretto of *Daphne* by Joseph Gregor, freudian overtones notwithstanding, may be nothing that special, Strauss responded with his usual adeptness. There is Daphne's long, beautiful aria "O bleib, geliebter Tag!" her ode to the sun and to the tree she grew and calls "brother." There is an informal duet for Daphne and her mother Gaea, in which Gaea tells her that she must prepare to become a woman. Strauss provides wonderful music for the sequence when Peneios, Gaea, and the shepherds await the coming of Apollo, especially Peneios' arioso "Mutter, ich seh ihn," as he spots Apollo in the distance, and the ensemble "Wisset, ich sah ihn," as Gaea warns Peneios not to expect to share in the laughter of the Gods and the shepherds tremble. There is the wild, sensual dance of the scantily-dressed thyrsus bearers, and Daphne's tender dirge to dead Leukippos ("Unheilvolle Daphne"), in which she at last understands the dead boy's heart. Also notable is Daphne's final aria, "Apollo! Bruder!," as she figuratively stretches her branches toward Olympus. Some of the best music is understandably reserved for Apollo, including his aria "Was seh ich?" as he sees a vision of beauty, Daphne, and is convinced she must be a Goddess; and his "Was erblicke ich?" in which he realizes that by killing Leukippos he also wounded Daphne, who mourns him. Strauss wraps it all up with a beautiful orchestral piece. Whatever its flaws, *Daphne* is a charming and unusual opera.

Strauss' last two operas, *Capriccio* (1942) and *Die Liebe der Danae*

(1944)—which was actually composed before *Capriccio*—represent the culmination of his art. The first, with a libretto by Clemens Krauss and Strauss himself, is a fascinating examination of the perpetual war between words and music—composer and librettist—in an opera. The second is a flighty but moving look at the amours and foibles of an aging Jupiter, written by Joseph Gregor. Both are among Strauss' greatest works, and while either could be his supreme masterpiece (certainly *Capriccio* is the more intellectual of the two, although *Die Liebe* is not exactly mindless), *Die Liebe der Danae* might have the edge simply on the basis of its sheer and continuous musical beauty.

Experiencing *Cappricio*, a "conversation piece for music in one act," is like being at an elegant cocktail party attended by cultured, thoughtful and amusing individuals and artists. The story takes place in 18th century Paris and the characters are the young widow Countess Madeleine, her brother the Count, both of whom are patrons of the arts, the composer Flamand, the poet Olivier, and the director La Roche, who is to mount Olivier's play. Strauss used *Capriccio* to make some in-jokes about operas, musicians, and artistes. At one point La Roche rants "one cannot remember one melody; one cannot understand a word for the noise of the orchestra! ... One waits in vain for the arias, they all sound like recitatives ... production is the solution, production is the secret." These complaints about over-large orchestras that drown out the singers, the scarcity of set arias, and an emphasis placed more upon the production than any other aspect of an opera were made in Strauss' day (and earlier) and are still being made today with, if anything, even more vehemence. La Roche also complains about "pale aesthetes ... [who] ridicule the old and create nothing new ... I want to people my stage with human beings." At one point a soprano hired for the evening devours a large cake practically in one gulp. The count consuls that "you must separate men from their works," while the countess concludes that "tending to love those who admire us, we often believe we love those we admire." The libretto is a combination of sparkling repartee and serious arguments about art. Strauss responded to it with music of great sophistication.

The opera opens with a superb andante of a string sextet, the music of which appropriately—considering the story's ending—seems to intermingle hope with futility. The music becomes Italian in style as La Roche waxes enthusiastically about Italian opera. There is a sudden lyrical outburst as Olivier reveals his feelings to the countess ("ihr quält mich, Madeleine"), and then Flamand's own love aria to the countess ("Sie sagen, dass ich euch liebe!"). In between Flamand, having set Olivier's sonnet to music, sings it as an aria ("Kein Andres") which becomes a trio when the countess and Olivier join in. Then there is a lovely duet for the Italian tenor and soprano, a cantilena entitled "Addio, mia vita," which is a bit more "modern" than the bel canto piece that it is suggested as being. The countess comments that the "Farewell to life" is "very cheerful ... the text does not seem to suit the music very well." This was a complaint often made about bel canto operas, that the music of each aria was virtually interchangeable, but ironically the music of "Addio, mia vita" is not nearly as "cheerful" as many actual bel canto (and Verdian) pieces that also deal with death and gloom. The fugue sequence in which Olivier and Flamand have a fascinating argument over whether it is words or music which are more important has a compelling musical background. Also notable is the Octet Ensemble, especially the latter half in which Olivier and Flamand make fun of La Roche and his grandiose plans, calling his ideas "Old-fashioned trash." This culminates in the director's raging and impassioned defense of his ideals and his call for artists to create great stirring works featuring real human beings — or else stop criticizing what he is forced to put on ("Hola, ihr streiter in Apol!"). The countess urges the poet and the composer to stop fighting and join forces to create a new opera in her aria "In scharfem Disput." Therein follows the beautiful orchestral interlude between scenes twelve and thirteen. The countess' final aria begins with a reprise of Flamand's sonnet aria, then becomes the masterful, deeply moving "Ihre Liebe schlägt mir entgegen," which she sings to her reflection as if wishing she were twins. With great irony the countess realizes that she loves both Flamand and Olivier, and that the poet and composer compliment each other like "words and music." She also realizes — and this is where the futility and pathos comes in — that if she chooses one over the other it will serve to break up the budding team and thereby prevent the creation of the great works of art that could have resulted. A romance, happiness, with either man is therefore impossible. This is why the score of *Capriccio* has such an underlying poignancy.

The score for *Die Liebe der Danae* has an underlying poignancy for a different but related reason. In both operas the hopes of characters to find love are stymied, in both operas there are triangles, but in *Die Liebe der Danae* it is loss of youth — well understood by Strauss who was seventy-five when he began its composition — that ultimately creates the impassable roadblock. Financially-strapped King Pollux hopes that his daughter Danae will make a good match with King Midas, but under Jupiter's orders Midas arrives in the guise of his attendant Chrysopher, while Jupiter shows up to woo Danae disguised as Midas. Four queens seduced and rejected by Jupiter warn Danae that the younger "Chrysopher" will make the better match. Midas unmasks for Danae by turning her whole room into gold; when they clinch Danae turns into a statue. Jupiter demands that Danae choose between him and Midas, and she chooses the latter. Danae, restored to flesh and blood, and Midas, stripped of his "golden touch," live in blissful poverty. Jupiter tries to tempt Danae away from his younger rival, but now that she is genuinely in love, Danae has no need of a god's wealth and glamour and eagerly remains with Midas. Jupiter sadly recognizes that his old days of pursuit and conquest have come to an end.

At the opening Strauss creates a wonderful juxtaposition of a chorus of creditors hounding and berating the bankrupt Pollux as he tries to placate (and defraud) them and guards try to push the creditors back. The scene begins with dualing choruses of guards and creditors, then Pollux comes out of hiding and joins in. Strauss cleverly evokes a twinkling "shower of gold" in an orchestral interlude. There is splendid music for Danae and Xanthe in scene two, as they discuss the former's rather erotic dream including aforesaid shower of gold and a young, lustful young God; especially the duet which begins "Wes Himmels Regen der Erde gibt." In scene three the music simply builds and builds in resplendent, almost overwhelmingly romantic intensity as the four queens tell how they came upon the golden palace of Midas in their travels and so on. The chorus harkens to the arrival of Midas' ship in the harbor in "Es biegt ums Riff" and Danae and the disguised Midas have a lengthy, informal duet with "Leuchtet mein Traum?" The act ends with a gorgeous duet between Jupiter (disguised as Midas) and Danae, "Gegrusst sei Eos!" There are virtually no recitatives in act one, just a constant flood of melody supported by Strauss' usual expert and rich orchestrations. Act two boasts such excellent pieces as an informal duet for Danae and Midas ("Niemand riefmich") as Midas confesses that he is the real King Midas and the two explore their uncertain feelings for one another, culminating in the splendid formal duet "Herrliches Spiel! Vollendet der Traum!" which ends with the kiss in which Danae is turned to stone. Jupiter and Midas argue with each other and try to break the spell over Danae ("Zu früh flüchst"), leading to Danae's lovely arioso ("Midas — Geliebter — bleibe mir hold!") in which she chooses him over Jupiter, and genuine love over riches and power. Jupiter rants that he is through with Danae, who will live in a "miserable hut" with Midas ("Treulose Danae!"). As in act one, the lyricism of act two is of an extravagant nature.

Notable pieces of act three include a duet for Midas and Danae ("So fuhr ich dich mit"), a gentle paen to pure love, as they renew their commitment to each other despite the meager circumstances of their existence. In her aria "Wie umgibst du mich mit Frieden" Danae sings that "Midas' poor hut is Danae's new kingdom," recognizing, like Humperdinck's *Königskinder* lost in the forest (see next chapter), that love has turned her simple surroundings into a peaceful abode. Jupiter tries to remind Danae of her feelings for him as well as rekindle those feelings in "Andre Nächte," while she thanks him for bringing her and Midas together in "Nimm denn Gold von mir." Jupiter accepts that it is his twilight and that Danae is surrounded by the "beauty of creation" in his final aria. Jupiter, King of the Gods, portrayed as an aging man desperate for one last fling with a fresh beautiful youth, emerges not only as sympathetic but even a little pathetic. *Die Lieber der Danae* is a symphony to the joy of love and simple pleasures, and also a knowing examination of the need to accept that one's youth — and its prerequisites and preoccupations (such as romantic adventuring) — is over. Whether Strauss was inspired to write such a ravishing score to make up for the deficiencies of Joseph Gregor's libretto is ultimately besides the point. Whatever the reasons, it may be Strauss' most personal and magnificent achievement.

Meanwhile, another composer who had been even more of a prodigy than Strauss was soliciting talk in Germany's musical circles.

7. The Final Chords of Romanticism: Germany, Austria, 1900–1950

Austrian composer Erich Wolfgang Korngold (1897–1957) was a child prodigy whose ballet *Der Schneemann* premiered when he was thirteen years of age. His father Julius was a famous music critic and had important contacts, but it was Korngold's talent that led such composers as Mahler, Strauss, and Zemlinsky (with whom he studied; Zemlinsky also orchestrated *Schneemann*) to proclaim him a genius. His operatic output was comparatively small — he became better known as a film composer when he fled to Hollywood during World War Two (Korngold was Jewish) — but noteworthy: Of his five stageworks, at least three are twentieth century masterpieces.

Korngold's first two operas, *Der Ring des Polykrates* and *Violanta* premiered on a double-bill in Munich in 1916, when the composer was only nineteen. *Der Ring des Polykrates* deals — lightly — with a married couple in 1797 who come afoul of a jealous friend, Peter, who covets their success and happiness and tries to destroy them. The title refers to the mythological King Polycrates who sacrificed a precious ring to appease the Gods, just as the jealous man, Peter, hopes the husband will sacrifice his wife — to him.

While ultimately *Der Ring des Polykrates* is minor Korngold, it is all the more amazing when one realizes this work — which might have been considered a mature piece for another musician — was composed when Korngold was only fifteen! Since the story doesn't really call for much intensity, there is only a soupçon of the highly dramatic flourishes which would empower his later operas. Like Strauss, Korngold was able to take a smaller orchestra and make it sound much larger, and this despite his efforts at deliberate simplicity. When writing about this opera most critics cite the wife Laura's aria "Kann's heut nicht fassen," in which she reads in her diary about her long-ago relationship with Peter, as the opera's highlight — it strains to be Straussian — but the work contains much better music. Laura

92

and husband Wilhelm are given soaring romantic duets, there is a lively duet for the men which is a bit Rossini-like, and, best of all, there is the quartet for the two romantic couples (the husband and wife each have a servant/confidante who are also in love with one another). On a whole *Der Ring* is quite charming, and contains just a few hints of what was in Korngold's operatic future.

Violanta takes place in Venice during the Renaissance. The heroine wants revenge upon the great lover, Alfonso, because her sister committed suicide over him. She hatches a plot with her husband, Simone, to lure Alfonso to their home whereupon Simone will murder him upon her signal. (An interesting aspect of the plot is that Violanta will not sleep with her husband until Alfonso is dead.) But Alfonso reveals to Violanta that he is not just the conscienceless rake that she imagines him to be, and the two fall in love. When Simone rushes forward to stab Alfonso, Violanta throws herself in front of him and takes the blow instead. The two men stand in shock above her body as celebrants of Carnival Night invade the palazzo. Although composed only a short while after *Polykrates*, *Violanta* is a major leap forward, with Korngold demonstrating a sure grasp of dramatic technique. He employs a big sound clearly modeled on Wagner but with its own twists and sensitivities as well as a gentle, persistent flow of eroticism. Korngold's lyrical gift is arguably stronger than Strauss's. *Violanta* is more than just creditable (especially considering the composer's youth), it is a stirring and memorable achievement.

Much of the score consists of very handsome and wonderfully arranged recitatives and ariosos, but there are also several excellent numbers. These include Alfonso's aria "Sterben wollt ich oft," in which he sings of his essential loneliness and the emptiness and disappointment of his life. The opera certainly builds up a lot of suspense as we await his first appearance. There is a beautiful duet ("Der Sommer will sich neigen") as Alfonso arrives at the palazzo singing of love and summer and Violanta responds with some cynicism, and another, even lovelier duet ("Wie schön seid") in which Alfonso is even more romantic and Violanta begins to melt a bit toward him. But these are not even the main love duet, which is the absolutely ravishing "Reine Lieb, die ich suchte." In this piece Alfonso and Violanta each realize that they've finally found the lover — the grand passion — that has so far eluded them, reflected brilliantly in Korngold's ecstatic music. Although *Violanta* may not be quite as good as Korngold's later operas, it is much more than just a blueprint for them, having a richness and vitality all its own.

Korngold's next opera, *Die tote Stadt/The Dead City*, widely considered to be his masterpiece, premiered in 1920. The main character Paul, is mourning his dead wife, Marie, when he meets a woman, Marietta, who strongly resembles her. As he begins a relationship with this doppelganger, he refuses to accept that she is a different person entirely and excoriates her. She responds with taunting bitterness and he strangles her. But everything except the first scene turns out to have been Paul's dream, a way for him to realize what a terrible mistake it would be to start a relationship with a woman who so resembles the wife he is still obsessed by. He decides to leave the "dead city" and try to go on with his life.

Die tote Stadt is a grim, fascinating, almost unbearably poignant study of grief and obsession. Korngold's music is sensual and positively aches with emotion. It is perhaps more bombastic and "Wagnerian" at times than it needs to be (these very rare occasions border on triteness), but this does not prevent it from being very rich in both the musical and emotional sense. The ending, when Paul seems determined to move on with his life, is not really a happy one. For one thing, his grief is still too palpable (which is certainly made clear in the music), and one senses that Paul will have trouble ever finding a new love due to his religious and sexual hang ups. In at least one production of the opera Paul commits suicide at the end, although this is not part of the actual libretto.

It is from *Die tote Stadt* that there comes one of opera's all-time most memorable duets, "Glück, das mir verlieb," which Paul and Marietta sing in act one. Marietta sings an "old song" (Paul later joins in) in which is expressed the sentiment that it's a cold, cruel world with a difficult passing but that love can help us weather it and can, in fact, transcend death. In that sense, it is a love duet. But while this is the most famous piece in the opera, it is only one of several splendid numbers. The duet that ends act two, "Schändlich entweiht," is another major piece that incorporates a three note love theme that is heard elsewhere in the opera. Marietta "seduces" Paul into longing for a living Marietta instead of a dead Marie and they fall rapturously into each others lips and arms. As Korngold's music reaches triumphant heights, it becomes one of the most passionate and erotic duets ever composed. The music of the prelude to act two, which also employs the three note motive, mixes musical and psychological themes adeptly, and is unusually orchestrated to sound like both a literal and emotional storm.

Act one boasts Paul's aria, "Nein, nein sie lebt," in which he tells his friend Frank how he's found another woman who is the living image of his dead Marie. Korngold brilliantly goes from excitement to sorrow to anticipation to joy as Paul narrates how he has gone from walking with a shadow of Marie to encountering her alive in the flesh. Then there is Paul's arioso, "Ich will den Traum" (which is foolishly cut from some recordings) as he refuses to heed Frank's warnings and anticipates "Marie" crossing his threshold. Marietta gets a splendid introduction as the music swells romantically and joyously and Paul cries out "Wunderbar!" at her appearance. Act two's most famous number is the aria (Pierrot's Lament) "Mein Sehnen, mein wähnen," sung by Fritz, one of a number of traveling players. In this haunting piece about yearning for the past and lost loves the music deepens the simple lyrics and makes it a soulful aria of regret and wistful sorrow. Other notable act two numbers include Paul's aria "'S war meine Gattin," in which he tells Marietta that she is only a shadow of Marie and that she has degraded the image of his last love; and Marietta's response, "Paul, du leidest," in which she complains that she can hardly help it if she is carefree and young and attractive to men. The outstanding music in act three includes the children's chorus of the procession ("O Süsse Heiland mein") and the sublime counterpoint of the lovely piece Marietta sings between verses of the chorus. (It is interesting that Paul and Marietta's "morning after" is played against a religious procession.) As the adult chorus of the procession sings in Latin, Paul cries out rhapsodically about the religious fervor surging through the city ("Nun die historische Gruppe!") Paul then sings an aria comparing his love for Marie to holy faith ("Aberglaube? Nein, kein Aberglaube!") as Marietta counters with a gorgeous piece, "Ich aber lebe," in which she sings with deep feeling of her own life of hardship as compared to Marie's easier time of it (notwithstanding a presumably early death.) It isn't that Marietta has no compassion for the dead woman but is understandably sick and tired of constantly being compared unfavorably to her. Paul's poignant final aria ("O Freund, ich werde"), in which he tells Frank how his "dream of bitter reality" has awakened him, leads into a reprise of the act one duet, this time sung as a solo.

Das Wunder der Heliane/The Miracle of Helen (1927), although not necessarily a great advance on *Die tote Stadt*, is fine and admirable on its own terms. Korngold's longest and most ambitious opera is full of familiar "Korngoldisms," reminding one mostly of *Die tote Stadt*, yet it also has its share of magical moments, many passages of great beauty and tenderness. Korngold outdoes *Die tote Stadt* in some tremendous, vibrant, powerfully instrumentalized orchestral passages that are highly effective, but there are also stretches of empty bombast along the way, and there simply aren't as many sublime moments as there are in *Die tote Stadt*. Still there is one soaring soprano aria "Ich ging zu ihm" that utilizes the operas's impressive main theme, and is prime Korngold, and also a magnificent final duet, as well as other notable arias and duets. One may briefly be reminded of *Turandot* during the overture to act three, but some Korngoldians feel Puccini's final opera has some music that was influenced by *Die tote Stadt*, so perhaps turnabout is fair play. In any case, Korngold's fans may eternally argue over which opera is Korngold's masterpiece, *Das Wunder der Heliane*, or *Die tote Stadt*. Actually, the real battle may be between *Die tote Stadt* and Korngold's final opera, *Die Kathrin*.

Die Kathrin premiered in Stockholm in 1939. Kathrin is a young woman who meets a sensitive young soldier, Francois, falls in love, and becomes pregnant just as his company is transferred. The two finally catch up with each other at a nightclub, where Francois is furious to see Kathrin being "entertained" by the club's lecherous owner, Malignac. (Why can't romantic heroes in opera ever tell that their girls are being seduced unwillingly instead of immediately assuming they're unfaithful?) Later each mistakenly believes that the other has shot Malignac to death. (He has actually been killed by his jealous mistress.) Francois goes to jail for the crime, and again the lovers lose touch until a few years later, when the freed Francois wanders into the town where Kathrin is living with their young son. The boy is overjoyed to meet his father and vice versa, and all ends happily. The story of *Die Kathrin* may seem sappy, but Korngold's music makes what could have been stock situations into very moving episodes. *Die Kathrin* is probably the most continuously melodious of Korngold's operas. The recitatives are so full of melody that it is hard to distinguish them from the formal arias, especially in act one.

The duet for Francois and Kathrin in act one ("Wenn Herz dem Herzen Treue halt") makes it seem as if the two really do fall in love at that very instant. A particular act one highlight is Kathrin's "letter" aria ("Ich soll dich nicht") in which she writes to Francois to break it off with him only to avoid further heartbreak. Kathrin is also given a notable solo in "Mein Mann hat mich vermieden," as the transferred soldier she adores has unwittingly left her alone, jobless, pregnant and utterly bereft. The powerful orchestration adds depth and a tragic air to the clichéd situation. Francois is also given some fine arias in act one. He muses that he would rather be a "soldier of love" instead of war, enjoying his freedom, singing and girls, in "Es ist ja wahr." He reveals that Kathrin is the woman he's always been looking and longing for in "Da bin ich trei." His arioso "Schau, der sommerregen," sung just before the two make love, is a burst of tender sensuality — love, sex, youth and happiness all bound up together in Korngold's wonderful music which specifies that their lovemaking is pure and beautiful, much more romantic than lustful.

Scene one in act two, which begins and ends with the comical banter between a lady innkeeper and a vagabond dickering over prices, has a lot of quirky charm. There is an insinuating tango interspersed with bassoon punctuations, and a nice arioso for Kathrin ("Zu ihm!") expressing her desire to be reunited with Francois. The jazzy chanson sung by Francois and the girl

Chou Chou at the club ("Voici mesdames, messieurs") about living life to the hilt actually sounds better when a dejected Francois reprises it in a slower tempo. When Chou Chou lovingly warns Francois that he better be faithful after all she's done for him ("Verdient eigentlich gar nicht") the music reflects her trying to be light on the surface while her true deep feelings burn below. Malignac is given a fine aria in "In einer Viertelstunde" as he anticipates sensual joys with fresh young Kathrin and wishes his adventuring could go on even after death — ironically just a few minutes away — whereupon he'll return like the proverbial phoenix. The piece expresses his delight in pursuit and pleasure fulfilled. Kathrin's aria, "Ja! Ins Dunkel fällt ein Licht," in which she determines to keep hope alive for the sake of their unborn child as Francois is dragged off to jail contains an especially sublime phrase that Korngold develops into a full-blown duet in act three.

Act three opens with a theme that signifies Kathrin's longing for and ultimate belief in being reunited with Francois, a theme that reoccurs moments later when Kathrin tells her son that he will "suddenly see your father's face." Korngold expertly underlines the upsetment and devastation Kathrin feels upon learning that Francois was innocent of the crime of which he was convicted. Kathrin and Francois' duet "Du bleibst, Francois" employs the wonderful theme mentioned above, but if this wasn't enough Korngold ends the opera with yet another profoundly beautiful duet ("Bei dir ausruh'n im Abendschein") as the couple determine to forget the miseries of the past and have a long future with their child. Yes, Francois shows up on the very day that his son finally asks why his mother always sets an extra plate at the table, but the libretto doesn't take itself too seriously. The town tailor who wants Kathrin to marry him also wonders why Francois has to show up that very day and if Kathrin would have found him better husband material had he had a spell in prison. An opera that could have been corny is actually touching because its sentimental situations are brought to life by a poignant and compelling score.

Richard Strauss, who was always supportive of Korngold, had deemed the younger man a genius when the latter was the ripe old age of eleven. Although Julius Korngold had written negatively about *Tosca*, Puccini didn't hold it against his son and he and Erich eventually became good friends. Puccini responded favorably to Erich's playing selections from *Violanta* at a tea sponsored by Julius. Puccini was also a great admirer of *Die tote Stadt* and at one point proclaimed that "with regards to modern German music, my biggest hope lies with Erich Wolfgang Korngold." Julius would later tell people the possibly apocryphal but not entirely improbable story that Puccini had wanted his son to help him revise *La rondine* but that Puccini's death prevented this collaboration. Even Max von Schillings, who was "an acknowledged anti-semite" admired Korngold's music and mounted *Die tote Stadt* in Berlin.[1] Gustav Mahler liked Korngold's music, as different as it was, probably for the same reason he admired Pietro Mascagni's, that underlying core of deep sensitivity and a sometimes startling and sad eroticism.

Eugene D'Albert (1864–1932) was born in Glascow, studied with Arthur Sullivan, and became a devotee of Wagner and German music in general. In Vienna, D'Albert became a pupil of Franz Liszt, and eventually embarked on a highly successful career as a concert pianist. In his later years D'Albert devoted his time almost exclusively to composition, everything from songs to symphonies. D'Albert composed several operas, but only one of them has stayed in the international repertory for any length of time: *Tiefland/The Lowlands* (1903). Sebastiano wants to marry a wealthy woman, so he orders his mistress Marta to wed the simple peasant Pedro, telling Marta that she will continue to be his mistress under her "husband's" unsuspecting nose. When Pedro finds out the truth, he wants to return to his mountain home, but Marta, who has genuinely come to love him, tells him she wants to go with him. Sebastiano's marriage plans having failed, he comes to take Marta back, but Pedro refuses to give up his wife and strangles Sebastiano during a struggle.

Because the subject matter of *Tiefland* is pure verismo, some critics have claimed that D'Albert shows the influence of Puccini and Mascagni in his music; the opera might have been much more effective if that was the case. Despite some fine moments, the score lacks variety, and certainly isn't intense enough to bring its rather tawdry story to life in a vivid enough fashion. D'Albert relies too much on an assortment of motives making the music seem repetitive; worse, the themes rarely develop into full-blooded, major arias. There is some nice background music — the wedding theme — in scene ten as Marta and Pedro prepare to go to the chapel and Marta talks to the child Nuri, who reminds her of her innocent former self. The four note theme that opens the overture and runs through the opera is vaguely haunting. Sebastiano's brindisi-like song and dance ("Hüll in die Mantille dich fester ein") comes at an inappropriate moment, near the end of the opera, cutting all the tension that's been building, although it greatly helps that the lyrics make clear that under the surface gaiety Sebastiano is sexually taunting Marta. Rudolf Lothar's libretto has many interesting facets. For one thing, it is the man, Pedro who has romantic fantasies for a woman — he longs and prays for a wife — instead of the other way around.[2] Marta is an especially dysfunctional character; at one point she wants Pedro to kill her and tries to goad him into doing so, never thinking of what would undoubtedly happen to him afterward. When Pedro wounds Marta with his knife in an angry moment, she cries out "Ah, rapture!" Sebastiano is one of the true creeps of opera, exploiting Marta from age fourteen onward. A nice touch at the end after the duel to the death has Pedro comparing Sebastiano to the dangerous wolf he had previously triumphed over. D'Albert's music is too cool and delicate for such tormented and passionate characters.

Engelbert Humperdinck (1854–1921) is most famous as the composer of *Hänsel und Gretel* (1893). When his choral ballade *Die Wallfahrt nach Kevlaar* (1879) won the prestigious Mendelssohn prize, he was able to travel the continent on the prize money, whereupon he met Richard Wagner in Naples. In 1881 he became the great composer's assistant, helping to prepare the score of *Parsifal*. Humperdinck's second best-known opera *Königskinder* premiered in 1910 at the Metropolitan in New York, where it was very well-received. Much of the music had been written for a "melodrama" of the same name which premiered in Munich in 1897 and employed a type of pre–Schoenberg "Sprechgesang" developed by Humperdinck. When this earlier version failed to catch on, the composer turned it into a more conventional opera, and a masterpiece. A wandering prince comes across the goose-girl in the forest and gives her his crown, but she is unable to leave with him because of a witch's spell. With the aid of the Fiddler, the goose-girl breaks away and goes off to find the prince. Townspeople await the arrival of their new king, unaware that the prince is already among them. When the goose-girl arrives with the prince's crown and the prince joins her, the townspeople declare them impostors and throw them out. Desperate and starving in the woods, the prince sells his crown for a cake that has been poisoned by the witch. The Fiddler finds the young couple dead.

The first two acts of the opera consist mostly of lyrical recitatives with some melodious ariosos, especially the music for the Fiddler, which tends to soar more than the rest. The goose-girl is given a lovely climactic aria in act one ("Vater! Mutter!") in which she calls on her dead parents to help her find the prince that she loves. Similarly, the most memorable music in act two occurs at its climax, when the prince sings "Wird sie erscheinen" in the hopes that the alleged royal personage arriving at the stroke of noon is his beloved goose girl — it is! The evocative and gently grim overture to the much darker act three, hinting at the tragedy to come, is one of the best pieces in *Königskinder*, and indeed act three, which is full of tunes, has the most beautiful music in the opera. Highlights include the Fiddler's Song ("O du liebheilige Einfalt du"), in which he suggests he and the children of the forest wait until springtime to search for the prince and goose-girl; and his aria "Wohin bist du gegangen," in which he reveals how much he misses the goose-girl himself. With the duet "Weisst noch das grosse Nest" the goose-girl and the prince become every poor couple valiantly trying to make the best of their pitiable lives and surroundings, knowing they deserve better and hoping for same. The opera has a moving wind up with the Fiddler's lament ("Ihr Kindlein") and final song "Und spielt ich die lezte," which he sings to the memory of the dead lovers. Underneath the seemingly silly fairy tale of *Königskinder*, there are fascinating and tragic subtexts of, for instance, good destroyed by the venal; poor people downtrodden by the hypocritical wealthy or middle-class; appearances being subjected to misinterpretation (no one believes the prince is the King's son because he's dressed in rags); and the tragedy of circumstance, not to mention the idea of children and the truly innocent being able to see the truth. The fact that the lovers are quite literally children themselves makes it that much sadder.

Although nowadays he is not as well-known as Richard Strauss or Korngold, Franz Schreker (1878–1934) was considered a leading composer of opera in Germany for a period of at least twenty years, and indeed was seen as Strauss' chief rival. He was born in Monaco, studied in Vienna, and received accolades for his ballet *Der Geburstag der Infantin*. He then composed a number of operas. Schreker's masterpiece is *Der ferne Klang/The Distant Sound*, which premiered in Frankfurt in 1912. The title refers to a ghostly noise that the musician Fritz hears in his mind and which he hopes to find the source of, as he is sure that when he does it will somehow ensure his fame and fortune. At that time he plans to marry his girlfriend, Grete. In the meantime Grete's father has actually lost her in a bet to an innkeeper who wishes to take her for his bride. Horrified, Grete runs off and falls into bad company. Ten years later Fritz discovers her again, but is shocked to learn she is a very successful courtesan, and stalks off. More years go by and Grete is now a common whore. Fritz has somehow switched from musician to writer and has succeeded in having a play mounted, but he is also very ill. Grete comes to see him and Fritz at last hears "der ferne Klang," the sound of true love, but too late; he dies.

Der ferne Klang is about the desperate search for elusive happiness and fulfillment. Fritz and Grete are young people who have everything to hope for but who wind up leading miserable and lonely lives. Despite the coincidences and romantic nature of the plot, *Der ferne Klang* is all too cruelly realistic. The highlights include Grete's act one aria, "Ach, wie schön," in which she contemplates suicide alone in the woods after running away from home. In the following piece the music generates a lot of mystery, even magic, over an old lady who offers to help Grete ("Liegt ein Schönes"), but only leads her into a life of prostitution. In act two Grete sings of dissolute, pleasure-driven life and the distant, hopeful sound she hears ("Im Walde entschlief"), and proposes a competition: whoever tells the best story will win her hand. The count's story about a king tormented by a crown that burns whenever he feels passion ("So hört: In einem Lande") is one of the best pieces in the opera, reflecting the count's own passion for Grete and his hurt at her mistreatment of him. Fritz is given an impassioned outburst when he sees Grete in "Wie aus ferner Zeit," which leads into a beautiful ensemble ("Zur rechten stunde kammst"). Act three contains a major aria for Fritz ("Wie seltsam das ist!") as he listens to the birds in his garden — D'Albert creates an aviary effect musically — and reviews his life and unhappiness. The haunting theme for the "distant sound" plays again as Fritz and Grete are reunited and the opera ends with Fritz' death.

Schreker turned to the supernatural for his final opera, *Der Schatzgraber*. Schreker delivered a full-fledged romantic score full of velvety, tuneful music to suit this enchanted but very dark fairy tale. It concerns an innkeeper's daughter, Elis, who covets a princess's magic jewels which can keep a wearer forever young. Ensnared in her nefarious plotting for the jewels are a court jester and a minstrel named Els. Before the story has been concluded there have been a few murders, Els is nearly hanged for crimes he did not commit, and the innkeeper's evil if beautiful daughter winds up with the jester instead of the handsome minstrel in order to avoid the "death" penalty. Act three contains some inspired love music with interesting orchestral effects, and the powerful prelude to act four is also notable. The opera was very successful.

Austrian composer Franz Schmidt (1874–1939) was much admired for his oratorio *Das Buch mit sieben Siegein* (1938) but was also responsible for *Notre Dame* (1914) an admirable operatic version of Victor Hugo's *Hunchback of Notre Dame*. The libretto, co-authored by Schmidt and Leopold Wilk, is very workable, although the characters are somewhat one-dimensional; Esmerelda becomes the central character instead of Quasimodo. Schmidt's lush, romantic, well-orchestrated score is comparatively "modern" in style, almost jazzy at times, especially in its use of blaring horns and organ. Schmidt differed a great deal from Strauss in that he designed his scores so that the singers would never be drowned out by the orchestra; Hugo von Hofmannsthal was always irked by Strauss' penchant for drowning out his words. Esmerelda is introduced with a beautiful orchestral flourish that embodies comments made about her that "she moves with lovely grace, proud and majestic as a queen." There is an excellent intermezzo in act one that expands upon this theme. Esmerelda and her lover Phöbus are given two duets: the charming "Wie leuchtest du so hell"; and a major love duet, "O komm in meine Arme nun." Dramatic touches include Phobus being stabbed right after the love duet, and Quasimodo grabbing Esmerelda as the priests chant in Latin in the background. The opera was rejected by Gustav Mahler for the Vienna Court Opera but was eventually mounted at the Hofoper in Vienna.

When Max von Schillings (1868–1933) was in his twenties he met Richard Strauss, who did his best to promote the younger man's music. Like Strauss, Schillings, at least in his early career, was greatly influenced by Wagner, and even more by Strauss. As general music director of the opera house in Stuttgart he premiered many modern works, including some by Strauss and at least one by Schillings himself. A successful conductor, he was appointed intendant of the City Opera in Berlin in 1933. Schillings had already come out with the operas *Der Pfeifertag* (1899) and *Moloch* (1906) when he met the writer Beatrice Dovsky in 1911. Schillings had been interested in setting her drama about Lady Godiva to music, but Dovsky instead suggested a poem she had written about Mona Lisa, subject of Leonardo Da Vinci's famous painting.

The real Mona Lisa had been Lisa Gherardini, born in 1479, who married thiry-five-year-old Francisco del Giocondo when she was all of sixteen. Dovsky's poem, and the resulting libretto, imagines that Lisa has been forced into an unhappy, arranged, passionless marriage with a wealthy, much "older" man. This man, Francesco, keeps his most precious possessions (after his wife), his pearls, in a locked vault which not even air can enter. He is tormented by the fact that Lisa wears an enigmatic smile in the painting of her done by Leonardo, but that she never shows this same smile to him in real life. When Francesco learns that Lisa has taken a lover, Giovanni — who has seen the "Mona Lisa" smile and then some — he locks the man in the vault and throws the keys in the river; Giovanni suffocates. When Lisa learns that the keys landed in her stepdaughter's boat and not in the water — that she could have saved Giovanni from his terrible death — she enacts a cruel vengeance on her husband. She pretends that Giovanni was never in the vault and asks Francesco to get her his pearls. Then she locks the door on him. Forever.

If the plot alone did not reveal *Mona Lisa* as German verismo, it is made more explicit by the fact that the second act, wherein Lisa gets even with Francesco, takes place on Ash Wednesday. Ever since the violent events of *Cavalleria* took place on Easter Sunday, composers wishing to repeat the success of that opera have used religious holidays as a frame of reference. (Remember, Wolf-Ferrari's *I gioielli della Madonna* takes place on feast day.) It worked for Schillings, too, as *Mona Lisa*, his final opera, was his most successful. Previous operas had been influenced by Wagner and Strauss, but now Schillings was working in the mode of the Italians, albeit with uneven results. Schillings style is romantic, fluid and rich, starting with the dark, velvety overture with its sinister undertones, but it mostly lacks the intensity of true verismo. There is delicate music for Lisa's introduction, coming from church, and lyrical passages for Francesco as he sings of his pearls ("Seht hier des Meeres") and as he expresses his desperate desire to know the enigma of Lisa's smile ("Dieses Lächeln! Ja!"), and, best of all, a passionate love duet for Lisa and Giovanni ("Also waren's eure Augen dach"). There is an amusing juxtaposition when a chorus of celebrants praising the sensual enchantments of Venus come across a procession of nuns wailing about the Virgin Mary — and sing at the same time! Immediately following this choral brouhaha there comes a chorus of monks promising that hellfire will surely rain on Florence before the day is over. Lisa's stepdaughter and servant girl are given a pretty duet, "Grüner, grüner, blaublühender Rosmarin," in which they sing of how time is passing by without their finding love. But the best, and certainly most energetic, music in the score is Lisa's act two aria, "So! so! Hab' ich dich!," in which, half-crazed, she maniacally chortles over her revenge on the husband who brought out the "devil" in her. There is also an interlude in Act two which is meant to depict doomsday and in several powerful passages nearly succeeds.

Mona Lisa was first presented in Stuttgart in 1915; it played the Metropolitan eight years later, and all over Germany and other countries in the years between and after. In 1923 Schillings married soprano Barbara Kemp, the first Mona Lisa, after finally getting a divorce from his first wife. Schillings is occasionally written about as if he were a monster, using his position as intendant at the Berlin Opera, as well as President of the Prussian Academy of the Arts (1932), to bash anyone with whom he had crossed swords, especially if they were not in favor with the Nazis. Whatever the case, Schillings did not have time to do too much damage; he died of cancer not long after both these appointments.

Hans Pfitzner (1869–1949) was born in Moscow because his father had found work there as a violinist, but he spent his formative years in Germany. He composed several operas but his best-known is his masterpiece *Palestrina* (1917), about a crisis in the life of the sixteenth century composer Giovanni Perluigi Palestrina. Palestrina is in mourning for his wife, Lucrezia. Cardinal Borromeo warns Palestrina that if he can't compose a polyphonic mass that the Pope will find devout, the Council of Trent may ban all such music altogether. Palestrina is too depressed to work — his son Ighino and pupil Silla think he's old-fashioned and past it — but in a burst of energy inspired by angels and the spirits of his wife and great composers of the past, he completes the new mass overnight. He refuses to hand over the score, however, and is imprisoned because of it. But wishing to spare him punishment his choristers give the mass to his jailers and it is a triumph. Borromeo and the Pope come to congratulate Palestrina.

Only the lack of some magnificent set arias prevent *Palestrina* from being outstanding. This is not to say that there aren't some spectacular orchestral passages and interesting vocal writing scattered throughout its three and a half hour length. Scene three of act one has some strong music as the Cardinal nearly begs Palestrina to write music inspired by God that will (to put it simply) wipe away the threat of new-fangled heathen compositions. Borromeo is given a very long recitative-aria ("Es drohet nichts von eitlen Dilettanten") that is a masterwork of the form with a big, lush (if never quite Wagnerian) effect. While it never soars in the melodic sense, it is extremely attractive and compelling music. The sixth scene has Palestrina inspired by heavenly angels who sing a beautiful choir of "kyrie eleison" as he takes up his pen and begins composing his mass. This scene incorporates some melodious passages from the real Palestrina's "Missa Papae Marcelli." As Palestrina finishes his mass, and dawn rises and he falls asleep, there comes from the orchestra a pounding, rhythmic, slowly rising crescendo, a vibrating wave of music of nearly overwhelming force and beauty that creates a truly magnificent effect. As Ighino is amazed that his father composed the entire Mass in one evening, and Silla is skeptical that it will do anything for Palestrina's reputation, the act ends with a powerful reprise of this music. In act two, scene five is often amusing, with various clerical factions arguing with each other to such extent that it creates pandemonium. The scene presents the clergy as childish, narrow, hysterical, and sniggering. The best music is given to Morone, especially the aria "Vorn Wunsch erföllt," in which he sings of his noble mission. Act two ends with the Spanish, Italian, and German servants of the clergy rioting and attacking one another; the furious Cardinal has soldiers kill some of them and escort some of the living ones "to the rack." In the touching ending of act three Palestrina is unable to share in everyone's joy over the reception of his Mass because (as it is intimated) his late wife isn't there to share his triumph with him. The opera seems to be making the point that this tormented artist is much closer to God than any of the pious clergy who have been threatening him and arguing with one another like a bunch of jackasses. Ighino is given a nice arioso about his father ("Nun bist du mir"), while Pope Pius the Fourth sings praises to Palestrina, comparing his music to the song of angels, in "Wie einst im himmlischen." Pfitzner had his troubles along the way: he was thought, rightly or wrongly, to be a Nazi, and his very open contempt for radical music and atonalism made him many enemies. However, he was feted on his eightieth birthday in Salzburg.

Alexander Zemlinsky (1871–1942) was born in Vienna and created a society there to promote new music by young composers. In his lifetime Zemlinksy was better known as a conductor than a composer, but he did come out with quite a few operas. His best-known work — actually one-act literaturoper — *Eine florentinische Tragödie* (1917) sets a translation of Oscar Wilde's play *A Florentine Tragedy* to music. A business-obsessed merchant named Simone comes home to find his wife Bianca "entertaining" the handsome Prince Guido, and tries to sell him some rare and expensive goods. A lot of suspense is generated over whether or not Simone is that gullible or if he's merely playing games with the couple. Eventually we learn the truth, when Simone half-seriously challenges Guido to a sword fight which quickly becomes deadly. The opera builds to a terrific climax — Simone kills Guido — and has a grotesque postscript: Bianca is excited and aroused as never before by her husband's violent passion, and the two are erotically reconciled with the corpse of Guido sprawled at their feet. The punch of the ending makes academic the fact that all three characters are thoroughly unlikable.

Zemlinsky drenched Wilde's highly poetic words in intense and richly orchestrated music. Simone has the most speeches, so he gets all of the arias. Early in the opera, he rapturously describes a beautiful robe of cut-velvet in which he hopes to interest Guido ("Jetzt fällt mir ein"), and later, with honied words, importunes Guido to play his lute, singing praises of the magical instrument ("Nicht doch mein Prinz"). His aria "Wer spricht von Tod?," after he overhears the tail end of Bianca wishing he were dead, creates sympathy for the aging, unloved merchant, although it's evident that he doesn't really treat his wife very well. While handling Guido's sword, Simone tells of how he killed some robbers on the road, and how indeed he kills anyone who tries to take what belongs to him ("Ei, welch ein Schwert!"). Bianca and Guido, in the meanwhile are given an informal love duet, "Ach, löse deines Haares." The opera is quite effective if comparatively minor.

Although Ferruccio Busoni (1866–1924) was born in Italy (and is therefore considered an Italian composer by some people), he spent more time as an adult in Germany than anywhere else, grew to love the German composers such as Mozart and Bach, and wrote several German-language operas, all of which premiered in German opera houses in Dresden, Zurich, and the like. Busoni wrote his own librettos as well as the music. Two short operas premiered on a double bill in 1917: the one-act *Arlecchino* and the two-act *Turandot* (almost a decade before Puccini's masterpiece on the same subject). Although the former also uses characters from the commedia del arte, it is not as good as Mascagni's *Le maschere*. For one thing Busoni's music is rather heavy-handed for such light fare — the adventures of Arlecchino as lover, warrior, husband, and hero. Still, there are some nice things in the score, not necessarily in the major arias but in certain themes and background pieces. The best music is the processional and dance music at the end of the opera, which displays the wistfulness that Busoni completely failed to capture in his senseless and uninteresting libretto. The character of Leandro is supposed to be a parody of an aging, overweight, over-emphatic and hokey tenor, but his music (meant to parody romantic arias), including the piece "Venus sieht auf uns her nieder"—which Columbina constantly interrupts to comment on how old-fashioned it is—is actually rather good. Some of the arias have evocative undertones, such as Abby's ode to the hills and wine of Tuscany ("Toskana!") and Columbina's "O, du bist so begabt," in which she tells Arlechhino the faithless that she'd make him a "perfect housewife."

The more successful *Turandot* is a perfectly fine fantasy opera which would be better known and admired today had Puccini's more ambitious, dramatic, and beautiful version not eclipsed it. It is entirely possibly that Puccini could have been influenced to a minor degree by this version's dramatic approach, and certain musical phrases. The story eliminates the characters of Calaf's old, blind father and the girl Lui and substitutes Adelma, one of Turandot's ladies, who has loved "Kalaf" since childhood and wants revenge for his disinterest. The Eunuch is made a major supporting character. The first scene of Busoni's *Turandot* consists of the entire first act of Puccini's version but only employs two characters.

Kalaf's first arioso in act one ("Peking! Stadt der Wunder!") at once exotic and majestic, pulls one right into the story, although the music that accompanies his seeing the severed heads and realizing that the grisly legend of Turandot is true is not terribly dramatic. Scene two features an amusing Gilbert and Sullivan style patter song ("Avant tout chose") in which Truffaldino, the Royal Eunuch, sings: "I would like to take these foolish suitors and convert them into neuters. Yes, If I only had the chance, it must be said, I'd see they forfeited more than their head!" The music for the three riddles scene is very suspenseful and well-handled. In act two, scene three, a woman's chorus begins to sing, of all things, "Greensleeves." While this is actually only a fragment, little more than a quote, it is still quite out of place in this score. There is an excellent musical interchange between King Altoum and his daughter Turandot when he comes to tell his daughter that she will "be humbled before the whole world" and deserves to be. The finale includes the splendid chorus "Was ist's, das alle Menschen bindet" in which it is suggested that love is "the power that unites all humanity." After the chorus sings out the word "Love!" a bunch of eunuchs begins to dance and giggle.

Doktor Faust premiered in 1925 and was Busoni's version of the Faust story. It suffers from one of the worst librettos in opera (in the theatrical sense), courtesy of Busoni, whose alleged antipathy towards Wagner must be called into question by his score. Busoni felt that his operas were a type of "epic" theater that was in sharp contrast to Wagnerian "music drama," but the score for *Doktor Faust* not only reveals that Busoni was influenced by Wagner but that he was trying too hard to sound like him, although the music betrays little of Wagner's melodic inspiration. After a rather shapeless overture, there is a five minute spoken speech introducing the opera and explaining the reasons for a new version of the Faust story. The music of the first prologue, as Faust receives a mystical book and key from three students, is eerie and suspenseful, and deliberately paced (the opera in general is very slow-moving). The tempo picks up as Faust calls for the names of and ultimately rejects each demon he has summoned, until he comes to the last one, Mephistopheles. The first more or less formal aria (scene one), "Er ruft mich," as the Duchess decides to respond to Faust's invitations, is hardly full of the passion that the Duchess would be feeling. Similarly, Faust's scene two aria, his paean to the materializing Helen ("Traum der jugend") is also disappointing. Busoni died before he could finish the opera, and the last sections were completed by first Philipp Jarnach and then Anthony Beaumont. Beaumont's version is said to be the closest to Busoni's own concept, which may be why Jarnach's is actually more effective. The Beaumont version of Faust's outstanding aria in the third and last scene in the opera ("Blut meines Blut") is not without interest, but is not half as effective nor as good as the Jarnach version. In this aria Faust bequeaths his life energy to his dead baby son, who becomes a living adolescent. The piece has a decided dramatic power and the whole sequence is moving and powerful, providing an excellent wind-up to the long-winded tale.

One of the most influential German composers was Arnold Schoenberg (1874–1951), pupil and brother-in-law of Zemlinsky, who developed and championed a controversial new kind of music, the twelve-tone or serial method which became known as atonalism. Put simply, in this music no keynote took precedence and the twelve semitones were given equal status.[3] To proponents of atonal music, the results were striking and original; to opponents the music lacked true melody and beauty and was a mere "stunt," essentially pointless. To them, it signaled the death of romanticism in music. For better or worse, Schoenberg created a revolution in music which affected many modern composers, made romantic advocates seem out of date and become horribly under-valued, and has had opera fans tearing their hair ever since. Some composers rejected tonal music altogether, while others simply adopted a form of modernism which eschewed the traditional lyrical values so dear to the hearts of most operagoers, creating music best described as "blathery." It is ironic then that none of Schoenberg's operas, which include *Erwartung* (1924) and *Die glückliche Hand* (1924)—his *Moses und Aron* did not premiere until 1954 — really caught on with the public. A bigger irony is that despite the influential nature of this "revolution" only a comparative handful of atonal operas have been composed, most of which were rejected by the public and sank without a trace. It took one of Schoenberg's protégés, Alban Berg, whose own version of serialism was somewhat different from Schoenberg's (and he had no problem with the occasional tonal passage when required), to come out with the only atonal work that is regularly performed, *Wozzeck* (1925), based on a play by Georg Büchner. Berg's *Lulu* (1937) has also become popular, although not to the same degree.

Wozzeck has many admirers, but it's hard not to wonder if the chief appeal of the opera is its frank, pathetic story and not the music. To put it simply: The title character has a lover named Marie who has a young boy, Wozzeck's child. When Wozzeck discovers that Marie has been unfaithful with a drum-major, he stabs her in the throat. Trying to get rid of the knife in a pond, he winds up drowning. The little boy, unaware that he is now an orphan, runs off with other children when one child announces the discovery of Marie's body. In some ways *Wozzeck* is almost a parody of an opera, surrealistic, borderline camp, with over-the-top caricatures who talk about their plight in broad strokes as if they're in a fairy tale. A good cast of singing actors can "flesh out" the one-dimensional characters, however. Despite the flaws in the heavy-handed libretto, also written by Berg, the basic verismo-like story is full of fascinating details and an occasional pithy line. ("You tear through the world like a razor," the captain says to Wozzeck, "we could cut ourselves on you.") By the third act *Wozzeck* has developed into an excellent piece of music theater, if nothing else. The music in each scene is in a different form: passacaglia, fugue, rhapsody, rondo etc. but when all is said and done it might be best described as effective background music. Berg did not intend that the average audience member would recognize, notice, or care about his use of these different forms. Berg "tricks up" traditional forms, such as the dance music in act two, scene four, but doesn't improve upon them. His use of quotes may be adroit, but no more so than many another composer. Although the music can be quite dramatic and emotional, it is never especially compelling, moving, nor melodious. There are occasional passages that sound tonal (act two, scene five) and even romantic, such as the music that bridges scenes two and three in act one. There is some nicely eerie music in act one, scene two, when Wozzeck and Andres are cutting firewood sticks in the field and Wozzeck has an attack of fear and panic. Marie's aria, "Hush a bye, baby" in scene three is lyrical but minor. When the drum-major grabs Marie in scene five — she initially protests — the music is almost comically overdone, too dramatic for the action on stage. The Chorus of Apprentices and Soldiers ("A hunter from the south") sounds like warmed-over Wagner. In act three the long silence before the moon rises before Wozzeck stabs Marie is effective at building tension, and the murder scene is the best and most dramatic in the opera. There is interesting rhythmic music in scene three, with Wozzeck in the tavern, betrayed by the blood on his arm, and some lovely dark passages bridging scenes four and five. This is the most romantic music in the score, potently encapsulating the tragedy of the story, and the death of both of the little boy's parents. The music of *Wozzeck* can be big and powerful but the vocal writing never matches that power. The opera has polarized audiences since it first appeared, but it's possible that the very same strange and distinctive music that turns off so many opera-goers ensured that *Wozzeck* was not over-looked, instead making it stand out from a host of operas whose librettos are just as grim and tragic but whose music is less "outlandish." At the same time, the libretto may be what's hooked many of the opera's fans; certainly that's the case with Berg's *Lulu*, which has one of the most fascinating stories and mesmerizing lead characters in opera.

Lulu began life as two plays by Frank Wedekind, which were also the basis for the silent film *Pandora's Box*. Lulu is a wild gal who goes from man to man, using male and female admirers alike to get what she wants, living life to the hilt, and even committing murder when it suits her. In a supreme act of either devotion or masochism, a smitten countess substitutes herself for Lulu in the prison hospital so the latter can go free. Lulu is finally reduced to prostitution and in the climax encounters her final client, Jack the Ripper! The ultimate effect is rather kitschy, like a Stephen King novel set to "operatic" music. Even for this blackest of comedies, some of the scenes, such as one with all of Lulu's suitors of both sexes hiding under tables, behind curtains, and the like, border on camp, and undoubtedly it is this factor that attracts some of the opera's converts. The plot is a sort of modern-day, franker *Manon Lescaut* with a much nastier, more sexual, and murderous Manon. With mostly quickly intercutting dialogue and very few monologues, it is very much like a play set to music. Berg's libretto plays around with stage conventions as well; Lulu's trial for the murder of her third husband, Dr. Schön, is presented in the form of a silent movie. The music that accompanies this isn't very memorable, but is exciting for the scene when Lulu shoots Dr. Schön.

The closest thing to an aria is Lulu's act one piece "Auf einmal sprint er auf." The love music for Lulu and her stepson Alwa nearly turns into a duet in act two, scene two, which boasts the best music in the opera: sensual, almost beautiful, with a decided power. The scene ends on a deliciously perverse note as Alwa pledges undying love to the woman who murdered his father. "Isn't this the sofa on which your father bled to death?"

asks Lulu. Oddly, in act three, the scene between Lulu and Jack also contains some romantic strains. All told, the music has dramatic intensity, color, and yes, emotion, if not a lot of melody. It is as melodramatic as verismo, but never as rich or romantic. The characters and events are so unpleasant that *Lulu* may be compelling but it is never moving. Only the countess is remotely sympathetic, and she's an idiot who helps get a murderess out of jail!

Understandably, composers have had a variety of reactions to atonal and modern music. Benjamin Britten described *Wozzeck* as "thoroughly sincere and moving music, extraordinarily striking." Britten wanted to study with Berg, but the authorities at the Royal College of Music found Berg's work to be "immoral."[4] According to Puccini, "today people move toward atonal music, and have fun doing handsprings in it, and the ones who are farthest off the true path think they are on the right road. And in the field of opera, we don't have even the tiniest victory. Three hours or more of music like that will kill you. It's fine in a concert, because it's followed by Beethoven and others (according to them, those men are relics of the past), who set your spirit straight and make you forget all the tired smears left behind by composers looking for something new, no matter what the cost."[5] Puccini was not alone in finding the worst thing about some modern composers wasn't necessarily the music they wrote, but that these same composers heaped derision on any music that had come before. Wolf-Ferrari commented "Why do many 'modernists' criticize everything in the past? Can anyone think of a saint who criticized all the saints who went before him?"[6]

Austrian composer Ernst Krenek (1900–1991), pupil of Schreker, had a certain minor influence with his best-known opera *Jonny spielt auf/Jonny Strikes Up* (1927), although he composed over a dozen operas in all in both Europe and the United States. Krenek was an experimenter who tried various styles and techniques to explore as many operatic options as he could, but he was never in the front rank nor necessarily deserved to be. The libretto of *Jonny spielt auf*, written by the composer, is flavorful but not terribly cohesive. Jonny is a black saxophonist with a hotel band who steals a priceless violin from the virtuoso Daniello, who is having an affair with the singer Anita. Anita is married to the composer, Max, who is devastated by her faithlessness, but eventually reconciles with her. Daniello is crushed by a train as Jonny and the violin prepare to leave for America. The story is a rather obnoxious and heavy-handed metaphor for New World (modern) Music overtaking stiff, European Old World Music. There seems to be no other reason to make Jonny — who is somewhat amoral, carefree, sexual and attractive — black except that he's a personification of New Music and because blacks were considered "exotic," their music hip, of the moment and sexy, in the 1920's. It is no accident that the famous classical violinist gets crushed under the wheels of a train while hep-cat Jonny gets to keep the violin (or fiddle, as he sees it) to play his own music. Yet on its own terms, the story is interesting, presenting people who are victimized by fate, circumstance and others' actions. The music holds it all together in perfectly swell pop opera fashion.

Generally looked upon as a "jazz opera," it is more accurate to say that the jazz in *Jonny spielt auf* is effectively incorporated into the mix; in any case, by today's standards the opera's "jazz" sections sound practically classical. Krenek undeniably has a sense of the theatrical which serves him well, and the music is appropriately urgent when it needs to be. A highlight is the exotically orchestrated and bouncy intro to scene three; mostly piano, horns and percussion with Jonny's sax thrown in for good measure. Scene three also has a snappy and irresistible jazz chorus ("Leb wohl, mein Schatz") that could have become quite popular as a separate number. Anita and Daniello's duet ("Seltsam, wenn Sie") has an undeniable power despite its not being melodious in the usual sense. In this number the two develop an understanding and appreciation of—not to mention an intense attraction toward—one another. One piece that is definitely melodious in any sense and stands out from the rest of the score to a marked degree is Jonny's majestic "Jetzt ist die Geige mein" in which Jonny crows about his new acquisition, the "fiddle."

Kurt Weill (1900–1950), student of Humperdinck, did a number of works in Germany before emigrating to the United States and becoming an "American" composer. His most famous work is *The Three Penny Opera* (1928), which isn't really an opera. Closer to the mark while still falling a bit short of it is his *Aufstieg und Fall der Stadt Mahagonny/Rise and Fall of the City of Mahagonny*, which premiered in Leipzig in 1930. Although it has played the Metropolitan and other major houses, *Mahagonny* is more of an entertaining political revue than an opera. It is reminiscent in some ways of Bernstein's *Candide* in that it's a broad, sometimes obvious, sometimes obtuse satire, with good music. This study of the corruption that overtakes the newly founded city of Mahagonny in the desert of America is full of interesting ideas, but gets a bit silly and childish, and goes on too long, becoming repetitive (the constant repetition of the word "Mahagonny" is in itself extremely irritating). There is an emphasis on vulgarity, commonness, and lewd behavior, reflected in some very frank lyrics with their references to syphilis, drugs, sexual organs, and prostitution, none of which would be considered shocking today but must have been pretty daring for 1930; this is definitely a young man's work. Additionally *Mahagonny* is provocative in its insistence that there is no afterlife. Weill's music is full of insolence, eroticism, the aforementioned vulgarity, but it has a cheap (if tuneful), vaudeville feel to it. It is often very pleasant, and sometimes better than that, but little of it is genuinely operatic. The most famous number, the "Alabama" song, is splendid, with an irresistible melody (made even more famous by Jim Morrison and the Door's excellent recording of it). Jim's "Deep in Alaska's snow-covered canyons," in which he sings of how hard he worked to have money to get to Mahagonny and how bitterly disappointed he is, is a true operatic piece, and the music in this entire sequence — with Jim's friends trying to restrain him and others trying to throw him out — is the best sustained music in the opera. There is more wonderful music in the scene when Jim works up the citizens of Mahagonny to rebel against the forbidden laws, beginning with a sinister men's chorus ("Brothers stand upright") and ending with a splendid chorale finale ("the dice roll"). The charged music of the men's chorus in act two as they sing of sexual licentiousness, reflects the energy, eroticism and abandonment of the lyrics, but Jim's act three aria ("let the night stay forever") in which he fears the dawn and what will happen to him, is nice but not nearly powerful enough.

"There is something even worse than death and worse than sleep: the vain and empty glory of living, of vague, senseless duties, thought up to lend a life some meaning," says Regina in Paul Hindemith's *Mathis der Maler* (1938). Hindemith (1895–1963) wrote about ten operas, the most famous of which are *Cardillac* (1926) and *Mathis der Maler*. Hindemith was born in Hanau, which is not far from Mainz, where Mathias Grünewald was 16th century court painter. *Mathis der Maler*, with a libretto by Hindemith, presents Mathias/Mathis against a backdrop of the 1542 Peasants Revolt. The opera is a heartfelt, ambitious failure, so obviously well-intentioned, and with such a poetic (if oftimes clumsy) libretto that you long to admire the work more. The characters, including Mathis, the Cardinal-Archbishop, Schwalb the leader of the peasants, his daughter Regina, and Mathis' love interest Ursula, are archetypes instead of fully-realized human beings. The theme of the opera is that art is next to God, and that Art and God can fill up an empty life, but the sheer massive religiosity of the piece may become oppressive to some listeners. The opera does make the point that priests and church officials can pervert the teachings of Christ.

Despite lovely moments and some excellent orchestrations, the music lacks true distinction, although there are certainly some memorable pieces. These include Mathis' duet with Schwald ("Was an Taten in dir aufblühen") after the latter tells Mathis that his painting will not be of much help in the war and he should take up arms. Part three has an attractive exchange and an almost formal duet ("Was dein Denken tötend mich prebt") between Mathis and Ursula as Mathis struggles to make her realize not only that he is too old for her but that they are not fated to be together on Earth. The chorus that ends part three, "Lobt Gott," as Riedinger, Ursula's father, vows to end the era of book burning and religious intolerance and the chorus praises God is also noteworthy. In part four the peasants cruelly toy with a count (whom they execute off-stage) and countess, whom they taunt and threaten with rape, the scene made more chilling because the music is light, almost "gay," like a very dark dance. Mathis appeals to the peasants not to become the very thing they most despise. There is also a beautiful quartet in part four ("Den Vater bedrückten") as Regina, the countess, Schwalb and Mathis sing together and separately of their fears and/or deepest desires. Just before this the peasants sing that even if they survive the upcoming battle, they'll only return to a "life of endless, dreary boredom at home." Ursula is given a fine aria in part five ("Was in mir Liebe war") in which she urges Cardinal Albrecht to end the bloodshed and misery and lead the church into new peace and understanding. Part six boasts a duet between Mathis and Regina ("Wie mürbe ist des Alters Pein") as he sings of the heavenly inspiration of music, lifting her depression, evoking images of musicians in the sky, to which Regina responds beatifically. This is not a strong melody, but the piece, with woodwind-dominated backgrounds, is nevertheless lovely. A fantasy dream sequence in part six with the sets resembling old paintings is theatrically effective but sort of stops the opera dead, even as it fits the "grandiose" scope of the work. Arguably the best piece in the opera is the duet between Mathis and Albrecht (in the guises of St. Anthony and St. Paul) in part six ("Dem kreis") which ends with a glorious, perfectly orchestrated "Halleluia."

Carl Orff (1895–1982) wrote a number of operas, oratorios, and music theater pieces, but his first work, the staged cantata *Carmina Burana* (1937) remains his best-known and most successful. This is a song cycle, the theme of which is that love and lasciviousness bloom in the spring and one perishes for lack of them. Almost all of the medieval *cantiones profanae* (profane songs), originally published in 1847 after being collected in a monastery, are about sex! The music is a potpourri of styles with passages that remind one of Mascagni, Janáček, and other composers. Some of the music is forgettable, but at its best it is playful, sexy and melodious. The most famous music in *Carmina Burana* is the opening chorus "Imperatrix Mundi" about the fickleness of fate, which is almost pop-like with its insistent rhythm and pulsating melody. The chorus "Chramer, gip die varwe mir," has a wistful orchestral background playing between verses that hint of the hope of true love beneath vanity and simple lust. Section two features a kind of ersatz

Italian verismo aria in "Estuans Interius," in which a baritone sings that he is "greedy more for lust than welfare, dead in soul." A drinking song, "In taberna quondo sumus" is a decidedly downbeat brindisi, an oddly unhappy ode to drunkenness that becomes more joyous as the men, presumably, get drunker. Throughout the work, Orff orchestrates well.

And then there's the strange case of Richard Wagner's son, Siegfried Wagner (1869–1930), another student of Humperdinck, who wrote music in the tradition of his more famous father without outright imitating him, and was a gifted and melodious composer in his own right. Employing massive orchestral forces drenched in romanticism, as his father did, Siegfried was able to summon delicacy and bombast with equal aplomb. While some might find his music derivative, with such influences as Verdi and Massenet as well as Wagner Senior, it is hard to hear such pieces as the marvelous and beautiful overture to *Bruder Lustig* (1905) and not feel that the work of Richard Wagner's son deserves better than the neglect into which it has fallen. Wagner Jr. composed more operas than his father, eighteen in all, including *Sonneflammen* (1912) and *Rainulf und Adelasia* (1922). Although most of these works were performed in Siegfried Wagner's lifetime, recordings of these operas are expensive and hard to come by, more's the pity. In the 1990's many of his operas were performed at a festival in Rudolstadt, the twin town of Bayreuth in eastern Germany.

As artistic director of the Bayreuth Festival, Siegfried had to wage a constant battle against two opposite forces, those who hated his father's music and influence and saw his son as the dead Wagner's representative on Earth, and the loyal, almost fanatic Wagnerians who felt a man from a younger generation, even if he was Wagner's own son, couldn't possibly understand Wagner Senior as well as they could. Siegfried took umbrage at the fact that people apparently pitied him because it was Richard Strauss, not Siegfried Wagner, who was seen by virtually everyone as the heir to Richard Wagner. Not one of Siegfried's operas became a part of the international repertoire while many of Strauss' works, such as *Salome*, were almost immediate international successes. Strauss had done much to support Siegfried's career, but eventually Siegfried's quite understandable resentment made a relationship between the two men impossible. Perhaps looking after and protecting his father's legacy prevented Siegfried Wagner from devoting as much time as he needed to promoting his own work. "I do not feel like a tragic figure," wrote Siegfried Wagner in his memoirs. "I rejoice every day that I had the good fortune to have a father such as mine." He mentioned his loving wife, children, sisters, the townspeople of Bayreuth, and his own inherited talent and humor. "Do you think that anyone who has so much to be grateful for can be a pitiable, tragic figure. I certainly don't!" Still,

Siegfried would not have been human if he hadn't wished he might have come out just a bit from under his famous father's daunting shadow.

As the Germans struck the last chords of lushly romantic music and struck brand new chords with controversial atonalism, over in Russia Prokofiev and others were striking out in their own directions.

8. Sound, Fury, Significance: Russia, 1900–1950

The most important Russian composer of the twentieth century was Sergey Prokofiev (1891–1953). Prokofiev began working on the scores of operas while he was still a student at the conservatory in St. Petersburg, where he was intrigued by such works as Puccini's *Tosca* and Boito's *Nerone*. One of his teachers, sixty-year-old Rimsky-Korsakov, led the composition examination in which Prokofiev took part. There are those who feel that Prokofiev was hampered by his always having to fashion his operas to the political situation in his native country whether he wanted to or not; the authorities would often dictate revisions that had to be made not just in his librettos but in his scores. His music was not always approved of by the Soviet powers-that-be, a situation aggravated by inevitable jealousy and "office politics" among the ministers of music. Somehow Prokofiev managed to compose a number of operas, but only one was successful in his lifetime. Many of his operas, including *War and Peace*, were not properly mounted until after his death. Prokofiev also composed several film scores and ballets, including the highly successful *Romeo and Juliet* and *Cinderella*.

The first of Prokofiev's operas to reach the public was *The Love for Three Oranges* (1921), a fantastic fairy tale about a prince who is nearly dying of melancholia. The basic idea of trying to distract this hypochondriacal fellow with humor — the doctors have told the King that only laughter can cure his son — is a sound one, but the plot goes off in rather idiotic directions. The prince goes off on a quest for three gigantic oranges, inside which are females who expire after the fruit is torn open. There are evil magicians and giant rats, and while the opera is more of an "eccentric" quirky piece than a comedy, it is never exactly amusing, except at the end when the princess Ninetta, transformed into the aforementioned big rat, shows up on the throne at the end. As someone observes, "She's come to take her rightful place, spell or no spell!"

While *Love for Three Oranges* probably remains Prokofiev's best-known and most popular opera — and it is very likable in its own unique way — it is hardly the best thing the composer ever did. The opera doesn't really come alive until act two, with the jolly march music, a truly joyful and infectious piece with melancholic undertones. Act three certainly gets no points for political correctness or even humanity (bear in mind Prokofiev wrote his libretto over eighty years ago): The Prince shows no concern for the dead women who fall out of the oranges, and refuses to marry the live one, Smeraldina, because she is a "negress" and he finds her "repulsive." The character Leander remarks that she came out black because the orange had gone bad! In the prologue of the opera a group of highbrows (representing tragedy), lowbrows (comedy), romantics (sentiment) and empty-heads (farce) all argue over what kind of opera they want to see. A group of "eccentrics" come in, pull the others apart, and introduce the opera. There is nice music in this sequence, but when everyone sings at once creating an unintelligible cacophony it's sort of canceled out.

The Gambler, which premiered in 1929, is one of Prokofiev's greatest works. It proves that Prokofiev was at least as skilled at "music theater" as (the later) Benjamin Britten, and Prokofiev is decidedly the greater composer of the two. Unlike Britten, Prokofiev also wrote his own librettos, as he did for *The Gambler*, from a short story by Dostoevsky. The story is an absorbing comedy-drama set in a gambling house, although the libretto (a kind of Vicki Baum scenario with assorted folks with problems interacting in a casino) never quite jells; it is Prokofiev's generally compelling score that brings it all together. While *The Gambler* is in no way a "number" opera, and the score may not necessarily be considered "great," it is always interesting and well-orchestrated, frequently lyrical, and has some wonderful dramatic effects. Some aspects of the story are not as well delineated by Prokofiev (in both music and text) as they could have been, but generally his work is superlative. One of the most amusing characters is Grandma Bubulenka (an elderly relative of a gambling general), who is supposed to be on her death bed. Instead she shows up at the casino and begins betting like mad as the general wonders if she'll leave anything for him to inherit. Her music and vocal writing are quite unattractive and unpleasant, as if to reflect the negative effect she's having on all the heirs who hoped she was dead. She is given an interesting aria in act three ("Hello Aleksy Ivanovich"), in which she asks a man named Aleksy, who is the tutor for the general's children, for his help. The music has an undertone of poignancy to denote the old woman's senility. The general is given an intense aria in act three ("Yes, gracious sir") as he nearly goes mad from being upset over money and the desertion of his lover, the greedy Blanche. Prokofiev is in top form as both librettist and composer in an excellent scene in act four when Aleksy bets — and wins — at the roulette and other tables, closing down one table after another, to the amazement, joy, and jealousy of others in the crowd, breaking the bank, as the music reflects all the suspense and excitement of the event. This is followed by a chorus of fellow gamblers who are delighted at what Aleksy has done and are overjoyed that someone has gotten revenge upon the casino ("He has won two hundred thousand!"). The final scene of the opera presents a kind of twisted love duet between Aleksy and the general's step-daughter, Paulina, which ends with a powerful discordant burst that makes it clear the relationship is doomed; the duet itself is a throwaway.

Semyon Kotko premiered in Moscow in 1940. The title character is a young soldier who comes home from fighting in World War One to his village in the Ukraine, where he hopes to wed his beloved Sofya. Her father, Tkachenko, collaborates with the Germans, naming Semyon and others as Bolsheviks and causing much misery. Semyon escapes only to return yet again with members of a resistance movement, who take the town back from the German interlopers. Tkachenko is led away to be killed and the various lovers of the town, including Semyon and Sofya, are reunited. Whatever his flaws as man and leader, Joseph Stalin at least preferred "number" operas and Prokofiev tried to provide him with one in *Semyon Kotko*, but the former was unimpressed and the opera disappeared quickly from the stage, a shame considering that it is one of Prokofiev's finest works. Prokofiev by now could bring situations and characters to life with great dramatic vitality, which he demonstrates throughout *Semyon Kotko*. There is a restrained power to the warm and mellow introduction, and the romantic dawn prelude of act three — as three couples in love appear on stage one after the other — is quite beautiful, leading into an informal duet for Sofya and Semyon ("Isnitsya mne opyat") as she relates a frightening dream and he attempts to comfort her. The lightness of the early proceedings of the opera, although there are foreshadows such as Sonya's dream, make the murders, the hangings in the village done by the Germans, that much more shocking and horrible. The outcry of the girl Lyubka, upon seeing the body of her beloved Tsaryou hanging from the tree, occurs as Tkachenko, the village traitor, calmly shouts for his bread and salt. Lyubka's aria ("Net, net to ne Vasilyak") gets across her numbness and disbelief with its pounding, repetitious quality. In the outstanding aria "Tak delo vikhodit" Semyon sings of how he has to flee his loved ones and forsake happiness because of the Germans. There is a lot of suspense as Semyon and his colleague Mikola rush off to cut down the bodies of the hanged men and murder the German guard even as their respective women worry if they can get away without being shot. The tremendously effective act three finale has villagers attempting to keep the entire town from going up in flames[1] as Lyubka, insane with grief, sings in a desperate and deranged counterpoint. Prokofiev's music is more than just bombastic background music, which is what lesser composers would have supplied. Act four, with its melodramatic "perils of Pauline" quality, is a bit of a let-down after act three, but it does have some fine moments, especially Remeniuk's majestic aria as he sings of his fallen comrades, the hanged men, and promises vengeance. This is followed by the chorus "Kak umru," as the dead men are buried, one of the first of the powerful, haunting choruses that Prokofiev became famous for. The piece is busy and pounding if not quite as memorable as those that Prokofiev would compose in the future. Frasya's aria, "Oy lyudi," illustrating the horrors inflicted by the Germans is disappointing. Act five features a pleasant quartet as the weddings of various couples are announced.

Admittedly, there are moments in the opera that give one pause. Semyon can be as stupid as Tkachenko is loathsome. Semyon had previously let the man escape, even though he was considered a security risk, because he was in love with his daughter. Tkachenko not only feels no gratitude, but gives Semyon's name to the Germans. In act five, Semyon chucks a grenade into a church to blow up the Germans; one can only hope there were no villagers inside. In an Italian opera, Tkachenko would not have been (presumably) killed off stage, but would have been stabbed and savaged in full view of the audience by an angry mob justifiably howling for blood. Instead of the music being upbeat, it would have reflected the absolute fury of the villagers. Prokofiev chose instead to simply push the villain to one side and end on a high note, which of course was his prerogative.

Without doubt Prokofiev's masterpiece is *War and Peace*, which premiered in 1944. It has been called practically a movie on stage, and indeed Prokofiev originally wrote some of the music for films and some as incidental music for the stage. A major love theme was original written for an unproduced play based on Pushkin's *Eugene Onegin*. Whatever its flaws, *War and Peace* is a monumental work and Prokofiev's equally monumental score captures all the tragedy and heartbreak that it cost the Russians to oust the French from their country. Prokofiev could not have been unaware of the music of Puccini, and to a lesser extent, Mascagni, and there are passages that betray a definite Italianate influence, although one of Prokofiev's later operas was more clearly cut from the Italian mold.

Scene one introduces the aforementioned love theme in Prince Andrei's aria ("A radiant spring sky") in which he worries if happiness is just an illusion and thinks of an image of a gnarled, mighty oak representing disillusionment. Whatever its origins, and despite the fact that it is perhaps not

as developed as well (as an aria) as it might have been, this is one superb —
and frustrating — melody. The melody plays again briefly in scene three
when Natasha wonders why her lover's family don't seem anxious to accept
her into the fold. Later in this scene she sings what appears to be the second half of Andrei's aria (the chorus, so to speak) as she sings rhapsodically
of how wonderful it would be if he were suddenly back and she could be
warmed by "his eyes, his face, his smile." That love melody recurs in scene
four, when Natasha thinks of Andrei so far away and handsome Anatol so
close by. We hear the love melody again in scene thirteen when Prince
Andrei is finally reunited with Natasha on his death bed but, unfortunately,
even here the theme doesn't turn into a major duet. Pierre briefly takes up
the theme again in scene thirteen as he asks about Andrei and then sings
about Natasha. The melody floats through the opera on a lyrical stream,
forms into a pool now and then into which we can dip our toes, and trick-
les onto the land for a tantalizing moment, but never quite gushes into a
full-blown spring, more's the pity. Or it might be better to liken it to a bird
on the wing that dips, trills, rises and falls, gently now, and then quickly,
twittering with passion about to burst, that soars heavenward but never
quite reaches transcendent height, at least for a long enough period. Still,
it is quite a melody, so wonderful, in fact, that you keep listening for it
throughout the entire four hours of the opera. (Many of Prokofiev's subsequent arias in later operas would be variations of it.) While this is the most
memorable piece, *War and Peace* has much else to recommend it.

There is the lovely duet between Natasha and Sonia in scene one, in
which they sing about the beauty of nature and their surroundings ("stream,
meandering over the bright stream"). Scene two boasts an evocative, sensual polonaise played at a nobleman's house, as well as a waltz number which
becomes an informal duet between Prince Andrei and Natasha ("one spring
night"). In scene three the music behind the interchange between Natasha
and Andrei's sister Princess Marya is a prime example of how to make recitatives interesting, lyrical and attractive (Tobias Picker and others take note!).
There is delicate, infectious, delightful dance music in the background of
scene four. There are times, although these are rare, when the score is merely
background music or else the characters "talk" instead of sing, but even then
Prokofiev hardly ever loses sight of the dramatic thrust of the piece. Scene
five has little music of distinction, which is also true of scene six aside from
Pierre's arioso "Everything Lost?" In general the vocal writing for Pierre is
quite good, including two excellent ariosos in scene seven. In the first, he
tries to explain to Anatol that he cannot treat women so cruelly in search
of selfish pleasures; in the second he reaffirms his romantic passion for
Natasha. The highlight of scene seven, however, is the magnificent chorus

representing the spirit of Russia defending itself against the invaders. While it is chock full of highly indignant passion, it is perhaps not as afire with understandable anger and hatred as, say, the chorus in *Il piccolo Marat*. The music that opens scene eight is suitably dark, ominous, and suspenseful, and later is used for Kutuzou's stirring rally-to-arms aria, "Splendid people!" There are two more outstanding choruses in scene eight: The Chorus of Smolensk Peasants, as they tell of how invaders burned their homes and left orphans in their wake; and the Chorus of the Home Guards as they rally to fight to the death and crush the enemy, a tribute to their leader Kutuzov (in this the "indignant" quality seems replaced by a more blatant warhawk-ism). There is an especially powerful reprise of this chorus (with a different arrangement) at the end of the scene; despite the jingoism, this is very moving.

Also notable are Andrei's aria "But I will tell you this," in which he sings that since they are fighting for their homeland they cannot be beaten, and the Chorus of Soldiers ("Just like the old days") and Chorus of Cossacks ("Like a whirlwind"). In scene nine no less than Napoleon is given an excellent aria ("It's different from other battles in the past") in which he wonders why this time he's having such trouble winning a war. The scene ends somewhat humorously with an unexploded cannonball landing near Napoleon's feet — he kicks it away as an aide runs off in terror. In scene ten Kutuzov is given a masterful aria ("When was the fate of this terrible calamity decided?") in which he sings that the retreat from Moscow, rather than a defeat, will ultimately lead to the vanguish of the French. As Pierre thinks he's about to be shot in scene eleven ("I am nothing but a twig caught in the wheel of some unfamiliar carriage") the music reflects his rapid, frenetic thoughts, but not quite his terror or despair. The opera ends on an exceptional note as the final triumphant chorus encapsulates the struggles, hopes, determination and hardship of the Russian people.

Of course, the love story of Natasha and Andrei sort of gets lost, diffused, throughout the long opera, so that the sequence when Andrei dies just as they find each other again hasn't any real impact. Soviet authorities insisted Prokofiev add many more patriotic sequences as World War Two had broken out and Russia had again taken up arms. At times the libretto seems just a bit simplistic and superficial, and the nationalistic phrases become tiresome — yet it's all quite moving due to the music and the sentiments it expresses so profoundly. Thus in the long run Prokofiev's art triumphed over the interference by the state.

Prokofiev's *Betrothal in a Monastery* premiered in Prague in 1946; six months later it was presented in Leningrad/St. Petersburg by the Kirov Opera. Don Jerome has arranged a marriage for his daughter Louisa to a wealthy old friend, Mendoza. Louisa is actually in love with young Antonio, while her brother Ferdinand pines for her friend Clara. Louisa's maid, who wants Mendoza and his money for herself, comes up with a convoluted plan wherein everyone will get what they desire, and disguises herself as Louisa. After a lot of running around and the mixing up of identities, everyone winds up in a convent where Clara has fled to pine for Ferdinand. With the monks' happy blessing, all three couples wind up married. Don Jerome consoles himself with the fact that if his daughter did not marry money, at least his son did, as Clara is an heiress.

Prokofiev gets things off to a rousing start with the delightful, quirky music of the overture, with which he creates the sensation that everything to follow will be a little off-key. The whole opera has a lyrical Italianate flavor, and through much of its length you could swear you were listening to a 19th century Italian opera, which Prokofiev was apparently trying to emulate. In this he generally succeeds, although his own special flavoring is always overlaid over the notes. Highlights include the exotic and sexy dance music at the end of act one; the sublimely melodious aria that Don Jerome sings in act two about Louisa and marriage; and the charming glass harmonica number that closes the opera as Don Jerome plays a wedding song on glasses for his guests. Some of the music, especially the romantic duets, are a little too reminiscent of the love music from *War and Peace*, although they are not without merit of their own. There are also some memorable arias for Clara and Antonio. Don Jerome's theme, which bursts into full flower in his aforementioned aria, is repeated throughout the opera and is one of Prokofiev's most inspired pieces.

The Story of a Real Man premiered in 1948 at the Kirov Theatre in Leningrad. Prokofiev's reputation had plummeted in the eyes of Soviet leaders, and he felt this tale of a Russian hero, taken from a well-known Russian novel, with a simpler compositional style, might gain him some supporters, and that *War and Peace* might again be looked upon with favor. It was not to be, although *Story of a Real Man* is a more than creditable addition to the Prokofiev canon. The hero, Alexei, is a fighter pilot who is shot down and literally crawls his way to a nearby village. Although his life is saved, both of his legs have to be amputated. Alexei makes up his mind that he will not allow his disability to prevent him from both walking and flying again, and after much struggle he achieves his goals. It seems incredible that *Story of a Real Man* didn't please Soviet leaders or the audience at the single by-invitation-only performance during the composer's lifetime. Perhaps some of the Soviet cultural officials in attendance were hoping for a more consistent strain of Tchaikovsky-like lyricism, but it is more likely that jealousy of Prokofiev's obvious and prodigious skill was the true culprit, and not the opera, for it is a love-valentine to the Russian people and the Russian spirit in general, and to the Russian soldier in particular. While Alexei is one-dimensional, defined only by his disability and his desire to return to the front, Prokofiev's music makes the whole story quite moving despite his somewhat clumsy and episodic libretto (co-written with Mira Mendelson).

The opera begins with another of Prokofiev's great choral pieces, the Song of the Collective Farmers, which uses a sturdy tree struck by lightning in its prime as a metaphor for the hero. This "sturdy" tune, expanded when the chorus is reprised in act one and in an entr'acte that follows, is Prokofiev at his finest. When the trio of Alexei, Grandfather, and Varya sing a dirge regarding their troubles and the sadness of life in general, Prokofiev's music seems to carry all of the burdens of Russian peasants down through the centuries. The composer creates an interesting contrast when a farm boy speaks (he does not sing) of how the Germans came to his village, routing peasants and sacking the town, taking away his father and brother, while a delicate waltz plays behind him. The grandfather is given a mediocre and hokey aria in which he complains about being the only man left to stay with the women, and act one ends rather flatly.

In act two, the Commissar, responding to the nurse's compassion for and worry over Alexei, sings a ballad in which he tells how his squadron had to walk on foot through the desert for days, illustrating the strength of the human spirit. The prelude to this ballad has an unexpectedly light quality that, rather than providing contrast, merely seems out of place. The same is true of a song that another hospitalized pilot, Kukushkin, sings about "Anguta" and how an injured tank driver has a crush on her. It's meant to lighten the mood but the mediocre piece is too forced, like something out of a musical. A rumba in act three is lovely and well-orchestrated, but its place in the story is not really clear. However, when Alexei convinces a senior physician that he is fit to fly by dancing a waltz with a lady at the sanitarium, the charming music works perfectly at this juncture, and does appropriately lighten the grimness of the proceedings. The waltz begins delicately and finishes with a soaring burst of modern orchestral touches that contrast nicely with the Viennese-style melody. Act three also has an informal love duet, a barcarole, for Alexei and his girlfriend Olga, who are separated by a great distance ("what stillness! How softly the moon shines..."). Trying to please his "masters," Prokofiev again filled his opera with nationalistic phrases that — while they can hardly be said not to fit the subject matter — become a bit grating and trivializing. Still, *The Story of a Real Man* does not deserve the neglect that it has been consigned to almost from conception.

Prokofiev also composed two more operas, *Maddalena* (his first), and *The Fiery Angel*, which premiered after his death; they are discussed in chapter 14.

Sergey Rachmaninoff (1873–1943) has always been better known for his orchestral pieces and for his conducting of operas than for his own operatic works, which were limited in number. He tried his hand at a few segments of operas in his youth, but his first full-length work, which premiered in 1893, was *Aleko*. This was yet another opera influenced by Mascagni's *Cavalleria rusticana*— it deals with hot gypsy passion and violent vengeance and is clearly a work of Russian verismo — and was written to satisfy a requirement for graduation from his music school. In fact Rachmaninoff was awarded the Great Gold Medal of the Moscow Conservatory for *Aleko*, which went on to have a fairly successful life in professional opera houses in London, New York, and elsewhere.

The Miserly Knight was Rachmaninoff's second opera and premiered in the Bolshoi Theatre in Moscow in 1906, the first half of a double bill. A Russian version of literaturoper, *The Miserly Knight* is basically a short verse drama by Pushkin set to music. The story, told in one act and three short scenes comprising an hour's running time, concerns a young knight, Albert, who is kept in poverty by the miserly ways of his father, the Baron. Albert appeals to a Duke to intercede on his behalf. The Baron tells the Duke that Albert has stolen from him and tried to kill him. In reality, Albert scathingly rejected the suggestion of an associate to murder his father for his money. Albert accuses his father of lying, the two quarrel, and the Baron drops dead at his feet. One presumes Albert will inherit everything and live happily ever after. Rachmaninoff's music is superior to the rather clunky libretto, whose characters are one-dimensional and which needs development of its basic father-son conflict. The composer's influences range from Saint-Saëns to Tchaikovsky to (briefly) Wagner. Musical highlights include the long, moody overture which becomes quite tempestuous and dramatic, drenched in romantic waves; and the Baron's masterful monologue which comprises scene two. During this powerful piece the Baron explains his point of view — that his callow son does not realize the terrible effort it took to amass his fortune — even as it betrays his conscienceless avarice. Rachmaninoff is in top form in this piece, a magnificent showcase for an ambitious baritone; in fact, Rachmaninoff intended that his friend Feodor Chaliapin, who created the title role of *Aleko*, sing the role of the baron for the premiere. A rift between the two artists occurred when Chaliapin told Rachmaninoff that his music was inferior to Pushkin's words. While Chaliapin was wrong about this, some of his misgivings were borne out when he finally sang the monologue in concert and got some of the worst notices of his career. Perhaps his lack of faith in the piece affected his performance.

Francesca da Rimini, was the second half of the double-bill with *Miserly Knight*. Slightly longer than the first piece, it consists of a prologue and epilogue with the ghost of Virgil and Dante, and in between two scenes of the tragic love story of Francesca and her brother-in-law Paolo. In the prologue there is a sleepy overture with sinister undertones, and a chorus of the damned that is sadly uninspired. Scene one contains Lanciotto Malatesta's plaintive aria in which he hopes to see some glimmer of affection from his wife before he departs; and scene two has a love duet between Paolo and Francesca that is attractive and passionate but lacking in distinction. The prelude to scene two is reminiscent of Tchaikovsky. There is good vocal writing in *Francesca*, but the opera is static, with a listless libretto. It would remain for Zandonai to create what is probably the best version of the story with his own *Francesca da Rimini* eight years later in Italy.

Nikolay Rimsky-Korsakov (1844–1908), along with Borodin, Mussorgsky and others, was a protégé of composer-pianist Mily Balakirev at the conservatory in St. Petersburg. His first opera, *The Maid of Pskov* premiered in 1873, and he followed this up with such works as *May Night* (1880), *The Snow Maiden* (1882), and *Mozart and Salieri* (1898). Rimsky-Korsakov composed several twentieth century operas, beginning with *The Tale of Tsar Sultan* (1900), from which comes "The Flight of the Bumblebee." *The Legend of the Invisible City of Kitezh and the Maiden Fevroniya* premiered in 1907 in St. Petersburg. It deals with a legendary city and a forest maiden who falls for a young man who turns out to be the Prince. There are attacks by Tartars, misunderstandings galore, and the death of virtually the entire cast who wind up in Paradise or Heaven. The romantic music of the opera, including the love duets, is quite attractive, but the other music for marches and battle scenes is less memorable, even mediocre. The final scene is drawn out to almost comical length.

In *The Golden Cockerel*, which premiered in 1909, the title fowl — which will supposedly warn of danger with its cry — is given to Tsar Dodon by an astrologer. An amusing farce/folk tale with a certain degree of satirical charm turns grim in act two with a battlefield strewn with corpses, including the tsar's two sons. Even taken as an allegory the libretto is rather nonsensical, and there are absolutely no characters to admire, care about, or root for. The music of act one is pleasant and skillful (especially a sequence with the tsar, his housekeeper, and a beloved parrot) but without any outstanding arias. Although quite a bit of the music in act two is unmemorable, it does boast the opera's best piece, The Queen of Shemakha's "Sbroshu choporney tkeni." In this she sings with little humility of how much she admires her own beauty. It's ironic that the most romantic and melodious piece in *The Golden Cockerel* is a love song someone sings, essen-

tially, to herself— even as she attempts to seduce the tsar! The queens' earlier aria ("Otvert' mne, zorkoye svetilo"), in which she introduces herself to
the Tsar and his army, and sings a hymn to the sun, is a little too reminiscent of the composer's *Scheherazade*, if not in the same league.

Like Prokofiev, Dimitry Shostakovich (1906–1975) was often a victim
of political circumstance. Violent attacks on his work, especially his opera
The Lady Macbeth of the Mtsensk District, in Pravda left him literally fearful for his life and forced him to change directions, afraid to tackle serious
works that might be seen as immoral or objectionable by the Soviet authorities. Shostakovich composed several operas, but his masterpiece is — as it
is generally known — *Lady Macbeth of Mtsensk* (1934). The title character is
the bored, sexually frustrated Katerina, who takes one of her husband
Zinovy's laborers, Sergei, for a lover. Katerina poisons Boris, her father-in-
law, after he discovers the affair and brutally whips Sergei. When Zinovy
returns home and takes the lash to Katerina he, in turn, is beaten to death
by her and Sergei. With two murders behind them, the lovers prepare to
marry, but on the wedding day Zinovy's corpse is discovered in the cellar
and the couple is arrested. On the way to Siberia Sergei rejects Katerina in
favor of another pretty convict, Sonyetka. Katerina murders her rival by
pushing her into the rushing river and then follows suit.

Fascinating and gripping, *Lady Macbeth* is a prime example of Russian verismo. For a storyline like this to work at all the villains or anti-
heroes have to have some redeeming qualities (aside from sexiness) and the
victims have to be unsympathetic, which they certainly are. Father-in-law
Boris, who berates Katerina for not bearing his son a child, and who warns
her not to be unfaithful, is perfectly willing to "pay a call" on his daughter-
in-law, betraying his son, until Sergei beats him to it. Husband Zinovy is
too shadowy a character to feel anything for. On the other hand, when
Sergei and the other laborers sexually torment the cook (this is before Sergei
hooks up with Katerina), Katerina wisely tells them off, reminding them
that women can be as strong and self-sacrificing as any man. (It would be
wrong, however, to read *Lady Macbeth* as a feminist opera.)

Although some might find *Lady Macbeth* more "music theater" than
opera, its score is far more effective, well-orchestrated, imaginative, flavorful, and varied than anything by Britten or others of his ilk. Critics have
argued over the opera's more outlandish moments, wondering if they were
missteps or examples of satiric "comedy relief" in an otherwise unrelenting
melodrama. The truth is simply that *Lady Macbeth* is an obvious black comedy with sections that are more serious than others, such as most of act four,
which if more conventional in musical terms has the kind of dramatic power
associated with the best verismo composers. Act one begins with a kind of

mocking, off-center parody of a chorus ("Cuvstuvyem!") as Boris' laborers assure him that they'll miss him when he's away in the most blatantly over-stated terms. The interlude between scenes two and three gives us the first intimations of the "circus/carnival" music that plays a strong role in subse-quent scenes, such as when Katerina and Sergei "wrestle" on the ground after she comes to the aid of the cook. Katerina is given a brooding, sensual aria ("Zerebyonok v Kobilke") in which she bemoans her loneliness, boredom, and lack of physical fulfillment. As Katerina and Sergei again wrestle and make love (Katerina's orgasmic sighs are signified by the sustained notes of the trombone) we again hear the carnival theme. The music is almost com-ically overwrought and overdone throughout this sequence, as if the com-poser was commenting that sex between these two predators, all hot and lusty but devoid of love and feeling, is a grotesque farce. In act two the scene when Boris flogs Sergei after he catches him coming out of Katerina's window is dramatically effective, although the whipping noises come too rapidly and rhythmically to be realistic.

Act three features the wedding day of Sergei and Katerina, who keeps staring at the basement stairs where they put her husband's body. A "shabby peasant" sings a bizarre brindisi ("U menya bila kuma")—this is quite good if not exactly comparable to Iago's brindisi in *Otello*—at the end of which he goes down those stairs to get more wine and discovers Zinovy's decom-posing corpse. This leads into a virtually maniacal interlude where the car-nival theme is at its most flamboyant and irresistible. The fact that Shostakovich chooses such wild and amusing "dance" music to follow up the discovery of a dead body gives more weight to the notion that this is a black comedy. The carnival music is hardly a love theme, but used to con-vey madness — mad passion, mad horror (at finding a smelly corpse), emo-tions completely out of control. Scene seven with the superb Chorus of the Police Sergeant and his officers ("Sozdan policeysky bis vo vremya ano") is clearly played for laughs as they complain of the lack of not only a good salary but good bribery money as well. A "happy" chorus of unhappy men is reflected in music that is both upbeat and solemn at the same time. This episode is like something out of Gilbert and Sullivan although the music is very different. In scene eight, the drunken wedding party, the priest keeps calling on the groom and everyone else to kiss the bride as if expressing his own sexual interest in her. This scene is especially well-constructed for the ultimate theatrical impact, as Katerina and Sergei try to flee once they real-ize the lock has been broken on the cellar door and the police arrive before they can do so. Instead of trying to bluff her way out of it, Katerina stu-pidly tells the sergeant to put the cuffs on her before the corpse has even been identified. (Possibly she confesses out of simple guilt.)

Act four is essentially played straight, with some tacit humor in Sergei's dog-like behavior in regards to women. The chorus of convicts ("Vyoristi odna za drugoy"), a reprise of which also ends the opera, is a grim but attractive piece that reflects their misery at being prisoners. The interchange between Sergei and Katerina as he tries to get her stockings away from her to give to his new babe Sonyetka is very well handled in both the musical and theatrical sense. Katerina's climactic aria ("V lesu") is hardly pretty and shouldn't be; it's a hollow, soulless, bleak song of a deep, frightening black lake in the woods (death), reflecting her mood as she realizes that even Sergei has left her. *Lady Macbeth* is a rather exhilarating experience.

Igor Stravinsky (1882–1971) wrote several operas — his most famous one did not come along until many years later and in another country — but he was most famous for his ballets, such as *The Firebird* and *The Rite of Spring*. Aside from these pieces, which had their detractors despite their success, Stravinsky was more the darling of the critics (and even that was not always assured) than of the public. Stravinsky's *Renard* premiered in 1922; this was a fifteen minute trifle — but with interesting moments and instrumentation — commissioned by the Princesse Edmond de Polignac (the same woman who had commissioned Falla's *Master Peter's Puppet Show*) for her salon. A boastful cock is saved from a fox by a cat and a ram, these roles enacted by mimes while their voices are supplied by singers situated in the orchestra. The piece opens with martial music, heavy on horns and percussion, and ends with the four animals singing — with great practicality — "And if my story pleased you, please don't forget my fee's due!" The sheer repetitiousness of the piece eventually becomes monotonous, however.

Stravinsky's *Oedipus Rex*, sung in Latin, premiered in 1927 in Paris. Stravinksy's quirky music is never less than interesting, superficially quite different from the later *Rake's Progress* but with definite similarities of style. Stravinsky doesn't necessarily aim for "pretty" melodies, but there are melodies in the opera, dissonant, strange and unique if never quite first-rate. Stravinsky's orchestrations are uniformly excellent. Still, the story of Oedipus deserves a magnificent score, which this isn't. That it is entirely different from Leoncavallo's treatment of the same subject need not be said. Like *Renard*, the music eventually becomes monotonous. You admire it without being moved by it, which is also true of Jean Cocteau's libretto. The more memorable pieces include the seer Tiresias' "Miserande, dico," in which he defends himself against the charges of Oedipus and sings "the king murdered the king"; Jocasta's "Nonn' erubescite, reges," in which she admonishes Tiresias and Oedipus for bickering in a "stricken city" and advises that oracles are not to be trusted; and the act two chorus that sings of Jocasta's suicide and Oedipus' self-mutilation, "Mulier in vestibulo." This last piece almost sounds at times like a college marching song, but it is as compelling in its way as everything else in the opera. The best piece in *Oedipus Rex* is the "Gloria" chorus that ends act one, as the people sing in praise of Queen Jocasta.

Stravinsky would be heard from again before the century was over. While in Czechoslovakia and elsewhere, many other composers were struggling to have their voices heard and to rise boldly and brilliantly above the musical mob.

9. Janáček and Other Europeans, 1900–1950

Leoš Janáček (1854–1928) was the most important composer of opera in Czechoslovakia in the twentieth century. Unlike most composers who make a name for themselves in the operatic milieu, opera was not a part of Janáček's youth and he did not even attend it regularly until middle-age. His first successful opera, *Jenůfa*, did not even premiere until Janáček was sixty-two. From then on he composed a series of generally well-received operas, some of which are masterpieces, until he was well into his seventies. Although his own works bear little real resemblance to them, his favorite operas included Puccini's *Madama Butterfly*, Charpentier's *Louise*, and Berg's *Wozzeck*.

Jenůfa/Her Stepdaughter premiered in Brno in 1904. A young Moravian woman, Jenůfa, has two suitors, Steva, whom she loves and who has impregnated her, and Steva's half-brother Laca, who slashes Jenůfa's face in return for her rejection of him. Jenůfa's stepmother, Kostelnicka, hides her away as she gives birth, but Steva refuses to marry her. A repentant Laca is willing to make Jenůfa his bride, but Kostelnicka is so afraid the baby will deter him that she drowns it. The truth comes out when the baby's tiny corpse is discovered on the very day they are to be married. A tormented Kostelnicka confesses and is taken away, and Laca reaffirms his commitment to and love for Jenůfa.

Although most of Janáček's biographers fall all over themselves disassociating the composer from the verismo movement, *Jenůfa* is clearly a work of verismo in both subject matter and style, and was just as clearly influenced by Mascagni and other veristi, although Janáček puts his own touch on it. It generally lacks the full-blooded intensity and soaring melodic invention of the veristi and indeed cries out for an Italian composer, although it is also true that *Jenůfa* contains some lovely things and the lyrical and dramatic moments outnumber the kind of "dead" blathery ones. One thing is for certain: Janáček's libretto for his opera, from the play by Gabriela

Preissova, is one of the finest ever written, although some may find the ending too pat. Jenůfa forgives her stepmother much too quickly, almost as if she's glad that Steva's baby is dead (certainly she's glad that the truth is out and Steva himself will suffer).

The more memorable moments include the spirited song of the recruits in act one ("Všeci sa zenija") as the men come in with a drunken Steva, who was fortunate enough not to be conscripted. Steva and the other men then sing a song ("Daleko, široko do tuch") with sad undertones beneath the superficial joyousness. The song is about a girl, standing beneath a tower made up of men, who catches her boyfriend, the handsomest, as the human tower collapses. Act one also has a beautiful chorus ("A ty Jenůfa") sung by the grandmother and then the whole ensemble. Janáček summons up some Mascagni-like dramatic intensity for Kostelniuka's act two aria, "Co chvíla," in which in a mad moment she decides to get rid of the baby. Jenůfa's prayer for her baby, "Ale modlit se musim," is notable, but the piece she sings when she learns her baby is dead ("Toz umuel")— her grandmother tells her the baby died of a fever — is perhaps too understated. The wonderful prelude to act three has a bouncy dance quality overlaid with sinister underpinnings. Jenůfa's final aria ("Odešli Jdi také!") becomes a moving duet with Laca as they realize that they can still find happiness together despite the tragedy.

After *Jenůfa*, Janáček's most-performed opera is *Katya Kabanova* (1921). Katya is a Russian woman who is married to a weak husband who is dominated by his mother and doesn't prevent her from mistreating his wife. Katya enters into an affair with the more sympathetic Boris, but is so guilt-wracked by it that she drowns herself in the Volga. Janáček also did the libretto for *Katya* as he did for *Jenůfa*, but *Katya*'s plot is not as fascinating or heart-rending as the former's. Katya is much too vague a figure, and her lover Boris is a complete cipher. While Katya's husband and his monster of a mother may be the true villains, Boris turns out to be a stinker as well, refusing Katya's offer to go with him when he is sent out to Siberia by his uncle. Worse, despite some nice moments, the music for *Katya* is not as good as the score for *Jenůfa*. The pretty love music for Boris and Katya in act two is lyrical and tender, but never develops into a major duet, and sounds derivative as well. The supporting character Kudryash is given a song ("Po zahrádce devucha jiz"), about a lovely maiden rejecting a handsome suitor who gives her many presents, that has an interesting undercurrent of anger. The music is quite effective in act three when the major characters take shelter from a storm in some ruins and a distraught Katya confesses her sin. Her death and the final moments of the opera are handled well, but not with the intensity they deserve. The whole opera is swathed in a certain dreariness that its defenders may claim is perfectly appropriate given the bleak quality of Katya's life. Strangely, the background music in act one as Katya's husband prepares to go off on a trip vaguely reminds one a bit of the oriental music from Puccini's *Turandot!*

Janáček's next opera — and his third most-popular — is *The Cunning Little Vixen*, which premiered in 1924. Centering on a vixen cub and a gamekeeper, Janáček's libretto (from a novel by Rudolf Tesnohlídek) presents cute little animals with highly active sex lives, and is basically about love, death and getting old, the passing of time, among humans and animals in a magical woodland setting. *Vixen* is a decidedly odd and flawed opera — almost more of a ballet — but it has too many excellent features to be overlooked. In the overture Janáček uses strings to create a sensation of scratching, clawing forest creatures scurrying about. Then there is the magnificent coming of dawn theme in act one which seems to encompass every hope, despair, heartbreak, and fantasy of humanity. (It is somewhat reminiscent of an act one aria sung by Katya in *Katya Kabanova* but is much more memorable.) In act two there is a charming sequence when the vixen meets a male fox and is romanced by him, Janáček's music evocative of tender, hesitant young love, at once hopeful and fearful. Janáček is adept at creating appropriate music for differing animals, and skillfully embellishes the action, but in the first two acts at least the arias are unmemorable at best and wretched at worst. In act three, however, there is some improvement in this area. The tramp Harastas is given a flavorful aria, "Dez sem vandroval," while the gamekeeper's arioso "Kam? Do lesa a dom," although not melodious, evokes what the man must be feeling as he sings about his dog — and himself — getting old and thinking somewhat sadly of his younger days so far off in the past. His final aria ("Nerikal jsem to?") as he remembers more of his past and looks forward to the summer, has a rather nice melody in spots. This leads into the beautiful and poignant music of the finale. While it can be said that Janáček's orchestral writing is superior to his vocal writing, when his music is wonderful it is very wonderful.

Although they are not performed nearly as often as *Jenůfa*, *Katya*, and *Vixen*, Janáček's last two operas may be the best he ever did. *The Makropulos Case* premiered in 1926 and *From the House of the Dead* in 1930. As usual Janáček wrote the librettos, after Karel Čapek and Dostoevsky respectively. *The Makropulos Case* is a weird story about a famous singer, Emilia Marty, who turns out to be over 300 years old due to an elixir developed by her father. Over the years she has been many different people and had many different love affairs. She involves herself in a famous, long-running lawsuit — and with a man named Albert Gregor — over an estate in an effort to retrieve the formula for the elixir. While the libretto is quite clumsy at times, the premise and story exert a strong fascination, and Janáček's music displays an almost Straussian lyricism and intensity. The somewhat dubious theme of the piece seems to be that living too long and having virtually everything life has to offer — sex, money, success, love — destroys your soul. But one senses that Emilia Marty/Elina Makropulos etc. was never an especially nice person, not because she was a mistress of kinky sex (as hinted) but because she was always self-obsessed.

Janáček's overture for *The Makropulos Case* is superlative, continuously arresting and unusual, the rare classical piece that manages to be both modern and romantic in nature. Janáček's employment of rapid violins briefly reminds one of *Vixen*, but the quirky and busy orchestration also includes bombastic horns dissonantly punctuating a more traditional lyrical melody. Although there are few set arias in the opera the music is continuously effective and occasionally blossoms into something quite special, such as Gregor's act one arioso "O, nechte mne domluvit!" as he passionately begs Emilia to tell him more about herself in an attempt to unveil her "terrible loveliness." The aged suitor Hauk has a nice arioso ("Ona byla cigonka") in act two when he remarks that Emilia is the spitting image of his lost love, completely unaware that Emilia just happens to be that exact same lady from his youth. In act three Emilia is given two outstanding ariosos, first when she realizes death is upon her and wonders why she was ever afraid of it ("Cítila jsem") and then as she observes that "it is a great mistake to live so long" ("Ach, nemá se tak dlouho žít!"). The choir and orchestral music heard during this final scene are also excellent.

From the House of the Dead is a slice of life in a Siberian prison camp, observing the prisoners as they interact and argue and tell each other the stories of why they were arrested. A friendship develops between a new upper-class prisoner Petrovic and a boy named Alyeja who becomes his surrogate son. This culminates in a moving conclusion when Petrovic is freed and must leave Alyeja behind. Although Janáček's libretto and characterizations lack true depth, the music more than makes up for it. *From the House of the Dead* may be his strongest opera despite its undeniable flaws. The strange thing is that there are really no set pieces that one can point to and label as outstanding; the opera just works as a whole for the listener or it doesn't work at all.

The long, rambling overture seems like snatches taken up and cobbled together from old notebooks. Janáček tends to repeat himself at times, but the recitatives — this is in no way a "number" opera — are adroitly composed. In act one he employs a big, brassy sound that at times seems to be used to generate more noise than anything else, although the big, booming effect at the end of the act at least makes sense when Petrovic's whipped, bloodied body is dumped into the courtyard of the prison. With its folk songs and choruses for the prisoners the opening of act one is reminiscent of *La fanciulla del West*, although Janáček's style is of course quite different from Puccini's.

From the House of the Dead is also full of much compelling music, such as when one prisoner, Skuratov, explains how he wound up in prison, and is constantly interrupted by another drunken inmate. Prisoner Shiskov is also given a long narrative of his past misdeeds. You're prepared to feel sorry for the man until you hear how he whipped and then murdered his wife, whom he mistakenly believed was a "tramp." When her father finds out the truth, he remarks "If I had known she was decent I could have got her a better man." Meanwhile another inmate, Luka, who is dying, expires at just the moment that Shiskov reaches the point in the story where he kills his young bride. It turns out that Luka was the man who supposedly corrupted Shiskov's wife and whom she really loved. While *From the House of the Dead* could be seen as little more than a collection of tales and episodes tied together by music that is occasionally mediocre and more often lyrical and inventive, it casts a strange spell and deserves to be more widely performed.

Antonín Dvořák (1841–1904) composed several operas but his most famous, *Rusalka* (1901), was composed near the end of his life. Rusalka is a water nymph who falls in love with a Prince and has Jezibaba the witch transform her into a human. The catch is that she cannot speak. The prince becomes attracted to her due to another spell, but is distracted by and eventually prefers a beautiful princess. Rejected, Rusalka runs away but the repentant prince goes after her. When they kiss, the prince dies and Rusalka returns to her watery form. Jaroslav Kvapil's libretto has many interesting aspects, such as how Rusalka's fellow water sprites reject her in fear that her perpetual gloom will start to affect them. It seems unfair that the prince willingly dies in atonement for his alleged "fickleness" when he only became aware of, and fell for, Rusalka due to the witch's magical contrivances. Dvořák's score abounds in lovely "folk tune"–like melodies, but a lot of the music is distressingly ordinary, such as in a scene when the gamekeeper and turnspit gossip about the prince and Rusalka. Often the music doesn't match the emotions of the characters, as if it were 19th century bel canto. This is most apparent when Rusalka sings an aria in which she recognizes that the prince loves another and she faces an uncertain fate ("O marno, marno, marno"); it should be an anguished outcry but instead Rusalka only sounds mildly dismayed or annoyed. Still, there are some memorable pieces, including the opera's best-known aria ("Mesicku na nebi hlubokem"), in which Rusalka urges the moon to send thoughts of her to the human she loves; and the prince's lovely aria as he sees Rusalka in her beautiful human form

("Vidino divná"). The music reaches a dramatically exciting crescendo as the witch mixes the brew that will turn Rusalka into a human being.

Jaromír Weinberger (1896–1967) composed such operas as *Wallenstein* (1937) and *The Outcasts of Poker Flat* (1932), from Bret Harte, but his biggest success was *Schwanda the Bagpiper*, which premiered in Prague in 1927, played the Met four years later, and remained popular for many years. *Schwanda* is based on various folk tales of the famous Czech bagpiper. Babinsky, the King of Thieves, shows up at the farm where Schwanda lives with his attractive wife Dorotka (whom Babinsky covets), and "steals" him away (also stealing love away from Dorotka) by promising Schwanda that he'll make his fortune in a nearby kingdom. The queen of this kingdom falls for Schwanda, but an angry Dorotka arrives and she and Schwanda wind up condemned to death. Schwanda saves them by exchanging the executioner's ax for a broom, and Schwanda sets everyone to dancing by playing his bagpipes. Next Schwanda and Babinsky wind up in hell playing cards with the devil, gaining their freedom when the devil is exposed as a cheater. Babinsky tries to make Schwanda think that twenty years has passed and that his wife has become an "old hag," telling him to forget her and pursue young women, but Schwanda is determined to be reunited with his wife no matter what (this makes the point that if Schwanda had rejected Dorotka, he would not have really loved her). Schwanda and Dorotka are finally reunited while the lonely Babinsky goes on his way.

Schwanda begins with a long, powerful overture that is evocative of woods and the outdoors (without the obvious woodwind bird cries aside from some piccolos near the end) that contains a hint of melancholy. There is another melancholy piece, a lovely duet between Schwanda and his wife ("Jetzt ein Herz") as she urges him not to give up hope as they about to be executed. Also notable is the slovak "Odzemek Dance," Schwanda's bagpipe music, which makes everyone, including the executioner, get up and dance. In the lengthy delightful trio that follows ("Siehst du was du für ein"), Dorotka berates Schwanda for his attentions to the queen as he protests and vows faithfulness and Babinsky urges Dorotka to forgive her husband. When Schwanda exclaims "may I go to the devil if I kissed the queen!"— down he goes to hell in a clap of thunder! Babinsky vows to bring Schwanda back from Hell after singing a wonderful love aria to Dorotka ("Dorotka, weine nicht!") Weinberger, who was excoriated in certain circles as a dreaded romantic traditionalist, has a little fun when the Devil picks up Schwanda's bagpipes and gives them a try, resulting in some horribly discordant music; the devil remarks "it seemed to me it sounded just a bit modernish." (It is amusing to note that this music is supposed to sound dreadful but still sounds better — to most ears, at least — than atonality.) This is followed by an excellent quintet with Schwanda and Babinsky celebrating the winning card game and the Devil and his familiar bemoaning their fate.

With its excellent and often very elaborate and powerful orchestrations, *Schwanda* is much more grand opera than folk opera, no matter the origins of its story. The score particularly highlights Weinberger's impressive contrapuntal abilities. *Schwanda* was a big hit and Weinberger lived off its royalties for many years. Fleeing Czechoslovakia due to anti–Semitism, he moved to the United States, where his career never quite caught fire. Forgotten, he took an overdose of sedatives in August, 1967. Opera fans will remember him for *Schwanda*, a lovely and brilliant work that is ripe for revival.

Bohuslav Martinů (1890–1959) was considered a major figure in Czech opera in his native land, but to many opera fans — unlike Janáček and Dvořák — he is almost completely unknown. He studied composition in Paris and returned there after the German occupation of his homeland. After that he became a true international figure traveling all over Europe and the United States, but somehow all this traveling did little to make Martinů an important figure in international operatic circles where it counted.

In 1937 Martinů's one act radio opera *Veselohra na moste/Comedy on the Bridge* premiered. Running only about forty minutes, *Comedy* is a trifle, but a pleasant one. Bureaucracy traps two couples on a bridge between two opposing armies where they have their own private war of bickering and jealousy. In a situation both absurd and comic, it seems that each person has a pass to go from one end of the bridge to the other, but the same pass isn't good to let them back in, nor will it allow them to exit the other side — thus they must remain on the bridge or, as one guard puts it, throw themselves into the water. Each of the four accuse his or her respective lover of having an affair when it turns out they actually have perfectly good reasons for venturing into enemy territory. The opera is entertaining and amusing (although it goes awry on one or two occasions) and Martinů's score is lyrical and well-orchestrated. However, aside from the victory march at the conclusion of the piece there's nothing especially outstanding in it. Martinů would be heard from again in the latter half of the century, however.

Pavel Haas (1899–1944) was born in Brno, Moravia, and became a student of Leoš Janáček in the 1920's. He was seen as being at the forefront of the Czech avant-garde. Most of his works are orchestral pieces, but he did compose one outstanding opera. *Sarlatan/The Charlatan* (1938) is the story of Dr. Pustrpalk, who travels with his shrewish wife Rosina and a whole slew of entertainers as he ministers his quack medicine to anyone who is willing to pay him. After being cured of her ennui, one lady, Amaranta, leaves her dull husband and decides to join the doctor's troupe, which hardly sits well with Rosina. Pustrpalk becomes quite famous, curing folk far and wide, but it all comes crashing down when he is unable to successfully operate on a monk. *Sarlatan* is engaging, colorful and quite different, even if the interesting libretto, written by Haas, has flaws. The characters remain mysteries, with the doctor's positive and negative characteristics canceling each other out, although he never seems truly evil. Act one highlights include Pustrpalk's lovely arioso, "Amaranta; ste Krasna," in which he sings with much enthusiasm of Amaranta's beauty. This is followed by a hilarious catfight between Amaranta, dressed in a huge crinoline outfit which prohibits her movements, and the hellcat Rosina. Pustrpalk has to cut off Amaranta's dress so that she can defend herself.

In act two Pustrpalk sings the sad and strangely sensual piece "Tam vesnice byla" in which he sings of an old miller who has lost everything, is dying, and whom he cannot help. But on his mind the whole while (accounting for the sensuality) is Amaranta. Pustrpalk claims that he is going to divide his loot equally with all his men in a piece ("A prece spolecne") that has a very compelling energy — and urgency — to it. After this there is an irresistible informal brindisi — it sounds like an earthy, dramatic folk tune — as the men drink to good fortune, leading into a brief formal chorus. Much of the music in the following scene is derived from the aforementioned tune, although at times it seems too disjointed, as if Haas were simply throwing everything in for effect. Also of note is the final chorus of act three, as Pustrpalk and his associates sing of their bizarre medical "triumphs" in comical terms of underlying self-mockery. By far the best piece in the opera is the outstanding "Wanderer's Song" chorus in the first act as the caravans travel across the stage in front of moving scenery. The chorus sings, essentially, that you must keep your sense of humor because you'll do enough crying at the end of your life, backed by music that is equal parts joyful and somber. Haas' vocal writing tends to be superior to Janáček's, at least to American ears, perhaps because Haas was less concerned with retaining Czech speech patterns. Haas might have gone on to write many more wonderful operas, but he was imprisoned in Theresienstadt by the Nazis in 1941. He had divorced his non–Jewish wife so that she and his children would be safe. Three years later he died in the death camp at Auschwitz.

Béla Bartók (1881–1945), one of Hungary's leading composers, only did one opera, but it's a dilly. Although Paul Dukas' operatic treatment of the Bluebeard Legend, *Ariane et Barbe-Bleue*, is a fine opera, Bartók's *Duke Bluebeard's Castle* is a certified masterpiece. Although there are no set arias as such in the work, you don't quite miss them. Bartók gets a very rich, impressive and powerful sound from the orchestra as the magnificent music expertly matches the "action," as well as Judith's emotional responses to what she is seeing. The opera manages to be suspenseful and dramatic because Bartók has theatrical flair as well as compositional genius and great orchestrative abilities. Despite one-dimensional characters, *Bluebeard's Castle* works on a dream-like level that can be quite affecting. Bartók creates wonderful effects to bring to life the mountains of jewels and then flowers, and the lake of tears, behind their respective doors, and these sequences also include some of the opera's best vocal writing, such as when Judith discovers heaps of gold and gems ("oh, be sok kincs!") or flowers ("Oh! virágok!"). When she opens a door to find a verandah that overlooks a vast kingdom, "Ah!" is all she sings as the music soars and transforms into an informal duet with Bluebeard as he describes his land in glowing terms and Judith gives brief a cappella responses. There is a particularly splendid duet as Bluebeard and Judith sing of the "radiant, royal, matchless beauty" of the glorious brides behind door number seven ("Szépek, szépek, százszor szépek"). In musical terms, *Bluebeard's Castle* was considered a very modern opera in its day; now it seems absolutely drenched in romanticism. Say what you will of the libretto, this works because of its music.

Zoltán Kodály (1882–1967) was a close friend and business associate of Bela Bartók, and the two were the premiere Hungarian musicians during their lifetime. Kodály had a special interest in Hungarian folk songs, and developed a form of music teaching that grew out of this interest. Kodály's stage works are generally considered singspiels and nominal operas. His best-known — primarily due to the orchestral suite that Kodály fashioned from it and which has become quite popular in concert halls — is *Háry János*, which premiered in Budapest in 1926. This was based on the somewhat romanticized adventures of the real-life Janos Háry, a soldier in the Napoleonic wars. *Háry János* approaches musical theater more than opera: the story is told in spoken dialogue, interrupted by songs and a few instrumental interludes. The music is tuneful and attractive, occasionally bouncy and "jazzy." The charming piece, "Viennese Musical Clock," gets across the fun and romantic quality of the hero and his tall tales. There is a notable intermezzo and a few pleasant songs as well. Modern-day audiences are more likely to become familiar with the music in the concert hall than in the opera house, except perhaps in Hungary.

Nicolai Bretan (1887–1968) was born in Transylvania and had a career as a baritone before turning to composing. In 1937, he came out with his best-known opera *Horia*. ("For lovers of old-fashioned opera, *Horia* is a stirring score, singable and expressive," opined *Opera News*.) In 1944 his wife's family was sent to Auschwitz where they were killed. That same year he accepted a post as director of the Romanian Opera; a post from which he was discharged four years later when he refused to become a communist.

Bretan's opera *Golem*, based on the legend of the rabbi who creates a man of clay, premiered in 1924 at the Hungarian Theatre in Cluj. In this version, the golem falls in love with the Rabbi's granddaughter, Anna, who is dying because the golem has kissed her. The golem wants Rabbi Löw to give him the power to procreate and become more fully human, and an argument ensues. In the conclusion of the piece, Rabbi Löw must destroy the golem so that Anna might live. Bretan works up a considerable amount of sympathy for the golem and ends the opera with a nice tribute to him sung by Anna. In addition he gives the golem most of the arias, such as "Fi voi un barbat bogat" in which he sings of the glorious future he foresees for himself and Anna if he becomes human. The opera's best musical moments come in two trios: In "Sub torna nu simti frigul," the golem expresses his poetic love for Anna, who has a vision that a "black bridegroom" draws nearer and nearer as her grandfather cries out in despair. In "Inima mea in durerata," Anna, Löw and his student Baruch sing praises to the sun and to life after Anna recovers from her ordeal. Bretan employs a big dramatic sound to tell a small but fascinating story. The golem's arias, while quite good, often lack the appropriate intensity and despair; Bretan was clearly not out to milk tears from the audience. Bretan was also clearly influenced by the music of Mascagni and other veristi; the scene in which the rabbi tears the parchment out from under the golem's tongue, causing the latter's death, is highly reminiscent of the climax of *Cavalleria*.

George Enescu (1881–1955) was born in Romania but died in Paris, where he spent much of his time, which is why he is often considered a French composer. His only opera is *Oedipe*, which premiered in 1936 at the Paris Opéra and was sung in French, further clouding the issue. Whichever nation he was most identified with, *Oedipe* is an excellent work that deserves to be heard more. This version of the famous Greek tragedy is in four acts, and covers the whole story from the birth of Oedipe until his old age when he is exiled with his daughter Antigone and is lifted heavenward by the Gods. Enescu's overture is redolent of horror and madness, the unthinkable, as in act one we hear Tiresias' prophesy at Oedipe's baptism that the child will grow to murder his father and marry his mother. This occurs in act two (the only section of the opera that has much stage action), and Oedipe learns the truth in act three, and blinds himself. In Act four he and Antigone find a sacred place of refuge and Oedipe tries to justify his actions to the gods.

Throughout the opera, Enescu's music is lush, sensual, and persuasive, with fine choral writing and excellent orchestrations — at times Enescu seems to be having fun exploring all the tone colors and instruments of the orchestra. The music runs the gamut from intensely romantic to wildly modern and everything in between. Generally, *Oedipe* lacks the strong melodic arias that might have made it more popular (although Oedipe is given some powerful pieces), but the music is often beautiful, especially in a long, brilliant choral piece in the middle of the opera and the magnificent — and quite melodious — finale wherein Oedipe sings to the gods and is gathered up to them to a sublime, powerful background. *Oedipe* was like nothing Enescu had ever composed before, and his successful careers as concert violinist and conductor left him little time to compose more operas. The original score of *Oedipe* was lost during World War One. The process of rewriting, completing, and fully orchestrating the opera took over a decade.

Major Polish composer Karol Szymanowski (1882–1937), said to be influenced by everyone from Chopin to Richard Strauss, composed one lasting opera in *King Roger*, which premiered in Warsaw in 1926. In twelfth century Palmero, a mysterious Indian shepherd is causing consternation in the court of King Roger. Eventually the beatific fellow "ensorcels" Queen Roxana, causing her to go off with him on a pilgrimage. King Roger abandons his throne to follow after the pair, and in what may be a dream sequence discovers that the shepherd is actually Dionysus in disguise. King Roger has "sacrificed" his queen to Dionysus and sings a hymn in praise of Apollo. In *King Roger* the story, and certainly the characters, are subordinate to the stage spectacle of a piece that is partly oratorio. Szymanowski's music is always smooth and attractive, often dramatic, but it never quite soars despite some interesting pieces. These include the scene when the shepherd tells Roger where he comes from. There is a compelling dance backed by flute, oboe and cymbal which intensifies as Roxana joins in vocally, becoming a duet with the shepherd ("W radosnym") that is loud and emphatic but, unfortunately, nothing very special.

Danish composer Carl Nielsen (1856–1931) studied at the Royal Conservatory in Copenhagen and became best known as a symphonist. He is the composer of two operas, *Saul and David* (1902), and his masterpiece *Maskarade* (1906), which premiered in Copenhagen where the opera takes place. Jeronimus wants his son Leander to marry his friend Leonard's daughter, Leonora. But both Leander and Leonora, who think they have never met, deplore the match because they have each met their dream spouse — actually each other in disguise — at a masquerade. (These masquerades are sort of the 18th century Copenhagen equivalent of modern-day raves with masks.) Jeronimus deplores the masquerades and all they represent, but Leander's mother Magdelone has a bit more latitude. She attends one of the masquerades where she has a flirty dance with Leonard. A secondary romance flourishes between the servants Henrik and Pernille. When everyone unmasks, the young lovers Leander and Leonora have a pleasant surprise — the person they love just happens to be the one their fathers have chosen for them.

Nielsen's score is consistently colorful and exuberant. Of special note are Magdelone's dance and aria ("Om jeg kan danse?") in act one, which leads into the equally delightful "Folle d'Espagne." Jeronimus is given an irresistible and rather poignant piece in which he mourns the changes in city life since the advent of masquerades and their "depravity — now everyone is equal." Even if one can't agree with his sentiments, the tune has a haunting tone as it echoes his dismay over growing old and forever losing a certain way of life ("Fordum var der Fred"). Henrik has a fine aria in which he sings that everyone in the country of darkness requires fun and good times — the maskerade — now and then ("I dette Land"), following this up with "Og pro secunda," in which he explains how the maskerade makes hard-working lower classes feel equal to their masters for a time, and no wonder they want to join in! Act one ends with a wonderful, exciting quintet of Leander, Henrik, Jeronimus, Leonard, and Aru as the young men insist that they will go to the maskerade and the others forbid them.

Act two is full of several notable lyrical pieces, but the music is especially good in act three; for instance, Leander and Leonora are given a lovely, delicate duet ("Ulignelige Pige") as they exchange names and declare their love for one another. There is a very evocative song to Bacchus sung by the tutor and chorus ("Naar Mars og Venus"), another celebratory piece with an undertone of sorrow, as if the celebrants are utterly desperate to be drunk and happy for that moment. In fact the whole opera has an undercurrent of pathos, with the masquerade being a metaphor for man's need to stave off death, old age, and fool himself into temporarily thinking that life is better than it really is. This subtext — as well as its light-hearted ribbing of class structure, youthful ways versus old, and so on — gives the comedy an added depth and feeling while Neilsen's music brings it all alive. Very popular in Denmark, *Maskarade* deserves to be better known throughout the world.

10. (Mostly) Gentlemen at Work: United Kingdom, 1900–1950

Opera was not particularly important in England until the arrival of Handel and his Italian-style operas. Another German expatriate, John Pepusch, wrote the music for the phenomenally successful *The Beggar's Opera* (1728), which is usually attributed to its librettist John Gay. Gay created the ballad opera as a reaction to the "Italian" operas popularized by Handel and others. Ballad operas predominated English culture up until the time of Gilbert and Sullivan. England's operatic composers included William Vincent Wallace, William Balfe, and Henry Rowley Bishop, but despite the fame of some of their compositions — Bishop composed *Clari*, from which comes the song "Home, Sweet Home" — none of these gentlemen became known as the Great British Operatic Composer. Indeed today they are generally completely unknown to the opera-going public. It was not until Benjamin Britten entered the scene that England at last had an opera composer of some stature that it could call its own. And then there was also Frederick Delius (1862–1934).

Delius was born of German parents but came into the world in Yorkshire, although he spent most of his adult life outside of England. As a young man he ran some orange groves in Florida — rather badly — where he became acquainted with native Negro melodies that stayed in his mind and influenced the subject matter of his operas, as did Florida itself. He ran wild in Paris, sampling the night life and the flesh pots, and contracted syphilis, from which he eventually went blind. In Paris during those Bohemian times he would take weekly trips to the morgue — perhaps in search of a lover who had disappeared from his life? His marriage was childless and possibly chaste. As he grew older, Delius and his wife seemed to dislike all composers' music except Delius.' Delius was championed by Sir Thomas Beecham, and among his professional admirers were Bartók and Kodaly. Delius tried to secure the rights to Oscar Wilde's *Salome*, but these were snatched away by Richard Strauss. Anti-Straussians looked to Delius as the antithesis of Strauss, the "ersatz Wagner" whom they thought was admired only in the absence of the real thing.[1]

The first of Delius' operas to be presented to the public was *Koanga* (1904). This is the story of the tragic love affair on a Louisiana plantation in the late eighteenth century between a mulatto slave girl named Palmyra, and a proud, defiant new slave named Koanga. The plantations owner's wife is Palmyra's half-sister, and contrives to stop the wedding between her and Koanga. Palmyra is kidnapped by the foreman's servants, and Koanga is hunted down after killing the foreman while rescuing her. After Koanga is killed, Palmyra commits suicide.

The libretto to *Koanga* was revised more than once, but still could stand improvement. Koanga and Palmyra are not as well developed as Porgy and Bess — a comparison to Gershwin's work is inevitable despite the vast differences between characters and situations — and Delius undoubtedly felt no true connection to the characters as Gershwin did to his own pair of operatic lovers. On the other hand, *Koanga* is no folk opera like *Porgy and Bess* — it is a full-fledged Grand Opera in the European tradition. At the same time *Koanga* is not quite as "tuneful" nor as memorable as Gershwin's work, although it contains enough nice music and fine moments to make it worthy of revival. These include the lovely overture that comes between the prologue, wherein Uncle Joe is importuned to tell the story of Koanga and Palmyra, and the first act (which has a notable quintet "I feel a strange foreboding"); Palmyra's charmingly orchestrated "Hail to thee mighty prince!" in act two, which turns into the chorus and ballet of Creole slaves; and Koanga's "Hear me God Voodoo," in which he calls down magical powers on the whites who kidnapped Palmyra and brings act two to a dramatic close. Act three contains such highlights as the prelude (which was originally used for *The Magic Fountain*) and Koanga's "This is the night of the new moon," which leads into a splendid dark chorus and a truly frenzied, colorful voodoo dance as the blacks "gash themselves with knives" for the blood sacrifice. In the epilogue, Renee's "let's stay up and watch the coming dawn of day" and the subsequent chorus — as well as the instrumental music that closes the opera — are among Delius' loveliest compositions.

Koanga's final aria and death scene isn't as powerful or dramatic as it should have been. Instead of building up to a strong climax of the love story with the deaths of the lovers, Delius seems to be frittering away in search of something that might work. Oddly, the beautiful orchestral interlude between act three and the epilogue has the dramatic intensity that would have been perfect for the climax. It is also strange that the particularly memorable theme we first hear in the prologue and which develops into the overture is never heard again until the beginning of the epilogue.

A Village Romeo and Juliet— a "music drama in six scenes"—premiered in 1907, and has a frankly bizarre libretto. It takes place in Switzerland in the mid-nineteenth century and concerns the son (Sali) and daughter (Vreli) of two farmers who are feuding over a piece of land. The two fall in love, then fall under the spell of the Dark Fiddler — clearly the messenger of Death — an ominous figure who lost his claim to the land in dispute. At the end of the opera Sali and Vreli sail off on a barge which the former deliberately sinks so they can die romantically in each other's arms. Typical of Delius, his libretto hardly boasts dramatic flair, but despite its flaws the story works on the level of a dream, making *A Village Romeo and Juliet* another sad and rather fascinating Delius Opera of Doomed Love. Baleful undertones permeate the richly orchestrated score, and the Wagnerian influence seems stronger than ever. Highlights include the dark fiddler's haunting theme, the orchestral bridge between scenes two and three, and the music of the dream sequence in scene four, which contains a wedding hymn that also has sinister undertones. The music really begins to take flight in scene four which also contains the brief duet "Nay, we will wander together" and Sali's tender arioso "We'll never, never part again." Scene five has an attractive chorus of merchants and patrons at a fair attended by the lovers, as well as a notable entr'acte, "A walk in the Paradise Garden," which would stop the opera dead were it not for the fact that the pace of the opera is continuously languid. The final scene has The Song of the Vagabonds ("In rain and sunshine") in which said vagabonds celebrate their wandering lifestyle, and the best piece in the opera, the beautiful duet "See the moonbeams kiss the woods," as the lovers decide to seek peace and eternal love in death. There are those who see the dark fiddler not as a sinister presence but as a metaphor for Delius himself, a kind of benign Bohemian urging the lovers onto a freer life communing with nature, and while some of this may be borne out in the text, it is in the music that Delius gets across the character's malignant and dangerous aspects.

Delius' final opera, *Fennimore and Gerda*, premiered in 1919. This was a triangle drama with two friends, Niels and Erik, falling for the same woman, Fennimore. The lady decides to marry Erik, but the latter's creative block and heavy drinking cause a marital crisis, resulting in Fennimore and Niels giving in to their erotic impulses. When Erik is killed Fennimore is too guilt-wracked to continue her relationship with Niels, but he finds happiness with a young woman named Gerda. None of this is half as interesting as it sounds. While Delius is always interesting and lyrical, *Fennimore and Gerda* is a distinctly minor work. Not awful, but it's as if

Delius were treading water, as if he collected leavings, discarded scraps of music, and put them together into something he hoped would be presentable. It is also much too "sleepy," lacking energy and dramatic thrust. In fact the rather clumsy libretto, divided into eleven "pictures," is almost antitheatrical. *Fennimore and Gerda* is pleasant, nothing more, and occasionally tedious. Among the more memorable moments are Fennimore's lute song ("Young Svaenhild sat above and sighed") in which the words mirror her own longing for travel and excitement. The love music for Fennimore and Niels is acceptable but second-rate for Delius, but the love music in the final "picture" for Niels and Gerda is perhaps the only time the score all too briefly takes flight. Erik is given an interesting aria in which he describes how he's drifting, can not paint, wants time, yet feels time rushing by, feels despair and so on, but Delius' music does little to give life to his words. Delius told Sir Thomas Beecham that "he had eliminated from it all that was unessential to the true development both of the drama and the music." Beecham was afraid Delius' "elimination" may have gone too far, resulting in the "non-lyrical nature of the whole piece." Some of Delius' earlier — and much better — operas were finally disinterred in the 1970's and these are discussed in chapter 14.

Ethel Smyth (1858–1944) is that rarity of the operatic world, a female composer of opera. Why did so few women compose operas or indeed classical music of any kind? It's likely that even talented women were discouraged from pursuing careers as musicians due to the basic sexism of the period. Women writers often felt they had to write under male pseudonyms, and indeed some couldn't get published unless they did. There is no way of knowing how many talented women composers may have been lost to the world simply because their families refused to send them to the conservatory. If the boys in the family had problems convincing their parents they should embark on a career as a composer, it would have been impossible for the girls.

Smyth was a colorful character who aggressively pursued her ambitions — as she had to — and sometimes set people's teeth on edge because of it. One intendant, when asked if he knew Miss Smyth, remarked that not only did he know her, but when he saw her he would "jump into a cab, drive to the railway station, and take the first train out of the city."[2] When Smyth complained that being a woman made it difficult for her to get her music heard, George Bernard Shaw, somewhat missing the point, asked her how she could say there was an objection to feminine music when Sullivan "whose music was music in petticoats from the first bar to the last" and Mendelssohn with his "ladylike music" were so popular?

Smyth found some sympathy in Germany. *The Wreckers*, her best-known work, premiered in 1906 in Leipzig. The opera has an excellent story, concerning folks in long-ago Cornwall who, like some modern-day terrorists, are perfectly willing to spill innocent blood because their own lot is poor. They actually pray to God for shipwrecks off the coast so that they can gain needed booty by looting them. Someone is lighting fires to warn the ships, however, and when his identity is discovered it turns out to be Mark, the lover of Preacher Pascoe's wife, Thirza. As Thirza has begun to help Mark in his compassionate mission, the two of them are imprisoned in a cave where they will drown when the tide comes in. The lengthy first act works up considerable suspense over the identity of the good samaritan, who Mark's new lover could be, and whether or not Pascoe is having a crisis of conscience. One problem with the libretto, however, is that "hero" Mark doesn't appear enough and is a cipher. It's hard to care about the two (only decent) characters because we don't get to know them well enough, therefore their plight at the end isn't nearly moving enough.

Smyth's music is generally not up to the level of the libretto, never quite magical or emotional enough, although there are good things in the score. A lovely theme for the character of Mark is buried in the attractive overture and accompanies his ballad "I'll sit beside his grave and mourn him," but unfortunately Smyth never develops it into a major aria on its own. The music in the first act begins to intensify as Thirza sings in disgust about the hypocritical congregation who pray to God for disaster and think of themselves as doing "God's work." Pascoe's aria, "Mid wild rocks dwelling," in which he tries to justify their evil to his young wife by talking of bloodshed previously done in God's name or at his bidding, is fairly strong. The chorus of villagers celebrating the fact that a new ship is about to crash on the rocks has a quirky, off-beat quality to it. (An Italian composer of the period would have made this chorus much darker and less "upbeat.") Most of the music in act two could be dismissed as warmed-over Wagner — and Smyth is obviously aiming at that effect — were it not for its attractiveness and the skill with which it's put forth. The set arias, while pleasant, fail to distinguish themselves until the exciting, excellent duet between Mark and Thirza "Blaze, fire of love in deathless splendor!" There is some perfectly nice music in act three, as well, but it never erupts into brilliance and it isn't moving, despite the poignancy of the situations. Thirza's "Think ye that I repent?" is notable, however, as is a particularly well-orchestrated chorus ("Mark the trump of doom") that leads into a final, informal duet "Turn on me those eyes full of sky and sea." At times Smyth's score sounds like ersatz verismo, and at other times, as noted, imitation Wagner (as opposed to music that has been influenced by Wagner). *The Wreckers* is certainly not a bad opera by any standards. Despite some genuinely nice moments, however, its music is simply not great enough to make it a lost masterpiece.

When *The Wreckers* premiered, the Kapellmeister had made incomprehensible cuts that infuriated Smyth. The next day before anyone else was in the building, she went in and literally stole away all the copies of the score, including the orchestral parts, and fled to Prague where another production had been arranged. She later realized what a mistake this had been. Not only had her actions been insensitive to the hard-working musicians and prevented a second performance, but other German opera houses were now on notice: Ethel Smyth was "difficult." When *The Wreckers* was revived many years later at Sadler's Wells, a nearly blind Smyth was in grateful attendance, although she had also gone deaf and could not hear a note of her opera.

Rutland Boughton (1878–1960) is best-known as the composer of *The Immortal Hour* (1914), his second opera (and the first to be produced), a fantasy that was once quite popular. Boughton studied for a while at the Royal College of Music, but could not afford to continue. He was interested in socialist and communist causes and established a very humble music festival of sorts in Glastonbury which managed to attract some well-known faces. There he put on no frills versions of his own operas and others. His third operatic work was the choral drama *Bethlehem* (1913), which tells the story of Mary and Joseph and the virgin birth. The opera has no real narrative structure; the libretto is merely a series of tableau with choral interludes. Highlights include the Angel Gabriel's aria "Hail Mary, full of grace," wherein he tells Mary of the joyful fate awaiting her as the Holy Virgin. Mary's "Now, sweetest Lord, I prey," sung over the baby Jesus is also of note. The best music, however, is given to Herod. His aria "I am he who reigns" showcases Boughton's orchestral abilities and dramatic flair as Herod struts for his followers. Herod vows that he is the King of the World and that no child, divine or otherwise, will usurp him, in his second major aria, "Unwisely and unwittingly." As for the rest of the music, much of it is pleasant but some merely sounds like pretty little English ditties and is about as impressive. Furthermore it's disconcerting to hear "Come All Ye Faithful," "First Noel'" and other famous carols interspersed (in expanded and reorchestrated form) throughout the opera as choral interludes. They are almost always far superior to Boughton's own music. In spite of this, *Bethlehem* is rather nice all told despite its flaws.

Gustav Holst (1874–1934) was born in Cheltenham, England, son of a Swedish father and Russian mother. Fairly forgotten by now, he achieved a measure of fame with his piece *The Planets* (1914) and also tried his hand at several operas. His chief influences were said to be Wagner and Sir Arthur

Sullivan, though you can hardly find a trace of them in his one-act chamber opera *Savitri* (1916). In this work the title character, in essence, manages to talk Death out of claiming the life of her husband Satyavan. Never mind that Holst's libretto has no action to speak of, his music rarely takes flight. Richer scoring might have helped the piece; in fact, some of the singing is done a cappella. Holst also composed *The Perfect Fool* (1923), *At the Boar's Head* (1925) and *The Wandering Scholar* (1934). The oft-recorded *Savitri* just doesn't work.

Frederic Norton (1869–1946) was an actor and baritone who was responsible for one of London's most popular musicals, *Chu Chin Chow*, which premiered in 1916. This was a very tuneful, operetta-like (near operatic, at times) piece inspired by the story of Ali Baba and the Forty Thieves, mostly orchestrated by Brian Fahey. "I Love Thee So" is a lilting love ballad, and the two most outstanding numbers are the knock-out ballad "I Long for the Sun" and the plaintive and evocative "Cobbler's Song." There is some Sullivan influence in the score (for instance, "The Robbers' March") and "oriental" touches are employed to good effect in such numbers as the dramatic "I am Chu Chin Chow" and "Behold." One can see this piece being successfully revived if the cast and production were carefully assembled.

Ralph Vaughan Williams (1872–1958) was a friend of Gustav Holst, and studied at the RCM. His operas include the ballad opera *Hugh the Drover* (1924) and the very different *Riders to the Sea* (1937). Taken from the one-act play by Synge, *Riders to the Sea* is one long dirge and outcry of anguish, an attempt to reconcile with and accept cruel fate and the agony of loss and life (and death). Vaughan Williams' atmospheric score is suitably bleak and dreary but also compelling and lyrical, if not terribly melodious. The closest thing to an aria is mother Maurya's "Bartly will be lost now," in which she reviews all the sons, husbands, fathers who have been drowned at sea. (This almost becomes comical — so many in the family have died you wonder why they didn't seek a new profession.) Ultimately, however, the opera engenders compassion in the listener; the story, after all, concerns a poor family that knows no other way of life or survival. The opera is in a sense a tribute to those families who have suffered so many unbearable losses, a situation that was quite commonplace at the time the story takes place.

Benjamin Britten (1913–1976) has always been an acquired taste that some opera-goers have no real desire to acquire, despite the fact that all of his operas have a certain theatrical flair and contain much interesting music. Britten was perhaps the first composer to take the "music theater/background music" concept of Debussy's *Pelléas et Mélisande* and build virtually his entire career around it. Britten's operas are essentially plays set to music (although not strict literaturoper) just as *Pelléas* was a play set to music. Britten's operas don't really sound anything like *Pelléas*, however — not just because of the essential difference in style between the composers, not to mention the stark differences in nationality — but because in musical and dramatic terms, respectively, Britten's works also have hefty elements of musical theater (one might almost call it Broadway) as well as of the legitimate stage. The music flows, all of a piece, in Debussy; that is not always true of Britten. Another essential difference is that Britten has often been accused of writing film scores instead of operas. Whatever one thinks of Britten, he is considered one of the most important and influential of British composers of opera.

Although the word "tuneful" is not one that normally comes to mind when thinking of Benjamin Britten, the word applies to his first stagework (if very few of his subsequent ones), *Paul Bunyan*. *Paul Bunyan* was originally conceived as an operetta that could be performed by high schoolers, but was expanded into more of a Broadway-opera hybrid along the lines of *Porgy and Bess* and *The Most Happy Fella* (although it bears little in common to those two much superior stage works). *Paul Bunyan* received its first staging at Columbia University in New York in 1941, and was rediscovered over thirty years later when Britten made some revisions to the score. It was successfully revived by New York City Opera in the 1980's, and has been performed elsewhere, but it has never entered the repertory of any major opera house. The problem isn't the music; the problem is the pretentious libretto by W. H. Auden which clumsily uses the folk tale of giant lumberjack Paul Bunyan as a framework for a tiresome political allegory. The score is a mix of folk songs, musical comedy numbers, ballads, snappy blues songs ("You don't know all, sir, you don't know all"), Gilbert and Sullivan pastiche ("My friends, on your leave, this Christmas Eve"), and the occasional operatic piece, all shot through with a lyricism that recalls Bernstein (whose first work *On the Town* did not premiere until three years later). Among the operatic highlights are "I guess that a guy's gotta eat," a fine aria in which a man describes his dreams and why they have not been accomplished; the love duet "trysting stone"; and the chorus "Great Day of Discovery." The plaintive, if minor, aria "Mother, poor, mother" has a nice ascending flute background, and there are two effective male choral numbers, "I hate to be a shanty boy," and the darker "It's too late." For the seventies revival Britten composed one of his most beautiful and memorable pieces, the lovely chorus that opens the opera "Once in a while a dream comes true."

Britten's *Peter Grimes* premiered in London in 1945 and its influence can not be underestimated. Many of the "music theater" pieces that have proliferated in the years since — a whole different type of opera from that practiced by Verdi and Puccini — can be traced directly back to *Peter Grimes*. (Although it must be said that Verdi planned to move away from number operas as early as *Aida* and finally did so with *Falstaff*.) When the young boy apprentice of fisherman Peter Grimes dies at sea, an inquest rules his death was accidental but suspicion still falls on the taciturn Grimes. Peter dreams of a quiet life with sympathetic Ellen, the one person who is kind to him. After the more or less accidental death of a second boy apprentice, there is little likelihood that the villagers will let Grimes "get away" with it a second time and it is suggested that Grimes set sail and sink his boat, which he does.

Peter Grimes is arguably Britten's greatest opera and, next to *Billy Budd*, contains his most memorable music. The overture to act one contains the fascinating woodwind sea theme which goes up and down the scale like a wave or a bird in flight, and dominates the chorus, "Oh hang at open doors," and the entire first half of scene one. The chorus "Look out for squalls" as the townspeople prepare for the upcoming storm is redolent of the bleak, weary hardships of life. The only problem with the excellent orchestral opening to scene two which depicts the storm is that it perhaps goes on too long. Another fine piece is the hymn in act two ("Now that the daylight"), sung behind Ellen's recitative ("I'll do the work. You talk.") as she sings to the silent second apprentice John. The sad music creates some sympathy for the boy, but as this is the only occasion when this happens (for either of the dead boys), it might well be inadvertent. Ellen's act three aria "Embroidery in childhood" — she sees her embroidery on a discarded jersey she gave the second boy apprentice and tries to avoid its significance — is one of Britten's best, better than the otherwise creditable act one aria when Ellen ("Let her among you without fault") responds to those who criticize her for associating with and helping Grimes. Grimes is given two major arias in "Now the great Bear" in which he ponders his future in the skies, and "In Dreams" in which he sings of the life he hopes to have with Ellen. Neither aria is of any great melodic distinction, but both are dramatically viable, as is Grimes' more melodic arioso "What harbor shelters peace?" The polka that plays in the background provides a striking contrast to the somber, evocative prelude to act three. Although it may not have a host of strikingly memorable arias, the score for *Peter Grimes* is continuously interesting and boasts several attractive interludes and ensemble pieces. Yes, there are times when it resembles a film score or smacks of musical (as opposed to music) theater. While generally it's a stretch for Britten to be truly lyrical in the classic definition of the term, he hits the mark in this opera possibly more often than in any other (aside from the hybrid *Paul Bunyan*).

The biggest problem with *Peter Grimes* is that while Grimes is pathetic and possibly crazy he isn't that sympathetic a figure, although Britten and librettist Montagu Slater try — and fail — to turn him into one. The deaths of the young boys are much more tragic, and while their deaths hover over the story (and at times) the score, they are not centerstage; in fact it could be argued that in the prologue, for instance, nothing in the words or music really comment on what a tragedy the death of the young apprentice has been. In fact, no one really seems to care about the boys (except maybe Ellen, more out of concern for Grimes perhaps), which helps make the muddled point that Grimes must be punished more for being "different," for being "apart" from the others in the village, than for being a possible murderer. Slater's libretto does little to make either Grimes or the other characters anything more than one-dimensional. *Peter Grimes* is an excellent example of fine, if flawed, "music theater."

There are many who see *Peter Grimes* as one of the greatest twentieth century operas, or at least a personal favorite — of the "modern" type. "My choice for the greatest opera of the twentieth century would be *Peter Grimes*," says Carlisle Floyd, composer of *Susannah*. "Its appeal, I feel is wider, musically and dramatically, than either *Wozzeck* or *Jenůfa* (which would be my second and third choices) with no sacrifice of musical or artistic merit. Compositionally speaking I find it astonishing, both in its musical invention and technical mastery, and the score always illuminates and transforms a superb libretto, never calling attention to itself even in the interludes."[3] Soprano Phyllis Curtin says "in my experience Benjamin Britten's *Peter Grimes* is a masterpiece of the century. Powerful story; brilliant musical realization of place and individual characters; wide musical vocabulary."[4] But "Peter Grimes" did not win everyone over at the time of its premiere, and even today it leaves many opera-goers cold, if for no other reason than its repellent main character. The lack of truly superb arias that stay in the mind is another deficit.

Britten's *The Rape of Lucretia* premiered at Glyndebourne in 1946. Roman general Junius is upset and jealous that his wife was unfaithful when the wife of friend and rival Collatinus (also a Roman general), Lucretia, remained chaste when the men were away from Rome. Hoping to prove that Lucretia is not as virtuous as he claims, Etruscan Prince Tarquinius rides to her home and asks for a room for the night. When he attempts to seduce her, she initially responds, thinking he is her husband. When she realizes the truth and rebuffs him, Tarquinius rapes her. The next morning Lucretia feels utter shame, like a fallen women — as if the rape were her fault. Devastated and guilt-wracked over what happened, Lucretia kills herself even though her husband "forgives" her. A chorus ties it in with Jesus Christ dying for our sins, and giving us hope that misery — such as this tale demonstrates — is not all there is to our lives. The staging at one point has the chorus telling what is happening as the singers mime the actions. Or else the chorus provides narration and the singers sing the dialogue. These devices are more effective than they might have seemed on paper. The libretto by Ronald Duncan is genuinely poetic and well-written if not that dramatic and at times airy and a bit pretentious. Britten's score is comparatively second-rate but often effective as background music.

Due to Britten's limitations as a composer, *The Rape of Lucretia* is never moving. Still, there are effective moments in the score. At the end of act one the female chorus slowly sings of sleep overtaking Lucretia and the other women in her household as the male chorus breathlessly sings of Tarquinius rushing through Rome on his way to Lucretia's home. This and other numbers are very well orchestrated. Tarquinius sings his aria "Within this frail crucible of light" as he looks down to admire Lucretia's sleeping nakedness, thinking the light is to be envied because it always sees her and when extinguished "lies with her as night"; this becomes a duet with the female chorus warning Lucretia not to awaken. The rape scene begins with a brief duet between Lucretia and Tarquinius as she tries to convince him she loves and wants only her husband, and develops into a dramatic ensemble ("Go Tarquinius!") that is highly effective. Britten seems to be attempting old-style Italian opera at times, and the music sometimes displays a certain sensitivity not normally associated with the composer. The music in the scene when Lucretia tells her husband what has happened to her is particularly dramatic and lyrical. The arias of the "male chorus" (actually one tenor) have no real melody but their interesting backgrounds make them seem portentous and eerie. Despite the grim story (which illustrates the "shame" and despair felt by rape victims, although that was probably just an inevitable by-product), the opera has its amusing moments, such as when Tarquinius irritates Junius by calling him a "cuckold." This results in a verbal battle of half-wits, as the two call each other such names as "pagan, dyspeptic pig" and "lewd licentious lout." *The Rape of Lucretia* may not be a great opera but it is excellent music theater.

Albert Herring premiered at Glyndebourne in 1947. This charming comic opera details what happens when a committee in a small British village has trouble coming up with a young lady virtuous enough to be Queen of the May, so wind up choosing a young man, the unworldly Albert Herring, to be May King. After some amusing complications including Albert's getting a bit drunk, disappearing, and sowing his wild oats with ladies in pubs, it all ends happily. It is hard to dislike *Albert Herring* in spite of the fact that it has little music of true distinction. In fact, some of the sparsely-orchestrated sections in the first scene remind one of a mediocre off–Broadway musical. The exceptions are the Vicar's aria (not denoted as such) "Virtue says Holy Writ,' which becomes a memorable if too brief ensemble piece, and the finale ("May King! May King!") another ensemble that leads into the pleasant ode ("Rejoice my friends") that ends the scene. The musical interlude before scene two with its subtle percussion and whistling woodwinds is initially interesting, but in scene two the "songs," "duet" and "trio" denoted as such are inferior to Albert's arioso "It seems as clear as clear" (in which he ponders whether or not he should get out from under his mother's thumb and look for a more exciting and masculine life), and the music for the entertaining climax when the formidable Lady Billows comes to give Albert the news of his selection as May King. His mother (Mum) is delighted, Albert's annoyed, they fight, and the children outside sing a song mocking the both of them. Act two has nothing but a couple of minor, sometimes derivative pieces to speak of, and the only notable music in act three is the quartet "All that I did," sung by Mum, Nancy, Vicar and Miss Wordswoth, as Mum thinks Albert is dead and the others try to console her. The polyphonic "Threnody" ensemble piece — a dirge for Albert — is not especially memorable. An interesting note is that in act two the teacher sings "Doe ray me" while instructing her students years before Richard Rodgers used the same device in *The Sound of Music*, although Rodgers' music is better. When Albert takes a sip of some lemonade which has been spiked with rum, Britten quotes from the Wagner's *Tristan und Isolde* love potion music.

"Music theater" may have dominated England during the hey days of Britten, but in the United States it was musical theater that was all the rage, as more and more real and nominal operas began to premiere on the stages of Broadway.

11. The Musical Theater of Opera: United States, 1900–1950

Just as many of its citizens had come from England, so too did much of the culture in the United States, which included the ballad operas so popular in the United Kingdom. But puritanical attitudes led to the condemnation of many of these entertainments, and their players, as immoral. In the late eighteenth century the term "opera house" came into vogue in America chiefly to separate it from the more common "theater," where all sorts of hideous vulgarities went on. Eventually European opera made its way to America, especially of the French variety, which was performed in New Orleans to such an extent that the city became known as the "American Paris." Now forgotten American musicians — James Hewitt, Micah Hawkins — composed their own operas such as *Edwin and Angelina* and *The Saw Mill*. As Americans expanded westward and cities began to grow, there came a time when every fairly large city had its own opera house; this was especially true after the Civil War. One of the best-known and most prestigious was the Central City Opera House in Colorado, which attracted many famous European artists. The Metropolitan Opera House opened in 1883 in New York, and presented chiefly operas by the European masters. In 1910 the Met premiered its first American opera, *The Pipe of Desire* by Frederick Shepherd Converse. This piece was followed by such works as Walter Damrosch's *Cyrano de Bergerac* (1913), Reginald de Koven's *Canterbury Pilgrims* (1917), and Horatio Parker's *Mona* (1912). None of them permanently established themselves in the repertory.

Even John Philip Sousa (1854–1932) got into the act. Born in Washington, D.C., Sousa was known as America's "March King" but also wrote several mostly forgotten stage works in the late nineteenth and early twentieth centuries. His operetta *The Glass Blowers* (a.k.a. *The American Maid*) premiered in 1909 and disappeared four years later; it was an odd choice for revival in 2000 at Glimmerglass, and the following year at New York City Opera. Most critics felt that it might have been better if this work had remained undiscovered. The main problem was the story, which, even updated with topical references, was creaky and deadly dull. The plot deals with a love affair between a working class boy and a rich girl and how they and the other characters get embroiled not only in a fight between labor and management at a glass blowing factory but in the Spanish-American War! Much of the music in *The Glass Blowers* is quite pleasant, if never outstanding, but the wait between numbers — those excruciatingly deadly and unamusing dialogue sequences — diminishes their impact. It is unlikely that more of Sousa's operettas may see the light of day any time soon. Sousa was not without talent, but he hadn't quite the soaring lyrical skill of Victor Herbert.

Although Victor Herbert (1859–1924) was born in Dublin and was employed as a cellist in Stuttgart in his youth, he moved to New York as a fairly young man when he was hired by the Metropolitan Opera Orchestra; therefore he has always been considered an American composer. Some of the music in his highly successful operettas, such as *Babes in Toyland* (1903) and *Naughty Marietta* (1910), from which comes "Ah, Sweet Mystery of Life," was considered to be on the cusp of opera. When it was announced by Oscar Hammerstein (who had started the Manhattan Opera Company to rival the Metropolitan) that he would be presenting an American Opera composed by Victor Herbert, even non-opera fans were galvanized. The world of opera — and the Metropolitan — was dominated by Europeans and this was seen as a way that America could be on the musical forefront for a change. There was a massive amount of publicity for Herbert's opera, *Natoma* (1911), which was expected to usher in a new age of American Opera that would be second to none. Herbert briefly considered setting David Belasco's play *The Girl of the Golden West* to music, unaware that Puccini would eventually do the same. Herbert's librettist, the native Californian Joseph Deighn Redding, would also compose an opera, *Fay Yen Fah* that premiered in Monte Carlo in 1925. He knew how to provide a text that could be easily set to music and take advantage of Herbert's lyrical gifts. When the libretto for *Natoma* was later excoriated by most critics, this aspect of Redding's art was all but overlooked.

Herbert finished *Natoma* but the Manhattan Opera Company had gone out of business, and the Metropolitan rejected the opera. The Met had just presented *The Pipe of Desire* and didn't want to risk another native product, which did not set well with Metropolitan regulars, so soon. Instead, the Philadelphia-Chicago Opera Company, which had its own Metropolitan Opera House in Philly, would premiere the piece. Mary Garden deigned to play the title role but infuriated many when she announced to the press: "The American man hasn't it in him to produce great music,"[1] explaining that she was doing Herbert's little opera because she did not want to be accused of standing in the way of the great "cause" of American opera. She praised certain aspects of *Natoma* but in the most condescending of tones. On the other hand, after the premiere Herbert received respectful and congratulatory telegrams from both Giacomo Puccini and Pietro Mascagni, who worshipped the all-powerful melody as much as Herbert did.

Natoma takes place in 1820 on the island of Santa Cruz under the rule of the Spanish. Natoma is an Indian maiden (with some Aztec blood) who has actually inherited the mantle of leadership of her mostly decimated people. She falls for a Naval Lieutenant, Paul Merrill, who initially is attracted to Natoma but then loses his heart to Barbara, the daughter of the Spaniard Don Francisco. Alvarado, a cousin of Barbara's, is also in love with her but she does not return his feelings, so he conspires to kidnap her. When Natoma, who has been like a sister to Barbara, learns of the plot, she kills Alvarado to prevent it, knowing she is fated to lose Paul in any case. Father Peralta takes her to the Church, where she vows to lead her people in retribution against those who have destroyed them, but the Father reminds her of her love for both Paul and Barbara, and persuades her to embrace the Christian faith.

Herbert's music occasionally employs native American melodies but generally takes them in different paths and harmonies. He provides haunting and evocative themes for Natoma: an Indian Theme of Fate, and a Love Theme that expresses her hope and longing for Paul. Act one boasts Alvarado's lilting declaration of love for Barbara ("Fair One, listen to my vow of love"), as well as a lovely duet for Paul and Barbara, "His voice awakes my very soul." Natoma has an outstanding piece in act two ("Within the hour the morning sun will flood the hills"), as does Paul with the stirring aria he sings to the assemblage "Columbia, bright goddess of the free" (which Herbert's biographer Edward Waters thought "bloated and pompous"!) There is also a snappy Habanera when Alvarado dances with Chiquita in act two, as well as a Dagger Dance that builds dramatically up to Alvarado's murder. While this music, one of the pieces based on a native American theme, may sound stereotypically tom-tom-ish, it is still snappy, engaging, and likable, and serves its purpose of distracting the audience so that the killing will have more wallop.

Herbert's music was praised by most, dismissed by a few, and not seen as true Grand Opera by a certain minority of nay sayers; most critics felt Redding's book was the main factor that prevented *Natoma* from being a masterpiece. In actuality, *Natoma*'s libretto is no worse than many in the world of opera (it's miles ahead of, say, the libretto for *La vida breve*) and it not only provides a strong framework for Herbert's tunes and dramatic recitatives, but in a strange understated way is rather moving. As Redding himself put it, "To me *Natoma* is somewhat allegorical in that she epitomizes the pathos and heartache of the disappearing race as against the influx of the Aryan tribes. Again, the work shows that two characters are virtually obliterated: the devil-may-care and romantic Spaniard and the Indian."[2] This theme comes across quite vividly in *Natoma*, but few if any critics got the point. It seems unlikely that, as has been suggested, critics in 1911 could have really been bothered by the fact that Paul throws over the dark Natoma for the fair Barbara, or that Natoma has contempt for a half-breed named José; old-time opera librettos — and critics — were rarely politically correct.

Herbert was not through with grand opera, and did one more short work, *Madelaine*, which was accepted by the Metropolitan Opera in New York and premiered in 1913. Only fifty minutes long, it was paired with *I pagliacci*, and suffered in comparison. Herbert surprised everyone by going modern and presenting a slight story of a French woman and her suitors in a style influenced by Strauss and certain Wolf-Ferrari operas. There were no set arias (until the soprano protested) and only occasional snatches of melody, an extremely early piece of "music theater" (as opposed to musical theater) years before Benjamin Britten. The score was by no means a bad one, however; it was just not expected from a master of melody such as Herbert and *Madelaine* was not a success with the public. Interestingly, most of Herbert's subsequent operettas would feature operatic material, such as the arias "Thine Alone" from *Eileen* (1917) and "When You're Away" from *The Only Girl* (1914), and such love duets as "You're the Only Girl for Me" (*The Only Girl*), "All for You" (*Princess Pat*, 1915) and "Life and Love" (*The Velvet Lady*, 1919).

Scott Joplin (1868–1917) and his six brothers and sisters were raised by his mother after his father ran out on the family. His mother took in laundry from one family in return for their providing music lessons for her son; Scott proved an adept pupil. Joplin's *Treemonisha* premiered in 1915 in Harlem and virtually disappeared for sixty years until it was revived by Houston Grand Opera in 1975. Joplin, known as the King of Ragtime, had trouble being taken seriously as an operatic composer not only because of his association with ragtime but because he was Black.[3] Throughout his life he struggled to have *Treemonisha* mounted, but finally had to resort to paying for a single performance with a solo piano background in a small theater two years before his death.

The story of *Treemonisha* takes place on a plantation in Arkansas, where a black couple, Ned and Monisha, adopt a baby girl they find under a tree and name her Treemonisha. The girl is educated by the couple's white employers, and this brings her into conflict with other blacks who pray upon the superstitious in the community. Treemonisha is kidnapped by these conjurers but manages to escape. Although Joplin, who also wrote the libretto, suggests that Monisha is more susceptible to the wiles of the conjurers because she's female, at the end of the opera the people of the community choose her daughter as their leader. When Treemonisha wonders if the men will accept her as easily as the women, the men assure her that they will and seem to mean it. This aspect is certainly ahead of its time, as is the basic theme of the opera that education will point the path to true liberty for black people. Treemonisha is a budding bleeding heart, however. Even though the kidnappers planned to throw her into a wasp's next, presumably killing her, she urges her angry neighbors and her father, who wants to send them to the next universe, to let them go free — with not even a slap on the wrist but a mere lecture.

Despite its good intentions, some fine music, and the politically-motivated posthumous Pulitzer awarded to Joplin, *Treemonisha* is not a lost operatic masterpiece, but it is a highly pleasant operetta with a well-meaning if stilted libretto. Joplin's influences include everyone from Lehar to Victor Herbert to Sullivan, and at times *Treemonisha* resembles a revue. The overture has a Broadway/ragtime feel to it with a mild classical overlay. Such pieces as "She is the only educated person of our race," and "The Sacred Tree," in which Monisha tells her daughter of her origins, very much remind one of Lehar. The latter piece, although pleasant enough, is very long and quickly wears out its welcome. "We're Goin' Around" is an irresistible, foot-stompin' chorus, but it smacks more of musicals than opera. "We will rest awhile" is a mere barbershop quartet and makes little impression. The duet between Monisha and Ned ("I want to see my child") reminds one of Herbert as well as of Lehar. "We will trust you as our leader" is another pleasant number but it, too, seems to go on forever. There is a triplet of outstanding pieces in *Treemonisha*, however. "A Real Slow Drag," which ends the opera, is a sturdy, attractive tune, an anthem disguised as a dance number. Ned's Sullivan-like "When Villains Ramble Far and Near" boasts a solid melody that makes it the second strongest piece in the opera. The best piece, and the only one which really stays in your mind, is "Good advice," sung by Parson Alltalk and the chorus, which transcends its spiritual origins and becomes the centerpiece of the opera, a truly beautiful number that resonates with power. The irony is that by naming his minister "Alltalk" Joplin seems to be indicating that religion is just another form of the dreaded superstition that Treemonisha feels will hold her people back, although the parson's advice is nevertheless worthwhile, and Treemonisha refers to the "Great Creator" at one point.

Jerome Kern (1885–1945) had composed a number of operettas and musicals before he contributed his masterpiece *Show Boat* in 1927. Although this highly influential musical introduced a solid storyline along with its numbers (Broadway shows previously had been in more of a plotless revue format) decades before *Oklahoma!* was lauded for doing the same, and has memorable music, it's hard to classify it as even a nominal opera. Some of the numbers, such as the lilting "Make Believe" and "Why Do I Love You?," lie somewhere between show music and operetta, but most are either torch songs or blues ("My Bill"; "Can't Help Lovin' Dat Man") or snappy dance numbers ("Life Upon the Wicked Stage"). "Till Good Luck Comes My Way" can sound like an aria if it's sung by a tenor, but there are really only two genuinely operatic pieces in the show: the magnificent "Old Man River:" an anthem for the downtrodden in general and black people in particular; and the soaring love duet "You are Love."

That same year brought the premiere of an opera that had been commissioned by the Metropolitan, *The King's Henchmen*, by Deems Taylor (1885–1966), who had been a protégé, of sorts of Victor Herbert, but switched in midstream from musicals and operettas to serious opera. The librettist was no less than Edna St. Vincent Millay, and her story has to do with a King who asks a trusted aid to ask for a maiden's hand in marriage on his behalf. But the henchman and said maiden fall in love, although theirs is not a marriage made in heaven. The King is furious when he finds out what has happened, and the henchman commits suicide not only in shame but in realizing that his wife has never really loved him. This and Deems' later opera *Peter Ibbetson* (1931), another Met commission, reveal a composer of assured lyrical and theatrical strengths. Olin Downes in the New York Times commented of *The King's Henchmen* that "Mr. Taylor's score proves his melodic gift, his spirit and sense of drama. In his first essay in the form of grand opera, he has succeeded in an astonishing degree in giving this text musical form and organic musical rhythms. He has composed with complete frankness and without aping any style."[4] The closing duet of the second act was singled out as an especially outstanding moment, but the King's aria "O Ceasar," in which he recounts the history of various Ceasars, and the beautiful funeral dirge "Nay, Maccus" are also memorable, among others.

Harvard graduate Virgil Thomson (1896–1989) probably had more success as a critic than as a composer. Thomson's *Four Saints in Three Acts* premiered in 1933. The opera is essentially a goof (an act four is less than four minutes long); the dreadful, incoherent libretto by Gertrude Stein seems to be making fun of opera on the whole and does Thomson's music absolutely no good. (Surely some of the singers who have recorded and performed this piece must have wished they had really great lyrics to sing!) An example of Stein's pseudo-clever lyrics: "as loud as that as allowed as that." Another example: "How many saints can be and land be and sand be and on a high plateau there is no sand there is snow and there is made to be so and very much can be what there is to see when there is a wind to have it dry and be what they can understand to undertake to let it be to send it well as much as none to be to be behind." A bigger problem is that Thomson's music is often quite nice but sometimes "folksy" and derivative and hardly special. It does not contain a lot of melodic inspiration and doesn't require great voices. Still, it has its moments: There are some nice orchestral passages at the end of the love scene in act two and at the beginning of act three that aren't ruined by words. St. Chavez' arioso "St. Ignatius might be admired"; "the Chorus of the Saints' Procession"; and the Vision of the Holy Ghost's "Pigeons on the grass, alas" (Stein gets points for those lyrics) and the aria "Not April fool's day a pleasure" (between tableau one and two) stand out in this score, but overall *Four Saints in Three Acts* tries the patience.

The same is true of Thomson's follow-up, *The Mother of Us All*, which premiered in 1947 and also had a libretto by Gertrude Stein. In some ways it is as atrocious as any half-baked "modern" piece. Susan B. Antony (1820–1906) finds that however persuasive she may be considered, men will not give women the vote, but finally she achieves her goal. There may be a fine opera in the life of Susan B. Anthony, but *The Mother of Us All* isn't it. Anthony is never developed as a person, let alone a woman; there are no actual characterizations or even attempts at such, in Stein's libretto, which has, like *Four Saints*, little narrative structure. It mixes characters living and dead from different eras, with "Virgil T." and "Gertrude S." commenting on the action. Stein's mostly nonsensical and off-putting lyrics undercut any message that may have been intended. Thomson's music is nominally "melodious" but never rises above a fifth-rate level; there is not a single outstanding nor even memorable piece in the opera. The score smacks more of a musical than of genuine opera anyway, which wouldn't matter if Thomson's music weren't so trivial. In general, Stein's lyrics make the music seem even worse than it is so that the whole effect — forgettable music, stilted lyrics — is simply irritating. That said, it should also be said that Susan B.'s aria "what is man?" intelligently dissects male fears and what they lead to, but the music is unmemorable and the lyrics a bit simplistic and dated: "[Men] fear women, they fear each other, they fear their neighbor, they fear other countries, and then they hearten themselves in their fear by crowding together and following each other [like] brutes, like animals who stampede." Since when are women immune to fear and the mob mentality? Thomson and Stein did not create operas; they created bad, immature parodies of operas. Composer Ned Rorem thought that Thomson was an influence on Aaron Copland, who said of *Four Saints* that it "made all other American musical stage pieces seem dull by comparison." However, when Copland heard *The Mother of Us All* he thought "It's as if a new musical idea hadn't occurred to him in ten years."[5]

A much more memorable 1933 opera than *Four Saints* was Louis Gruenberg's (1884–1964) *Emperor Jones*, from Eugene O'Neill, which premiered at the Metropolitan but did not enter the repertory. A black man, Brutus Jones, escapes from prison and winds up leader of the people on a Caribbean island, until he is hunted down and killed in the finale. Contemporary critics saw the opera as either a film score or a play with incidental music, but despite the lack of arias *Emperor Jones* is not without moments of lyricism. There is great dramatic vitality in the finale, a combination of singing and shouting by the title character with drums in the background that pound constantly and build the tension and his terror to the near breaking point. It is interesting to note that despite Gruenberg's acknowledged interest and belief in jazz and Negro folk music and spirituals as genuinely American music, Gruenberg generally eschewed the use of such music in his operas.

In 1935 Howard Hanson's *Merry Mount* became the fifteenth American opera put on at the Met during the tenure of general manager Giulio Gatti-Casazza. Hanson was said to be a "militant chauvinist" when it came to nationalism in music, and, echoing Gruenberg, felt that American composers had a wealth of material in Negro and Native American music, among others, that they should draw upon. That's why it's ironic that *Merry Mount* approaches European Grand Opera like few other American operas. (Hanson also cited Ottorini Respighi as one of his chief influences, but he was probably referring to the latter's orchestral works.) *Merry Mount* is a bitter and powerful examination of religious intolerance and its link with repressed sexuality. The main character — and villain — Bradford is the leader of a group of Puritans. He is tormented by sexual desire and to that end agrees to marry a woman he doesn't love. But a group of free-thinking cavaliers come to the area, and Bradford is instantly entranced by a beautiful woman named Marigold. Angered by his righteous attitude and mistreatment of a jester who amuses the children, Marigold suggests he might marry her — but to another man, her lover Gower. Humiliated, Bradford decides to declare war on the cavaliers. The latter are having a maypole ceremony which the puritans interrupt with violence just as Marigold and Gower are to be wed. Gower is killed and Marigold vows vengeance, as does an Indian chief who has been insulted and attacked by the Puritans. Bradford has a dream in which the devil, in the form of the dead Gower, tempts him with women and Marigold appears dressed in the guise of demonic and sensual

Astoreth. Bradford agrees to serve Lucifer and help destroy the Puritans for love of Astoreth and when he wakes up discovers that his community has been set afire by natives. Bradford blames first himself and then Marigold for what has happened, and the Puritans want to stone them both. Now thoroughly insane, Bradford renounces the Lord, takes Marigold up into his arms, and dashes with her into the flames.

The opera begins with a majestic, vaguely Wagnerian prelude whose solemnity and power creates the perfect ambiance for the story to come. In the chilling chorus, "Be as a lion, dread Jehovah," the puritans sing of how those who do not follow the path of the Lord and who disagree with their ways will be torn to shreds. Some might argue that the music for this piece is too beautiful when you consider the ugliness of the verses, but the music has a commanding, tenacious, stirring, rather sinister quality that is especially underlined when it is powerfully reprised at the end of act one. Another composer of the "modern" bent would have composed ugly music to go with the ugly sentiments, but Hanson was able to get across the impact of the verses while giving the audience something attractive to listen to. In the subsequent Puritan chorus "Praise we the Lord," the frenetic orchestration and booming background gets across a vivid sense of religious mania that borders on the pathological. The Maypole Chorus sung by the freer-spirited Cavaliers at the beginning of act two has a surprising strength and urgency to it, as does the Maypole dance which follows, which is almost licentious and demonic — reflecting the attitude of the Puritans towards these folk who dare to dance, drink, and make merriment — under its basic sprightliness. Bradford is given two important arias: In "Last night came one," in which he sings of how he fought off the demons of temptation in the night, the music gets across how genuinely tormented he is by these feelings he can't control. In act two's "Almighty Father," which employs the main theme heard in the prelude, he prays for release from his lust for Marigold. As for Marigold, her "Let them strike twice" after Gower's murder reveals her willingness and desire to die in her misery. She expands upon this misery in act three's "No witch am I," which in its way is a virulent denunciation of the puritans and all they stand for.

The opera boasts two notable duets: "Marigold! When the morning stars together" is sung by Gower and Marigold just before the aborted wedding; the bravura "Rise up, my love, my fair one" is sung by Bradford and Astoreth-Marigold in the act two dream sequence. This is the most impressive and beautiful piece in *Merry Mount*, with the romantic but doleful music reflecting the line "for love is strong as death and as cruel as the grave." The only really "light" piece in *Merry Mount* is the charming children's song ("Barley break! Barley break!") as the children play at being angels and devils in act one. *Merry Mount* may be a genuine American masterpiece, but not everything in the score works as well as the sections described above. The ballet music in the very long nightmare sequence in act two, although some of it is based upon themes heard elsewhere in the opera, is not particularly memorable (aside from the sexy dance of the wantons as they try to seduce Bradford), and the music as the puritans come to violently disrupt the maypole celebration is perhaps a little too tame, and there are other spots where the score doesn't quite come up to the emotional level of the stage action (although it must be kept in mind that *Merry Mount* is not exactly verismo). Richard L. Stokes libretto, based on Hawthorne's "The Maypole of Merry Mount," is rich with poetic ideas but not always as sure-footed in the theatrical sense as it could have been.

As with *Tosca*'s Scarpia, Bradford's frustrated lust leads to his making evil decisions. Unlike Scarpia, Bradford does not enjoy or revel in his sexual desires. The mystical/supernatural overtones of the third act — the devil brands Bradford's forehead with a red mark in his dream; Bradford reveals this same red mark, actually on his forehead, to his flock in the next scene when he's awake — are probably not meant to be taken too literally, but signify that with his intolerant and hateful attitudes Bradford had long since been overtaken by "Satan." Puritans would say that "Merry Mount" shows that sexual desire is the root of all evil; what it actually shows is that it's how a man or woman handles that desire that makes all the difference. In these days of fundamentalists and terrorists who refuse to countenance any thought or action that doesn't coincide with their own narrow ideology, *Merry Mount* is, if anything, even more relevant. The Seattle Symphony presented a concert version of the opera in 1996 on the hundredth anniversary of Hanson's birth with Lauren Flanigan as Marigold. A full-mounted revival at a major opera house is in order.

Although *Merry Mount* may have largely disappeared from the world's stages, another opera that premiered in 1935 has rarely been out of view since its inception, George Gershwin's (1898–1937) *Porgy and Bess*. The story takes place in the poor black community of Catfish Row in South Carolina around the 1920's. When Bess is abandoned by her lover Crown after he kills a man, the crippled Porgy takes up where Crown left off. Crown tries to take up with Bess again, but she tells him that she and Porgy have fallen in love; Crown takes her by force. Bess gets away from Crown but when he tries to take her away from Porgy, the latter kills him in a fight. Porgy is arrested, and while he is in jail a dope dealer named Sportin' Life convinces Bess that she will be left alone and unprotected again. Under the influence of drugs, she goes off to New York with him. Released from jail, Porgy finds out what has happened and determines to walk all the way to New York if need be to get back his beloved Bess.

Over the years there have been complaints about *Porgy and Bess* and its treatment of black characters. Understandably many blacks were tired of being portrayed as illiterate, poor, drug-addicted, criminal, sensual, and all the other stereotypes — to be honest, Bess is pretty much depicted as a low life and a tramp, at least in the beginning — but the characters of *Porgy and Bess* are also warm, compassionate, wise in the ways of the heart, and richly human in all their flaws and good points. *Porgy and Bess* is just one look at one fictional community during a certain time period; it can not and should not be taken as a statement on blacks in general. Another tiresome aspect of the story is that all of the "bad" characters, such as Crown and Sportin' Life, have no religion while the good characters do.

Another controversy about the work is whether or not it is actually an opera. Gershwin was seen as a Broadway composer, a tin pan alley tunesmith, not a serious composer. Much of the music was in a popular, even jazzy vein. Much of it was seen as "Negro" music — some of the score was inspired by spirituals — an attitude which brought along with it an inevitably racist condescension that was standard for the period. *Porgy and Bess* not only opened on Broadway but a revival cut all of the recitatives and turned it into more of a traditional musical, further muddying the waters. And opening an opera with someone playing the blues on the piano and a chorus doing "doo wahs" is probably not the best way to start if you want to impress the long-hairs. But *Porgy and Bess* is an opera — an American folk opera. It can not and perhaps should not be compared to the Grand Operas of the European masters, but on its own terms it is a legitimate operatic masterpiece. Many people, such as composer William (*A View from a Bridge*) Bolcom, think it is the greatest opera of the twentieth century.

Act one boasts such numbers as Bess' "Summertime" with its lazy sensuality; the snappy "A woman is a sometime thing"; the funereal "Gone, gone, gone," derived from spirituals but transformed by Gershwin into an attractive near-classical piece (the entire funeral sequence is invested with a kind of grandeur); and Serena's "My Man's Gone Now" as she sings of the man she loved that Crown murdered. This last is a particularly powerful tune although it could be argued that it may be too up tempo to completely get across the true pathos of the lyrics and Serena's situation, although the right singer can certainly put it across, turning it into a powerful widow's anthem, an outcry of despondency. Gershwin skillfully keeps the recitatives interesting and generally well-orchestrated between song numbers, although some music, including the music underscoring the fight scene and Crown's murder of Robbins, is a bit schlocky and forgettable. Some sequences, such as the crap game, simply go on too long. Although Porgy and Bess certainly have a presence and are important in the scheme of things, they don't actually have much to sing or do in act one. Porgy's emphatic theme, which seems to encapsulate the whole pathetic dynamics of the story, is first heard when Porgy comes through the gate.

In act two "It takes a long pull to get there" has a kind of quiet dignity to go with its nice melody. "I hates yo' struttin' style," in which Maria tells off Sportin' Life ("I'd sooner cuts mah own throat then call you frien' of mine"), is an excellent example of speech-song. The chorus "Oh, I can't sit down" probably inspired a lot of happy, up tempo choruses in works by other composers in the years following *Porgy and Bess*. Crown's "It ain't necessarily so" is an okay "chitlins and black-eyed peas" composition. Porgy is given three excellent pieces in act two. "I got plenty o' nuttin'" is an irresistible tune with a surprising undertone of pathos beneath its upbeat tempo. It could be taken as an anthem of a lack of ambition, except it actually reflects Porgy's contentment with life now that someone, Bess, is at his side and sharing life with him. "The Buzzard Song," in which Porgy defies the omen of doom, a buzzard, and openly declares his and Bess' sincere happiness, is a genuine operatic aria, and a memorable one. From start to finish "Bess, you is my woman" is one of the all-time great operatic love duets, the absolute crown jewel of the opera, moving, beautiful, a touch erotic — Gershwin at his finest. Bess' second, jazzier duet with Porgy, "I Loves You Porgy," is quite pleasant if not as memorable as the first. It helps that it ends with a reprise of Porgy's wonderful theme. "What you want wid Bess?" turns into an anti-love duet with Crown, sounds like jazz verismo, and is extremely sexy. The recitatives during the sequence between Crown and Bess on the island are especially lyrical. Some of the background music in scenes two and three of the second act (Crown and Bess; Bess reunited with Porgy) is reminiscent of the kind of thing you'd hear in Italian opera of the period. Scene four has the least operatic music, including a forgettable revival-type chorus ("Oh, Doctor Jesus"), although Crown's "Red-headed Woman" is catchy.

Act three is not as musically rich as the first two acts and falls back on a number of reprises (used to back up the recitatives at times), but there is still some good music. The chorus "Clara, Clara," a rather haunting and lovely dirge," is a combination of Italian-type opera and Negro spirituals. The death fight between Crown and Porgy is strictly Broadway-style dance music. "Oh, Bess, oh, where's my Bess" starts out as pure Broadway, but becomes an operatic trio when Maria and Serena join in with Porgy, each representing opposing viewpoints about Bess and whether or not Porgy should pursue her. Porgy's "Oh, Lawd, I'm on my way" which he sings as he starts for New York provides a fairly rousing and appropriate finish to the opera, but the real ending of *Porgy and Bess* is a reprise of that marvelous, highly evocative Porgy's theme with its powerful use of sensitive and dissonant chords. Porgy may be a pathetic figure in many ways — Bess' going off with Sportin' Life before she even finds out what's going to happen to Porgy does not portend well for their relationship in New York, assuming Porgy can even find her — but he is also quite heroic. If his mission is doomed to failure, as it probably is, that only makes his undertaking of it all the braver — and more heartbreaking.

Brooklyn-born Aaron Copland (1900–1990) was a great champion of new and American music. He felt that audiences could not expect composers to keep writing in the romantic idiom, which had had its day. "The way of the uninhibited and personalized warmth and surge of the best of the romanticists is not our way," he said. He argued that audiences should not expect the same kind of melodies from all composers, and that the flow and structure of certain difficult melodies would become apparent after repeated hearings. He felt people had become too dependent, as it were, on music of obvious emotion. "When a contemporary piece seems dry and cerebral to you," he wrote in his book on music, "when it seems to be giving off little feeling or sentiment, there is a good chance that you are being insensitive to the characteristic musical speech of your own epoch."[6] Still, Copland admitted that some composers wrote "uninspired or willful dissonances," but "if, after repeated hearings, a work says nothing to me, I do not therefore conclude that modern composition is in a sorry condition. I simply conclude that that piece is not for me." Copland felt that serious music was not meant to be a relaxant from the stresses of the day, but to "stir and excite you." There is no denying that much of what Copland had to say, although self-serving, made sense, but he was talking about music in general. In the opera house the rules were often very different from in the concert hall.

Operas were not very high on Copland's list of compositions, but he flirted with the form on two occasions; once in the first half of the century (*The Second Hurricane*, 1937), and once in the latter half (*The Tender Land*, 1954). The latter opera, which will be discussed in the next chapter, is a masterpiece, but the two-act children's opera *The Second Hurricane* is not entirely without merit. In Edwin Denby's clumsy libretto, which includes lengthy narration and dialogue sequences, several children are flown by helicopter to an area devastated by a flood and hurricane to help with the rescue effort. When a second hurricane approaches, the kids find themselves trapped on a hill and in a frightening predicament. At first, giving in to their fear, they turn on each other. Accomplishing more by working in concert, they discover the obvious moral of the piece: people need to pull together to get things done and survive. Copland's music, full of his trademark sensitivity, has the messy, running-about quality of children, and the lyrics are similarly rushed in juvenile fashion, which unfortunately makes them hard to decipher at times. The opera is minor Copland at best, but it does have some nice pieces. Gyp's song, "I wish I had a car," in which he expresses his desire to drive off the hill to safety, gets across his wistful, lonely frightened feeling quite well. Jeff's song, in which he tries to build up his courage, has a slight melancholic air beneath the bouncy surface melody. The girl Queenie is give a fairly romantic piece in act two as she begins to feel hope and the serenity it brings. *The Second Hurricane* is not in need of revival any time soon, but it does have its virtues. Benjamin Britten loved Copland's music and, according to Copland's biographer Howard Pollack, "composed *Paul Bunyan* under the stimulus of *The Second Hurricane.*"

Another native New Yorker, this time from Queens, Paul Bowles (1910–1999) became much better known as a writer but flirted with musical composition in his early years. His one operatic work is a "zarzuela" entitled *The Wind Remains*, which bowed in 1943, and has rarely been performed since. Loosely based on "In Five Years Time" by Federico Garcia Lorca, it has no real libretto to speak of (although two writers were credited with one) but is a series of tableau and songs interspersed with long musical interludes. Although there are some surprisingly compelling things in the score, the music doesn't quite have the passion, energy and soaring melodies of a true zarzuela, and Bowles' attempts to give it authentic Spanish flavor ring false. There is an attractive, somewhat jazzy woodwind and percussion prelude, and a pleasant duet entitled "Donde vas?" The music is generally well-orchestrated as well. But if *The Wind Remains* is any clue, the world did not really lose a major operatic composer when Bowles switched professions in midstream.

Robert Wright and George Forrest were the team behind the Broadway success *Kismet*, which in the 1950's employed melodies from various compositions by Russian composer Aleksandr Borodin (1833–1887). Sometime before that major success, Wright and Forrest decided to build a stage work around the music of Norwegian composer Edvard Grieg (1843–1907), resulting in the operetta *Song of Norway* (1944). Some of Grieg's most famous pieces were re-orchestrated by Arthur Kay — who also did the vocal arrangements — with Wright and Forrest adapting the music and providing the lyrics. Grieg's reputation suffered after his death because of the advent of anti-romanticism, and never quite climbed back to the popularity it enjoyed during his lifetime. The plot of the operetta has Edvard struggling to have his music heard while interacting with two women, his cousin, Nina (whom he married in real life, as he does in the operetta), and an opera singer named

Louisa. Another major player is Grieg's real-life friend Rikard Nordraak, another Norwegian composer who urged Edvard in the direction of nationalism in his music.

Louisa sings an attractive number, "Now," in which she proclaims that she only lives in the present. The lyrics are clever, but it makes little sense that Louisa would sneer at the "stolidity" of opera, complaining that it doesn't allow her to abandon "reserve" and sing with "verve." What exactly has she been doing at the opera? Perhaps she would have been able to "abandon" herself with verismo, still several years in the future.

The operetta is full of several fine "numbers" employing themes and melodies by Grieg: "Freddy and his Fiddle," based on a popular Norwegian dance; "The Hymn of Betrothal" that Mother Grieg sings at Edvard's engagement; and, especially, the enchanting love duet between Nina and Edvard, "Strange Music." In this most famous of Grieg's melodies, Edvard sings how he hears music at the sight and sound of his beloved.

Speaking of Broadway, Rodgers and Hammerstein's *Oklahoma!* had already helped transform the musical theater when their follow-up, *Carousel* came out in 1945. Based on Ferenc Milnar's *Liliom*, it studies the marriage of carousel barker Billy Bigelow and factory worker Julie Jordan, as well as a secondary relationship between Julie's friend Carrie and her stuffy beau Enoch Snow. When Julie gets pregnant, Billy panics over their financial situation and agrees to assist in a robbery with a buddy. When the robbery goes awry, Billy kills himself rather than go to jail. Possibly Rodgers' supreme achievement, the score of *Carousel* has an intensity and seriousness that lifts it above a mere tuneful operetta. As the characters interact on the stage during the carnival, and Julie spies Billy and is smitten etc., we hear the Carousel Waltz, which begins with a haunting phrase and increasingly evokes the frenetic energy of the crowd. "When I Marry Mr. Snow," sung by Carrie, is a lilting Broadway aria. The scene with Julie and Billy after Julie's boss and the policeman leave them alone together is an extended recitative, leading into "If I Love You," one of the great songs, a veritable love duet for Julie and Billy that is part of a full-fledged operatic sequence. The banter between the men and women preparing for the clambake (leading up to the bouncy "June Is Bustin' Out All Over") is also sung recitative with separate choruses divided into tenors, basses, and baritones. Carrie and Mr. Snow's dreamy picture of their future, "When the Children are Asleep," runs right into the sailors' uplifting chorus "Blow High, Blow Low" with no dialogue in between. Billy's "Soliloquy," wherein he imagines what his son will be like ("My Boy Bill"), and then realizes his child may be a girl, is excellent from start to finish (the "My Little Girl" section is especially sublime).

In act two, "That was a real nice clambake," a recitative-chorus, has a kind of soaring, operatic intensity. "Geraniums in the Window," wherein Snow sings of his shattered dreams of what might have been with the "unfaithful" Carrie, leads into the "Stonecutters" chorus, then the almost bluesy "What's the use of wond'rin'" sung by a Julie determined to stand by her man right or wrong. This number is punctuated by Julie confronting Billy (who's pretending to go on a treasure hunt but is really intent on robbery) and feeling the knife under his clothing. "You'll never walk alone," which Julie sings after Billy's death, has a wonderful poignancy and sensitivity. "The Highest Judge of All," in which a dead Billy demands better treatment in Heaven than he got on Earth, is essentially an operatic aria. Rodgers' music makes this a masterpiece and helps smooth over the problematic aspects of the libretto. Today it's hard to reconcile Billy's hitting Julie (even "inadvertently") with what we now know about wife-beaters. Billy's lady boss at the carousel, is obviously attracted to and possibly in love with Billy, but the book doesn't treat the lonely and feisty widow much better than Billy does. Despite the fantastic "heavenly" elements at the end, which don't quite work, and the European origins of the story, this slice-of-life could almost qualify as American verismo were it not for the fact that its music is of a different type altogether. But there is no doubt that in the most important ways *Carousel* is a genuine American opera. The emotional current, which consistently engages and carries along the listener, is on from the first note to the last, and Rodger's melodic invention never flags.

The same could be said of Frederick Loewe's (1904–1988) score for *Brigadoon* which premiered in 1947, although the musical may not be quite as ethereal, in any sense, as *Carousel*; nevertheless it's another legitimate masterpiece of musical theater and another bona fide American opera. Two Americans named Tommy and Jeff discover a strange village in the mists of Scotland. Brigadoon is under a spell which makes it appear only one day in each century. Suffering from unrequited love when his sweetheart marries another, villager Harry Beaton tries to flee the town — which would apparently have disastrous consequences — and while being chased is accidentally killed. Tommy falls for a girl named Fiona and reluctantly leaves her behind as the once-in-a-hundred-years day comes to an end. Haunted by his love for her, he returns to Scotland and discovers that their feelings for one another are so strong that Brigadoon temporarily reappears, allowing him entry and access to the woman he adores.

Alan Jay Lerner's libretto is very moving if taken as the story of the desperate steps people take to avoid pain and loneliness (including the insane spell that affects the town and keeps it "safe" from dangerous modern ways) and the power of love. The townspeople — although small town folk, they love sex and liquor and are hardly dull — seem very curious as to the Americans' coins, saying "look at the date" and so on, but this is the only real bit of curiosity they have about the future world they have awoken into. (With a hundred years passing for each day in Brigadoon, one can imagine these folks actually being alive to witness the sun burn itself out.) Far from being glossed over, young Harry's death, which affects both Tommy and Jeff, resonates throughout the entire second act.[7] Lerner's well-constructed libretto — act one climaxes with Harry's announcement that he intends to leave — is as fascinating as much in what it doesn't explore (all the various ramifications of the spell, for instance) as for what it does.

Some of the numbers in *Brigadoon* smack of operetta (Fiona's "Waitin' for My Dearie") and there are irresistible Broadway tunes such as "The Heather on the Hill." Saucy Meg's "The Love of My Life (she sleeps with a variety of stinkers in search of a hubby) is very frank and amusing, as is her excellent comic number "My Mother's Wedding Day," which immediately precedes a bagpipe funeral dirge for Harry, dramatically interrupting the proceedings. Despite its up tempo rhythm, Tommy's "Almost Like Being in Love" has an operatic intensity and when Fiona joins in it becomes a proper love duet. "From This Day On" is another love duet, this time bittersweet, for these same lovers as they part. "There but for You Go I," Tommy's love song to Fiona, is also in part a dirge for dead Harry who literally is "the man who had never known a love that was all his own." However, the chorus of townsmen as they run after Harry hardly gets across their extreme desperation — if Harry escapes, not only will the spell end, but apparently the lives of everyone in Brigadoon will end as well. The audience is left wondering why Harry didn't leave Brigadoon as soon as he realized his beloved was going to marry another. Perhaps he couldn't bear the thought of leaving the only home he knew and hoped his Jean would change her mind? Compelling questions, but ones that Lerner chose not to answer. As with *Carousel*, the music smooths over the rough patches of *Brigadoon*.

Not only were operatic-like musicals debuting on Broadway in this period, but so were legitimate operas. Some of these were composed by the prolific Gian Carlo Menotti (born 1911). Although born in Italy, Menotti only found lasting success — and for a time it was a major success — after he emigrated to the United States. Menotti grew up in Milan where he was steeped in opera and culture of all kinds and, at eleven, composed an opera entitled *The Death of Pierrot*. No less than Toscanini suggested that Menotti attend the Curtis Institute in Philadelphia. It was there that Menotti met his lifelong friend, companion, and occasional collaborator, Samuel Barber. Menotti composed his first professional work, *Amelia Goes to the Ball* in Vienna, and it was mounted by the Metropolitan Opera in 1938. Menotti then did an opera for NBC radio entitled *The Old Maid and the Thief* (1939) and returned to the Met with a piece entitled *The Island God* in 1942, which was not a success.

A frequent thing that was said about Menotti was that he wrote music which was "Puccinian," or in a "Puccinian vein, or "Puccini-like." Nothing could be further from the truth. Because of his Italian origins, and because many critics would seize upon any halfway lyrical composition as an oasis in a desert of modern music (or else they had little actual familiarity with Puccini), Menotti was wrongly touted as the American heir to the composer of *Madama Butterfly*. But despite his talent Menotti simply did not have the superlative and almost staggering melodic gifts of a Puccini. Another difference between the two composers is that Puccini composed many masterpieces, and Menotti — despite his large output — only one.

In 1945 Menotti composed two one-act operas which premiered in different theaters and then mounted them as a double-bill on Broadway in 1945. These were *The Medium* and *The Telephone*. *The Medium* is the story of a phony psychic named Madame Flora, or Baba, who enlists the aid of her daughter Monica, and a mute boy she's taken in, Toby, to fool and fleece her customers. But when she begins to feel ghostly hands and seemingly experiences other psychic phenomena, she suspects Toby is playing a trick on her. Increasingly unhinged, she murders him in a drunken rage. Menotti's score for this work is uneven, with some recitatives that are not well done, and other sections that are quite skillful. The sinister opening chords of the opera almost remind one of the piano accompaniment for silent movie thrillers, although Menotti employs more instruments; the strings which follow are a bit Straussian. In act one Monica inexplicably sings a lament for a lost lover, a "folk tune" that is actually a very nice aria, "the sun has fallen and it lies in blood." Baba eventually joins in for an informal duet. Mrs. Gobineau's arioso about the death of her son, "It happened long ago," would have been devastating if actually composed by Puccini. In act two Monica is given an upbeat aria, "Up in the sky" as she playfully sings and dances a waltz for Toby. This song is somewhat altered as Toby tries to communicate his love for Monica and she responds, still a bit playfully, by singing his adoration for him. Monica seems a bit stupid herself, more mocking of the boy than compassionate, although she may be trying to be so. The more powerful moments are given to the increasingly paranoid Baba, such as when she tries to convince three clients that she's a fraud as they beg her to continue communicating with their loved ones in counterpoint. She reviews the terrible things she's seen in her life in "Afraid? Am I afraid?" The scene when she whips Toby is dramatically handled but utterly repulsive. Whether *The Medium* is seen as a grotesque, heart-breaking and pathetic drama, or as a vulgar exploitation piece, it is essentially an opera about child abuse. In any case Toby is given little dignity, and the opera is second-rate music theater.

The Telephone was the light-hearted curtain raiser for *The Medium* and is actually more successful than the main event. Ben waits to propose to his girlfriend Lucy but can't get her to stop talking on the telephone. Finally he leaves, goes to a phone booth, and phones in his proposal. *The Telephone* is a charming and pretty concoction that — unlike a lot of brief comedies — is genuinely amusing. Highlights include Lucy's aria "Margaret, I was just thinking of you" — a long juicy chat on the phone — and Ben's aria in which he compares the phone to a two-headed monster and says he'd rather deal with another man or difficult in-laws. Lucy explains to a friend about her quarrel with Ben in the lilting "It all began on a Sunday," and it all ends with an effective proposal duet. Menotti got a lot of attention for these works — his association with Toscanini certainly didn't hurt — and it wasn't long before he began working on further operas for Broadway.

Kurt Weill had emigrated to the United States by the 1930's and come out with a string of big Broadway hits — *Johnny Johnson* (1936), *Knicker-bocker Holiday* (1938), *Lady in the Dark* (1941), and *One Touch of Venus* (1943) — making him a highly successful American composer. His 1947 Broadway work, *Street Scene*, based on Elmer Rice's 1929 stage play and with lyrics by Langston Hughes, was subtitled *An American Opera* and deserved to be. Although there is quite a bit of spoken dialogue in *Street Scene*, making it half-musical, half popular/jazz opera — it has much less dialogue than most musicals. The opera explores the interlocking lives of the residents of a tenement in New York during the twenties. Lonely Sam loves Rose, daughter of Anna Maurrant, who is mistreated by her husband Frank and is having an affair. Other characters move in and out, a baby is born, couples make love and break up, and Rose's married boss wants to keep her and put her in show biz. She wonders if this is the way out of poverty, but Sam urges her to go off with him instead. Frank Maurrant comes home early and finds his wife and her lover together, shooting and killing them. Rose cannot quite forgive her father for murdering her much more loving mother, although he insists that in his own way he loved Anna, too. Rose decides not to go off with Sam — yet — because she believes not following their own paths is what led to her parents' tragedy. Sam goes and cries as she walks off. Neighbors wonder if Rose will ultimately turn out like her mother and take up her boss's proposition.

The opera begins and ends with the snappy blues number "Ain't it awful, the heat," which has a *Porgy and Bess* feel to it. Anna's outstanding semi-operatic aria "Somehow I never could believe," in which she describes her disappointment in marriage and why she's having an affair (without admitting to it), has a haunting melody which gets across the character's quiet desperation and longing for something — and someone — better. It is especially poignant considering that she gets murdered not much later. Young Jenny's "Dearest friends and neighbors" is a delightful song describing her graduation day as the neighbors join in for a chorus of hope for Jenny's family, which is about to be dispossessed. The "wrapped in a ribbon and tied in a bow" refrain is particularly lilting. The bouncy tune is in ironic contrast to the feelings of Jenny's family — as happy as they are over her scholarship, they're mostly terrified of being turned out onto the street, reflected in the music's undertone. Sam's "Lonely house, lonely me" is another blues number, sung in a semi-operatic style, as he describes being lonely in a busy house, street and city, even with so many people around him. Sam and Rose's moving duet begins with Sam crying "Pain! Nothing but pain!" but Rose recalls his quoting Walt Whitman's poem "When Lilacs Last in the Dooryard Bloomed" and they sing a piece setting the poem to music. It encompasses their longings for a better life (if only in their dreams) and their deep affection and concern for one another. The "Ice Cream Quartet" sung by some neighbors is a rousing modern operatic quartet and ersatz brindisi. In act two Anna is given a poignant song to and about her young son, "Somebody's going to be so handsome," hoping he'll turn out to be fine and respectful of women and other people and not turn out like his father. Rose and Sam are given another outstanding, semi-operatic duet, "We'll go away together" as they think of running away from their troubles and lonely, unhappy lives. Sam's "Now love and death," in which he sings of the murders and the ones left behind to mourn, reprises the melody of Anna's "Somehow I never" and leads into a genuinely operatic chorale treatment of the piece. Frank Maurrant"'s "Rose! You're wearing a black dress/I Love her, too" becomes a duet and chorus with an almost Italian opera type intensity as Maurrant exclaims that despite what he did he loved Anna, and Rose sings "she was my mother — why did you kill her?"

One might ask is there perhaps too much sympathy for Anna? Her husband is a loutish disappointment, yes, but he does provide for her — and she cuckolds him, presumably in their own bed. Of course Frank should not have shot anyone, but Anna is not exactly a saint. Like everyone else in the opera, she is all too human. *Street Scene* may be only a nominal opera — although it does have arias and honest-to-goodness love duets — but it is moving and adult and in some ways ahead of its time.

The last great American opera of the 1940's also debuted on a Broadway stage, Marc Blitzstein's *Regina* (1949), based on Lillian Hellman's play *The Little Foxes*. Blitzstein's (1905–1964) previous work was the non-operatic political musical *The Cradle Will Rock* (1937), which is better known for the circumstances of its original staging — locked out of the theater the performers enacted the piece from orchestra seats in another empty house — than for its music. *Regina* explores the lives of the venal Hubbard family in the post–Civil War South. Regina's brothers contrive to steal some valuable bonds from their brother-in-law, Regina's husband, Horace, who unexpectedly comes home after a long absence. Regina's unhappily married sister-in-law Birdie is afraid that her niece, Regina's daughter Alexandra, will be forced to marry her son, Leo, whom even his own mother doesn't like. When Horace has an attack during an argument — his marriage to Regina is loveless and he stands in the way of an important business deal — Regina withholds his medication from him and he dies. Because of their theft of the bonds, Regina is able to blackmail her brothers into giving her a much larger percentage of the profits from the business deal they were used for. Remembering her father's warning about "people who eat the earth" and others "who stand around and watch," Alexandra leaves home over her mother's protestations.

Spoken dialogue is kept to a minimum in *Regina* and often has music behind it or is "sung speech." The first number in the opera is Addie the maid's "Want to join the Angels," a wistful, melancholy high-class gospel number which is followed by a ragtime version of the same tune. Both versions are them combined for an interesting, attractive — if noisy — effect. This is followed by a majestic intermezzo which is the overture proper. In "Music, music, music," which reflects the character's loneliness, Birdie sings that when people are nice to her it reminds her of music, remembering how much music mattered to her family in the past. Regina declares her philosophy of going after what you want with determination in "The best thing of all" while her daughter Alexandra wonders who her lifetime partner will be, and what falling in love for the first time will be like, in "What will it be for me?" At the opening of act two Regina repeatedly bleats "Addie, where are you?" and gives instructions in a monotone (these instructions are sung, but only in the same one note) which is meant to illustrate how shrill and irritating the woman can be to Addie, but it doesn't take long for the audience to get the point and become exasperated as well. Horace's "How are you, Addie?" expresses his contentment at being back home as the music reflects his utter physical and spiritual weariness. In a ballroom scene a chorus of guests sing sarcastically about the Hubbards and their back-stabbing ways ("Regina does a lovely party"), a bizarre brindisi in which the bitter guests hardly drink to their hostess' health. Addie's "Night could be time to sleep" is another high-class blues number as she sings to Birdie to let go of her troubles for the night so she can sleep, a lovely piece full of Addie's casual wisdom and compassion. Regina asks an old beau "Do you wish we had wed years ago?" during a waltz number in which she is not being sentimental but is rather showing her contempt for the man. The very effective finale to act two has Regina arguing bitterly with Horace, finally screaming that she hopes he'll die, she'll be waiting for him to die, as a horrified Birdie and Alexandra look on and the crowd dances a lively "Gallop" in the background for dramatic contrast.

In act three Alexandra, Birdie, Horace and Addie sing a gentle paean to the peacefulness of precipitation in the "Rain quartet," which uses rain as a metaphor for helpful, caring people versus those who, like the Hubbards, "eat the earth." In her aria "Lionnet, Lionnet," Birdie fondly remembers and longs for the past when her estate, Lionnet, was in its glory, then launches into an embarrassing confession of her internal anguish, recognizing that her husband Oscar married her for her family's cotton, that she doesn't like her own son, Leo, and that she drinks intemperately to blunt the pain. While the music is almost recitative-like, improvisational sounding, it builds in power along with Blitzstein's lyrics. Regina excoriates Horace and reveals her utter loathing for him, leading to his fatal attack, in "It took me a while to find out." Brother Ben reacts to Regina's blackmail demands over the theft of the bonds in the snappy "Greedy Girl," which not only combines an operatic style with a Broadway ambiance, but manages to give it all a honky-tonk twist. Not to be outdone, Regina puts her brothers in their place with "Tomorrow I shall go straight to court." The affecting windup has Alexandra tell Regina that she's leaving and that's that as Regina rages and the chorus sings a gospel piece "Is a new day a-coming?" in the background.

Lillian Hellman was initially pleased with the adaptation. "Marc has done a really wonderful job," she said. "And it really is an opera, you know, not just a play with a few songs added." However, when the show closed abruptly it brought out Hellman's negative and jealous reactions and she stopped speaking to Blitzstein. Virgil Thomson, also jealous of Blitzstein's achievement (which Thomson himself could not have been capable of), attacked it viciously in the *Herald Tribune*, claiming that the opera was "not very musical ... raucous in sound, coarse in texture, explosive, obstreperous and strident."[8] Thomson's use of language was probably better than his employment of the orchestra.

If nothing else, Menotti had started a trend and Blitzstein's *Regina* ended the decade with a flourish. Operatic musicals had paved the way for actual operas on Broadway. In the next decade there would be a new wrinkle — operas on television. And more.

12. The Bright Lights of Opera: United States, 1950–1959

Hard as it may be to believe today, opera was once integrated far more into the cultural life and daily entertainment of average Americans. This is not to say that all Americans flocked to the opera houses any more than they do today, but opera wasn't quite as dissociated from the popular culture as it seems to be now. In the forties and fifties Mario Lanza[1] became a movie star — and an opera singer to reckon with — without ever setting foot on the stage of an opera house. Opera was regularly featured in movies — frequently opera singers were characters — and such famous singers as Lauritz Melchior regularly guest-starred in motion pictures (albeit they were often no longer in their glory days). In anthology films featuring a variety of entertainers, — comedians, crooners, long-legged beauties and so on — opera singers, almost always included, would invariably be called in to do a number. Most Americans knew that *I pagliacci* referred to a sad clown and a loser in love, even if they had never seen Leoncavallo's opera — the term had entered the popular lexicon. Many people may have preferred swing music or the big bands or Sinatra, but they were not totally unaware of opera. When television began in the late forties and slowly entered the homes of most Americans throughout the fifties, there were many live presentations of operas. Opera singers, who had previously been featured in many a radio broadcast, showed up regularly on such shows as *Ed Sullivan* up until the sixties. With the coming of rock and roll came the Great Divide. Nowadays we have the Three Tenors (and pitiable knock-offs like the almost unknown "Three Sopranos") and the equally pitiful Andrea Bocelli. But at least more people are actually going to the opera house.

The one American composer who was most associated with opera throughout the fifties was Gian Carlo Menotti. Five years after the *Medium/Telephone* double-bill garnered him much attention, he was back with *The*

Consul (1950). *The Consul* is about a woman, Magda, who desperately tries to get a visa so that she can get out of her oppressive European nation and join her husband, John, who was forced to flee from the secret police. When their baby dies, John risks re-entering the country so that he can reunite with Madga, but when he's captured she's overcome with hopelessness and commits suicide. Act one begins with spoken dialogue and a record playing in the background as John, injured, rushes into the apartment, making *The Consul* seem like music theater from the very first; in fact the music often smacks of Broadway and film scores. Scene one consists of mostly bleary and inept recitatives punctuated by two pleasant ariosos and a very attractive trio ("Now O Lips say good-bye) sung by Magda, John and his Mother as John prepares to flee. He urges his wife to have courage — "be like the sleeper who knows his dream is a dream." Two interesting pieces in scene two at the consulate have one character singing plaintively as another interrupts or translates: the foreign woman's "Grazie, mio signor" has the woman pleading in Italian to the secretary to be allowed to visit her daughter, who is in trouble, as Mr. Kafner provides a translation; later Madga tries to explain her situation to the same uncaring secretary in "Explain that John is a hero." The recitatives in this sequence are much more lyrical than before. The scene ends with an acceptable quartet ("In endless waiting rooms") with lousy, pretentious, pseudo-poetic lyrics, written by Menotti, which obscure more than they illuminate.

In the first scene of act two, Mother's gentle lullaby to her grandson ("I shall find for you") is not as poignant nor as harrowing as it should have been, considering the baby dies just a moment later. Mother's aria "I'm not crying again," a dirge not for the baby but for her son John whom she'll never see again, is forgettable. In scene two the whole business with the magician performing tricks and hypnotizing people to the annoyance of the secretary is meant to lighten the tension and the mood (after the death of the baby) but is irritating, with second-rate music to boot. We're asked to believe that the magician can hypnotize people into dancing, but can't hypnotize the secretary into letting him in to see the consul? Magda's aria "To this we've come," an outpour of anger against red tape, is, like the aforementioned lullaby, another example of Menotti muffing the opportunity to come up with powerful music to match his harrowing situations. Magda tearing up and throwing around "papers, papers, papers!" is theatrically effective, however, as is most of this particular sequence until the end of the act. Magda's arioso, "Oh the day will come," when "neither ink nor seal shall cage our souls." is a more effective piece, an ersatz Puccinian outburst which always gets applause, although it's nowhere near the level of the real thing. *The Consul* is never especially moving because the music isn't up to the demands of its heartbreaking story. In its day *The Consul*, a product of its times, was very successful and even managed to garner a Pulitzer Prize that it hardly deserved. Its tale of the horrors of the Iron curtain and the oppressiveness of the police state struck a chord that was anything but musical. It is often compared to *Tosca*. It has already been stated in this volume that in no realistic sense should Menotti be compared to Puccini. Similarly, in no way, shape or form is *The Consul* in the same league as Puccini's masterpiece. Told that Menotti was being touted as the new Puccini, *Regina* composer Marc Blitzstein, who did not agree, said "At the outside, a present day Wolf-Ferrari."[2]

However, Menotti created his own twentieth century masterpiece with his next opera, *Amahl and the Night Visitors*, which premiered on NBC television in 1951, making the composer even more famous, and imprinting his image as The American Opera Composer in the minds of most of his fellow countrymen. In this the three wise men on their way to see the baby Jesus encounter and change for the better the lives of the young crippled boy Amahl, and his poverty-stricken mother, who is tempted by the jewels they carry. Not only is this Menotti's best libretto, but this time he responded to his own words with the best score he ever composed. The tender mood of the piece is immediately set by the admirable, sensitive overture, which consists of the opera's main theme as well as various themes heard later in the opera. Amahl's aria "Damp clouds have shined it," his presumably fanciful description of the night sky, contrasts nicely with his mother's immediate follow-up, "Oh, Amahl, when will you stop telling lies"; the lyrical sweetness of the former set off against the heavy intensity of the mother's weary response. Amahl is given another lovely aria in "I am a shepherd" as he relates the bitter circumstances of his life. The song of the shepherds as they greet each other is a bit derivative, but also quite pleasant, nicely contrasted with the chorus of "Thank yous" from the three Kings. The wonderful Dance of the Shepherds which follows is first played on his pipes by Amahl and then taken up by the orchestra. The brief intermezzo between the shepherd's leaving Amahl's house at night and the coming of dawn employs the lovely opening theme which represents the mother's love for Amahl. King Melchior's aria "Oh woman, you can keep the gold" employs this same theme, connecting the mother's love for her son to Melchior's for the Christ child and vice versa. The mother courts temptation to steal for the sake of her child in the effective piece "All that Gold." Amahl and his mother are given a lovely parting duet "What to do with your crutch?"—Amahl's suddenly being able to walk would be hokey were it not for the fact that it fits the tone of the piece which is, after all, about a Christmas miracle. The most outstanding piece in the opera is the beautiful quartet "Have you seen a child the color of wheat?" as the three kings sing of Christ and the mother sings of Amahl; it works splendidly on both the melodic and emotional fronts. *Amahl and the Night Visitors* has a wonderful overtone of perhaps unrealistic hope combined with a certain melancholy air. *Amahl* used to be shown regularly on television during the Holiday season. Now children and their parents are more likely to be treated to a mindless bit of treacle backed by rap or hip hop.

Billed as Menotti's "musical drama," *The Saint of Bleecker Street*, which takes place in New York's Little Italy, premiered in 1954. In this, Annina is a devout young woman whose visions and alleged holy powers are the talk of the neighborhood. Her brother Michele is extremely, almost maniacally, protective of her and afraid that she will be exploited. His girlfriend Desideria accuses him of having incestuous feelings for Annina, and is stabbed to death in response. Michele becomes a fugitive, and the dramatic conclusion has him bursting in just as Annina becomes a nun and then dies.

Annina's death at the very moment of her greatest happiness is somewhat moving, but Menotti's libretto is simply too muddled to work. If it has anything going for it, it would be that at least it's unpredictable. Annina is not really developed as a character and Michele proves to be a jackass — Menotti takes the most intelligent character in the opera and completely undercuts him and his viewpoint. He never shows the slightest remorse for the death of Desideria and in fact, barely gives his victim a thought. Michele at first seems to represent common sense and new ideas versus dumb, traditional, superstitious values (like, oddly, the earlier *Treemonisha*) and isolationism among immigrants, but Menotti transforms him into an idiot, an almost "evil" figure and murderer. Some people may simply interpret this as Michele showing his true demonic colors — Michele the demon lusting after his pious sister (or does Annina seek to submerge her own feelings for Michele by taking the veil?) — or is the opera simply a study of a man driven literally crazy by his beloved sister's religious fanaticism? Menotti throws in a dash of piety, a soupçon of Tennesee Williams (or Lillian Hellman) but hasn't the real gifts to make it come together in any sensible fashion. And yet this pretentious mess was also given a Pulitzer.

On the other hand, much of *The Saint of Bleecker Street* works perfectly well in the theatrical (if hardly the intellectual) sense, such as the sequence when two women waiting to speak to Annina break into a cat fight just as the priest comes out to announce that Annina has begun to have a vision. At the end of scene two a woman frees Michele from bondage and kisses him passionately as he sobs. Dramatic, yes. Even sexy. But profound? No.

Although musically *Saint* is an improvement over *The Consul* (but not

Amahl), it is still not on the level of the Great Italians, although some of it was certainly influenced by Puccini and Mascagni. While the story decidedly veers into verismo territory with the stabbing death of Desideria, *Saint* is awfully slow at times and lacks the energy of true verismo. Annina's visionary aria "Oh sweet Jesus, spare me this agony" in act one builds in power and is effective despite its melodic unevenness. The orchestral introduction to the second scene is a lively piece full of the rhythms and excitement of Mulberry Street settings with some somber undertones. Annina and Michele argue over her taking the veil, leaving Michele to give up her life and love to God in the memorable duet "Sister, I shall hide you." In act two Desideria warns Michele that "Love can turn to hate" and his love for her should matter more than his love for Annina. Michele's "I know that you all hate me" — another arresting if melodically uneven aria — encapsulates his feelings of being apart from the superstitious "old country" immigrants he lives among when he has no true connection to Italy. In act three the music for Annina and Michele, beginning with his arioso "Where are my hopes and dreams" is good, including the brief duet at the end ("Everything has changed") as he begs her not to take the veil and leave him and she insists that she can not resist God's voice. Certain critics admired *Saint* but audiences did not flock to it. Menotti did a few more operas after this, but none of them really took hold with the public. In the seventies he wrote *Goya* at the suggestion of Plácido Domingo.

By the 1950's Igor Stravinsky had emigrated to the United States, becoming a Russian-American composer. His first opera written in this period was *The Rake's Progress*, which premiered in Venice in 1951. It is based on a series of prints by William Hogarth and has a libretto by W. H. Auden. The hero, Tom Rakewell, is tempted away from his true love, appropriately named Anne Trulove, by money and licentiousness, encompassed in his shadowy servant, appropriately named Nick Shadow, who is in reality the Devil. Tom winds up married to a bearded lady named Baba, sees his star rise and fall, and eventually winds up in a nuthouse. Through all this Anne remains true, but in the end Tom dies. It should be obvious that despite the similarities *The Rake's Progress* is not Gounod's *Faust*. Stravinsky responded to this libretto with suitably quirky music in what was called a neoclassical style, but which also might be called ersatz baroque. Some might feel that Stravinsky surpasses Britten by virtue of the fact that at least his vocal lines, while not necessarily outstanding, do give singers a real chance to show off what they can do with their voices. Of course *The Rake's Progress* is an opera for smaller voices who could never handle the demands of Verdi or Puccini.

The highlights include the weird but rather joyous chorus of whores and "roaring boys" in act one, "The sun is bright," which has an air of delightful ribaldry with sinister undertones. Tom's second act aria "Vary the song" has a compelling opening and a slight melody that is at first elusive but then rather lovely, with an effective background that adds immeasurably to its success. The act two finale, as Baba unveils and reveals her beard, which includes her aria "I have not run away" and the chorus of townspeople ("Ah, Baba!") features music that could be described as darkly glorious. In act three Sellem the auctioneer's aria "Who hears me, knows me" has an interesting, snappy section ("La! Come Bid!") that reminds one of Sondheim (who, of course, came much later) and his use of repetition. Shadow is given a highly dramatic aria "I burn! I freeze!" as he goes down for the count after losing a throw of the dice with Rakewell. Anne's lullaby and chorus "Gently, little boat," as she brings peace to the madmen in the asylum, is one of the best things in the opera. *The Rake's Progress* is an unusual work — inventive, clever, and humorous — that lives or dies by its singers and production. By 1962 Stravinsky was so firmly ensconced in the United States that he was writing an opera for CBS TV, *The Flood*, about Noah's Ark, which aired in June of that year. It did not have a life beyond that, however.

Aaron Copland's only full-length opera, *The Tender Land*, premiered in 1954 at the New York City Center. The libretto by Horace Everett was very loosely inspired by depictions of midwesterners in James Agee's book "Let Us Now Praise Famous Men." Laurie Moss is about to graduate from highschool and anxious to experience life on her own terms. She is afraid she might wind up stuck with the same lonely, loveless life of her widowed mother. When her grandfather hires two drifters, Martin and Top, to work on the farm, Ma Moss is afraid they may be the men who assaulted a young woman a while before, but they are cleared by the sheriff. Laurie and Martin fall in love and decide to go off together, but Top convinces Martin that a life on the road is no life for a girl. Martin and Top go off on the sly, leaving Laurie behind. Heartbroken but determined, she decides to go off on her own. This exquisite gem of an opera is aptly named, for the music is permeated by tenderness and compassion. As well, the score is drenched in a sense of pervasive loneliness, brought out in compelling fashion by Copland. While *Tender Land* may not fit into the verismo mold, in its own way the score is quite emotionally raw and almost painfully sensitive. Ma Moss' arioso "Two little bits of metal" immediately gets across the woman's longsuffering, weary, but loving, hopeful attitude, especially where her daughter is concerned. Laurie expresses her growing desire to experience life and see the wide world in "Once I thought I'd never grow as tall as this fence." When Martin and Top encounter Grandpa and get acquainted with him it results in the Broadway-style trio "A stranger may seem strange." The first act ends with the superb quintet, "The Promise of living," as the cast sing of working together to bring in the Harvest. This piece seems to encompass human hope and harmony and faith in nature, as well as thanksgiving to the Lord. It is a piece of great beauty and remarkable sensitivity.

The chorus-dance that opens act two, "Stomp your foot upon the floor," is quirky, bouncy and well-orchestrated, with certain dark undertones forecasting Ma Moss' unfounded suspicions concerning the two new hired men. The music for Martin's aria, "I'm gettin' tired of travelin'," in which he sings of his desire to settle down with a wife on some land, is full of a gentle fatigue as well as loneliness. While Martin and Laurie may seem to fall in love awfully quickly, both are at the point where they need a new adventure and some romance in their lives; this results in a creditable love duet, "The plains so green." In act three Martin gets anxious over his future in "Daybreak will come in such short time," the music for which gets across his conflicted feelings over Laurie and tortured uncertainty about what he wants out of life. Martin and Top are then given an effective pseudo–Broadway number in "That's crazy!," in which the latter tries to convince Martin that it would be ridiculous to subject Laurie to a struggling life on the highway. Laurie sings that "the sun is coming up" on a land that seems new now that she has found someone to share her life and quiet thoughts, and has an impassioned piece in "Perhaps I did love" when she realizes Martin is gone for good. In Ma Moss' final aria, "All thinking's done," the weary mother decides that she will find hope and sustenance in the child, Laurie's younger sister, who remains home with her.

The ending of *The Tender Land* is deeply moving. Like the mother, you can't help but wonder what will become of Laurie out in that big wide world... *The Tender Land* had originally been commissioned by Rodgers and Hammerstein and was to have been televised on NBC, but the network rejected it. Perhaps for this reason neither composer nor librettist was ever completely satisfied with the work, and kept tinkering with it, adding and subtracting some numbers and toying with two act and three act variations. A two-act chamber version employing a reduced orchestration (not done by Copland) premiered in 1987, but since the orchestration of the original is relatively "light" this version for only thirteen instruments seems unnecessary, although it may engender more performances in smaller houses. The trouble with this is that original version is vastly superior, bringing the music to vivid life in a way that the chamber version doesn't.

When Copland became a teacher at Tanglewood's Berkshire Center in Massachusetts, his students included Robert Ward, Alberto Ginastera, Ned Rorem, and Thea Musgrave, all of whom went on to compose operas that are discussed in this volume. Another pupil was William Flanagan

(1926–1969), a suicide, who was eulogized by Copland. Flanagan had always been very touched by the Mother's closing aria in *Tender Land*.

Jerome Moross (1913–1983) was a Juilliard-trained musician who tried his hand at film scores and ballets as well as music theater and nominal opera. His 1954 Broadway musical *The Golden Apple* has long been considered an opera by some because of its through-composed score. It is an opera, just not one with very much genuinely operatic music. Homer's tales of Ulysses and associates from the "Iliad" and the "Odyssey have been updated to after the American Civil War and turned into a satire. The libretto by John Latouche is clumsy and unmemorable, and Moross responded with music that is equally dismissible but for a couple of numbers, one of which is admittedly outstanding. This highlight is "Coming Home Together," a duet for Ulysses and Penelope during their long-awaited reunion as they reaffirm their love for one another and sing about how wonderful it is to share life and everyday pleasures. Helen of Troy's "Lazy Afternoon" is an insinuating, smoky, sleepy Broadway number that never quite became a standard. Penelope muses about Ulysses when he is far away in another fine piece, "Windflowers," and there's a silly but entertaining "Hawaiian" number in "Goona Goona Lagoon." But these pieces are vastly outnumbered by songs that are mediocre or even worse. Wisely Moross ends the opera with a reprise of "Coming Home Together" so the audience could at least go home humming the best number in the show.

A much happier musical experience was provided by Harold Rome in his Broadway musical *Fanny* (1954), based on Marcel Pagnol's Marseilles trilogy. Rome did a number of musicals both before and after *Fanny,* but in none of them did he reach the ecstatic heights of *Fanny,* whose intensely romantic story brought out every bit of romance — and operatic flair — in Rome's musical nature. It seems hard to believe that some critics actually criticized the book (by S. N. Behrman and Joshua Logan), because it brilliantly compresses all the drama of Pagnol's three plays and provides ample opportunities for lyrical flight. *Fanny* trades in the right kind of sentiment and not only has an exquisite score, but is warm and deeply moving. The story deals with Marius, who loves Fanny but longs for an adventure at sea. He and Fanny have a night of love, but Marius leaves the next morning. Pregnant, Fanny marries the older man Parnisse who loves her and is willing to say the child is his own. When Marius, lonely and homesick, comes back to Marseilles, he realizes that the child must be his and stakes his claim. Even his father Cesar is against him on this. Eventually Parnisse dies and Marius, Fanny — and their son — are reunited.

The title sung, delivered by Marius to Fanny after she confesses her love to him (in another fine piece, "I Love You") is not only one of Broadway's most ravishingly beautiful love songs, but one of the great twentieth century arias, full of Marius' desperate need to see the world and his equally desperate desire not to devastate the woman he loves. There is also what is essentially a love duet between father and son in "I Like You" (immediately followed by Fanny's aforementioned declaration of love for Marius). Cesar's "Welcome Home," in which he reminds Marius of the pleasures of coming home after being away, embodies real pathos in that Cesar is unaware that Marius is planning to run away the very next day. Marius and the chorus express his longing for adventure in the stirring "Restless Heart" and Cesar poses the question "Why be afraid to dance?" to a lilting waltz number. Cesar has a tender piece singing about his baby grandson in "Love is a very light thing," while Marius tells Fanny how the thought of her haunted and comforted him as he sailed in "The Thought of You." Fanny explains why she isn't free to run off with Marius in her arioso "Other Hands, Other Hearts." ("Think of this," she says to him. "Each night there's a woman who would love to lie down next to you, and smell your hair, and fall asleep in the warmth of your body.") "Be Kind to Your Parents," which Fanny and her son sing to one another, is a bit out of place, but even it has a sensitive undertone below the bouncy exterior melody. When Joshua Logan, who directed the Broadway production, did the same for the film (which tragically eliminated the songs except as background music), he wanted to call it *Joshua Logan's Fanny* until wiser heads prevailed. Wise heads would book a Broadway or opera house revival of *Fanny*. Its scope and the operatic construction of its music — some songs simply blend into one another as if they were a series of lyrical recitatives, ariosos, and duets — make *Fanny* a very high-class example of musical theater.

Opera fans have always been divided over Frank Loesser's 1956 Broadway production *The Most Happy Fella*. Some respond favorably to its excellent semi-operatic score (most of the dialogue is sung, and there are a few genuinely operatic arias and duets), while others simply shrug as if to say, "It's okay, but what is it compared to Verdi and Wagner?" There's no argument there. *The Most Happy Fella* is a different ball game from Grand European Opera. As an example of one kind of American opera, however, it is without peer. Based on Sydney Howard's play *They Knew What They Wanted*, it deals with a middle-aged vintner, Tony, who gets a young and pretty "mail order" bride (whom he had previously sighted in the restaurant where she works) through subterfuge. Instead of sending "Rosabella," as he calls her, his own photograph he substitutes a picture of his handsome foreman, Joe. Rosabella (her real name, Amy, is only revealed at the very end) is dismayed at the truth, but goes ahead and marries him, after a brief night of passion with Joe. Tony nearly throws her out when he learns that she's pregnant by Joe, but true love triumphs in the end and the two stay together. A secondary romance is carried on between Rosabella's friend Cleo and Tony's employee. This secondary romance is the stuff of musical comedy while the primary love story between Tony and Rosabella is the stuff of opera. And *The Most Happy Fella*, with its constant flow of wonderful melody, really is an opera. Many of the very few dialogue scenes are underscored with music, and even the dialogue in those scenes without music are delivered in musical cadences.

The horns that sound in the greasy spoon where Rosabella works as the show proper begins after the overture set the mood from the start: this is a show about loneliness and the things it drives people to do, and this theme continuously reverberates through Loesser's score, even in waitress Cleo's opening comic number "Ooh, my feet!" with its underlying pathos. The centerpiece of the first scene is Amy's touching "Somebody Somewhere," a virtual anthem of loneliness as Amy sings of her longing to find someone she can share her life with. The loneliness also sounds in "I don't know nothin' about you," when Amy sings the words of the rather pathetic but impassioned love letter Tony has left for her on the table along with an elaborate tip. "Standin' on the Corner (watchin' all the girls go by)" is a snappy Broadway number in scene two that seems like a sharp contrast to Cleo, Tony and Amy's loneliness — the men in this number seem to sing of casual, mindless relationships — but even this has a touch of wistfulness ("Haven't got a girl, but I can wish..."). The one character who doesn't seem lonely, except for the open spaces, is foreman Joe, whose ballad "Joey, Joey, Joey" reveals his need to escape, to explore and have adventure (like Marius in "Fanny"), a flight from commitment of any kind, the antithesis to the other characters and numbers.

The title tune, sung by Tony to his friends and neighbors as he relates his budding pen pal romance with Rosabella, is essentially a brindisi in tone if not subject. "Abbandanza" and "Great Big Italian Spozelitzio" are two more formal drinking songs. Tony's ode to "Rosabella" is a dramatic love aria, while his "Mama! Mama!," in which he tells his dead mother of his sublime happiness, is a magnificent aria that is quite poignant and highly dramatic. The main love duet is Tony and Rosabella's "My Heart is So Full of You" which is beautiful and also touching. It may be "Opera Lite" to some ears, but there is no denying its soaring effectiveness. There is also an excellent trio for Tony, his sister Marie, and Cleo, near the end of the opera ("She's gonna come home with me") as Marie tries to stop Tony from preventing Amy's departure and Cleo tries to stop Marie from interfering. There are also a number of arioso and smaller duets that add insights into the characters. Joe's "Don't Cry" ballad as he tries to comfort a disappointed

Rosabella after she first learns the truth leads into their lovemaking, but the music meant to illustrate their mounting passion is a bit flat (comparatively speaking) and certainly doesn't smack of Italian opera. The Spanish-flavored "Fresno Beauties" sung by the male chorus surrounds Rosabella and Joe's informal duet "Cold and Dead," a haunting interlude between the two as they recognize that their night of passion was an utter fluke and they have nothing to say to one another. There is a nice juxtaposition between the frenzied chorus and the "monotonal" downbeat duet. The songs for the secondary couple, Cleo and Herman (the splashy production number "Big D"; "I Made a Fist"; "I Like Everybody") are perfectly okay Broadway numbers but mere "crowd-pleasers"; they lower the tone and integrity of the work. However other numbers, such as Rosabella's ballad "Warm All Over," in which she expresses her tender feelings for Tony; "How Beautiful the Days," a quartet illustrating the growing romantic feelings between Tony and Rosabella and the innermost fears of Marie and Joe; and "Young People Gotta Dance," a waltz during which Marie tries to infect her brother with her own negativity (due, of course, to her own loneliness), while not operatic per se, are outstanding pieces that fit very securely into the tone of the work.

The characters in *The Most Happy Fella* are flawed, which only makes them more interesting. Amy may not be an out and out gold-digger, but would she really have gone out to marry Tony — good-looking or not good-looking — had he not been a well-off property owner? Tony is as self-centered in some ways as he is unrealistic. While his anger at Amy for sleeping with Joe is understandable, he never openly acknowledges that by dishonestly sending the wrong picture he was the architect of the whole affair. Marie is seen as a villainess — she can be tactless and unkind — but she also has a certain degree of common sense. *The Most Happy Fella* is an authentic American masterpiece.

Another Broadway masterpiece of 1956 — and another example of prime American opera — was Leonard Bernstein's *Candide*. This was based on Voltaire's fascinating, absurd, and darkly comic satire of the eighteenth century detailing the often grotesque adventures of the lovers Candide and Cunegonde. They encounter a wide variety of characters in their travels and travails, including an untrustworthy governor, an Old Lady who has lost half of her rump, among other things, the philosopher Pangloss, and many others. The original libretto was written by Lillian Hellman, with a number of people, especially Richard Wilbur, contributing lyrics. Hugh Wheeler and Stephen Sondheim contributed material to revisions in the seventies and eighties. The libretto is pretty faithful (certainly in spirit) to the source material, but what works on paper doesn't always work when it's staged. The book is often quite amusing, but as subtle as a sledgehammer and often too silly for its own good. Yet beneath the comic overstatement, *Candide* gets across the ugliness and loneliness of life and the desperate, foolish hope that fills and sustains us all. What makes it all work, however, is Bernstein's rich, delightful, and endlessly melodic score. Bernstein was assisted with the orchestrations by Hershy Kay. It is undoubtedly the first musical to have a snappy patter song about the spread of syphilis, and there are many other notable pieces. In "Glitter and Be Gay," which is a kind of mock bel canto piece, Cunegonde rails against the emptiness of her glitzy fate and surroundings while rather reveling in them, too. The melody rises above the parodic level in Candide and Cunegonde's duet "You were dead, you know" after they discover the other is still in the land of the living. The Governor spells out the anti-romantic facts of life to Cunegonde in the fascinating "My Love." To a devilish tango the Old Lady explains to Cunegonde how she learned to cope and survive in "I am easily assimilated." The music is even better in the second act, such as the very funny and inventive "Quiet"— several characters are utterly bored to death — and the wistful, lovely ballad "Eldorado." "Bon Voyage," sung by the nasty Governor to Candide is another inventive piece, and Bernstein's music creates a feeling a waves and rowing as an ensemble sings of "The Simple Life" on a raft. "What's the use" is a delightful song in which assorted scam artists who have to pay off bosses, police, blackmailers and so on observe with disgust that crime just doesn't pay. The Old Lady sings of her troubles as Candide empathizes in the "Gavotte" while Pangloss sings to the admiring ladies at the gambling tables. "Candide's Song" ("Nothing More than This") is a sweet, sad outcry of disillusionment, while the deeply moving "Make Our Garden Grow," sung by Candide and the entire company in the finale, proves the finest number in the opera. In this piece Bernstein makes splendid use of dissonant chords a la Copland. The theme of the song (as, indeed, of Voltaire's novel) is to make the best of whatever life throws at you. It has a palpable undercurrent of pathos and desperation as if the music were saying "please, let nothing else horrible happen."

Meanwhile there were operas being composed for actual opera houses. One of the most important American composers in this regard was Carlisle Floyd (born 1926), whose folk opera *Susannah* came out in 1955 and has been part of the repertoire in many major and minor houses ever since. (Ironically, it premiered inauspiciously at the Florida State University.) *Susannah* is a story in the Apocrypha updated to modern times and relocated to backwoods Tennessee. The heroine is an attractive young innocent who is branded a harlot by her community due to a boy's lies and her bathing in a baptismal creek. She is denounced by the new reverend, Blitch, who eventually seduces her and discovers that far from being a fallen woman she is actually a virgin. He tries to convince the Church Elders that Susannah has been wronged, but he is rebuffed. When Susannah's brother Sam learns what happened, he tracks down Blitch and shoots him. Sam flees. The community will continue to ostracize an embittered and lonely Susannah.

Blitch is given three effective pieces, including his stirring introduction "I am the Reverend Olin Blitch" in which he is joined by the congregation. He entreats sinners to confess in "Come, sinner, tonight's the night" and is humanized even as he slaps the make on a tired Susannah in "I'm a lonely man, Susannah." Sam's aria "It's about the way people is made, I reckon," is an okay song about people's need to believe the worst of others. This leads into the finale of act one (which continues the melody of Sam's aria but in more powerful orchestral terms) which creates an almost palpable atmosphere of the utter despair and extreme anxiety Susannah feels at having the entire valley turn against her when she's done nothing wrong. Sam's "Jaybird" song, which he sings to amuse his sister, has a sort of wistfulness to it but is wisely kept brief. Susannah is given two major pieces in the opera. In act two she sings a blues-influenced folk tune which reflects her desolate, confused state of mind, an attractive piece if not really a "great" aria ("The trees in the mountains are cold and bare"). However, the best number in the opera is her act one aria "Ain't it a pretty night" as she imagines the rest of the wide world out there and all of its possibilities. The sad melody is as full of as much homesickness and fear as it is hope and anticipation. This aria is a fine one that becomes outstanding when interpreted by the right soprano, for instance Phyllis Curtin, who sang the role of Susannah at the World Premiere and afterwards. If there is anything that prevents *Susannah* from being a truly major opera it is the lack of variety in the music and the comparative scarcity of melodies. Yes, *Susannah* is only ninety minutes long but there have been shorter operas that have much more melodic inspiration (*Cav* and *Pag* immediately come to mind). And occasionally the music lapses into musical theater effects. Still, *Susannah* has its own power as a noteworthy and lyrical study of religious hypocrisy. There would be greater works in Floyd's future.

For instance, *Wuthering Heights*, which premiered in 1958, and while much of the score is film-type music, it is nevertheless a sterling effort, much more ambitious and more beautiful than *Susannah*. Bronte's novel is one of the most romantic ever written, and it may seem strange that a more or less modern composer such as Floyd would attempt an adaptation. But Floyd's style, while different from the 19th century romantic composers, is not without its romantic aspects. Certainly Floyd was never a composer who disdained lyricism. The many memorable moments in *Wuthering Heights* include Hindley vowing to make Heathcliff a slave, and a duet for Cathy and Heathcliff in which they vow that "nothing will part us as long as we live." Nelly advises Heathcliff to "Take off your frown" and engages in wistful musing on his origins, then later warns Cathy that Heathcliff has "come back for only one thing." Edgar asks his beloved to "Marry me, Cathy," vowing that he'll make her forget Wuthering Heights (and Heathcliff, of course). The scene when Heathcliff wins Wuthering Heights in a card game is extremely well handled. There is an impressive quartet for Cathy, Heathcliff, Isabella, and Edgar, in which all their twisted relationships and passions are reflected in the music. Cathy's final plaintive aria has her bedridden, pregnant, wishing she was out on the moors. Isabella is given an outstanding aria regarding Heathcliff ("He's exploded my world") but the best music in the opera is understandably reserved for a ravishing, intensely romantic informal duet (actually successive arias) for Cathy and Heathcliff ("Oh, Heathcliff, I can breath again") when they're out on the moors. It's as if there's something about these two star-crossed lovers — and the bleak, misty romance of the moors — that brings out the best in composers. Bernard Herrmann's music for this scene in also superb in his version of *Wuthering Heights*, which adds a certain spookiness that Floyd's score is devoid of (this is discussed in the next chapter). Floyd would be back in the next few decades with several other works, including one that would rival *Wuthering Heights* as his masterpiece.

Floyd's music generally seems completely original. Says the composer, "I am honestly not aware of influences in my own writing as disingenuous as that may sound. On occasion I have been conscious of appropriating a Coplandesque sonority or rhythmic turn but melodically I have always felt that, for better or worse, what I heard and wrote was completely my own. That however is to be expected, I feel, since the lyric impulse (or lack of it) is always the most personally revealing aspect of a composer's musical language."[3]

Douglas Moore (1893–1969), like Floyd, is an American composer who is known by one lasting work — in this case *The Ballad of Baby Doe* — which may or may not be his best opera but is certainly his best-known. Moore had previously composed a creditable one act *The Devil and Daniel Webster* (1939) and the ambitious *Giants in the Earth* (1951), which won a Pulitzer Prize, among others, before *Baby Doe* premiered in 1956. The opera is the true story of Horace Taber, who became rich, built an opera house (the aforementioned Central City Opera House in Colorado), divorced his first wife Augusta and married his mistress, Baby Doe, gambled everything on the country retaining a silver standard, and lost everything when it switched to gold. Through it all Baby Doe remained faithful to Tabor and eventually died a poverty-stricken death. Some sequences in John Latouche's libretto are a bit suspect, dramatically contrived, such as discarded Augusta going to a ball to honor Tabor, and Baby Doe's mother (Mama McCourt) traveling to see Augusta to seek her help for a nearly bankrupt Tabor, but even these scenes are effectively handled. While the libretto is poetic and generally well-done, neither Tabor nor Baby Doe really come fully alive in either the text or the music. Moore's music veers from musical theater to Verismo Lite to a Massenet-like delicacy to occasional attempts at Grand Opera–style effects. It is often skillful, occasionally clumsy, but in general quite likable, tuneful and attractive with a few blathery sections. Baby Doe is given several nice numbers. Her "Willow Song" is a wistful song of lost love, while "I knew it was wrong" is a tuneful aria in which she tries to explain her love for Tabor to his wife. Her delicate — in fact, silvery — ode to silver, "Gold is a fine thing, but..." is especially well orchestrated. Her "The fine ladies walk" about the unloved wives who have jealous contempt of her is mediocre, but her closing aria, "Always through the changing," about the eternal nature of love and her unchanging devotion to Tabor, is excellent. Doe's best aria is the well-known "Dearest Mama," as she writes to her mother about her seemingly hopeless love for Horace Tabor. Tabor's "For my beloved bride," in which he presents her with Queen Isabella's jewels, is pure Broadway, but his love song to Baby Doe, "Warm as the autumn light" is more on the mark. This melody should have been used for the love duet instead of the one Moore actually chose, "She's not going, my heart," as Taylor and Baby Doe embrace. The first confrontation between Augusta and Tabor over Baby Doe borders on lower case verismo, while there is a minor European feel to a scene between Baby Doe and Augusta, with Tabor joining in, in the first scene of act two. Whatever its flaws, *Ballad of Baby Doe* is undeniably pleasant and memorable.

Moore's one-act farce *Gallantry* premiered in 1958. *Gallantry* is the name of a mediocre soap opera which is interrupted now and then by commercials for household products. In the main soap opera story, Dr. Gregg confesses his passion for nurse Lola as he's about to operate on his patient Donald, who turns out to be Lola's fiancé. She then learns that the good doctor is married, and the two argue during the operation. *Gallantry* is melodious and very pleasant indeed if never especially amusing, the idea itself being funnier than its execution. The highlights include a creditable duet as both doctor and nurse each wish to "escape from the joy of romance"; the nurse's pretty love song ("so good to see that you love me"); the nurses's "Now, Dr. Gregg!" in which she tells off the doctor in lively "dramatic" fashion; and Donald's aria "I thought I heard a distant bird" which he sings when he comes out of the anesthesia.

Jack Beeson's (born 1921) *The Sweet Bye and Bye* premiered in 1957. Inspired by Aimee Semple Mcpherson, the libretto deals with Sister Rose, a young woman in a key position with a group of revivalists in 1920's Atlantic City. Rose has fallen in love but knows that Mother Rainey, the head of the group, and the other followers, will never let her leave to be with her boyfriend, Billy. She fakes her own death to get away, but Mother and the others find her and drag her back. When Billy goes to rescue her, he is murdered by Mother Rainey, but, incredibly, the only one the congregation excoriates is Sister Rose. A strong condemnation of religious hypocrisy and mania, *The Sweet Bye and Bye* boasts a libretto that fascinates despite the fact that the characters are one-dimensional. The story cries out for a much better and bigger score than Beeson delivered. Like so many "modern" composers Beeson seems loathe to move the audience — and the ending should certainly move us — with his music. Beeson's music is often lyrical (a surprise to those who are only familiar with his *Lizzie Bordon*) and occasionally pleasant, but rarely very melodious; in fact much of it is simply shrill. The better moments include Billy's aria "My heart is at last sure," in which he proclaims to Rose that he's finally found the one woman he can truly love and be faithful to. It's rather lovely, but Beeson doesn't develop it as well as it could have been. Ironically, the hymn "Yours in harmony," sung by Rose and her flock, is the prettiest number in the opera. Rose's aria "Listen to me!" is musically undistinguished but makes a good point: that belief in an after-life to the exclusion of all else, including happiness on earth, is worse than childish. Billy's kind of quirky aria "They've won you back again" has a daunting vocal line but little else to recommend it. "Take My hand," the act two love duet for Billy and Rose comes closest to the display of soaring lyricism that this opera could have used much more of. Perhaps the best thing in the score is Rose's beautiful arioso over Billy's dead body, "My heart grew whole."

Beeson came out with the better-known *Lizzie Borden* in 1965. While it is not surprising that the opera should be rife with "horror movie" music, need it have been so entirely unattractive? There are a couple of forgettable lyrical pieces, but this is an opera that succeeds — if it succeeds at all — by its excellent libretto. The music is perfectly okay as background material for the dark story unfolding on the stage, but that's about all. Nevertheless, there are some critics who, digging with desperation, found some things to admire in the score, albeit their praise was somewhat reserved. The opera should not be considered the last word on the famous murder case. The latest and most plausible theory for the murders — not put forth in the opera — is that they were committed not by Lizzie but by her sister.

Like his friend Gian Carlo Menotti, Samuel Barber (1910–1981) had a lifelong interest in music beginning at a very early age, and composed his first opera around the age of ten. As an adult, he composed three operas, two of which had librettos by Menotti. Their first collaboration was *Vanessa*, which premiered at the Metropolitan in 1958. The libretto seems to be cobbled together from every Bette Davis movie ever made: Vanessa lives in a big house with her mother, the Baroness, and her niece, Erika. For twenty years Vanessa has been waiting for her lover Anatol to return to her, but when he finally shows up Anatol is actually the son of her now-deceased lover. Erika and Anatol Jr. bond immediately, if briefly, but eventually a stronger relationship develops between Anatol and Vanessa. The two fall in love at the same time that Erika learns she is pregnant by Anatol and attempts suicide. Anatol and Erika marry and go off to Paris, leaving Erika to sit in the old house awaiting the return of her Anatol; everything has come full circle. In some respects the music of the overture is reminiscent of a score for a 1950's horror/sci fi film with an added lyricism. The most famous piece from the opera is Vanessa's act one aria "Do not utter a word, Anatol," which she sings when she believes her lover has finally arrived at her door. She sings with her back to Anatol, not wanting him to look at her unless he still loves her. While not especially melodious, the piece is shot through with restrained passion and genuine longing. Act two features an interesting, if minor, hymn in "In morning light let us rejoice." In act three the love duet for Anatol and Vanessa, "Love has a bitter core, Vanessa," is second-rate although it eventually bursts into full-blown lyricism; it sounds better as the overture to act four, scene two. In general the music for the last two acts is superior to the music for the first two; even the recitatives in the latter acts are handled more felicitously. There is some fine ballroom dancing music interspersed through act three, with the "band" music reflecting the emotions of Erika and the Baroness in its changing orchestrations. Anatol and Vanessa are given another effective duet in act three ("Take me away from this house, Anatol!"), and the doctor is given a fairly lovely aria as well ("For every love there is a last farewell"). The final quintet ("To leave, to break") is another effective piece.

Barber is not a melodist on the order of Puccini, and the lyricism of the opera is derived more from lush and romantic orchestrations, and the occasional soaring vocal line than anything else, although the vocal writing is not first-rate. Another problem with *Vanessa* is that the characters are too thinly and yet at the same time broadly drawn to pull us into the story. This lack of characterization and depth makes the libretto, despite its admittedly fascinating aspects, little more than a soap opera. Menotti also wrote the libretto for Barber's very short (nine minutes) chamber opera *A Hand of Bridge* (1959). Barber would be heard from again.

Robert Kurka (1921–1957) struggled to finish his own opera, *Good Soldier Schweik*, even as he struggled with the leukemia that killed him four months before its premiere with the New York City Opera in April 1958.

Hershy Kay helped with the arrangements of the music, which employs only sixteen instruments — brass, winds, and percussion only — severely limiting (for Kurka's talents, at least) the impact of the music and the development of melody. Even for 1958 *Good Soldier Schweik* was an obvious and trite military satire, and while the music is pleasant at times, tedious at others, it is rarely memorable. Lousy orchestration ruins Schweik's "Oh, there's no denying" in which he tells how he plans to serve the Emperor. Some of the music, such as Schweik's asylum song, "I never felt so good before," sounds awfully derivative; the baroness' "Brave Soldiers" rips off Weill's "Poor Jenny" from *Lady in the Dark*. However Schweik's piece "Oh the generals and colonels" as he prepares to go to war is pleasantly bouncy and the small orchestra is well employed. The best pieces come near the end: the hymn of heartsick, half-dead, fighting men ("Wait for the rugged soldiers") isn't bad at all, and Schweik is given a lyrical final aria ("I'll take a quiet road") as he essentially deserts for a "clear stream where soft breezes blow," one of the nicer things in the opera. Undoubtedly sentiment over the composer's tragic early death gives more luster to *Good Soldier Schweik* than it deserves, but Kurka showed promise and his "jazz" opera is an amusing theater piece with a tender finale.

Lou Harrison's six act (but only fifty-two minute) opera *Rapunzel*, based on the poem by William Morris, premiered in New York in 1959. Harrison had suffered a nervous breakdown in 1947 from the usual things that beset artists, and composed the piece while recovering. There are three characters: the imprisoned Rapunzel of the long hair (soprano); the Prince who discovers and falls in love with Rapunzel (baritone); and the witch (mezzo) who constantly intones "Rapunzel, Rapunzel, let down your hair." The strange thing about *Rapunzel* is that although it's a twelve-tone opera it doesn't sound like one. Harrison makes expressive use of a small orchestra, especially in the work's final minutes. Much of the singing is done a cappella, and there is the occasional lyrical outburst. These include the prince's arioso "If it would please God," expressing his desire to hear Rapunzel sing; and Rapunzel's aria "My Father taught me my prayers." The latter is especially tuneless, although the a cappella opening makes the slight orchestration that follows seem even more effective. (Leontyne Price performed this aria at the International Conference of Contemporary Music in Rome in 1954; Harrison was given a Masterpiece Award. Go figure.) The Prince's "Now let us go, love" begins promisingly, with a shimmering background to it, but becomes blathery fairly quickly. Despite the delicate and admirable instrumentation of the opera, *Rapunzel* is monotonous and essentially unmemorable.

During the next decade operas like *Rapunzel* would become more the norm than the exception, but there were still some surprises along the way.

13. A Mixed Bag:
United States, 1960–1990

The forty years of American opera from 1960 to 1990 truly presented a mixed bag, everything from operatic musicals to music theater, from the occasional lyrical flight of fancy to operas-of-incidental-music where the music was very much incidental. There came a new breed of opera composer, and a new breed of opera fan, and indeed a new breed of opera in which the designer and director — always thinking of concept, concept, concept — became chief cook and bottle washer. These people made inroads and began to influence commissions and repertory, even as they remained (and this has not changed) vastly out-numbered by the more traditional opera enthusiast.

In a development that could only be described as bizarre, men and women who had never heard a score by Verdi began to compose operas. Librettists were culled from popular fiction, Broadway, or somebody's back yard. The musical values of opera became so diminished that composing an opera — at least of the modern variety — was seen as something that virtually anyone could do. Fans of these operas were snatched from the theater circuit, where they came to be excited by brash theatrical techniques, some admittedly excellent librettos (good theater), and of course — need we mention it — splashy production values. The score, if it were even considered, became secondary.

In the 1980's came what Peter G. Davis, *New York* Magazine's music critic, dubbed the "CNN School of Opera," where music theater works were based on the lives of real individuals and often built around political events. Generally these pieces attracted audiences who were interested primarily in the person or the politics, not the opera — to them it was the message not the music. Christopher Keene, then-director of the New York City Opera, the very company that put on many of these CNN operas, commented "American operas are not music-driven in the sense that the works of the classic repertory are, and as a musician I regret that."[1] Composers of limited ability — or at least with little flair (and little real interest) in matters operatic — began to collaborate with savvy, self-promoting directors or entrepreneurs to create operatic "works" that were little more than artsy fartsy projects and could hardly be described as works of art. But this transformation didn't happen overnight. And along the way there were twentieth century operas that still tried to preserve some operatic dignity and decorum — and a fair amount of decent music.

Robert Ward's (born 1917) operatic version of Arthur Miller's *The Crucible*, which premiered at New York City Opera in 1961, while imperfect, was not without merit. The story concerns the Salem witch trials of 1692, compared by Miller to the McCarthy hearings of the 1950's. The score, occasionally verismo in style, consists primarily of melodious and melodramatic recitatives and ariosos. There is an attractive hymn, "Jesus, my consolation," in act one, and Elizabeth Procter's recitative-aria regarding her husband John and how he must free himself of (lover and ex-maid) Abigail, in act two. In act three the scene between angry John and still-loving Abigail almost turns into an anti-love duet (a la a duet in Puccini's *Edgar* where one party is in love/lust and the other is full of hatred), but only Abigail's early passages are lyrical. Judge Danforth's invocation "Open Thou my lips, O Lord," before the trial in the meeting house is not exactly the "Te Deum" from *Tosca* although it perhaps aspires to that effect, as many modern day pieces have. In act four black maid Tituba's aria "The Devil say he's coming," doesn't really fit the mood of the piece and sounds like it would be more at home in *Porgy and Bess*. The nice mini-duet between John and Elizabeth when John says he will "confess" to stay alive should have been a full-fledged duet. John Proctor's arioso "And there's your first marvel" as he refuses to buckle under and sign a confession leads into the powerful conclusion of the opera.

Ned Rorem's (born 1923) operatic version of August Strindberg's *Miss Julie* (1965), was commissioned by the New York City Opera and subsequently vanished. Little wonder, for Rorem betrays no particular skill as an operatic composer, although his adherence to tonality when such was unfashionable is not only admirable but courageous. Unfortunately, the music of *Miss Julie* is mostly dull and languid with inept vocal lines and poor orchestrations and does absolutely nothing for Strindberg's fine drama. The libretto by Kenward Elmslie is like a Cliff Notes version of the play. There are a few nice enough (if unmemorable) lyrical moments, but not enough of them, and clumsy orchestration usually undermines whatever limited melody there may be. In fact, much of the score is simply pitiful. The opera begins inauspiciously with obligatory dissonant strings and "banging" noises, which continues during, and completely mars, the opening chorus. Perhaps the best thing in the score is a duet, which is referred to as a "folk song," but is actually better than that. But it, too, is nothing outstanding.

Carlisle Floyd of *Susannah* fame remained very active throughout the sixties, seventies, and afterward. His memorable one-act *Markheim* (1966) is based on a story by Robert Louis Stevenson and takes place in London in 1880. A desperate man, Markheim, who has fallen from grace, murders an ornery pawnshop owner, Creach, who cruelly taunts him, whereas the devil appears to tempt Markheim into doing further evil, such as murdering Creach's maid to cover his tracks; after a great internal struggle, Markheim resists and faces his punishment. The character of Creach, who is not even named in the story, is developed much more by Floyd than by Stevenson. He is sanctimonious and nasty to Markheim more out of his own unpleasant and envious nature than out of sincere righteous indignation, and Markheim kills him as an act of passion, anger at his insults, as opposed to the calculated robbery-murder at the beginning of the story. This makes Markheim a bit more sympathetic and the victim less so. Despite the trite God versus Devil religious overtones, the opera is moving because at great cost Markheim chooses to do the right thing instead of murdering Creach's maid and getting away with the money. The opera ends with him crying out to the woman: "I have killed your master! Go call the police!" which is also how Stevenson's story concluded. Floyd reinvents the piece as a verismo-style opera — the music is intense and there is much exclamatory vocal writing — consisting largely of lyrical recitatives with occasional "aria"-like outbursts. The opening has a nice counterpoint of the Scrooge-like Josiah Creach shouting at carolers to "go away! I'll give you no money!" against the background of a typical carol. The highlights include Markheim's aria of regret and lost dreams ("And I hadn't known it was Christmas Eve") as he thinks back on his happy childhood and the life of poverty, degradation and decadence he has fallen into; Creach's "Here are all your treasures," as he points out all the family heirlooms Markheim pawned and never reclaimed, underlining the abyss he's descended into; and best of all the Stranger/Devil's "Please yourself!," in which he urges Markheim to give into every ultimate sin and then repent before death. It seems he is more interested in men doing evil during their lifetime than he is in gaining their immortal souls. *Markheim* is a very compelling piece.

Floyd's *Bilby's Doll* premiered in 1976 at Houston Grand Opera, and takes place in a Puritan colony in Massachusetts. Doll Bilby is a young woman who was brought over from France as a child by her foster father, Jared. Titus Thumb wants to marry Doll, but she rejects him, telling him that her parents were burned as witches and she may carry the same legacy. A man named Shad who claims he is a demon marries her instead in a profane ceremony. Jared's wife Hannah, who has always been jealous of Doll, condemns her as a witch and Doll is arrested. Titus again appeals to Doll to renounce her alleged heritage and marry him. The minister, Mr. Zelley, tells Doll that Shad is no demon, but his estranged mortal son. Initially shattered by this revelation, Doll returns to her delusions, and dies in childbirth.

If ever there were a prime example of American verismo, *Bilby's Doll* is it. There is as much, if not more, exclamatory vocal writing in the opera as there is in *Tosca*, and the music is at times not only strident but positively shrill (in a way that classic verismo rarely is, oddly enough). The music goes far beyond folk opera in its full orchestrations and sheer intensity, which is also a trademark of verismo. There is also a complement of tender, lyrical, and often highly dramatic arias, the most outstanding of which is Titus' proposal aria ("I picked these wildflowers on the way") with its soaring, exultant vocal line. (We know Doll must have some deep dark secret if she can resist such a rhapsodic proposal.) There is also some excellent music for the sequences involving Doll and her alleged demon-lover, such as the duet in which they vow to be faithful, which is at first a bit monotonous but eventually builds in power. Bilby and Hannah arguing over Doll is pure verismo, if less artful than the classic variety. Whatever its flaws, the opera is very skillfully done and has many effective and powerful passages, while in addition there are fascinating facets to its story.

Catherine Malfitano created the role of Doll in Houston. She told USOpera: Floyd "wrote these huge soliloquies that had long, extended vocal lines with much more disjunct intervals, that soared over a huge orchestral sound. It was highly dramatic.... There were some very sexy scenes with Jacque Trussel (Shad) that we played in body stockings. While this worked well from a distance, I remember a rather silly photo of us in one of the major magazines in which you could see the painted nipples and so forth."

Floyd's *of Mice and Men*, which premiered in 1970, may be the only serious competition for the composer's *Wuthering Heights* as far his masterpiece goes. This is a major work of American verismo with an occasional Mascagni-like intensity. Floyd did a fine job of adapting Steinbeck's classic novella for the stage, and his score boasts several memorable pieces. George is given two outstanding arias in act one: "My life would be so simple by myself," in which he thinks how much easier it would be for him if he didn't have Lennie to look after; and "One day soon we'll save up enough," about his dream for a farm to live at and keep and own — their own home; this becomes a duet with Lennie. Lennie is also given a nice piece in "It was somethin' I could stroke" about his pet mouse and his need for something to hold and love. Although it could be said that the music is perhaps too intense for the bit when he accidentally crushes the mouse, it could also be argued that this is a devastating moment for the simple-minded Lennie and the music reflects his emotional state. While the opera drops the compelling scene in the novel between George and the black man who lives by himself, a black ballad singer is given a creditable song of homesickness, "Movin' On." In act three Curley's wife and Lennie have an informal duet in the barn, leading to her piece "Now I'm heading straight for Hollywood," detailing her probably unrealistic dreams for the good life, success, and the attention she craves. Lennie accidentally kills her a moment later. This character is never known as anything other than "Curley's wife" and gets hardly any sympathy. While there is too much empty melodramatic music in this sequence, the prelude to scene two is legitimately powerful. There is a dramatically effective if morally problematic finale as George shoots the doomed Lennie to keep him from the tender mercies of the search party — any way you slice it, this ending packs quite a wallop. Whatever its flaws, *Of Mice and Men* is one of the few modern operas that can wring a tear from the audience.

Ironically, Floyd does not in any way see himself as a composer of verismo operas and fairly bristles at the thought. "I always protest," says Floyd, "because I am not a particular admirer of the so-called Verismo school, especially Mascagni. If, as Paul Henry Lang claimed, you consider *Carmen* the true verismo (small letter 'verismo') opera than I would happily agree that I write verismo operas. However I think that the reason writers term my operas as being verismo is really my choice of, and approach to, libretto subjects, and that stems from my being steeped in mid-twentieth century American dramatic writing. I was brought up with the plays of Williams, O'Neill, Inge, and Miller and that is my heritage. When I began writing operas I also felt that, to widen the audience for operas in this country, we had to create the kind of dramatic immediacy that people were accustomed to seeing on the stage as well as in films. That also happened to coincide with my own personal sympathies."[2]

Floyd may have grown up with the works of Williams and O'Neill, but he also began composing operas during a time when the musical establishment of this country was looking to the future not the past, and the last thing any American composer wanted to be associated with was the late nineteeth/early twentieth century verismo movement of Italy, especially as many of those composers were considered unfashionable, or worse, old-fashioned. Floyd is not alone in wanting to disassociate himself from verismo and in not realizing how closely some of his *music*— not just his choice of libretto — resembles verismo, for few American composers of his generation bothered to study it. This is not to say that Floyd was consciously or even unconsciously influenced by Mascagni or other veristi — he is probably not even that familiar with most of their work — but that in intensity and vocal declamation there is often a similarity to verismo music in certain of his scores, as noted.

This whole tiresome business of being scared of being labeled a verismo composer might go away if those music critics who liked verismo — and there are more of them than anyone imagines — would not only come out of the closet but drop the patronizing or apologetic tone they use when writing about these works. They fall over themselves reminding everyone of how "unfashionable" these composers are, only reinforcing the negative attitudes that drove them into the verismo closet — and made American composers of verismo so antsy — in the first place. Fashionable, unfashionable — who cares? If something works, it works. If it's a work of genuine flair or distinction or even genius, just say so and be done with it.

In addition to the operas discussed in this volume, Floyd is also the composer of *Willie Stark*—"it is the opera of mine that people bring up most frequently as wanting to see revived," says Floyd[3]— and, more recently, *Cold Sassy Tree*, which engendered a great deal of favorable comment. In November 2004 Floyd, whose works are continually represented on American stages more than any other American composer of opera, was awarded the National Medal of the Arts in a ceremony in the Oval office.[4]

Samuel Barber resurfaced in 1966 with his second full-length opera, *Antony and Cleopatra* from Shakespeare. Commissioned by the Metropolitan Opera, the work was chosen to be performed on the gala opening night of the Met's new house in Lincoln Center. This caused some consternation among those opera fans who felt a wiser choice could have been made from among the hundreds of classic operas that had been performed by the famous company. While *Antony and Cleopatra* is not as bad as legend would have it, the fact is that it hardly made for an auspicious opening of the new Metropolitan Opera House. Basically Barber composed what would have been a perfectly fine score for a motion picture based on Shakespeare's play. With the exception of a few scenes, Barber rarely gives this great romantic story the power and beauty that it deserves, but there is enough nice music in the opera to make it fairly interesting, and at times even compelling and haunting. As with *Vanessa*, the lush, romantic orchestrations almost hide the fact that the melodies aren't terribly special. The music for the first meeting of the title characters in scene one is much too languid and devoid of passion to be effective. In act two there is some exciting music behind the scene when Cleopatra demands to accompany Antony to war, but the love duet "Oh take, oh take those lips away," although it may aspire to be a latter-day "My Heart at thy sweet voice" from *Samson and Delilah*, is distinctly second-rate. Barber basically muffs the scene when Eros, Antony's sword bearer, kills himself instead of killing Antony, as Antony requested. This lack of inspiration in the score continues as Antony tries to kill himself, learns his Cleo is still alive, and so on; none of it is powerful or moving. But Barber is much more on target in act three, especially when Ceasar mourns over his fallen opponent and friend Antony's body, and the music is filled with the power and passion that it requires ("O Antony, I have followed thee to this"). There is a beautiful prelude to scene two, and the death-by-asp sequence is handled extremely well by Barber, with Cleo's "Give me my robe" aria even managing to be melodious. The opera ends with a powerful chorus derived from this aria. Act three's music was good enough to send most of the audience home happy.

A side trip to Broadway: Mitch Leigh's score for *Man of La Mancha* (1966) is so outstanding that it's one of the few latter-day musicals that is regularly presented by opera companies. Leigh was a student of Paul Hindemith and studied at the Yale School of Music; *Man of La Mancha* remains his greatest — and perhaps only — success. His later shows folded out of town for one reason or another, though it is unlikely that the scores were the problem. The libretto by Dale Wasserman skillfully blends the heartbreaking life of the real Cervantes with the story of his greatest work, *Don Quixote*; the framing device shows Cervantes in prison telling his companions the story as it unfolds on stage. Almost unbearably poignant, the play has genuine depth, reflected in the superb score, if you're in tune to what it's saying. The crazy, romantic actions of Don Quixote are not necessarily meant to be taken literally; if *Man of La Mancha* has a theme it is that "we all need our illusions," as Tennessee Williams once put it. *Man of La Mancha* is about the importance of those illusions, of fantasy and hope — even, and especially, when there is no hope. To some people Don Quixote is just a crazy old coot who won't face reality, but as a romantic symbol he has much more power. Highlights include Aldonza's "It's all the same," a bitter discourse on men and her miserable life; "The Golden Helmet of Mambrino," in which Don Quixote waxes about a common barber's shaving bowl that he sees as a magical object; and Aldonza's ballad "What do you want of me?" which she asks of Don Q (this was a late addition to the show). The title song is intensely dramatic and melodious (it becomes a duet with Sancho Panza); and "The Impossible Dream," detailing Don Quixote's mission in life, is a stunner; there haven't been enough bad singers doing inferior versions of the song to strip it of its power. "Knight of the woeful countenance" (during which Don Quixote is knighted) and "To Each His Dulcinea," in which the padre sings his understanding of what drives Don

Q, are also excellent numbers, as is "Aldanza's song" ("I was born in a ditch to a mother who left me there"), a powerful number that encapsulates the woman's belittling and sordid existence. Perhaps the finest piece in the score and one of the most beautiful show tunes ever is "Dulcinea," sung by Don Quixote about the "common kitchen slut" Aldanza whom he was reinvented as an untarnished, wonderful princess. Their relationship is the most moving in the show. While few of the numbers are genuinely operatic in the formal sense, the score is so compelling and holds up so well under operatic treatment that many opera singers, including Plácido Domingo, have performed and recorded *Man of La Mancha*.

Marvin David Levy's adaptation of Eugene O'Neill's *Mourning Becomes Elektra* premiered at the Metropolitan Opera in 1967, appeared there the following season, and then disappeared for three decades until it was revived by the Chicago Lyric Opera in 1998. In 2004 a notable production of it starring Lauren Flanigan was presented by New York City Opera. O'Neill's story (adapted by Henry Butler) is an updating of the tale of Elektra (Lavinia), Clytemnestra (Christine), Agamemnon (Ezra), and Orestes (Orin), with generous hints of brother-sister incestuous feelings thrown in for good measure. Christine murders her elderly husband after her lover Adam fails to do so, and her children get vengeance upon them both. Although *Mourning Becomes Elektra* had its champions from the first, few critics thought it a work of musical distinction. Over the years Levy fiddled with the score to imbue it with the lyricism that might have pleased some critics — and certainly the audience — and brought snickers from others addicted to modernism and atonalism. The new version of the opera is by far the best, although it still has its troubling aspects. For instance, one could still sleep through the entire first act and not miss anything of musical importance; there certainly isn't a melody to be heard (when one seems to appear it vanishes just as quickly, unsustained by Levy). And there are times when the opera comes off like nothing so much as a parody of verismo, with overwrought characters simply shouting at one another, the music bombastic and aimless, unrelated (in very un–verismo-like fashion) to what's happening on stage. But the music improves as the opera progresses — there are some genuinely dramatic and impressive moments — and such memorable pieces as Christine's "Adam, my love," the quartet "You bring the gift of love," and Lavinia's "It is I who need to speak," among others. By opera's end, one is pulled in by the fascination of the story and by music that often bolsters it, at least in a theatrical sense. But while listening to Levy's score, whatever its pleasures, one can not entirely shake loose the sensation that O'Neill's original play can really stand on its own and needs no embellishments, musical or otherwise.

The same may be true for O'Neill's drama *Desire Under the Elms*, but the operatic version by Edward Thomas, which premiered in Connecticut in 1978, is more successful. Thomas has committed what to some may be the unpardonable sin of writing genuine melodies and distinct arias in what is essentially a scaled down but romantic style, and *Desire Under the Elms* is all the better for it. The story deals with the conflict between father Ephraim Cabot and his son Eben, who hates the older man because of his mistreatment of his mother. Ephraim comes back to the farm with a new young bride, Abbie, about Eben's age, and before long the two younger people — initially distrustful and at odds — have become lovers. Ephraim is overjoyed when Abbie presents him with a son, not knowing that the child is really Eben's. When Eben comes to believe that the child is only meant to secure Abbie's hold on the property he covets, he threatens to leave. Thinking the child has come between them, Abbie smothers it in her sleep. Eben gets the sheriff, Ephraim finds out the truth, and orders his son off the farm. When the sheriff takes Abbie away, Eben says that he helped her kill the child, as he has no desire to live after her death.

Although *Desire Under the Elms* is the stuff of Grand Opera, Thomas' folk opera version, with help from librettist Joe Masteroff, does a fine job of bringing O'Neill's story and characters to life. While there are sections of the score which are uninspired or underdone, there are also many memorable moments. These include Eben's compelling aria "Oh, there's a star," in which he sings about the woman of easy virtue that he goes to see on a regular basis; and Abbie's "Ain't the sun strong?" during which she tries to kindle the passion she knows Eben feels for her, which becomes a notable duet. A trio in act two ("Stones — A-pickin stones") is excellent and theatrically effective, as Cabot gets lost in musings of the past while Abbie stands near the bedroom wall and tries to sense Eben on the other side even as he does the same. There are some rich, vibrant orchestral passages, such as when Ephraim appears just as Eben and Abbie finish arguing in act one. Ephraim is given some notable arias, such as "You be my Rose O'Sharon" which he sings about his new bride; and "My fist wife," in which he reviews his life and why he and his three sons hate one another. Ephraim is also given an effective monologue, "Down to the very last straw," in which he proclaims that he'd rather have everything he owns burn than wind up belonging to somebody else. Abbie's lullaby, "Sleep my son, sleep," is especially effective set off in counterpoint with the dance melody of the party's celebrants. The brief love duet that ends act two — Eben and Abbie at last give in to their passion — is disappointing in that it hardly reflects the utter sensual abandonment that the two are caught up in at the moment. To be fair to Thomas, *Desire Under the Elms* is not Italian verismo, although the story might make it seem so at times, and Thomas seems, perhaps unconsciously, to be striving for a raw veristic approach in certain sequences that may simply be alien to his musical nature. In any case, *Desire Under the Elms* is worthy of revival, more so than *Mourning Becomes Elektra*. Although Thomas calls it a "folk opera," there are moments in the score that are much richer and more powerful than that categorization might signify.

Native New Yorker Nicolas Flagello (1928–1994) was performing as a concert pianist — and composing music — before the age of ten. He studied at the Manhattan School of Music, and was a member of the faculty there until 1977. Flagello probably paid the price for writing music in the tradition of the great Italian romantic composers of the past, music which was not modern or dissonant or atonal enough to get him the attention of others who were less talented but more adept at composing along trendier lines. His *Piper of Hamelin* (1970), which seems quite influenced by Mascagni in some sections, is a case in point. The townspeople of Hamelin, besieged by rats, hire a piper to get rid of them, readily agreeing to his price, but after he does the job, they renege on the payment. In response, the piper uses his music to lure away their children. (The townspeople whine that they would have paid full price had they known what the piper would do, but it doesn't say much for them that they reneged in the first place.) Eventually the town and the piper come to an agreement, the children are returned, and all is well with the world. To bring the rat invasion to life, Flagello uses scurrying flutes and strings that are very effective without being too intense, this being a children's opera. The townspeople salute the piper after he says he'll rid the town of rats in the attractive chorus "Hail to the Piper!" There is a charming instrumental march of the rats and mice as they follow the piper out of town as he plays his pipe in act two. The Mascagnian intermezzo that begins act three is not bad but unfortunately it ends just as it starts to get really interesting. In the opera's most outstanding piece, the Piper explains that he is the "spirit of music" ("I am that which you cannot see"), which is immediately followed by a moving chorus of returning children reciting notes ("Sol sol la sol sol") as the townspeople sing their thanks to the piper in counterpoint ("We thank thee"). *The Piper of Hamelin*, while not on the level of *Amahl and the Night Visitors*, is nevertheless a charming piece that in a different world might have become a perennial. Flagello won much praise for his full-length 1982 opera *The Judgment of St. Francis*, which was produced in Assisi, Italy and which made full use of his expressive and melodic gifts.

Dominick Argento's (born 1927) song cycle *From the Diary of Virginia Woolf* won a Pulitzer Prize, and he also has written orchestral work and several operas, including *The Voyage of Edgar Allan Poe* (1975) and *The Aspern*

Papers (1988), which was telecast on PBS. His best-known opera is *Postcard from Morocco* which premiered in 1971 at the Minnesota Opera. *Postcard* presents a variety of people or types—"Lady with a Hat Box" "Man with Old Luggage" etc.—waiting and weirdly interacting at a train station. John Donahue's poetic but pretentious libretto suggests that their suitcases contain whatever they most wish to hide about themselves. The immaturity of the script pretty much compels the opera into being a collection of bits and pieces of interesting music with no real coherency. Among the more memorable musical moments are the foreign singer's smoky aria "Ooo, Conjoura sa malika," which is a kind of classical torch song, and Mr. Owen's (with chorus) climactic "I'm Captain of this Magic Ship." Argento creates an interesting piece entitled "Souvenirs de Bayreuth" using snatches of various great Wagner melodies as played by a shipboard honky-tonk band. While not a "great" aria as such, the Man with Old Luggage's "Well, I'd never buy new luggage" is strangely melancholic, an effect created not by the melody but by its string and clarinet background. Argento's music has a quirky appeal— he is a composer of undeniable ability—but the bad book makes the opera seem tiresome more often than not, unfortunately.

Although it, too, has an unusual libretto—written by the composer this time—Argento's one-act chamber opera *A Water Bird Talk*, (1981) in a theme, six variations, and coda, is much more successful. This short work, loosely based on a Chekhov story, presents a lecturer on water fowl who reveals more about himself and his family, loveless marriage, and general unhappiness than he ever does about birds. This is the story of a middle-aged man, bitterly disappointed in life, who breaks down during a "dull" lecture which turns out to be not so dull, and which even becomes a bit chilling as the lecturer cries out in anguish: "I want nothing at all! Not now! Not ever!" Argento's often tender and always compassionate music keeps what is essentially a lengthy monologue almost consistently absorbing and creates sympathy for the protagonist. (Of course, we don't hear his wife's side of things!) Variation II, the "Roseate Tern," has a delicate lyricism and some nice ariosos. Argento provides some lovely music that occasionally takes flight. Argento was born in Pennsylvania and studied at Baltimore's Peabody Conservatory, Rochester's Eastman School, and in Florence, Italy. He is one of the founders of Minnesota Opera, which was originally called the Center Opera Company.

Thea Musgrave was born in Scotland in 1928 but has lived in the United States since 1972 and can therefore be classified as an American composer. Some of her later operas were premiered at the Virginia Opera Company in Norfolk, with whom she has formed a happy alliance, being married to the director, Peter Bart. While she may never achieve a Puccinian level of popularity, and her scores are not especially melodious, her work has nevertheless become increasingly assured and effective since her first opera, *The Decision* in 1967. *The Voice of Ariadne* premiered at the Aldeburgh Festival in 1974, and then was performed at Lincoln Center three years later. The libretto by Amalia Elguera was taken from a Henry James short story. Count Valerio, who has invited guests to view the unearthing of a statue on his property, is disappointed to find only an empty pedestal inscribed with the name Ariadne, whom he hears calling to him. Listening to gossip from a jealous Marchesa, the countess fears that her husband has fallen for another as he becomes increasingly obsessed with "Ariadne." Mr. Lamb, who loves the countess from afar, advises her that there is a special kind of love that asks only for the beloved one's happiness. That evening the count, hearing Ariadne's voice in the distance, tries to call her to him, but to his surprise hears another voice also imploring Ariadne to fulfill his wishes. It is the countess, whose selflessly desires only her husband's complete fulfillment. The count realizes that his own wife is the fulfillment of his dreams, the true image of Ariadne, and the two are reunited in new love and understanding.

Musgrave responded to this most romantic of notions with music that is a far cry from romanticism in the classic sense, but plainly exhibits her theatrical flair and good (if non-melodious) vocal writing in a score that has both tonal and atonal portions. At times the music throbs with mysticism and at other times simply throbs. The more interesting passages include the Marchesa's sinister act two aria regarding her love rival, the Countess, and Valerio's act three musings on the effect of the mysterious missing statue. Musgrave pretty much muffs a grand opportunity to write a fine aria in the sequence when Mr. Lamb advises the countess to love selflessly (as he has obviously done), as the music is quite forgettable here, but she more than rises to the occasion with a quite lovely duet for the count and countess ("Together") in which they reaffirm their love and which brings the whole supernatural business full circle in a satisfying fashion.

The Voice of Ariadne received some respectful reviews, but *Newsweek* was off the mark when it claimed that the opera had "a rich melodic line," although it must be considered that the terms "melody" and "melodic" become highly subjective when it comes to many atonal and modern operas. Many opera-goers, especially those addicted to the works of classical, romantic composers, are utterly baffled when critics talk about melodies and "fine vocal writing" in pieces like *Voice of Ariadne* or, say, *Lizzie Borden*, works which they find mostly or absolutely devoid of great arias (and which, to their ears, sound more like background music or film scores). How can an opera have great vocal writing if there are no melodies? they ask. The answer is that there are different types of good vocal writing.

The best, of course, is for those bravura arias by the likes of Verdi and Puccini that so thrill the audiences when well sung in all the great opera houses of the world (and which many modern composers simply seem incapable of or at the very least disinterested in). But even non-melodious vocal writing can be effective at showcasing a particular voice or getting across an emotion or point of character. Some critics admire vocal writing, or *prosody*, that retains certain inflections of natural speech or a particular language, even though it may sound like nothing special to the typical opera fan. The London *Financial Times* critic felt that the score for *Voice of Ariadne* had a "rightness in matching of emotional pitch to actual tessitura, a sense of where in the voice to find a particular shade of feeling." (Of course Puccini and other composers could do just the same thing and also provide an honest-to-goodness melody.) None of this adds up to great melodies, however. And what good is polyphonic writing (employing more than one vocal or orchestral line at the same time), if each strand is unmemorable?

As said before, critics and composers nurtured in a modern and/or atonal idiom have no real sympathy or appreciation of romantic music (and they could argue, vice versa); hence an aria that may be quite mediocre to the average opera fan is "melodious" to them. What does the public prefer? The tens of thousands of worldwide stagings each year of works by Wagner, Verdi, Puccini, Floyd, Strauss, and so on as opposed to the limited productions of *Moses und Aron* and many other modern works, pretty much tells the story. But composers like Musgrave should not be dismissed too quickly. Sometimes there's method to their madness.

Musgrave's *Mary, Queen of Scots* was commissioned by Scottish Opera and had its world premiere at the Edinburg International festival in 1977. Musgrave also prepared the excellent libretto, based on the play "Moray" by Amalia Elguera. Mary's half-brother James (the Earl of Moray) and the soldier and advisor Bothwell are both jealous of the influence the handsome Darnley has on the queen. Mary marries Darnley, who proves a drunken wastral, and alienates both Bothwell and her brother, eventually banishing them both. Darnley believes vicious gossip that the queen is actually pregnant by court secretary Riccio, and murders him. James returns to seize the throne, and Mary unwisely calls on Bothwell to aid her, but he seduces her instead. The public turns on Mary, but as she flees the country, a loyal subject, Gordon, murders James; Mary's infant son will now be king.

Although many listeners may find it a mixed bag, *Mary, Queen of Scots* emerges as a highly effective piece of music theater in the Benjamin Britten mold. Musgrave adds flavoring to the score by incorporating several period songs and dances, while her own music ranges from almost jazzy background punctuation — shrill horns, banging drums, other weird effects that can't quite disguise a certain blandness — to wonderfully orchestrated sequences that serve to heighten the dramatic interest. Throughout the opera the music creates and sustains an almost palpable tension. Highlights include Darnley's semi-lyrical love arioso to Mary set to a 13th century French Dance Royale; the lively dance to William Dunbar's period song "Of a dance in the Queen's Chamber"; and Darnley and James' respective arias "I am born to be King" and "Now I shall rule!" in act two. The scene when Darnley breaks in and stabs Riccio is extremely well-handled. James speaks the words, "Mary, are you hurt" as the strings stir portentously behind him. The finale to act two, pitting Mary against her half-brother, is also riveting, as is the climax of act three, when the two siblings face each other for the final time. The opera packs a dramatic wallop largely because Musgrave's music, whatever its limitations, fills it with great vitality.

Musgrave's *A Christmas Carol* premiered in 1979. Among the highlights are when Scrooge's dead sister sings the pretty and spirited aria "Do you remember, little man?" taking him back to their childhood. A happy piece in which the singer invites people to celebrate ("Good day, a Merry Christmas to you all!") has poignant undertones, and leads into a delightful dance as he continues to sing and the celebrants laugh. With drums pounding in the background, Ebeneezer gives into a burst of passionate anger in the exciting "I can not bear it!" Scrooge is handed another dramatic outburst ("Spirit!") when he screams at the Ghost of the Future who is tormenting him. Bob's arioso about Tiny Tim, "As good as gold and better," is notable, as is an effective trio ("We are poor...") detailing a vision of the possible dismal future for the family. *A Christmas Carol* is a minor work, but a pleasant one that's easy to take. The scenes are handled with dramatic flair by Musgrave, though some might feel that the music is practically "incidental." There would be more interesting works from this composer in the 1990's.[5]

Another side trip to Broadway: Leonard Bernstein and Alan Jay Lerner (of Lerner and Loewe fame) teamed up for what should have been a triumphant theatrical experience in 1976 with the Broadway show *1600 Pennsylvania Avenue*, which took the audience through the upstairs-downstairs lives of various administrations in the white house, with vignettes of various presidential couples as well as of the domestic staff. Whatever problems there may have been with the libretto, musically speaking Bernstein was in top form. In fact, the main reason that *1600 Pennsylvania Avenue* is of note is because it illustrates that Bernstein saved his best music for his musical projects, not his operas, although there is much material of an operatic and semi-operatic nature in this show. The highlights include the bouncy, crowd-pleasing "Potomac River"; President Jefferson's snappy and amusing

"Sunday Luncheon Party March"; and the lovely romantic ballad "My Sweet Little Seena" sung by Lud about his wife. Their child, Little Lud, is given one of the finest numbers, "If I was a dove," a poignant lament against racial inequality. "I Love This Land," the patriotic ballad sung by the president and chorus at the end of the show (never does it suggest mindless patriotism) incorporates Bernstein's wonderful opening theme and rings poetically with its downbeat Coplandesque chords. Lucy Hayes is given a catty song, "First Lady of the Land," about the President and Mrs. Grant that is semi-operatic in structure, and "This fire," sung by Seena as she worries that Lud will run into trouble each time he leaves, is essentially a lyrical recitative that turns into an informal duet. The same is true of "Try to sleep," which features a troubled bedtime duet between James and Eliza Polk. The most outstanding — and most operatic — number in *1600 Pennsylvania Avenue* is the stunning "Take care of this house," as the First Lady sings to Lud that the white house and what it stands for is "the hope of us all." There are moments in the score that remind one of Loewe, Gershwin, Bernstein's own *Candide*, the aforementioned Copland, and even Massenet, but whatever Bernstein's influences, *1600 Pennsylvania Avenue* is one of his finest efforts.

If only that were the case with Bernstein's only full-length opera, *A Quiet Place*, which first surfaced in Houston in 1983, then, after revisions, played La Scala and Washington D.C.'s Kennedy Center in 1984; little has been heard of it since. *A Quiet Place* began life as the excellent 1952 one-act pop/jazz opera *Trouble in Tahiti*, which examined the lives of a husband and wife, Sam and Dinah, who have drifted apart and have trouble communicating, suffering from what eventually became known as "suburban malaise." The title refers to a typically silly technicolor musical of the period that Dinah goes to see one afternoon, then again at the end of the opera with her husband. *A Quiet Place* is both an expansion of and sequel to *Tahiti*, and opens with Dinah's funeral after she has been killed in a car accident. All of the scenes from *Tahiti* are incorporated into *A Quiet Place* as flashbacks. Bernstein himself wrote the book for these scenes, while Stephen Wadsworth contributed the rest of the libretto. Added characters include Sam and Dinah's now-grown son, Junior, his sister Dede, and her bisexual husband Francois, who was originally Junior's lover (and may still be) before moving on to his sister. The touching if bizarre premise apparently has Francois and Dede marrying out of mutual love for Junior, who is emotionally disturbed and somewhat helpless (although it's a question if Francois' falling for his sister might have exacerbated or even engendered Junior's instability). At one point, after reminding Francois how they met in a gay bar, Junior tells him that he, Junior, and Dede are not really brother and sister and have repeatedly had sex, which is probably a crazy delusion of his. The plot is very American in its sophistication; unfortunately Wadsworth's libretto, meant to be profound, is instead arch, pretentious, and borderline campy, a black comedy fraught with phony "significance." It presents a "fucked up" family but doesn't really explore their psyches with any depth.

The opera begins with the tiresome dissonances and percussion effects that seemed almost de rigueur for some trendy American composers during this period. Sam's long aria, "You're late," in which he berates his children at his wife's funeral is a big, blathery mess that would remind one of Broadway if it only had a melody. This is followed up by an unmemorable trio wherein the two children (and their shared male lover) sing about their father's neglect. Junior's sarcastic "Hey, Big Daddy" is a standard jazz number in which he blames Sam for Dinah's death. Only the orchestral music at the end of act one is mildly memorable. Scene two of the second act consists of the first half of *Trouble in Tahiti*, and contains the two most outstanding pieces from that opera (and subsequently from *A Quiet Place*). The first is Dinah's "I was standing in a Garden/There is a garden," in which she sings of a mystery lover and dream prince, originally Sam. This lovely aria is full of romantic regret and disappointment and severe dissatisfaction with life as well as a fear of what the future might hold. At one point Dinah sings "then love will leads us to a quiet place," giving the sequel its title. This is followed by a duet for Dinah and Sam ("Why did I have to lie/Long ago") in which they sing of how once upon a time they meant so much to each other and now don't even want to have lunch together (each has made up an excuse to get out of it). In scene three we're briefly back to the present day and an acceptable if second-rate aria for Francois ("I've been afraid") in which he makes his true commitment to his wife, Dede, and avows his love for her. Scene four presents the second half of *Tahiti*, and features two unusual and compelling pieces for Sam and Dinah. In the sharp, energetic "There's a law," Sam sings about how there are winners and losers in life; this is a bright, attractive Broadway-style number with a certain operatic intensity. (Dinah's "There is a garden" is briefly interrupted by the "winner" music from this song, suggesting that Dinah desperately needs to escape from Sam's constant ambition and self-absorption.) Equally entertaining — and just as much a Broadway number — is Dinah's "What a movie!" in which she rants about the "technicolor twaddle" *Trouble in Tahiti*, an amusing spoof of MGM's moronic south sea island musicals. Act three returns to the present day. The opera ends on a touching note as the four troubled characters reach out to one another and try to come to an understanding of each other's weaknesses. Junior's aria "You see, Daddy," movingly illustrates his mental unstableness as he reaches out for (and receives) closeness from his father. (One can't help but recall that neither Dinah nor Sam, who argue early in *Tahiti* over who will go see Junior perform in his school play, ever do show up at the school.) Not a "great" aria as such, but poignant and effective. However, a poignant five minute wind up does not make up for the mediocrity of most of *A Quiet Place* in both libretto and music. Oddly, Bernstein handles the recitatives well in *Tahiti* but the recitatives are fairly wretched in the sequel. It was as if in trying to write "serious" material Bernstein forgot everything he knew about crafting good music. *Trouble in Tahiti*, a tuneful and notable study of people who are living the American dream and who still aren't happy, lives and breathes; *A Quiet Place*, despite its fascinating psychosexual additions, dies stillborn.

At the opposite end of the spectrum from *Trouble in Tahiti*, *1600 Pennsylvania Avenue*— and indeed everything else, which may be its only *raison d'etre*— lie the minimalist operas of Philip Glass (born 1937) the first of which was *Einstein on the Beach* (1976). He followed this up with *Satyagraha* (1980) and *Akhnaten* (1984) to form a trilogy of works tied to historical figures, but more interested in alleged ideas than drama. These operas have no real plot. Glass also based an opera on Poe's *The Fall of the House of Usher,* which was almost universally excoriated. However, in certain outré circles his work became popular enough for Glass to win a commission from the Metropolitan, which startled many. The result was *The Voyage*, which premiered in 1992. (According to Elise K. Kirk in her book *American Opera*, Glass received more money "in today's currency" for composing *The Voyage* than Verdi did for *Aida*!)

Most of Glass' work (ironically his score for the horror film *Candyman* is rather good) is kitschy, deliberately repetitive, and monotonous. *Einstein on the Beach* consists of very long sequences of sounds that go on at great length without the slightest variation. It is no surprise that Glass' collaborator on this and other ventures was director Robert Wilson, who has done more to singlehandedly schlock up operatic productions (shamefully at major venues like the Met and elsewhere) than perhaps any other untalented individual. To be fair to *Einstein* it is in no way a traditional opera, but more akin to ballet, with a chorus, actors, and especially dancers on stage performing various movements. To divorce the music from the action makes little sense (true of a great many modern operas) but a recording of *Einstein* was nevertheless released. It is hard to imagine anyone achieving any pleasure from listening to it for any length of time.

Wilson and Glass and their sycophants of course see them as serious artists willing to try new things and experimental forms regardless of whatever criticism they may get, and one supposes they should be given credit for that. But after a time an intelligent and gifted artist will see that something isn't working (not just for the public at large) or is vastly inferior to the already established forms. Glass and Wilson talk about "the changing face of opera," which they spearhead, but not only is it unlikely that the works of Glass will ever achieve the popularity or critical status of operas by Verdi, Wagner, Puccini, etc., but that they will even enter the repertory of any major or minor company. According to *New York* Magazine's Peter G. Davis, Glass' music was "for an audience more accustomed to using its eyes than its ears ... designed to avoid the sort of listener concentration demanded by traditional opera. Since the easily digested repetitive rhythmic patterns and accessible harmonic formulas of minimalism posed no problems to a generation reared on rock's simple beats and uncomplicated chord progressions, Glass and his imitators made capital from a musical language that would lurk subserviently in the background." Unfortunately, Glass and his proponents could not be disposed of that easily.

Henry Mollicone, a graduate of the New England Conservatory, was a musical assistant for *1600 Pennsylvania Avenue* and is associate director of the Ernest (*Macbeth*) Bloch music festival in Newport, Oregon. His full length opera *Hotel Eden* premiered in San Jose in 1989, and he has also composed a number of one-acts. These include the frequently performed *The Face on the Barroom Floor* (1978). In this piece a long-ago tragedy about a woman who was accidentally shot when two men fought over her is repeated in the present day when a discussion ensues over how a beautiful woman's face (the same woman shot in the past) wound up painted on the floor of a barroom (the woman's lover did the painting as barter). A trio of singers play two roles apiece, acting out both modern-day and long-ago stories. This modern, less intense verismo piece is very nicely done, with highly lyrical and well-orchestrated music as well as admirable vocal lines. Highlights include Madeline's aria "He came to the west to find fame and gold," a song about young star-crossed lovers with an effective accompaniment of flute, piano and violin; Larry's mock dance/aria "The face on the barroom floor"; and a lovely trio for Madeline, John and Matt singing about the portrait as Matt paints it on the floor ("He paints the portrait of his love.") *The Face on the Barroom Floor* is different and decidedly appealing. Mollicone would do more operas in the nineties.

Stephen Sondheim grew up a child of money and privilege and had the great good fortune of being nestled in the bosom of the family of Oscar Hammerstein of Rodgers and Hammerstein fame. This, of course, led to an association — and eventual collaboration — with Richard Rodgers (Sondheim wrote the lyrics for Rodgers' *Do I Hear a Waltz?* after the death of Hammerstein). Connections may have started Sondheim off on his career at a fairly early age, but luckily he had the talent to survive and prosper. Sondheim is reportedly not a big opera fan, but his favorites include Puccini,

Porgy and Bess, Britten, *Pelléas et Mélisande* and *Wozzeck*. Probably Sondheim's greatest work is *Sweeney Todd*, which premiered in 1979. It is undoubtedly his most operatic score, with genuine arias, duets, quartets and so on. It has as much lust, bloodshed and irony as any verismo opera, and an excellent, well-constructed libretto by Hugh Wheeler. The anti-hero of the story, who takes the name Sweeney Todd, has come back to London to gain vengeance on the corrupt judge who coveted his wife and had him sent to prison. Now the wife is dead, according to old acquaintance Mrs. Lovett, and this judge wants to marry Todd's daughter, Johanna. Todd sets up a barber business above Mrs. Lovett's meat pie shoppe. When he just misses a golden opportunity to slit the judge's throat as he sits in his barber chair, Todd goes crazy and begins murdering most of his customers. Good meat being scarce, Mrs. Lovett decides to use the corpses in her meat pies, which attract a lot of new business. (Todd only begins killing innocents after she comes up with her grisly idea.) Mrs. Lovett sort of adopts a little boy named Toby who wants to protect her, and Todd's young sailor friend Anthony finds and falls in love with Johanna. Todd finally manages to kill the judge, but also murders a filthy beggar who turns out to be his wife, not dead after all. After throwing Mrs. Lovett in an oven for lying to him, Todd is killed by a vengeful Toby. As in many an opera, much of the cast (aside from the young lovers) are dead by the end of the story. It could be argued that *Sweeney Todd* is a bit too cold-blooded and borderline campy at times, and that one loses all sympathy for the title character once his obscene killing spree begins, but *Sweeney Todd* at least gets major points for originality. There really is no other musical — or opera — quite like it.

As for the music, Sondheim's score is consistently melodious and inventive. The orchestrations by Jonathan Tunick are so perfect and adept that Tunick can practically be considered the co-composer of not only *Sweeney Todd* but the other musicals he worked on with Sondheim. Among the more memorable pieces are Johanna's wistful aria "Green Finch and Linnet Bird," reflecting her feeling of entrapment; the "Pretty Women" duet sung by Todd and the judge as the latter gets prettied up in anticipation of a marriage with the former's nubile daughter; and "Pirelli's Miracle Elixir," the closest thing to a brindisi as Toby touts his master Pirelli's liquid cure-all. Joanna and Anthony are given a fairly nice duet in "Kiss Me" but it doesn't compare to Anthony's love aria to "Johanna," one of Sondheim's most haunting and lovely compositions. This song is reprised in act two in a bizarre contrapuntal quartet as Todd first sings his own, alternate version of the song as he slashes the throats of his customers, the sound of their bodies being dumped down a shoot (the barber chair conveniently tips backward over a trapdoor) providing an effective punctuation — similar to the whoosh of the guillotine blade dropping at the end of *Dialogues of the Carmelites*. To complete the quartet the hag (Mrs. Todd) sings a hyper-dramatic "City on Fire" and Johanna comes in with a reprise of "Kiss Me." The celebration of the success of "Mrs. Lovett's Meat Pies" sung by Toby, the customers, and the gorgon herself, is another quasi-brindisi, a reworking of "Miracle Elixir." Two of the opera's best pieces are very different in tone. "We all deserve to die," which Todd sings after the judge escapes his wrath, is a powerful and chilling outcry of rage and insanity, while the light-hearted, hilarious "A Little Priest" details the results of both as Todd and Lovett make jokes — Sondheim's skill with lyrics are displayed at their best here — about the meat pies and how they taste according to the professions of the men whose flesh they are comprised of. "By the sea," which Mrs. Lovett sings to Sweeney as a sort of seduction attempt, dreaming of the life they could have together, is an okay Broadway-type number, which is also true of Toby's "Not while I'm around," his love song to his mother figure Mrs. Lovett, although the boy's being such a pathetic, trusting figure gives it an added poignancy, and its melody is quite nice. The song adds a touch of manipulative but welcome humanism to the terrible story. (There is no attempt to generate pathos over Todd's many innocent victims.) We can tell what Mrs. Lovett thinks of the child when she responds "what a sweet, affectionate child it is." When Toby kills Todd one might wonder if the child was as "sweet" as all that, but a boy locked in a basement with a lot of dead bodies and, presumably, body parts is entitled to go a little crazy. Sondheim and Wheeler are not interested in creating a tear-jerker, so the audience is not moved by *Sweeney Todd* until perhaps later when they have time to think about that lonely little boy and the miserable life he faces, probably a worse fate than the little boy in *Wozzeck*.

Although Sondheim's *Sunday in the Park with George* (1984), is considered by some to be closer to an opera than *Sweeney Todd,* due to its many recitative-like passages, it is a much less successful work. It deals with the painter Georges Seurat and his obsessing on his famous piece *A Sunday Afternoon on the Island of La Grande Jatte* to the exclusion of all else, including personal relationships. Never has Sondheim's own obsession with the musical device of repetition, employed in all of his scores, been more in evidence. Despite unusual and interesting moments in the idea and in James Lapine's libretto, the mostly forgettable music sinks *George* almost from the start. This was not the case with Sondheim's next work, the fascinating *Into the Woods* (1987). The idea of this is to take several familiar fairy tales (with one new one added), intermingle them so that they take place at the same time in the same woods, give them a happy ending for act one, and then in act two show that the characters of these stories did not necessarily live "happily ever after." The woods is meant to be life and the uncertain journey we take through it, while the giants the cast encounter are metaphors for life's unexpected disasters. Sondheim's lyrics are rife with double-entendres. Some of the tunes are very pleasant indeed — Jack's dirge for his cow ("Goodbye Old Pal"); Goldilocks' "And he showed me things," in which the wolf sounds like a pedophile — and at least two are prime Sondheim: "Agony," wherein two married men sing about the charms of Cinderella and imprisoned Rapunzel; and the poignant final number "No One is Alone." The witch's "Children Won't Listen" ("children can only grow from something you love to something you lose") is an aria that would have more impact if delivered by a genuinely operatic voice.

Although it had been composed some decades before, mostly during the mid-forties, Bernard Herrmann's operatic version of *Wuthering Heights* premiered in Portland in 1982. Then as now Herrmann is best known as one of the premiere film composers in Hollywood. Because of his association with Alfred Hitchcock and his excellent scores for *North by Northwest*, *Vertigo*, and *Psycho*,[6] as well as for such fantasy films as *Jason and the Argonauts* and *Journey to the Center of the Earth*, Herrmann was generally not seen as a composer of romantic music in the vein of Max Steiner or Erich Wolfgang Korngold. His music may have had a more "modern" sound to it, but in his early days in Hollywood he scored a number of romantic movies and proved as deft at that as he did at scoring thrillers and fantastic films.

The libretto for Herrmann's opera was written by his wife at the time, playwright Lucille (*Sorry, Wrong Number*) Fletcher. Wisely, only the first half of Bronte's masterpiece is covered. The opera begins with the literally haunting three note theme (in Herrmann's usual tortured woodwinds and strings) that is meant to represent the undying love of Cathy and Heathcliff. Then there are some effective, dissonant "horror movie" chords for the prologue, in which Heathcliff's tenant Lockwood ventures to Wuthering Heights and has his ghostly experience with the dead Catherine. The music for the prologue is bleak but lyrical, with Lockwood given two pretty if downbeat ariosos. After Lockwood tells him of his supernatural close encounter, Heathcliff sings the dramatic aria "Oh, Cathy, come in!"

Much of the music of act one is very reminiscent of Frederick Delius, who himself had contemplated composing an opera based on *Wuthering Heights*. The recitatives are generally melodious; although some are merely serviceable. Act one contains the opera's major piece, a duet between young Cathy and Heathcliff ("On the Moors") which creates in musical terms the special magical feeling that the moors engender in the couple. After the duet proper comes an orchestral piece — a ravishing nocturne of horn, harp and woodwinds that is one of the finest pieces ever composed by Herrmann — that contains the main love theme of Cathy and Heathcliff. (It is heard again at the end of the lovely prelude to the opera's final encounter between Heathcliff and the living Catherine, and is the background music for Cathy's third act aria.) This is the same music that Herrmann used as the theme for the film *The Ghost and Mrs. Muir* in 1947. Herrmann began working on the opera three years before this film came out, and it is highly unlikely that he wrote this music specifically for the film and then simply "lifted" it for the opera; rather the other way around. While *The Ghost and Mrs. Muir* is a lovely, charming picture, bolstered by the superb Herrmann score, the depth and richness of the music indicates that the theme was originally written for the dark love story of Cathy and Heathcliff, not the much lighter romance of the dead sea captain and Mrs. Muir. The supernatural aspects of the latter tale is probably what encouraged Herrmann to use the music for the film; probably he felt his opera might never see the light of day and indeed it wasn't staged until after his death, although he himself conducted a complete recording of the work in 1966. Herrmann also used some music from the opera as the love theme for the film *Jane Eyre* (1944) with Orson Welles and Joan Fontaine. This music, in altered form, is first heard behind Cathy's opening aria in act one ("I have been wandering") and the informal duet that follows and also plays in the background of Cathy's act two aria in which she recognizes, after marrying Edgar, that Heathcliff still has a hold over her heart, body and soul.

Not all of the music in *Wuthering Heights* was recycled by Herrmann. Edgar is given a very pretty love song to Cathy in act two, as is Isabella (to Heathcliff), who warbles "Love is like a wild rose branch, friendship like the olive tree," the music of which has something of the awe she feels for Heathcliff. Isabella is also given two dramatic solos in the third act: "How I love it," referring to the home she left as she compares it to the horror of living at Wuthering Heights with Heathcliff, and "Heathcliff, I love you," which is an outcry of her tortured, conflicted feelings for the man she married. Heathcliff is given his own outcry in act three, "Catherine Earnshaw, you shall not rest as long as I am living." Even the lighter pieces in the opera, such as a chorus of carolers in act one, have a downbeat, poignant undertone that perfectly reflects the mood and atmosphere of the story.

The final scene is extremely effective even though Herrmann and Fletcher decided to stretch it out quite a bit. We hear that haunting three note theme again, then a sepulcher voice against the wind. There is a reprise of Heathcliff's "Oh Cathy, come in!" Then those ghostly notes are repeated, the soft, fading voice of Cathy, Heathcliff crying out, repeated and repeated, each time softer and lower until the opera ends with a final soothing chord that seems to offer some measure of comfort to the audience if not to Heath-cliff. This ending — the whole story of *Wuthering Heights*— does not speak of "horror" but of pain. And that pain is brilliantly captured in Herrmann's wonderful music.

Herrmann accused Aaron Copland of plagiarizing his score for the film *The Devil and Daniel Webster* (1941) for Copland's *Lincoln Portrait*, which debuted in 1942, but both men admired each other's music.

William Mayer (born 1925), a Yale graduate who trained at Juilliard, is responsible for the opera *One Christmas Long Ago* and many orchestral works, with musical influences ranging from Bartók and Barber to Stravinsky and Kern. His best-known work is *A Death in the Family*, from James Agee's novel, which premiered at Minnesota Opera in 1983. The story, which is steeped in loneliness, obsession with the past, and aging, examines the effect of the unexpected death of a man, Jay, on his family, especially his wife, Mary, and young son, Rufus. Bayer gets points for a sensitive, often lyri-cal, occasionally Coplandesque score, which contains some pastiches of gospel songs and folk tunes, but there is also a lot of flat, uninspired vocal writing and recitatives; the skillfully done libretto, also by Bayer, helps turn the work into a rather good, if flawed, piece of music theater, however. One of the best and most moving sequences occurs near the end of act one, with little Rufus interacting with the old, senile grandmother, and the highlight of the score is a near-duet between Mary and Jay ("But when two people love as we do") in which they sing of the gulf in their marriage that they are sure their love will diminish. In an appropriate touch, Mayer has the couple sing a supposedly "existing" song to each other instead of a bona fide love duet. (Mary says that the tune is from an "operetta.") In the first scene of act three the music gets across Mary's anxiety as she waits for word of Jay's condition after she learns he's been in a traffic accident, but it isn't mov-ing, and the sequence when she learns the terrible truth from her brother Andrew isn't very well-handled. The prayer ensemble that follows ("Who shall tell the sorrow") doesn't quite work and goes on for too long. Mary's arioso "And what if he was drunk?," in which she hopes that Jay died happy as he rushed home to his family, is okay, but it's tantalizing to think what other composers could have done with the same material. While *Fanfare* claimed that Andrew's "butterfly aria," ("There were a lot of clouds"), in which he describes how a butterfly landed on Jay's coffin, is "touching, mes-merizing music," it's actually very minor and forgettable. Despite all these problems, *A Death in the Family* works, but not as well as one might have hoped for.

Anthony Davis was born in Paterson, New Jersey, in 1951 and studied at Wesleyan and Yale; in 1992 he became Professor of Music in Afro-

American Studies at Harvard University. He is best known for his 1986 work *X: The Life and Times of Malcolm X. X* is an "opera" about the life of controversial civil rights activist Malcolm X, showing some of the experiences that shaped his attitudes and convictions. Davis starts the work off with a jazzy "film score" type overture, and much of the score sounds like jazzed up gospel revival stuff, pop/rock music with classical pretensions. Scat, rap, even "mystical" music is thrown into the mix. While some of this is perfectly effective in a theatrical — and even a musical (if rarely "operatic")— sense, much of the score is simply monotonous, uninspired and dull. The aria Malcolm sings when he's in jail ("I would not tell you what I know") is typical "horror movie" music, derivative and forgettable. Malcolm's sister Ella's song "My Side of Town" is snappy but also derivative. However, in act two, the prisoners' chorus with oboe background ("In the Devil's Grip") is rather compelling, although it isn't long until we're back to the blather. Some moments are a bit more lyrical than most of the score, such as the informal duet for Malcolm and his brother Reginald, "Your past was stolen," and Elijah's "An X you must claim" is quite pleasant. The "We are a Nation" chorus is melodious and dark. Like a film score, the music at the end of the opera creates suspense and tension in the moments leading up to Malcolm's murder. The libretto is imperfect, although it does try to cover a lot of material in interesting fashion. *X* is all right as a theatrical event or (biased) historical document, but as an opera it's all too weak. More because of its subject matter and political ramifications than its music, *X* became the third-best-attended production at New York City Opera in the fifty years since it opened its doors. Clearly encouraged by this development, Davis came out with a "science fiction opera," *Under the Double Moon* (1989) as well as *Amistad* in 1997, and other works as well.

During all this operatic flux and flow in America, the composers of Europe were not standing still, and opera-goers in other countries found themselves with the same almost alarming assortment of musical styles as more and more opera houses filled with people who had little true interest in hearing scores of distinction.

But the traditionalists were not about to lie down and die.

14. Kitchen Sink International: Europe, 1951–1990

In Italy, Ildebrando Pizzetti (1880–1968) was determined not to follow blindly in the footsteps of other Italian composers like Puccini and Mascagni (although to a certain extent he wound up being influenced by them, especially the latter, nevertheless), and initially wrote operas in which carefully wrought recitative took precedence over any lyricism. Pizetti did a version of *Romeo and Juliet* around the turn of the century which was later destroyed, and had a major success with *Fedra*, which also premiered at La Scala, in 1915. Pizzetti did several more operas of varying degrees of success, which is why he may have eventually fallen back on a more traditional type of Italian scoring.

Pizzetti's *Assassinio nella cattedrale/Murder in the Cathedral* from T.S. Eliot's play about the death of Thomas Becket, premiered at La Scala in 1958; in a way it was considered his comeback. Although Pizetti wasn't really known as a verismo composer as such — and the subject matter of *Assassinio* is hardly veristic — the Mascagni/verismo influence is clear in this work, which, as mentioned, came late in the composer's career.

Assassinio, understandably, has a very dark score, beginning with a sinister, suspenseful overture that pulls you into the action. While some of the music is uninspired, there is very effective choral writing but no set arias in act one until Becket delivers an outstanding piece ("Signore, noi non siam state felici") in which he reacts to four temptations delivered by men who have come to his study to ensnare him. Bookended by Becket's notable Christmas sermon ("Figli cari di Dio") is an attractive intermezzo. Other highlights include the soprano aria "Neppur' oggi" and a sensitive, contrastingly delicate final chorus. Pizzetti admirers suggest that *Debora e Jaele* (1922), based on a biblical story, is more typical of Pizzetti and probably his greatest work, but *Assassinio* remains his best-known. Decidedly in the romantic Italian tradition, its very virtues are what doomed it to comparative obscurity after its initially successful run. Today Pizetti is all but forgotten outside of Italy.

The "concept" opera as typified by the works of Philip Glass and Robert Wilson was alive and well in Europe, notably in the works of Luciano Berio (born 1925). Berio's best known work, *Un re in ascolto/A King Listens* (1984), is one of those modern operas that really doesn't make much of an impression unless it's seen in the theater. The work contains some effective choral writing, as well as some arresting and occasionally attractive background music — it resembles a film score with singing and is not bad on those terms. In other words, Berio has come up with a good, even at times exciting and compelling soundtrack, if not an opera (Berio himself refers to it as "a musical action."). The music is not without melody (albeit of the synthetic, unmemorable variety) and it positively strains for lurid emotion. Some listeners will find it hard to get past the opening sequence, wherein everyone on stage sings at once not in harmony but in total discord, resulting in a chaos that quickly becomes, as does the opera itself, monotonous.

The piece has its defenders, however. Patrick J. Smith of *Opera News* judged it a "vital, moving exploration of an impresario's last moments, surrounded by his creations and memories.... There is an inevitability here that finally gives *Un re in ascolto* its stature as one of the more important operas of the past quarter-century." The general opinion of Berio, however, is that he is a kitschmeister who's work is of little lasting importance.

Spain and South America. Although he had passed away in 1946 Manuel De Falla — or at least his music — resurfaced in 1961 with the premiere of his scenic cantata or oratorio *Atlántida* at a concert in Barcelona. (The following year it was presented at La Scala.) De Falla worked on the score of this for almost twenty years, and it was still unfinished upon his death; Ernesto Halffter completed the score. De Falla fashioned his own libretto from a poem by Jacinto Verdaguer. The story mixes together everything from the boy Christopher Columbus to the lost continent of Atlantis, to the Great Flood to Hercules, three-headed monsters and dragons, and ends with the grown-up Columbus' voyage to the New World. Little of the incredible mythological action is reflected in the music, which completely lacks the excitement and sense of wonder that the convoluted story calls for. Mostly the chorus simply sings about events, in music that is lyrical but generally of little distinction. The Hymnus Hispanicus that opens the piece has a beautiful and compelling theme, however, and Queen Isabella is given a sweet and memorable aria in part three. The music is occasionally reminiscent of Martinů. There are sporadic moments of interest in the score, but not enough to be stretched out over eighty minutes. Lacking the energy and variety of Orff's *Carmina Burana*, it is unlikely that *Atlántida* will ever rival that work's popular appeal.

Alberto Ginastera (1916–1983) made a reputation for himself in his native Argentina with two ballets in the 1940's. Twenty years later he was getting attention with his operas, especially *Bomarzo* (1967), which premiered in Washington, D.C. The opera was not a good bet to become a permanent part of the repertory because of its essential atonality. The opera follows the life of Pier Francesco, The Duke of Bomarzo, who is a hunchback, from his tormented childhood until his death at the hands of his nephew. In between the Duke kills his brother because he believes he was intimate with his wife. The Duke is a sympathetic figure up until the time of the murder. At the time of the premiere Ginastera proclaimed, "I see Bomarzo not as a man of the Renaissance, but as a man of our time. We live nowadays in an age of anxiety, an age of sex, an age of violence. Bomarzo struggles with sex, submits to violence, and is tormented by anxiety, the meta-physical anxiety of death." Ginastera felt it necessary to defend what some saw as the excesses of what was being called "the topless opera." Four dancers resigned from the production due to the orgy ballet at the end, prompting choreographer Jack Cole to say "I can only conclude they come from strange households" and conductor Julius Rudel to declare "You can't be square about this opera." The mayor of Buenos Aires canceled the premiere at the Teatro Colón because he deemed the opera "unfit for showing."[1]

Some of the controversy was over the opera's homosexual content, which consisted only of the Duke's intimation that his black slave might love him in more than the platonic sense. Later the Duke kisses the statue of the minotaur on the lips because he thinks of the disfigured monster as a soul mate and therefore his only possible "lover." All of the brouhaha over the sexual content of the opera may have obscured the fact that the only thing truly controversial about it was the music. The largely inaccessible score would not drag in disgruntled opera patrons, but the nudity might. Stripped of all the publicity, *Bomarzo* emerged simply as an excellent piece of music theater with a score that few people would ever want to hear again, and certainly not if it was divorced from the spectacle on stage.

The overture is as full of tiresome "sound effects" as it is music, although the orchestra is cleverly used to achieve these effects. There's a certain charm to the song of the shepherd boy in scene one, much of it supplied by the sweet voice of the boy soprano. As the boy declares he would not change places with the wealthy hunchbacked duke we hear the duke's own musings on his life and times. We hear this song again at the end of scene seven when it is incorporated into an interesting horn and percussion dance called the "Galliard," which builds into some of the more memorable music in the score. The courtesan Pantasilea's song ("Ninguna ciudad del mundo") is almost a parody of an Italian aria, comically lacking in romance and melody, yet it's repeated four times and never gets any better. The staging of scene four (as described in the libretto) is especially good, however. Pier Francesco's self-consciousness about his hump is dramatically magnified by having actors with humps act as his image seen in mirrors all over the courtesan's room. They writhe and grimace as his discomfiture increases. Repulsed by himself, he rejects Pantasilea's advances.

In scene six a very creditable, well-orchestrated chorus ("Rox gloriae") attends the ceremony in which Pier Francesco is proclaimed the Duke of Bomarzo. The best thing in the opera, it owes something to the famous coronation sequence in Mussorgsky's *Boris Gudonov*. In scene eight Ginastera muffs the opportunity to write a great aria (which may have been beyond his talents) as Pier Francesco delivers an ode to his new-won confidence and vanity to a portrait of himself; except for some mild incidental music in the background, Ginastera doesn't even set the speech to music. Scene eleven's dream-orgy music is so undistinguished that it is presumed the naked bodies on the stage kept the audience from noticing it. The vocal music for the Duke, while it produces no great arias or any genuinely memorable music, does encapsulate in emotional and dramatic terms his despair over his life and deformity. All of this results in good theater but not great opera, although there were critics who fell all over themselves to be hip about the "topless opera." In some ways *Bomarzo* was superior to *Wozzeck*, with which it had many similarities.

Opined *Saturday Review*: "With his superb feeling for orchestral textures and instrumental scoring, what emerges is music of strength, character and dramatic impact." In other words: good theater. *Time's* music critic wrote that "there can be no doubt that Ginestera has powerfully achieved his effects, combining orchestral wizardry and forceful vocal writing to carve out the contours of jarringly dramatic emotion." On this the critic was accurate, but the very same thing could have been said of, say, Puccini and Wagner, whose music had the additional quality of being something you would actually want to listen to over and over and over again.

Francis Poulenc (1899–1963) was born and died in Paris. His most famous opera, *Dialogues of the Carmelites*, premiered at La Scala in 1957. The opera takes place on the eve of, and during, the French revolution and focuses on a young woman named Blanche, daughter of aristocrats. Her mother died in child birth after she and Blanche's father were caught in a frenzied mob, resulting from a panic after some fireworks caught fire and exploded. Blanche, who can't shake a persistent feeling of dread that has been with her all her life, joins an order of the Carmelite nuns, and there is happy. But as the violent events of the French revolution proceed, her intangible fears become all too real; the convent is sacked and Blanche goes into hiding, disguising herself as a maid in the house she grew up in. When she learns that the nuns have been arrested, instead of staying in hiding and saving herself, she goes beatifically to join them on their march to the guillotine, and is beheaded along with the others.

While *Dialogues* boasts one of the most literate librettos in opera (also written by Poulenc), it is a question if it can really be considered intellectual. Is it the story of a frightened (possibly emotionally disturbed) young woman who conquers her fear of both life and death through her love of God and like companions? Or a story of a bunch of mentally-ill women, the worst of whom is Blanche, and some of the more insane aspects of religion? Blanche could have joined her brother in exile and lived out her lifespan but chooses to die a hideous death instead. In truth, at the end of the opera Blanche is running from life and its turmoils into death, the simplicity of non-existence, so that there will be no more fear! Someone other than the devoutly Catholic Poulenc may have been able to turn *Dialogues* into something more penetrating than the simple, albeit fascinating, study of martyrdom that it is. Poulenc saw a frightened woman overcoming her fear through faith and going off to Heaven where she would be free from terror. Others see a helpless, emotionally fragile girl sacrificing the rest of her young life via grisly decapitation. *Dialogues* is only one of several operas — *Andrea Chenier* immediately comes to mind — in which religious fervor allegedly banishes the fear of the guillotine.

That said, *Dialogues* is a noteworthy opera with many lovely things in it. The first scene contains themes that continue and are developed throughout the opera; the lyrical strain in the recitatives comes prominently into display with Blanche's "Mon père, il n'est pas d'incident si négligeable," in which she reveals her desire to become a nun, that everything seems to propel her in that direction. In scene three, the (rather stupid) Sister Constance's aria "Oh! Soeur Blanche" is perhaps the only real moment of joy in the opera, as she remembers the fun she had dancing at her brother's wedding. Scene four presents a very powerful depiction of the painful cancer death of the sorely-tested Mother Superior as she is attended by the cold and practical, somewhat tight-assed, Mother Marie, and a dismayed Blanche. Poulenc handles this all with great and grim dramatic panache, possibly because he had to watch his own male lover slowly dying of a lengthy illness while he was working on this very scene. As the Mother Superior dies, we even hear the "guillotine" music playing lightly in the background, a nice bit of foreshadowing. In act two, when Blanche's brother comes to beg her to leave in the second scene, the music is so intense that it borders on verismo; it is also, at times, oddly romantic, considering the principals are siblings and the libretto, at least, does not betray any hint of incest. The new Mother Superior's aria in scene six ("Mes filles, voilà-que s'acheve notre premiere nuit de prison"), in which she joins them in a vow of martyrdom and sings of her love for them, is the most sustained bit of (non-instrumental) lyricism in the opera. Although Poulenc may have been straining for a Puccini-like effect here, the music is not on that level, and, while memorable, lacks a certain power as well, considering the bleakness of the situation.

The most outstanding piece in the opera is the "Salve Regina" chorus sung in Latin as the nuns march forward to have their heads lopped off one by one as we periodically hear the grotesque whoosh of the descending blade of the guillotine. However, the modern "beat" in the background, especially during the first half, almost makes the piece a touch campy. Poulenc used the music for famous heroines in grand operas, such as Massenet's Thais and Verdi's Desdemona, as models for varying characters' vocal writing, but Poulenc's music is rarely on the same level. His over-reliance on leitmotifs makes much of the music sound repetitious. Lastly, for an opera which is as much about terror as faith, little of the music reflects that terror. In contrast, Mascagni's *Il piccolo Marat*, also set during the French revolution, has a score shot through with it. It is interesting to observe that the only (religious) survivors at the end of *Dialogues* are Mother Marie, who initiated the vow of martyrdom, and, of course, the priest.

"I have done relatively little twentieth century music," Richard Bonynge told this writer, "as we [Bonynge and his wife Joan Sutherland] really enjoy living still in the nineteenth century, [but] *Les Dialogues des Carmelites* has given me enormous pleasure; both musically and dramatically it creates an extraordinarily moving effect in the theatre. Otherwise I fall back on the great Puccini operas and my own special favourites which will make you laugh. The operettas of Lehar and Kalman."[2]

Little did anyone realize that a Frenchman named Claude-Michel Schönberg (born 1944 in Vannes) would compose a kind of French "opera" that would change the face of musical theater first across the channel and then across the ocean. *Les Misérables* (1980), based on Victor Hugo's novel, was not that big a success in France, but the tide was turned when the Royal Shakespeare Company put on a production of it in London. Because of that production's big success, the show was pre-sold to Broadway audiences who believed something that made that much money had to be good. The success on Broadway was even greater, ushering in several shows that were, like *Les Miz* (as it was called), through-sung (little or no spoken dialogue) like operas but whose music was another story altogether.

Pop and rock operas were nothing new, of course. The Who's *Tommy* of the seventies had started out as a record album with some creditable popular numbers and wound up as a Broadway show where all that seemed to matter was the production, with even the one or two good songs wiped away by very bad orchestrations. Andrew Lloyd Webber's *Jesus Christ Superstar* also began life as an album before becoming a kind of concert/road show; even it boasted a couple of pleasant numbers (such as Mary Magdalene's "I don't know how to love him" and Jesus' "I only want to say"). But *Les Miz* was the one that really made an impact on musical theater and was mistaken for an opera by hundreds of thousands of theater-goers. People who would never be caught dead at the Met would walk out of previews in New York smiling broadly and say "Why, it's like an opera!" flushed with pride that they had sat through something "cultural" without falling asleep. The through-sung nature of *Les Miz* made it seem like an opera to the uninitiated, but to any halfway serious opera-goer the pop sensibility of the composer put paid to that theory. To be fair to Schönberg the pop music of *Les Miz* is often very facile and melodious. The most famous number, "I dreamed a dream" is an attractive (if not greatly original) pop ballad with operatic undertones. "A Heart Full of Song" is a pretty duet (then trio) with an operatic-type structure that needs an entirely different orchestration and different singers. "Do you hear the people sing" is a stirring anthem and probably the best piece in the show. There are other pleasant numbers — and a number of forgettable ones — which are all but ruined by some of the strained pop voices of the various casts. But the main problem with *Les Miz* isn't even the music. Victor Hugo's huge tapestry of a novel is too long and heavy for a pop sensibility to bring to life with any veracity. It requires serious and profound operatic treatment. People who wouldn't be caught dead at the opera may have enjoyed *Les Miz* but most serious opera fans were bored.

On the other end of the musical spectrum was Oliver Messiaen's kitschy *Saint François d'Assise*, which premiered in 1983. Generally considered more oratorio than opera, it depicts — in excruciating detail — St. Francis' journey towards spiritual benediction. *Saint François* is a test of endurance not because it is over four hours long, but because it contains little music of real inspiration or value. The score features uninteresting vocal lines backed and punctuated by blaring brass and discordant, jangling percussion, a kind of borderline atonalism that results in monotony. The backgrounds are at odds with the "melodies" and have a sing song childish air to them. If Messiaen hoped the orchestration would somehow enliven his dreary vocal writing, it is too much the same thing — over and over again — to do the trick. The instrumental passages sound like demented children at play, and the music never seems to reflect the meaning of what's being sung. The music for the Angel is more comparatively "lyrical" than most, but still isn't memorable. In act two, the Angel plays ethereal music on the viol for St. Francis, backed by a chorus singing one note (not surprising in this work). The choice of instrument is more interesting than the music, as the viol does make a sweet, compelling sound that can best be described as "celestial." These passages are briefly intriguing, but the musical interlude that follows is unimpressive, badly orchestrated, and not in the least "heavenly," undoubtedly drawing unintended guffaws from some listeners when St. Francis proclaims that he was "overwhelmed, dumbfounded" by the "unbearable sweetness of the music." He is so overwhelmed that he passes out at this point, along with much of the audience.

Although throughout his career Messiaen listened carefully to birdsong and tried to capture it in his music, he completely muffs the "grand concert of birds," which never takes flight; it's simply percussive noise suggesting bird-like chaos instead of music that takes off in winged glory. Act three's chorus "Je suis cet après" is moderately more interesting than usual, being one of the more "powerful" pieces in the opera. This piece, in which God speaks to Francis, actually works in theatrical terms — the bombastic first half is followed by a section in which the chorus simply intones the word "François" softly for a nice contrast — although it hardly compares to the great chorale numbers of the past. The theme of the opera is put forth in the choral number (with the chorus representing God): "Many desire my heavenly kingdom, few consent to carry my cross," which is nicely set to music by Messiaen. St. Francis' conversation with God has the best music in the opera. Oddly, *Saint François* ends with a kind of Broadway-style chorus. Are the final notes quite pleasing or is it just one's joy that the opera is finally over? Criticism of *Saint François* may be pointless, because it is a work that is not aimed at the average opera fan but fashioned instead for those who come to it hoping for a transcendental spiritual experience, and who probably couldn't care less about the quality of the music. Then there are those immature, inexperienced critics who will praise *Saint François* because — not having heard that many great operas, for one thing — they have yet to learn that Great Art need not be ponderous. Sadly, there are people who will sit through four hours of Messiaen's opera and, although they're as bored as everyone else, will congratulate themselves and feel all puffed up on having successfully endured what must be a great work of art because, after all, real art — to them at least — is measured in tedium. And of course, to further dazzle the impressionable, *Saint François* features a massive orchestra and huge chorus, holy cow, not to mention a splashy production at its American debut at San Francisco Opera. But there is nothing — no effect, no sound, no instrumentation, no heavenly choir — absolutely nothing in *Saint François d'Assise* that hasn't been done better by much more talented operatic composers.

Writing of the production of the opera in San Francisco, *The New York Times* opined: "For all its shimmering wonder, the score can be exasperating. In some of his statements about opera in general ... this devout composer sounded artistically arrogant. The score does run on at times in ways that diminish its musical impact. You wish the Messiaen had given at least some consideration to the conventions of musical drama that serve as checks to musical indulgence. In his elevated spiritual realm, Messiaen comes close to seeming above it all."[3]

Germany. Arnold Schoenberg's *Moses und Aron*, upon which he had worked for years, finally premiered three years after his death in 1954 as a concert in Hamburg. It has since been staged at Covent Garden and the Metropolitan. God informs Moses that Aron will be his voice even as Moses is God's voice. The pair confront their people, who have been enslaved by the pharaoh. They scoff at this new God's invisibility, but marvel when Moses' leprous hand is miraculously healed — proof the "invisible" God exists. Aron promises them that they are the chosen people, the promised land will be full of milk and honey, and so on. In act two, the people are so impatient for Moses to return with his revelations that they nearly tear Aron and the elders apart. Then comes the Golden cafe and pandemonium. Moses (Ideas) and Aron (Image) have a protracted pseudo-intellectual philosophical discussion until the end of the act. Act three, which was not scored, continues the argument, ending with Aron's death. Moses is almost a spoken (or "pronounced" or "yelled") role.

Despite its being presented by major houses and championed by prominent conductors, *Moses und Aron* has not really caught on with the public and probably never will; it isn't just that its atonal language is difficult to decipher and adjust to, but that for most ears even repeated hearings won't make the music any more attractive, especially when compared to the tonal music of all the other operas there are to chose from. Much of the music, while it sometimes manages to nearly approximate the emotions of the characters, sounds like it should be the background score for a film set in an insane asylum. The orchestrations are often interesting, but the nearly complete lack of melody makes the score monotonous. Still there are individually dynamic moments, such as the "galloping" music that signifies the approach of the tribal leaders and the Ephraimite. Some of the more arresting moments include the chorus "Er hat uns auserwählt" which has a handsome harmonic sound to it. However, the "Dance of the Butchers," although provocatively named, with its trumpets, woodwinds, and variety of percussion instruments, is not as interesting as one might have hoped. Frankly, Schoenberg, who seems to be throwing in anything and everything to see what will work, seems more limited than other, tonal composers would have been.

The second act has a great deal of action, mostly centering on the golden calf and consequences of its appearance, including the slaying of a young man who objects to it, all leading up to a section called "an orgy of drunkenness and dancing," as it is headlined in the libretto, which is also vivid in its way but ultimately disappointing. Four naked virgins are sacrificed, their blood captured in jugs, followed by a wild "orgy of destruction and suicide" — with rape and murder mixed in for good measure — with background music that isn't nearly dark, frantic, or sinister enough but sounds more like bad modern-dance music. The death cries of the virgins, the naked people running about, are almost comical. The chorus of the Elders, "Selig ist das Volk," is one of the more attractive numbers in the score; even here the orchestration seems improvisational (or spontaneous). *Moses und Aron* can be reasonably entertaining as music theater if it's well-staged and has energetic dancers and interesting choreography. But it does make one wonder: do people go to this opera for Schoenberg's music — or for all the nudes on stage?

But it was not Schoenberg's *Moses und Aron* but rather his pupil Alban Berg's *Wozzeck* which was on the mind of Bernd Alois Zimmermann (1918–1970) when he composed his own atonal work and *Wozzeck* imitation, *Die Soldaten* (1965). Marie is torn between Stolzius and the wealthy Baron Despartes, an army officer, but Stolzius enlists in the army himself when he learns about his rival, vowing revenge, and Descartes discards Marie. After a dalliance with a count, Marie is passed along to Despartes' servant, who apparently has his way with her. Stolzius murders Despartes when he finds out about this, and allows himself to be killed in return. Marie becomes a beggar on the street. At the end of the opera her own father doesn't recognize her as he reluctantly hands her some change. We hear the sound of marching soldiers goose-stepping along, a pretentious reminder of the soldiers who despoil and discard young girls.

Because the ending delivers a dramatic wallop, it probably makes the opera itself seem a lot better than it is to the impressionable, but the story is really no more "modern" than *Tiefland* or even *Cavalleria rusticana*. Zimmermann's abysmal music distances the listener from the story and characters instead of pulling him in. The opera begins with obligatory dissonant horror movie music that at times provides an arresting cacophony but says absolutely nothing about the story and seems to go on forever. The music is generally inappropriate for (or unrelated to) the actions and emotions of the characters. Marie's wondering at the end of act one if she should forsake love and only wed to better herself is accompanied by music better suited for a battle scene of London during the blitz. Similarly, in an act three scene between Stolzius and a male soldier named Mary the music is almost comically exclamatory despite the utter banality of the action and dialogue, more overwrought than anything in verismo opera, which at least used intensity for a purpose. One of the more effective moments occurs during scene one of act two, when the frenetic, jazzy music as soldiers and others dance in a coffee house is entertaining and deliberately humorous, capturing the mood of the men who sing of "freedom," reflecting their utter surrender. *Die Soldaten* has its admirers, but it's not even on the level of its obvious model.

Hans Werner Henze's *Elegy for Young Lovers* premiered in 1961 in Germany (its first performance in English was two months later at Glyndebourne). The main point of interest in this opera is, ironically, its story, written by W. H. Auden and Chester Kallman. Meant to be the sort of thing once scripted by Hugo von Hofmannsthal, the work is dedicated to his memory. Alas, von Hofmannsthal's librettos were set to music by the genius Richard Strauss, and Henze, as prolific as he may be, is not in Strauss' league. It could even be said that Henze's virtually "incidental" music distracts from the somewhat fascinating events enacted on stage instead of adding to them.

The story focuses on a self-absorbed poet named Gregor Mittenhofer, whose entourage includes his much put-upon patron and secretary, Carolina; his Doctor, Wilhelm; his young lover Elizabeth; and a psychic widow named Hilda who was been in mourning since her tragic wedding day. One of the libretto's most interesting elements is the discovery, after forty years, of Hilda's husband's body in the ice in the Alps, not far from the inn where the opera takes place, but this aspect of the story is not really expanded upon. Instead Elizabeth and the doctor's son, Toni, fall in love, enraging Mittenhofer, who feigns acceptance. At the end the two lovers die in a storm on the mountain (sent on a search for Edelweiss by the devious Mittenhofer) and Mittenhofer finally finishes the poem he's been working on, which of course is entitled "Elegy for Young Lovers."

The score does have some "fun" moments, such as when Carolina and the Doctor sing a duet describing how the lives of poets are utterly dissected after their deaths ("The Poet dies"), but even here the lyrics are more effective than the music. Even the better pieces — Mittenhofer's arioso "Everything must be paid for eventually"; Elizabeth and Hilda's vaguely lyrical duet about the disappearance of the latter's groom, "How I came here one yesterday"; and Elizabeth's outburst "False, father, false to you!" — are hardly memorable. An act three intermezzo (to cover a scene change) manages to get across the sense of things unraveling, but is otherwise just loud, brassy and ultimately boring, like the opera itself. Henze's using different instruments to denote each character is not exactly novel, and a moment when Hilda goes a bit mental, said to be modeled on the mad scene in *Lucia di Lammermoor*, does not compare favorably to anything in Donizetti's oeuvre.

Henze has written many other operas besides *Elegy*, but his appeal seems limited primarily to Germany. As of this date, he has certainly not caught on in the United States, perhaps because there are enough American composers writing works that are every bit as uninteresting, making imports unnecessary. *Opera News* opined "The biggest problem with *Elegy* is Henze's music, residing in the compositional wasteland somewhere between the Duncan Yo-Yo and the Hula Hoop. Though challenging and possibly rewarding to perform, it is tedious to listen to, and definitely not to be confused with entertainment."[4]

Victor Ullmann (1898–1944) was born in Prague and studied with Schoenberg. He was arrested by the Nazis and placed in the Czechoslovakian concentration camp Terezín, which the Nazis employed as a "show place" to try to fool concerned parties into thinking that the prisoners of the Third Reich were treated well. Working with a libretto from a fellow prisoner, Peter Kien, Ullmann composed his opera *Der Kaiser von Atlantis* while in the camp. While the circumstances of its composition would lead one to hope that *Der Kaiser* was a lost masterpiece, such is not the case, although it is without doubt a creditable effort.

The story has to do with an Emperor Overall, modeled on Hitler, who so outrages Death that Death decides to quit in protest so that no one can die. A soldier and a girl from opposing sides in the battle meet and fall in love. Death is importuned to go back to work but only on condition that the Emperor Overall is his first victim; The Emperor sings a sad farewell to life. The opera was deemed inflammatory by the Nazi authorities who refused its performance in Terezín; Ullmann and Kien were transported to the death camp at Auschwitz and killed (on the same day as the Pavel Haas). The Schoenberg influence is not much in evidence in Ullman's score, which is generally tonal and even romantic in between some tedious stretches. The arias are not as immediately accessible as, say, Puccini's, but they are melodious in a more modern sense. They include Death's aria "Das waren kriege," as he thinks of the days and glorious wars gone by, and the Drummer's "Hallo! Hallo! Achtung! Achtung!" as he announces "a great and blessed war of all against all" in the name of the Emperor, which includes a distortion of the German national anthem.

Major pieces include the duet between the soldier and the girl Bubikopf

("Schau, die Walken sind vergangen") and especially "Der Kaiser's Abschied" as he sings farewell. While the lyrics of the aria may not refer to it, and the singer is a parody of Hitler, the music of the farewell is permeated with the depressing, hopeless, despairing atmosphere of the concentration camp, making it all too clear what the song is really about; it is simply heartbreaking, all the more so because it is real.

Russia. Prokofiev worked on *The Fiery Angel* on and off for eight years in the 1920's, but it didn't see the light of day—or a night in an opera house—until 1954, when it premiered in concert form in Paris. Its first staged performance was at La Fenice in Venice the following year. The bizarre libretto, scripted by Prokofiev from a novel by Valery Bryussov, has to do with a woman, Renata, who has an obsession with her imagined guardian angel, Madiel, whom she comes to believe has come to earth in the form of her lover, Heinrich. Heinrich has disappeared and she enlists the aid of a man named Ruprecht to find him. After encounters with magicians, demons, a duel between Heinrich and Ruprecht, and the unexpected appearance of Faust and Mephistopheles, Renata enters a convent only to encounter her "fiery angel," Mephistopheles, for the final time. *The Fiery Angel* is a seriously flawed opera by any standard, but as in anything by Prokofiev, it contains a lot of interesting and impressive music. There is the powerful entr'acte between scenes two and three in act two, which evokes a sense of magical forces barely restrained, just out of sight, too terrible to be contemplated or released. This music continues throughout the interchange between Ruprecht and the magician Agrippa as the former asks for help and Agrippa tries to deny the existence of magic and demons and so on. A great touch has skeletons (which Ruprecht can not see) crying out "You lie!" twice at Agrippa's denials. There is some fine music in act three as Renata and Ruprecht talk outside Heinrich's house, culminating in Renata asking the latter to kill her former love; later she begs Madiel to forgive her for ever thinking he was Heinrich in her aria "Prosti... prosti...." The entr'acte between scenes one and two which depicts the duel features music which is lush, sensual, throbbing, and suspenseful, and as richly orchestrated as ever.

The Fiery Angel goes completely awry and loses all of its intensity with act four and the comical appearance of Faust and Mephistopheles, who seem literally dragged in from another opera, and completely implodes with act five, set in the nunnery. There is a lot of hysterical, borderline ludicrous business with possessed nuns, and Renata being accused of sleeping with the Devil. The music is so intense, loud, and busy, positively thick with noise—especially with those choruses of screaming nuns—one can't help but think of "sound and fury, signifying nothing." While the music of *The*

Fiery Angel always seems combustible, on the verge of exploding, in act five it is over the top. What starts out as a fascinating psycho-sexual, quasi-religious, supernatural drama (albeit a pretentious and muddled one) turns into an utter burlesque. What's worse, as the libretto sinks — or stinks — the music also fails to impress.

This is not the case with Prokofiev's first opera, *Maddalena*, which finally premiered on BBC radio in 1979, sixty-eight years after it was composed. It is a hour-long one-act opera in four scenes, the last three of which were orchestrated by Edward Downes. Stenio tells his friend Gennaro that he is tormented by his love for a paramour who refuses to tell him her identity. The woman turns out to be Gennaro's wife, Maddalena. The two men decide to kill the faithless harridan, but she manages to get them to kill each other. The implication seems to be that Maddalena is a succubus, a demonic female who leads men to their ruination and death.

Maddalena is Russian verismo in both style and subject matter. (Prokofiev, along with certain others, is considered by some musicologists to be too "serious" a composer to write verismo, but even a cursory hearing of *Maddalena* makes clear that this is not the case.) Although *Maddalena* is obviously an early effort, the music still has a decided stature. It is very effective as a theatrical piece, although it is not in the league of such verismo works as *Cavalleria* and Korngold's *Violanta*. The second half of scene two has some wonderful, poignant love music ("For that whole day") for Maddalena and Gennaro. Scene three, when Stenio confesses he's fallen in love with a woman who torments him alternately with rapture and jealousy, is adroitly handled, aquiver with tension, and proof that Prokofiev had a certain theatrical flair from the very first.

Czechoslovakia. Although it had been presented in concert as early as 1934, Leoš Janáček's *Osud* (Fate) did not have a stage premiere until 1958 in Brno. The libretto of the short (approx. 80 minutes) piece had been subject of much tinkering over the years, and it remains the weak point of the opera. Essentially the story is about a composer, Zivny, who is reunited with and marries Mila, his former lover and the mother of his child, against the strenuous objections of Mila's mother. During a struggle with her now insane mother who lives with them, Mila falls to her death along with the old woman. A devastated Zivny puts the whole bleak story into an opera, in which he is the main character, but proclaims that the end is not yet written to the students at the university who are going to perform the work. When a storm breaks out, he imagines that he can see his wife, cries out, and falls to the floor in a heap in a flat and abrupt conclusion. The libretto has some interesting concepts but they are poorly developed. Despite the fine contribution from Janáček the opera just doesn't work and is never moving.

The musical highlights include the beautiful, exhilarating overture that positively bristles with noise, rhythm and melody, as well as the subsequent chorus ("Shine on us, sunlight") in which the crowd celebrates the sunshine of the day as it affects everyone in a positive manner, imbuing them with romance and a feeling of health. There is some wonderful choral music as a bunch of schoolgirls ask Dr. Suda, an acquaintance of Mila's, to accompany them on their excursion. Suda is also given a frenetic ballad, "Sun in the heavens up on high," while Zivny's long monologue about the consuming quality of his past relationship with Mila ("the past, the past") is passionately mounted and effective without being especially melodious. Act three features a chorus of students, "Listen to the thunder," singing from the score of Zivny's opera-within-an-opera. (At the end of act two when his wife is killed, Zivny wonders why there was no thunder to warn of danger to his wife, which is why he reacts so violently to the thunder at the end of the opera.) There is also a notable aria from the opera-within-an-opera ("Endless the pain I must suffer") in which the character meant to be Zivny sings of the death of his wife.

Bohuslav Martinů's *Ariane/Ariadne* premiered in 1961 in Gelsenkirchen. Seven youths, including Theseus, sail to Crete to kill the minotaur. While waiting for the minotaur to appear, Theseus meets Ariane, who is also waiting for the minotaur. She has fallen in love with the creature, even though she's only heard his voice. She can, however, see handsome Theseus, and the two fall immediately in lust. When the minotaur appears, he looks exactly like Theseus. "I knew he would look like you," declares Ariane. Apparently the minotaur takes on the appearance of those who would try to slay him. The city drummer announces the wedding of the king's daughter, Ariane, to the stranger, Theseus, who has killed the minotaur. Later, when Theseus is king, he has to sail off on further heroic adventures, leaving his heartbroken Queen Ariane behind. This little gem of an opera features a blend of extremely skillful recitative, ariosos, and highly dramatic "background" music. The absolutely joyous sinfonia that opens the one-act — Ariane's theme — is irresistible. The invigorating second sinfonia, a martial-type piece into which is woven a trumpeting dance theme, is also infectious. Theseus is given a notable aria in the prologue, but the opera's showcase is the outstanding aria given to Ariane in scene three, as her husband sets sail and she plans to commit suicide. As Martinů biographer Brian Large puts it, "Ariadne sings a poignant threnody in the form of a rondo with ornate bel canto episodes in the style of a cabaletta." This long, languid, evocative piece is beautiful and despairing in equal measure; the first few bars of the opening sinfonia play over the last note of the aria, the quality now ironic instead of joyous. It's a shame that *Ariane* isn't a bit longer with a more detailed libretto as the music is memorable and the story introduces but fails to develop a lot of fascinating psychological elements.

The Greek Passion, based on the novel *Christ Recrucified* by Nikos Kazantzakis, premiered in 1961. The story takes place in Lykovrissi, a small Greek village where each year parts are assigned among the townsfolk for the Passion play. The shepherd Manolios is chosen to be Christ; a widow, Katerina will be Mary Magdalene; and her lover Panait, Judas; and so on. When a group of refugees arrive at the outskirts of Lykovrissi, Grigoris the village priest refuses them help, fearing they might spread cholera, among other reasons. The actors assigned to the Passion play begin to merge with their roles, Manolios becoming more Christ-like as he urges the villagers to help the desperate, starving refugees against the orders of Grigoris and the village elders, who are particularly enflamed because Manolios wants them to share their wealth with the refugees. In addition, Manolios and Katerina grow very close, although only in a spiritual sense. Angered that Manolios has come to see himself as a substitute for Jesus, Grigoris excommunicates him, whereupon he is murdered by a jealous Panait. *The Greek Passion* is a study of religious hypocrisy and empty traditionalism with certain political overtones. Although the situations and characters are flavorful and the conclusion moving, the religious aspects of the story are often limiting and pretentious.

The musical style of *Greek Passion* is a hodge podge of lyrical recitatives, sung speech, majestic ariosos, Greek tavern songs, interspersed with a considerable amount of spoken dialogue (sometimes people talk and sing over one another), making it a kind of Czech zarzuela. One thing that Martinů does not provide in his score is major arias and strong melodic development, which becomes very frustrating for the listener. While *The Greek Passion* is a compelling and interesting work, there are times when Martinů takes a serious misstep, as both the libretto (which he co-wrote with Kazantzakis) and score have their share of awkward, clumsy and unconvincing moments. Sometimes the music is too bombastic (there is a clear Wagnerian influence in certain passages) and overwrought, and there are strained attempts to be "modern." Yet the music is almost always of interest and is adeptly orchestrated (occasionally over-orchestrated) throughout. Martinů does provide a wonderful haunting theme for Manolios/Christ/the Holy Mother, which is heard briefly in the overture and then repeated throughout the opera. This theme is used as a backdrop for Manolios act three aria ("God moves in silence"), but is not the main melody. Katerina's equally minor act three aria ("It's you"), sung when Manolios arrives at her door and she mistakes his innocent intentions, is made more interesting by having a harmonica tune from the tavern in the village nearby playing in the background.

Although composed in 1937, Martinů's one act opera buffa *Alexandre bis* did not premiere until 1964 in Mannheim Germany. Twenty-eight years earlier Martinů had contacted the French author André Wurmser and asked him for a story he might set to music for the 1937 World Exhibition. Martinů suggested that the libretto might contain a singing cat, which amused him, but not Wurmser, who countered with the possibility of a singing oil painting. Martinů liked this idea, and the result was *Alexandre bis*. The slight plot, if you can call it that, deals with a man, Alexandre, in 1900 Paris, who decides to shave his beard and dress up like a mythical cousin and seduce his own wife. This results in a nightmare sequence in which two Alexandres (the dull husband and the lively lover) wage war with one another while the wife, Armanda, writhes in both ecstasy and horror. Armanda has been resisting the passes of another man, Oscar, but at the end of the opera finds herself much more open to them. By reawakening passion in his wife, Alexandre has made her more susceptible to the charms of other men!

A comment on the monotony of wedded bliss and sex devoid of passion or variety, the opera is not as interesting as it sounds, largely because musically Martinů is only treading water. A dance of the demons in the nightmare sequence isn't bad, and there's a pleasant duet between the maid Philomene and the portrait of her employer (which not only sings but comments wryly on his model's actions throughout) as they excoriate what they think is the faithless Alexandre as he sneaks out of the house with a suitcase and razor ("Jak dá se to chá pat!"). Otherwise, *Alexandre bis* is forgettable. Why the twenty-eight year delay between composition and premiere? World War Two got in the way.

Nicolae Bretan's short opera *Arald* premiered in May 1982 at the Romanian Opera in Iasi. While Bretan's earlier one-act opera *Golem* was influenced by the Italian veristi, *Arald* was obviously composed under the influence of Wagner, and in addition, sounds much more Slavic than *Golem*. In *Arald*, the title character, a variation on Orpheus, comes to a seer or Pagan priest to beg him to bring his beloved Maria back to life. Maria is resuscitated, but only so that she and Arald can spend eternity together in death. *Arald* boasts Bretan's strong melodic ability (even if the melodies occasionally sound recycled), his vocal writing and orchestrations are both rigorous, but the lack of action in the libretto is limiting and nothing in the score really jumps out at you; more variety in the music would have been welcome. Nevertheless, there are some good arias, such as the poet's introduction "Arald pe un cal negru zbura" and Arald and Maria's formal duet "Din noaptea vecinicei uitări."

Finland. Aare Merikanto's (1893–1958) only opera, *Juha*, premiered after his death in 1958. Merikanto had every reason to think he'd have great success as an operatic composer. His father Oskar was a successful musician and composer of opera and he also founded what eventually became known as the Finnish National Opera. Aare wrote his first opera *Helena* in 1912 but it was never staged and he tore up the manuscript. The public did not take to the other music he composed, and he was unable to make a living at music; instead he became a teacher. He composed *Juha* in the 1920's and was disheartened when it was rejected by the Helsinki Opera company. The libretto was then turned over to composer Leevi Madetoja, whose own version of *Juha* premiered in 1935 — another nail in Merikanto's coffin. Now after his death his version of the story is frequently performed while Madetoja is better-known for his 1924 opera *Pohjaaisia*.

The story of *Juha* deals with a middle-aged farmer whose younger wife Marja is tempted and led astray by a wealthy and handsome merchant with whom she runs away. Ensconced in the merchant's household and now pregnant, Marja soon discovers that she is only the latest in a long line of his conquests. She eventually goes back to Juha, who believes that she was taken by force. Taking her back to the merchant to demand the child, Juha attacks the man in a rage. When Marja has to explain that she left with the merchant willingly (to keep Juha from killing him), a disheartened Juha commits suicide.

Merikanto's opera is well-orchestrated and dramatic, at times reminiscent of early Janáček, and has a certain verismo-like quality both in the subject matter and the intensity of the music. While there are moments in the score that are pretty and lyrical, Merikanto never really gets a handle on a memorable melody. There's an attractive dance of fiddle and flute, and a very long intermezzo that strikes a note of sustained and imminent menace. The conclusion is powerful: it ends with a few sweet notes trailing off after a burst of passion and musical thunder as Juha takes his own life.

Switzerland. Frank Martin (1890–1974), one of Switzerland's most important composers, fashioned several stage works, of which the best-known is *Der Sturm*, based on Shakespeare's *The Tempest*, which premiered at the Vienna Staatsoper in 1956. While not necessarily a truly major work, *Der Sturm* creates interest with its compelling, improvisational-sounding overture; Prospero's tuneful and lovely act three aria "Hin sind meine Zauberei'n"; and its simply but effectively orchestrated music.

In the meantime, as Europe was bristling with so many different styles of music and types of operas, the operatic scene was more lively in the United Kingdom than it had ever been before, with brand new works from Benjamin Britten and a host of new composers, not to mention the rediscovery of some of Frederick Delius' finest operas.

15. Old Music, New Bottles: United Kingdom, 1951–1990

Ralph Vaughn Williams had been working on and off on his operatic version of John Buchan's *The Pilgrim's Progress* for forty years before it finally premiered in 1951. This is a very deliberately-paced piece in spots, which brought the composer some criticism, and others noted that it seemed more of an oratorio than an opera. It recounts the pilgrim's journey through various lands until he arrives at the celestial city. Despite the pilgrim's lengthy trek, not much happens during the two and a half running time. Even when he enters the land of Vanity Fair where the inhabitants, worshippers of Beelzebub, try to tempt him with all manner of pleasures, sensual and otherwise, the opera doesn't get especially "sexy" (although undoubtedly there have been or will be productions with naked breasts and the like to keep the audience awake). Of course, sexiness is not exactly the point of the opera, which is so awash in religiosity and piousness that it can be quite tiresome to those of a less beatific bent. Yet Vaughn Williams composed much lovely music for the opera, in particular the Pilgrim's beautiful aria "O fool that I am," in which he realizes he can escape from the jail in which Beelzebub's followers have imprisoned him by using the Key of Promise, reminding him that God is always with him. The chorus of sinners who lead the pilgrim to jail ("Hold him, the traitor!") is effective, and there is a charming duet between the pilgrim and a woodcutter's boy he happens upon ("He that is down need fear no fall") on the way to the Delectable Mountains (this section had originally premiered as a one act in 1922). A duet between the pilgrim and a singing bird soprano ("The Lord is my Shepherd") in Act four is notable, as is the final chorus, "Holy is the Land." While some portions are unmemorable, most of the music is at the very least pleasant and well-orchestrated, if never quite outstanding. One of the work's best pieces, the Porter's aria "Into they hands, O Lord," with its delicate wood-

236

wind background, is only performed to cover the scene change when there's no intermission between acts one and two. Whatever its shortcomings, *The Pilgrim's Progress* is an ambitious piece, providing a veritable catalogue of the assorted strengths and weaknesses of the composer.

The year 1951 also saw the premiere of one of Benjamin Britten's most admired operas, *Billy Budd*, based on Herman Melville's famous story of the young seaman who is executed when, due to his inability to express himself, he strikes a superior officer who has slandered him. The novel was adapted by E.M. Forster and Eric Crozier. Much of the opera's power comes from Melville's story, although Britten's score is more "listenable" — that is, a recording of it can bring pleasure when it is listened to apart from the libretto or visual element — than others by the composer. But the occasionally Coplandesque music in this music theater piece is still a mixed bag. In scene one, the vocal lines are virtually all exclamatory, almost shouted gruffly by virtually every character, making it sound like tuneless verismo, and at times it comes off as almost desperate and kitschy. The more lyrical moments include the chorus' "Oh, Heave!" which is interspersed with recitation in the opening moments and hints of the grim events to follow; Billy's "Billy Budd, King of the Birds!," an almost-aria which is declarative and sturdy; and the sequence with the friend comforting the novice who's been whipped, the chorus joining in to sing "We're all of us lost, lost forever in the endless sea." This last piece certainly captures the lonely despair of the shanghaied sailors' predicament. Billy and the chorus's "Star of the morning" at the end of the scene, about Captain Vere, who will lead men on to victory against the French, is also notable. Scene three features Claggart's aria "O, beauty, O handsomeness, O goodness!" in which he sings of his hatred and jealousy of Billy and his need to destroy him. This piece seems modeled on other "evil men" arias like Scarpia's in *Tosca* and Gerard's in *Andrea Chenier*, although it doesn't approach their lyrical level. At the end of the act Billy's actual happiness despite his situation ("this life suits me." he sings) and his simple hopes for the future ("I'm soon to be captain of the mizzen!" he declares) are poignant given what we know to be his subsequent fate.

In act two, the chorus "This is our moment" that is sung throughout the first half of the scene as the ship pursues and fires upon the French, only to lose them in the fog, is such a melodious and robust composition — one of Britten's finest — that it almost comes as a shock. Billy's aria in scene three ("Look! Through the port comes the moon-shine astray!") is well orchestrated, but it doesn't compare favorably to other "doomed prisoner" arias (again *Tosca* and *Andrea Chenier* come to mind) because its weak vocal line fails to sustain interest. However, Billy's final aria "And farewell to ye, old Rights o' Man!" is probably the strongest piece in the opera (although it's still not exactly a "tune.") In this piece Billy professes peace and contentment over his sad fate and "land of her own where she'll anchor forever." Vere's final aria "For I could have saved him" uses a variation of the same music to somewhat lesser effect. The scoring heard behind the men as they react unfavorably to the death of Billy, coming close to rioting, is very effective movie music. Britten did make a major misstep in assigning the role of the boy Billy to a baritone instead of a tenor. He did this because he saw Captain Vere, who wrestles with the moral dilemma of whether or not to execute Billy, as the main role of the opera and not the title character — the main role in Britten's operas usually went to his lover, the tenor Peter Pears.

Britten's *The Turn of the Screw*, from Henry James' novella, premiered in 1955. Typical of Britten, the ersatz baroque score is a combination of the inventive and the uninspired, sometimes atmospheric, and at other times jarring in a way that only shatters the atmosphere. In act one, the interesting "variation three" orchestral passage between scenes three and four leads into the Governess' reaction to her surroundings ("How beautiful it is"), creating a feeling of loneliness, serenity, repressed fear, and hope for the future. Later, Flora and Miles sing an oddly compelling children's song in "Tom, Tom, the piper's son," and Miles has a "haunted" solo with his ghostly tune "Malo." When the governess is certain that the ghost of Quint has "come to look for Miles" it introduces the note of pedophilia which is found elsewhere in Myfanwy Piper's libretto. There is some effective "fantastic" music in scene eight when the ghosts of Quint and Miss Jessel appear to Miles and Flora, including Quint and Jessel's duet ("On the path, in the woods"), although Quint's first aria ("I am all things strange and bold"), despite its excellent lyrics, is perhaps a bit too "up tempo" to be disquieting. In act two, the second scene has an attractive ensemble with the children, Mrs. Grose and the governess backed by bells: "I shall never write to him," in which the governess says she won't write to the childrens' father regarding the ghost's influence over them. After Miles obliquely challenges the governess to act, the orchestra, now dominated by the bells, plays an off-kilter piece that reflects the woman's conflicted, troubled, and frightened feelings. Despite some fine moments, *The Turn of the Screw* is not a terribly effective rendering of James' fascinating story. The ending is not moving and it should be. Britten was undoubtedly loathe to write what might be misinterpreted as a common tearjerker.

Britten's final opera was *Death in Venice*, which premiered in 1973. Thomas Mann's brilliant novella was adapted by Myfanwy Piper, who had also done *Turn of the Screw*. Vacationing in Venice, the writer Aschenbach becomes fascinated by and then to his horror sexually obsessed with a fourteen-year-old boy, Tadzio. The story of the writer's anguish, moral conflict, and eventual disintegration are played against the corruption of Venice itself, as city officials downplay the facts about a cholera epidemic so as not to frighten away tourists. Piper does an excellent job of dramatizing and compressing Mann's story, but Britten doesn't really follow suit, too often losing all of the values of Mann's work in a sea of monotony. The music is generally devoid of true emphatic and sustained melody and the vocal writing is so uninspired as to be pitiful. The tedious sung speech of *Death in Venice* should not be compared to the interesting recitative approach of other composers.

As in all of Britten's operas there are some lovely moments, usually in the instrumental passages (making this a reasonably fine movie score), and to be fair the music does seem to get across the age, fatigue and decay of both Aschenbach and Venice. The often colorful, if muted, orchestrations (Britten shows particular adeptness with percussion instruments in several sequences, such as after Aschenbach purchases some strawberries) are painted in colors both gloomy and pastel. There is suspenseful, effective background music for "the pursuit," as Aschenbach follows the boy and his family around Venice, and a strangely melancholy and tauntingly sinister "Laughing Song" of some strolling players. In this last piece the somber notes sung in Italian by one man are repeatedly followed by an upbeat chorus ("Ha! Ha! How ridiculous you are!"), creating a compelling effect. If nothing else, *Death in Venice* is an interesting piece of music theater.

Mann's novella has often been misread as simply a book about pedophilia instead of one man's moral crisis, and the opera has been especially misinterpreted due to the composer's own proclivities. Although Britten lived for many years with Peter Pears, biographers suggest that he was as much, if not more, interested in boys than he was in men. Whatever the truth about Britten, Aschenbach seems as tormented by his erotic feelings for a boy as he does in Mann's novel (the story describes his struggle between wallowing in these feelings and rejecting them). Britten's homosexual relationships with other consenting adults such as Pears are one matter — perhaps the operatic version of *Death in Venice* is meant to explore his own conflicted feelings over his relationships with minors.

Even as Britten was coming increasingly to the forefront of British composers in the 1950's, the works of another, very different English composer were starting to be rediscovered, Frederick Delius. His *Irmelin* is a true nineteenth century opera in that it was composed in the 1890's, but as it didn't premiere until 1953 in Oxford it is fit for discussion in this volume. The Princess Irmelin, like Mascagni's Isabeau, angers her father by rejecting all suitors in favor of a dream lover who has yet to appear. Meanwhile

Prince Nils, disguised as a swineherd, is following a silver stream which he believes will lead him to the princess that he has dreamed about. After briefly hooking up with a band of outlaws led by Rolf, Nils makes his way to Irmelin's side and simply wanders off with her just before her wedding to a knight, presumably to live happily ever after. Obviously a fairy tale opera like *Irmelin* is miles away from the likes of *Death in Venice*, and Delius, who also did the libretto from a Hans Christian Andersen story, responded with an intensely romantic score. Despite its age, the score has a somewhat modern sound to it. While there is an obvious Wagnerian influence, Delius has his own distinct style (besides using a much smaller orchestra).

In act one, the chorus of young lovers in the woods ("Away, far away"), joined by Irmelin with "Could I but stray" as she longs to be among them, leads into the excellent aria "Ah, but he will come," in which she imagines making love to her long-awaited dream prince. Act two features Rolf's ballad of his youth "Nigh forty years ago ..." and a rather sexy chorus of women as they try to entice Nils into staying with the gang ("Come, let us sing and dance"). The introduction to scene five contains the wonderful "silver stream" theme, which begins with a lightly tripping flute and bursts into full lyricism — you can hear the rippling of the water recreated by the orchestra — as Nils finally sees the stream. This leads into Nils' "Oh joy" upon finding the stream with a chorus of nay-saying wood nymphs behind him urging him not to go on. Act three boasts a long beautiful love scene, which includes Nils' ballad, "Listen to my dreams," in which he tells how he came to the princess' side, as well as an informal duet between him and Irmelin. There is an especially lovely prelude to scene two, which builds to a dramatic and passionate intensity (generally the music is more romantic than passionate). After both Irmelin and Nils sing an arioso about how their finding the other has led to a new existence for him/her, there come two excellent formal duets: "Am I dreaming" and "The dawn is breaking." It is interesting to contemplate what fortunes Delius' reputation and career might have enjoyed had *Irmelin*, his greatest opera, been heard by the public during his lifetime.

Almost twenty-five years would go by before another lost Delius opera was unveiled, *The Magic Fountain*, which premiered on BBC radio (and was recorded) in 1977. Like *Irmelin*, *The Magic Fountain* was a product of the 1890's. Sailors in the 16th century are nervous as they sail with the Spanish nobleman Solano to "shores paved with gold." Solano survives a shipwreck and winds up in an Indian village in Florida. The Indian maiden Watawa does not trust Solano, but Chief Wapannacki offers to lend her to him as a guide to the Fountain of Youth in exchange for gold. Watawa explains the situation to old seer Talum Hadgo, who councils her to trust her heart when she says she wishes to kill Solano in vengeance for what the white man did to her people. But as the two search the Everglades for the fountain — and find it — they fall in love. Watawa warns Solano that Talum told her the waters kill those who are "unprepared," but Solano dismisses it. To show her faith in him, Watawa drinks from the fountain — and dies. Solano, responsible for the death of his beloved, drinks from the fountain so as to join Watawa in death and the afterlife. (Ironically, a white man has destroyed Watawa just as the white man destroyed her people.) While Delius' skills as a librettist were sufficient for the languidly romantic *Irmelin*, he betrays little dramatic flair in his book for *The Magic Fountain*, but in many cases, especially the affecting conclusion, the music makes up for it.

The highlights include the chorus of sailors ("At last a breeze!") in act one, as they express their delight that the ship will move in the wind (which becomes a disastrous storm.) Act two has a beautiful prologue depicting the Indian village in the calm of dusk, followed by a brief "humming chorus" of Indians (which is nothing like Puccini's humming chorus in *Butterfly*). Watawa is given a poignant arioso as she dies ("See how the moon-beams flood..."). Also memorable are the act three love duet ("Watawa, I cherish doubly now they love") and Solano's ecstatic outburst as he spots "The fountain! The fountain!" However, Watawa's act three aria 'What can it be?" in which she struggles with her hatred of — and growing love for — the white man never really gets off the ground.

Delius' one-act opera *Margot-la-Rouge* — a genuine twentieth century piece — finally surfaced via another BBC recording and broadcast in 1981. In 1902 Delius had entered this in the same Sonzogno competition that had been won by Mascagni's *Cavalleria rusticana* twelve years earlier. *Margot-la-Rouge* did not win the prize and nothing more was heard of it for seventy-nine years. The title character is a sexy woman of ill-repute who hangs out in the Parisian cafe where the action takes place. Her former lover, a sergeant named Thibault, comes to blows with her new lover and is stabbed to death when he tries to defend her from the man's attack. She then kills her new lover with the sergeant's bayonet. Although the music flows along with Delius' usual skill (and an occasional Wagnerian-style flourish), Delius did not truly have the temperament for verismo. Indeed, the music is so comparatively "delicate" that the stabbings — two deaths! — would go completely unnoticed as far as the score is concerned if the listener were not already familiar with the libretto. *Margot-la-Rouge* is an attractive, if minor, work for Delius, boasting a beautiful overture and a nice aria for Thibault, but the centerpiece is the lengthy love duet for Thibault and Margot-la-Rouge which builds and builds in passion and intensity. (Delius later recycled this music into a concert piece using words by Walt Whitman). The opera is an unlikely bet for revival.

William Walton (1902–1983) was born in Lancashire, England the same year that Delius completed *Margot-la-Rouge*. For most of his career he concentrated more on film scores than operas, but he did come out with two works, a one-act called *The Bear* (1967) and the three-act *Troilus and Cressida* (1954). The opera is not based on Shakespeare's play but comes from Chaucer and other sources, and depicts the star-crossed relationship between the title lovers during the Trojan War. Cressida is daughter of the high priest of Troy. When she is taken to the Greek camp in exchange for a Trojan prisoner, Greek Prince Diomede falls in love with her. Her lover Troilus' messages to the camp have been destroyed, so Cressida mistakenly believes he has deserted her and agrees to marry Diomede. When Troilus is killed by Cressida's traitor father during a battle with Diomede, she commits suicide with her lover's sword. Cressida is truly one of the most tragic heroines in opera, her fate twisted about by men who give her no say, denounced as a whore by Diomede merely because she had previously fallen in love with her fellow countryman, Troilus, and her own father even murders her lover.

Walton's score is handsome, evocative, well-orchestrated, and often quite powerful, even if there are times when it lacks the required amount of passion and pathos. Highlights include Cressida's act two aria "At the haunted end of the day," in which she realizes that she can't get Troilus out of her mind, is tormented by recurring visions of him, and finally emotionally surrenders to her "conqueror." Troilus' burst of passion over Cressida ("If one last doubt"), also in act two, whereupon he urges her to find refuge "close to my body" is a rather sexy piece. Troilus is given a lovely act three aria ("Sooner would leafless boughs"), an "I-could-never-forget-you" song which borders on a musical theater–type number but is quite good in spite of it. The sequence when celebrants begin to arrive due to the upcoming nuptials of Cressida and Diomede culminates in an excellent orchestral fanfare. This is followed by a notable sextet with a strong undertone of foreboding as all of the major characters sing out their deepest thoughts and feelings. Cressida's final aria, "Turn, Troilus, turn," is an effective dirge for Troilus after his murder, leading into the dramatic, poignant suicide of Cressida. The quirky vocal line of Troilus' act one aria "Is Cressida a slave," in which he prays to Aphrodite, reminds one a bit of Stravinsky.

Michael Tippett (born 1905) has composed several operas, the most famous of which is *The Midsummer Marriage*, which bowed at Covent Garden the year after Walton's *Troilus and Cressida*. The simple premise is that of a father who objects to his daughter's choice of boyfriend (or indeed any boyfriend) as he can't handle her emerging sexuality, told in symbolic, mystical terms that border on the surrealistic and employing two sets of lovers. The story, such as it is, enfolds as a magical woodland fantasy or dream. The rather awkward libretto, written by the composer, was roundly denounced in 1955, and even today it could be dismissed as a pretentious "new age" opera were it not for Tippett's fine music. The libretto is obviously not meant to be held up to intense scrutiny, but manages to be quite properly theatrical in its way, and accomplishes its main purpose of serving and showcasing the music. While Tippett perhaps lacks a melodic gift of Puccinian proportions, his music is almost consistently dramatic, at times "grand" and majestic, with real moments of genuine beauty and compelling loveliness. His vocal writing can be gorgeous. It could even be said that the score is a kind of "baroque" music worked over in a twentieth century style and sensibility. What *Midsummer Marriage* has in common with *Troilus and Cressida* is that on occasion the music has a "Broadway" feel to it.

Highlights include Mark's act one aria (with male chorus in the background) "You, you who were with me," telling how he was in despair when Jennifer left but is now energized and reborn (Mark and Jennifer are the primary lovers). In act two there is a charming, delicate interchange ("They're gone now, Bella") between the secondary lovers Jack and Bella as they discuss getting married and their life together. Scene two has a lengthy dance sequence consisting of three interlocking ballets concerning the hare and house, fish and otter, and hawk and bird. The ballet music is acceptable but unexceptional and goes on for too long; the best parts are the dramatic flourishes that indicate the beginning of each new ballet. In each ballet, it being leap year, the female dancer is the predator and the male the prey. Act three has a fine contralto aria for the medium Sosostris in "Who hopes to conquer." Some of Tippett's vocal music, such as Mark's act one arioso ("Ah, the summer morning dances in my heart") and Jennifer's aria ("Is it so strange if I resent") allows the singers to show off in bel canto fashion. After a shaky start, Tippett's fine and unusual score won the opera many converts, although some remained unconvinced. Richard Bonynge says that "my wife (Joan Sutherland) had her fill of modern opera in the 1950's when she sang a *Midsummer Marriage* of Tippett and Britten's *Gloriana* as well as several first performances of modern works by British composers. She did, however, enjoy creating the British premiere of the *Carmelites*, especially working with Poulenc."[1]

Michael Nyman (born 1944) is a former critic and minimalist who has composed film scores, and several operas for television and the stage. *The Man Who Mistook His Wife for a Hat*, a chamber opera based on the case study by Oliver Sacks, premiered in London in 1986. Dr. P., a music teacher and opera singer, suffers from visual agnosia, and is a patient of Dr. S., a neurologist. Dr. P cannot perceive images or pictures as normal people do. He grabs for his hat, but puts his hands on his wife's head instead, convinced that her head is his hat. The two things that help him get along in life are music and his wife. The opera gets across without overstating it the awful toll that her husband's condition has taken on Mrs. P. While at first she seems to be in denial, she actually fears that her husband will have to retire, which she knows would kill him. Says Dr. S: "My only prescription is more music."

The Man Who Mistook His Wife for a Hat is an opera that should not have worked but does. The libretto by Christopher Rawlence is excellent and Nyman's music — whatever it is — is very effective and poignant, despite its generally upbeat tempo. The score could be described as classical music — mostly Schumann and Schumann pastiche — filtered through a pop sensibility or vice versa, or maybe modern-day baroque. It does not require operatic voices. When Schumann's "Ich grolle nicht" from "Dichterliebe" is sung by Dr. P. it sounds vastly superior to anything composed by Nyman. Some of Nyman's music is appealing, but it also becomes repetitive and monotonous after awhile. The poignancy may be supplied by the storyline and by Schumann. This may be a "stunt" opera, but it is very interesting and effective on its own terms. At one point, Mrs. P turns on the TV and Dr. S asks her husband to describe what he sees. He recognizes a photo of the composer, Nyman, at the piano (a jarring, egocentric touch), but confuses a "torrid" Bette Davis movie with first the news, then a suntan commercial, then wrestling. Despite these amusing touches, The Man Who Mistook His Wife for a Hat is ultimately quite moving.

Where the Wild Things Are (1980) by Scottish composer Oliver Knussen, is pure, unfiltered kitsch. Commissioned by Opera National, Brussels, and based on a book by librettist Maurice Sendak, it has plot similarities to L'Enfant et les sortilèges but there the resemblance ends. An imaginative little boy named Max fantasizes about strange creatures and angers his mother with his impossible behavior. He travels to a land where "wild things" kick up a rumpus with him. The only lyrical passages in the opera are quotes from classical composers, especially Mussorgsky and Debussy. There are attractive sounds and arresting moments, but not a melody to be heard, primarily because the score — which is admittedly skillfully orchestrated in parts — is more about background effects than it is about music. Some of the score sounds like a parody of Moses und Aron, and other such works, which may well have been intended by Knussen. (Just what opera lovers needed, a parody of a parody!) A performance of the opera is probably fun to watch with all of its colorful animals and action, all the costumes and dancers, but the music is neither compelling nor original, but sounds more like noise trumped up by a desperate composer devoid of genuine operatic resources. Knussen adds nothing new to either the atonal or modern bag of tricks. In spots the score reminds one of an eight year old banging tin cans together and hoping to blindly produce music. Perhaps, like children, *Where the Wild Things Are* should be seen and not heard.

Australian composer Richard Meale (born 1932) was for many years at the vanguard of the avant garde in his homeland, and was credited with introducing works by such modern composers as Messiaen and Schoenberg to Australian audiences. Therefore it was a surprise and disappointment — and to some a delight — when Meale's first opera, *Voss* (1986), turned out to be a masterpiece in a decidedly tonal and lyrical idiom. Based on the novel by Patrick White, the opera explores the relationship between the German explorer Johann Ulrich Voss (based upon the real-life Ludwig Leichhardt) and his patron's niece, Laura Trevelyan, as Voss explores the interior of Australia in the mid–1800's. Voss and Laura first meet and make a connection at a party. Voss gathers together a number of men who will accompany him on his journey, including young Harry Roberts, who is willing to follow him anywhere, and a guide named Judd. The libretto by David Malouf is an often bizarre series of tableau depicting events back home in Sidney with Laura and her family juxtaposed with scenes of the expedition in the outback, which comes to a disastrous end. Some of the party are killed by aborigines, one commits suicide, some die of exhaustion and exposure to the elements, and Voss himself is beheaded. Years later, at the unveiling of a statue of Voss, the only survivor, Judd, and Laura finally meet.

Whatever the strengths or weaknesses of the admittedly poetic libretto, this is an opera that rises and falls by its music. The scoring is proof positive that a composer can play around with harmonies, rhythms, instrumentations, and tempos etc. in a highly interesting fashion (as many atonal composers do) yet remain tonal, lyrical and most of all listenable. Meale's employment of the orchestra is masterful. And while *Voss* may not be a "number" opera in the traditional sense, it does have a host of formal and informal arias and duets. Among the highlights, are Laura's aria, "I was alone in the desert," in which she relates a dream to the accompaniment of lush strings which, oddly, creates a strange underwater effect; Harry's aria "Morning's dawn upon the trees" which becomes a stirring ensemble; and Voss' outstanding "old-country song" which he sings to Laura in German. This is a beautiful romantic piece full of longing and a decided loneliness. Voss and Laura are given a sensitive duet in "I will be followed across the continent" and Voss composes a letter to her in the mesmerizing piece "My dear Miss Trevelyan." There is an interesting moment when Voss asks Laura to pray for him and she tells him that she does not pray. "You do not believe," asks Voss. She replies with a list of the things — wood, sunshine, etc.— that she does believe in.

Voss sings an attractive prayer, "Almighty God" in act two. His last aria, "I have always been alone," is a powerful diatribe with a dramatic and thunderous background. Harry's plea to Voss to "Take me with you" is memorable, as is Laura's beautiful arioso that ends act one, "I will follow." Meale occasionally uses snatches of 19th century Australian parlor songs for flavoring and background in act one. In act two, there are bizarre renditions of these same tunes to reflect the unraveling mental states of the expeditioners. The sumptuous score for *Voss* is continuously interesting and different. If it is essentially a "film score," as some may claim, it is a film score with excellent vocal writing (far above the level of most modern opera composers such as Bolcom and Picker, for instance) and genuine melodies. *Voss* deserves to be heard in every major opera house. *Mer de Glace*, Meale's follow-up to *Voss*, premiered in Sydney in 1991.

There was one more decade to the twentieth century. It would contain just a few surprises and quite of bit of interesting music.

16. The Final Decade — and the Future: United States and the World, 1990 into the 21st Century

American composer John Adams (born 1947) came to attention with his opera *Nixon in China*, which premiered in Houston in 1987 and concerned the meeting between Nixon and Mao Tse-tung in 1972. Hardly likely to become a popular repertory item, *Nixon in China* was not as controversial as Adam's next full-length stage work, the music theater piece *Death of Klinghoffer*. Only six years before the opera premiered in 1991, Palestinian terrorists hijacked the cruise ship *Achille Lauro* and in an act of monstrous cowardice murdered an elderly Jewish vacationer in a wheelchair, Leon Klinghoffer. The opera attempts to detail these events, but while Alice Goodman's poetic libretto may occasionally be obtuse, pretentious, and downright clumsy, with minimal characterization, it is superior to Adams' music, which betrays Adams' extremely limited resources as a composer of opera.[1]

The Death of Klinghoffer could have been powerful stuff, but Adams' limited pop sensibility and warmed-over Brittenesque style make him the wrong composer for the work. Despite an occasional pleasant or mildly lyrical moment, the music never takes flight, and the ugliness of the story is no excuse; Leon Klinghoffer deserved better. The opera begins with a musically pretentious Chorus of Exiled Palestinians which explains their anger over Israel, but the music distances us from them instead of drawing us up into their feelings. It should be made clear that *The Death of Klinghoffer* does not, as charged, seem to be biased in favor of the Palestinians and against the Jews; the terrorists' viewpoints are simply musicalized, as such, to explain their actions. Therefore, it makes little sense to distance the audience from them the way that Adams does. The Chorus is not well-orchestrated; and if Adams meant for it to be unattractive, he succeeded.

This chorus is followed by a "prettier" Chorus of Exiled Jews which is vaguely romantic but also monotonous. The influence of Britten is clear in the Captain's act one monologue, "It was just after one fifteen." This isn't a bad piece, almost haunting, but there's not enough variety in the "melody" or background to keep it from becoming boring. The bouncy chorus "Is not the night restless for them?" is busy, noisy, and almost campy, pop music gone awry, Andrew Lloyd Webber on uppers, and ultimately quite uninteresting despite its energy as compared to the rest of the score. The British Dancing Girls' act two number "I must have been hysterical" is like sixties off-Broadway schlock. Goodman's lyrics often give certain arias intrinsic power (Leon Klinghoffer's "I have never been a violent man" and "May the Lord God," for instance), but Adams' essential lack of major talent eventually does them in. Omar's "It is as if our earthly life" has a kind of vigor in its ascending chords and increasingly intense synthesizer background, but even it is not that memorable. Marilyn Klinghoffer's "aria" about her dead husband is moving due more to the excellent lyrics and grim situation than it is to the unimpressive vocal line or the music in general. This aria, at least, can be taken as a tribute to Leon Klinghoffer; the opera, alas, can not. Adams' latest opera, *Doctor Atomic*, is about the director of the Manhattan Project J. Robert Oppenheimer, and was commissioned by the San Francisco Opera.

John Corigliano's *The Ghost of Versailles*, with a libretto by William Hoffman, premiered at the Met in 1991. It might best be described as a quirky potpourri, a modern but melodious interpretation of classic opera filtered through a "romantic" sensibility. The opera was hailed as a masterpiece by many, but also received more negative critical reaction than it perhaps deserved, but it may be because of the convoluted nature of the story than its music, which is generally better than we have come to expect from modern-day operas. The piece could also be described as some good music lost in a sea of silliness were it not for the fact that the libretto, despite some tiresome detours, is quite imaginative and, at times, thought-provoking.

The fascinating premise has the ghost of Beaumarchais meeting up with the ghost of Marie Antoinette in the after-life. Pierre-Augustin Caron de Beaumarchais was the real-life literary figure who wrote plays that were later turned into operas by Mozart (*Marriage of Figaro*) and Rossini (*The Barber of Seville*). In *The Ghosts of Versailles* he creates a new opera-within-an-opera, utilizing characters from the Mozart and Rossini works, in an effort to help Marie Antoinette come to terms with her life and early death, and indeed possibly change time to avoid her execution. He even enters his own opera at one point to try to get things back on track. It makes little sense for Corigliano to have been hammered by some critics for doing pastiches of various musical styles (Richard Strauss and Gilbert and Sullivan are the first that come to mind), as well as for incorporating musical quotes, when other composers have done the same and been hailed for it. In any case, Corigliano's score is often inventive, consistently interesting, and features that rarity in modern operas, some very good vocal writing. Early in the opera a woman yawns "another evening at the opera," while a gentleman friend replies "I'm so bored." Corigliano and Hoffman obviously did this whole piece as a labor of love with tongue in cheek and a decided wink for the opera lover, but some of the critics didn't take the work in the proper spirit. Perhaps *The Ghosts of Versailles* wasn't "serious" enough for them, like *The Death of Klinghoffer,* but Corigliano's music is certainly superior to Adams.'

Outstanding numbers include the villain Bégearss' "Oh, the lion may roar" in act one, a highly dramatic number with a sinister throbbing background that adds to its effectiveness. "Come now, my darling," is a charming love duet sung by Rosina and Cherubino, which is reprised by Beaumarchais and Marie Antoinette for a quartet. Marie's tune "Once there was a golden bird" is contrasted with her less lyrical but intensely dramatic aria "They are always with me," referring to the victims of the French revolution with their heads on pikes. In act two Susanna and Rosina are given a notable duet, "As summer brings a wistful breeze," in which they warble of lost years and regrets, and there is a memorable ensemble piece, "Remember the chestnut trees," for two romantic couples. The trial of Marie Antoinette is quite intense and theatrically effective, and the evocative intermezzo between scenes is quite good. "Oh God of Love" is another very memorable ensemble piece after the family is reunited. In her final, very moving aria, "I suffered here," Marie Antoinette decides to accept the past as it actually occurred. She realizes that Beaumarch tried to save her life even though she did not love him. Now she realizes and tells him that she does love him, and faces the guillotine once more with the certain knowledge that their love will now endure. One sequence in the opera that goes on too long takes place at the Turkish embassy and features the singer Samira and her dancing girls. The opera begins to go awry with the entrance of Samira, and the mid-eastern musical pastiche she sings and dances to is mostly unmemorable.

Philip Glass and Robert Wilson were back in 1991 with their opera, *White Raven,* which was commissioned by the government of Portugal to "commemorate the 500th anniversary of the country's golden age of global exploration," as Peter G. Davis put it in *New York.* "The visuals looked tired, heavy-handed, and recycled, a collection of bland tableaux with little to challenge the mind or stimulate the imagination," wrote Davis. "Ditto for Glass' score, with its usual simpleminded syncopations, sappy tunes, awkward vocal writing, and gummy orchestration. No one in the cast (of the 2001 American premiere at Lincoln Center) gave an especially distinguished performance, probably because no one had any distinctive music to sing."

Robert Saxton was born in 1953 in London, where he was counseled by Benjamin Britten, and then studied with such composers as Robin Holloway (at Cambridge) and Luciano Berio. His opera, *Caritas*, based on the play by Arnold Wesker (who also wrote the libretto), premiered in 1991 at the Opera House in Wakefield. The story takes place in the 14th century in Norfolk, and centers around the Peasants' Revolt and a young woman named Christine Carpenter who suffers dearly due to a crisis of faith. The style of the opera reminds one a bit of Thea Musgrave, in that the tension in the music, which has occasional lyrical tendencies, serves to create suspense. Saxton employs such tricks as switching from live music to recorded at the climax. As the composer puts it, "at the climax, when Christine has lost her reason, the chant's final transformation into recorded vocal noise not only illustrates her tragedy, but also objectifies this (adding another perspective) by no longer being 'live' and thereby underlines our sense of her isolation."[2] The composer was praised for his instrumental writing and the opera itself was seen by many as being a creditable and powerful modern-day piece of music theater.

Thomas Adés (born 1971) was born in London and studied at the Guildhall School of Music, and then with Robin Holloway at the King's College in Cambridge. He has composed chamber symphonies, music for string quartets, and other pieces, and — at last — an opera entitled *Powder Her Face*. Commissioned by the Almeida Opera, it premiered at the Cheltenham Festival in 1995. Kent Nagano, who will apparently conduct anything, conducted the U.S. concert premiere of the opera in Berkeley; it premiered in New York at the Brooklyn Academy of Music (which will apparently *present* just about anything).

Powder Her Face purports to be the life story of the notorious real-life Margaret Whigham, a.k.a. the Duchess of Argyll, who was castigated by the prudish judge for her outré sexual tastes at a sensational divorce hearing in 1963. This seems to be the main *raison d'être* for the opera, which never bothers to do much to illuminate the actual person beyond a few campy attributes. The very poor libretto by Philip Hensher aspires to be a lowercase *Lulu* but despite a few theatrically effective bits here and there hardly works at all. There is an amusingly grotesque moment in scene four when the anonymous waiter whom she has just paid for his sexual favors tells the oblivious Duchess that they've actually done this once before, and scene seven, when the Duchess rants about Blacks and Jews in the streets, buying houses, illustrates how the same people who are so wild in youth often become just as narrow and disapproving as their critics as they grow older.

The score by Adés, although sporadically effective, doesn't help much. The music of scene one, while not especially riveting or memorable, does get across in a rather sensuous if blathery manner the deep depression felt by the Duchess, who's feeling all dried up and old. The murky, melancholic, jazzy interlude between scenes two and three is dramatically viable, and there's efficiently grim and somber — if again, unmemorable — music for the penultimate scene when the Hotel Manager evicts the desperate 78-year-old Duchess from her suite for nonpayment of rent. As for "arias," The Electrician (as Lounge Lizard)'s song "Who said it mattered?," is flavorful and borderline melodious. The Maid (as Waitress)'s number "Fancy. Fancy being rich" is a good example of an okay modern-day aria in that it has no real melody to speak of but is well-constructed, managing to get across the emotions of the character, her envy and anger, while even emitting a certain, if limited, strain of lyricism. There are other arresting moments in the score and at times an interesting use of the orchestra, including such unusual "instruments" as a popgun and a fishing reel for the percussionist. And there are quotes from *The Rake's Progress*.

Alas, none of this adds up to greatness — or is even very good. On a whole the project never gets beyond a mediocre, tedious childishness. The self-conscious music and scatter-shot libretto serve to push you out of the story and away from the characters instead of pulling you in. Adés music is often pointless in its effects, arresting without having any true subtext or relationship to what's happening on the stage. It is the kind of fifth-rate stuff that only impresses those who have only cursory knowledge and appreciation of great classic opera. *Powder Her Face* is kitsch. Adés adaptation of *The Tempest* debuted in 2004.

Not so kitschy, but a bit polarizing, was Stephen Sondheim's Broadway show *Passion*, which also debuted to mixed notices in 1995. The show was a combination of songs, underscored spoken dialogue sequences, and plain spoken dialogue. *Passion* has to be taken on its own terms. As many opera fans have noted, this study of unrequited love hardly compares on the musical level with another famous study of unrequited love, Mascagni's *Cavalleria rusticana*. On the other hand, Sondheim's work (setting aside the fact that it may not be fair to compare it to a genuine operatic masterpiece) is a delicate, lovely, lyrical work that will deeply move some while leaving others utterly cold.

Giorgio is a soldier who is in love with a married woman named Clara.

On the base that he has been assigned to, Giorgio strikes up a friendship with Fosca, the plain, quiet and deeply depressed cousin of his superior officer. (When Fosca comes upon the ruins of a castle she says "I find it lovely—probably because it's ruined.") As their friendship deepens, Fosca becomes utterly obsessed with Giorgio, but Giorgio finds it impossible to return her feelings. With sheer persistence, Fosca eventually wins over the disinterested object of her obsession. While this aspect of *Passion* is not completely convincing—for one thing you can't imagine Giorgio would really want to make love to Fosca—the show is nevertheless quite effective. The characters in James Lapine's excellent book are realistically imperfect: Fosca's self-pity becomes quite tiresome after awhile; and Giorgio shows his own selfishness by refusing to understand Clara's reluctance to leave her husband for him when doing so would mean that she would also lose her child.

Although *Passion* is not through-sung, it resembles certain operas in that the music is all of a piece. Instead of there being variety to the numbers, one main melody swims through *Passion* and every other tune is essentially a variation of it. The love duet for Giorgio and Clara, "All This Happiness," is nice but perhaps a bit too "pop" to be memorable. Fosca's solo numbers are superior: In "I wish I could forget you," she dictates a letter for Giorgio to "write" to her. "Loving you is not a choice, it's who I am (and not much reason to rejoice)" is a sad, heartfelt examination of how it feels to love someone knowing your feelings are not returned. *Passion* is probably one of those shows, initially unsuccessfully, that will gather more devotees–who are not necessarily unaware of its flaws—as the years go by. Whatever one thinks of its score, Sondheim's lyrics are characteristically superb.

In 1995 there came a pop opera by Stewart Wallace entitled *Harvey Milk*, which detailed a gay man's journey—the real-life San Francisco city supervisor Harvey Milk—to self-acceptance, enlightenment, and death through intolerance. Milk and San Francisco Mayor George Moscone were murdered in 1978 by homophobic former city supervisor Dan White. *Harvey Milk* is certainly an interesting and at times invigorating and very colorful theatrical experience, it just isn't a memorable opera. The libretto is generally well-constructed but occasionally a bit too "kitschy," with a foolish and inappropriate kind of *Will and Grace* sensibility. (One lesbian character in the Stonewall riots scene is simply referred to in the libretto as a "dyke.") Milk was an opera fan and we can hear notes from *Tosca* as he attends the Met for the first time as a young man, as well as some Wagnerian strains, the only real opera you'll hear in this "opera." Some of the pieces, such as the Drag Queens' "We are the Stonewall Girls" and the Rioters'

"Out of the Closets and into the Streets," are okay Broadway and rock/pop numbers. The Parader's "Thank you San Francisco" is pure Broadway of a derivative, lesser kind. Many of the arias are just "opera" filtered through a pop sensibility. Harvey's politically incorrect "Who are these men? Who are we? We are the men without lives," referring to opera queens, could have been a strong piece if Wallace's orchestrative skills weren't so limited. Scott's aria "I dunno," explaining why he stays with Harvey, becomes a rather nice duet with the latter, although one might wonder why this love duet contains the line "and the ones you love after me" after they affirm their love for one another, which seems to completely undercut the commitment they have made. *Harvey Milk* has value as a theater piece and to a lesser extent as a human or historical document, but it's not something most opera fans would want to listen to repeatedly.

Thea Musgrave's vital, vigorous score for *Simon Bolivar*, which premiered at Virginia Opera in 1995, is arguably her greatest. Shot through with sheer nervous drive, the score sustains an almost constant state of tension. It is full of intense, highly emotional vocal lines that must be a strain on lesser voices. Some of Bolivar's arias have an anguished, positively tortured undercurrent. The energy of the music pulls the listener in right from the beginning, and Musgrave keeps things interesting with such flavorful additions as explosions, clacking swords, and literal and figurative fireworks. A particularly powerful recitative by Bolivar is followed by a contrastingly delicate parlor piece that eventually results in a pretty and unusual informal duet. There are passionate ensemble pieces and arias which blend into the whole. The music becomes much more lyrical, of course, when Simon interacts with females, including a flowing, romantic duet with a sinister undertone. Compelling and dramatic from start to finish, the score for *Simon Bolivar* is a very dark and exacting one.

One composer who has made certain inroads into major operatic venues is the heavily self-publicizing Tobias Picker. His works include *Emmaline* (1996) and *Therese Raquin* (2001), and he is currently working on an opera that was commissioned by the Met. Another secret to Picker's success? He picks good stories to set to music that is, unfortunately, mostly mediocre in nature. The *Wall Street Journal* calls Picker "our finest composer for the lyric stage," but if a composer has a limited melodic gift, how can this be true? As is true of many other contemporary operatic composers, Picker is probably better at orchestration than he is at composition. With *Emmaline*, Picker had one of the most fascinating stories to tell in all opera, and had the great fortune of working from a libretto by J. D. McClatchy. McClatchy's excellent libretto moves the story along and hits all the high points with such great skill that it's tempting to say that *Emmaline* is really

McClatchy's opera. Judith Rossner's novel, from which the libretto was fashioned, is based on the true story of a woman who meets, falls in love with, and marries a young man who turns out to be her own son. Picker seems influenced by everyone from Stravinsky to Copland to Sondheim, and probably would make a good composer for films. The music for *Emmaline*, too often blathery and uninspired, is more full of "melodiousness" than of melody. To be fair, there are times when the music of *Emmaline* is very pleasant, but it never soars. The individual listener will have to decide if this is because Picker is somehow afraid of being too emotional, or more likely simply lacks the kind of talent that includes a deep well of vivid and brilliant melodic invention.

Emmaline does get off to a fine start with an evocative, attractive overture, which also plays over the final scene and becomes Emmaline's final aria, "Everything I have is gone"; it works better as orchestral mood music than as an aria. The staccato, dissonant music of scene two is meant to get across Emmaline's confusion and the noisy unpleasantness of the mill, but it's also quite unpleasant to have to listen to. Act two's love duet for Emmaline and Matthew works well in pop-opera terms, with Picker's gift at orchestration serving him well as it generally does. However, when "Rock of Ages" is sung by the townspeople in act two, many in the audience may be thinking "at last — a real tune!" Reinforcing the theory that Picker would be better at composing films than operas is the wonderful and intense background music for the post-revelation confrontation between Emmaline and her husband/son Matthew. The ending to the story is tragic and grotesque, but without really great music its impact and moving nature is severely muted, and the conclusion seems drawn out as well. One can only imagine this great story with every sequence being bolstered by the music of a truly outstanding operatic composer.

Picker's skill at orchestration also serves him well in the similarly tuneless *Therese Raquin*. This time the libretto was fashioned by Gene Scheer, from the novel by Emile Zola. In Paris in 1864 Therese and her lover Laurent murder Camille, the man that she was raised with and whom she married, and are ultimately haunted and destroyed by their inhuman act. Camille's arioso "The Seine moves like a melody" is okay, but one wishes that its melody were better. A sequence in scene two when Camille enters and a champagne party begins (before the champagne has actually been served) has a throbbing, rhythmic background which makes it pleasant and interesting, but this is not the same as a lyrical recitative; and one background for an entire scene indicates limited resources on the part of the composer. However, there is a genuinely effective ensemble as Laurent and Therese sing secretly of their love and thwarted plans to rendezvous while in the midst of several preoccupied persons who, oblivious to the clandestine lovers, sing of other matters. The love/death duet (while Therese and Laurent sing of their love for one another Laurent hints it would be best if Camille were out of the way), "A scent of violets," has a pretty background which will impress the undiscriminating, but an unremarkable vocal line. The orchestral passages at the end of the piece adroitly blend the romantic with the sinister with some more excellent instrumentation.

In act two Therese's aria "My Wedding Day" is a perfect illustration of the anti-melodious aria that never comes to terms with a melody, wandering all over the lot in search of a tune, not only blah and forgettable but even irritating. Similarly, Therese's "white dove" aria, in which she longs for peace and an end to her nightmares, is pretty much a bust, and the piece sung by Camille's ghost ("Betrayed!") is a shameful mess. A potentially decent duet between Laurent and Therese on their wedding night is also muffed, then the melodramatic music descends into a lot of banging, banging, that is neither evocative nor even musical. Therese's final aria, "Never forgive me," in which she tells all to her paralyzed former mother-in-law is, however, above average for this opera, leading into an effective finale. Despite the few moments that work, *Therese Raquin* is only a fair-to-middling ersatz-verismo piece that just doesn't work as Grand Opera and is not that great as "music theater," either. Furthermore, a pop-Broadway-musical theater veneer, while not necessarily overt, clings to the whole project and cheapens it.

One might argue: doesn't Picker have the right to compose music that may not be very melodious but functions perfectly well as film-type background music, as many other composers do? Is Picker's work any worse than that of some of these other composers? In one sense, Picker's work is no worse than many; in others, it's much worse, because — unlike some of those other composers — Picker works with stories and librettos that cry out for more traditional music, even for "number" operas, which he probably isn't capable of providing. There have been many twentieth century operas that are not necessarily fountains of melody, who do not consist of one hit number after another, and whose great strength is the orchestral abilities of the composer (Bartók's *Bluebeard's Castle* comes to mind), but Picker's operas are not in that league, and have realistic librettos that require a different kind of score. And, to put it bluntly, Picker is no Bartók. It's not that we wait in vain for an aria, but that when one comes it's almost always a disappointment.

But *Emmaline* and *Therese Raquin* are works of Verdi or Wagner compared to some of the pop operas that have been generated by any minimally skilled composer who thinks he can slop one together, and by opera houses or other venues who are willing to mount such tripe in order to seem "hip." Such a piece is Michael Daugherty's *Jackie O*, which was produced by Houston Opera Studio in 1997. This presents a series of tableau presenting the former first lady and her friends and foes, including Liz Taylor, Andy Warhol, Grace Kelly, and so on. There is no real plot; *Jackie O* is really just an excuse to celebrate our celebrity-obsessed culture, and on any terms is pure unadulterated kitsch.

Jackie O begins with an overture with an annoying, somber solo cello (with snare drum) that quickly wears out its welcome. "The Happening" at Warhol's factory in the sixties, is instantly disposable pop music, and the chorus "Jackie's Coming" is so dreadful that it's almost impossible to listen to. "The Painter's Credo" sung by Warhol as he paints Jackie isn't bad, however, having a nice melody and an interesting orchestration. "I Am Curious (Yellow)," sung by Aristotle Onassis, is okay Andrew Lloyd Webber–type stuff, as is Jackie's "All His Bright Light." "At the Lido" is a pitiful attempt at a "trio" between Onassis, Maria Callas, and Jackie; attempts at ersatz operatic-style recitatives are disastrous. The use of opera singers may fool some into thinking that the "Flame Duet" is opera, but it doesn't make the grade. Perhaps *Jackie O*'s nadir is "Smash That Camera" which pits Jackie versus a tap dancing photographer. The final number, sung by Jackie ("Ask not what your country can do for you") is a pleasant pop tune. It all sounds like good clean fun — on the stage it may be — but musically this is fifth-rate all around.

Daughtery, who wrote a symphony inspired by Superman comic books, is not untalented, but he seems to know pop culture and little else. The music of *Jackie O* betrays no familiarity with the music of great and serious operas by the immortals. Daughtery is typical of modern composers who feel a need to explain their music in the liner notes of the CD for those who don't quite get it. Thus we are told that the "Flame Duet" between Jackie and Maria Callas is "a vocal tour de force for two sopranos." Well ... not quite. Once upon a time the notes were written by critics or someone who actually appreciated the music, but nowadays the composer himself leaves nothing to chance when it comes to letting us all in on his "genius." If *Jackie O* is ever mounted again, great voices need not apply.

The only thing worse than the music of *Jackie O* is Wayne Koestenbaum's silly libretto, which mostly provides camp instead of illumination. The lyrics, meant to be clever, are more often dumb. Some of them simply list things — numbers, letters, celebrities, drinks, items Aristotle can buy — instead of examining character. Most of the people who see and enjoy stuff like *Jackie O* will not get the operatic references that Koestenbaum occasionally drops into a lyric. Koestenbaum does provide one nice bit of spoken dialogue for Jackie: "Now Jack is a myth when he would rather have been a man."

If ever any subject should have been turned into an actual opera, it was the sinking of the Titanic, turned into a Broadway musical/ersatz opera by Maury Yeston. Yeston has undeniable melodic — and musical — ability, but most of the music in *Titanic* (1997), while often very pleasant, is distressingly "pop" and rather second-rate. The fact that the performers have pop voices doesn't help the few numbers that strive to be something more than modern-day Broadway-style ditties. The score includes a couple of agreeable waltz numbers ("I Have Danced"; "No Moon"), a snappy ragtime pastiche ("Doing the Latest Rag"), but "To Be a Captain" ends just as it gets interesting (and other melodies are never satisfactorily developed), and "We'll Meet Tomorrow" illustrates the main problem with the work.

This last number has husbands and wives saying goodbye to each other at the lifeboats as they all wonder if this will be the last time they ever see each other. The situation is terribly moving; this powerful moment needs much more powerful music than a merely serviceable pop tune. The same is true of the following, somewhat derivative "Still," in which older couples sing of how much they still mean to each other after many years of marriage. Yet Yeston rises to the occasion at least twice in *Titanic*. "Godspeed Titanic (Sail On)" has a certain nobility and inevitable poignancy as the doomed ship sets sail on its fateful voyage. And the touching "Lady's Maid," which examines the aspirations of the men and women traveling in the lowest decks, expertly personifies what America meant to the desperate immigrants sailing from Europe in hopes of a better life. The trouble with Yeston's *Titanic* is that the subject matter requires not a composer of mere talent but one of genius. In spite of this, *Titanic* won the Tony for Best Musical in 1997.

Not quite an opera, but more than a musical, was Jason Robert Brown's *Parade* which premiered in 1998. *Parade*, which was sub-titled *An American Opera*, illustrates the point that in the 1990's and earlier, musical theater was providing the melody and inventive scoring that was all too often lacking in straight opera. More to the point, *Parade* is one of the only — probably the only — genuinely excellent pop operas. An indictment of Southern intolerance masquerading as Southern pride, *Parade* is based on a true story of a Jewish man, Leo Franks, who was convicted in 1913 of murdering a little girl, and after having his sentence commuted from hanging to life imprisonment, was killed by a mob. The story was filmed in 1937 as *They Won't Forget*. Brown also supplied the lyrics, while Alfred Uhry contributed the book. The excellent orchestrations were done by Don Sebesky. It isn't just that Brown comes up with some winning melodies (albeit mostly in a pop style, although there are operatic-type numbers, Broadway numbers, blues songs, and so on), but that there's a cleverness and sophistication to the way he presents them. He often uses counterpoint, two melodies at once, to contrast or compliment certain emotional ideas. For instance, Leo's "How can I call this home?" relating how alienated he feels in Atlanta, "the land that time forgot," is counterpointed with a chorus of southern celebrants. Lucille's "What am I waiting for?" in which she acknowledges that she married well but that something is still missing, is counterpointed with "Leo at work" doing math at the pencil factory and deciding, ironically, "this is wrong, this is wrong." Frankie's moving eulogy to the murdered thirteen-year-old, Mary, ("It don't make sense') is counterpointed with the choral dirge "There is a Fountain." Often the music is used to create a contrast to the mood of a particular sequence, such as in "Feel the Rain Fall," an effective blues number as the governor questions a witness who may have lied; the spirited tune and its delivery is in contrast to the serious nature of the questioning. Granted that some of the pseudo-rock numbers are tiresome, and some of the music is mediocre, there is also much to admire in the score.

The first number, "The Old Red Hills of Home," as the Young and Old Soldiers sing of the Old South's way of life and how it's worth fighting for, is a masterful and intense pop-opera piece with an irresistible melody. The final number, "All the Wasted Time," although dismissed by some advocates of the show, is a beautiful and powerful love duet for Leo and his wife Lucille as they reaffirm their love; this also has an operatic intensity and structure. In between there are other memorable numbers. Lucille is given an impassioned defense of Leo's character in "You don't know this man." Mary implies that Leo is "interested" in her in "He calls my name," a "pretty" melody on an ugly subject (pedophilia, rumor pandering, or both) which only makes it more chilling. Leo's bouncy "Come up to my office," has sinister undertones as it suggests that the Leo of the other girls' testimony has an unnatural interest in them; the music here has a dark underscoring beneath the Broadway tempo. Mrs. Phagan's "My child will forgive me," her dirge for her daughter, is perfectly nice and attractive, even if it's really just a "country/western" tune. Whatever its flaws, *Parade* should have had the success and reputation of the highly over-rated *Les Miserables*. As for Leo Franks, most historians seem to agree that he was railroaded.

The same year that *Parade* debuted, there was a flurry of press reports creating some anticipation for Andre Previn's operatic version of *A Streetcar Named Desire*. Throughout the history of opera, composers have used stage plays as the basis for their works, but the vast majority of these plays were dated or mediocre works that would have been completely forgotten were it not for the musical version which superseded it. But with *Streetcar*, Previn was dealing with a certified American masterpiece. There was precedent: operatic versions of masterpieces by Eugene O'Neill, for instance, had already been performed. But the general consensus was that if music did not add to what was already a riveting evening at the theater, what was the point in adapting the play in the first place? By that criteria, Previn's *Streetcar* is truly pointless. All of the opera's power comes directly from Williams' play, with only an occasional bit of sensitivity and lyricism in the music.

Streetcar is basically in the verismo-style — sometimes the music is too overwrought for some of its simple dialogue scenes, notwithstanding the emotions below the surface — but lacks the great melodies that are associated with the genre. Blanche's aria "I want Magic," in which she explains how she fudges the truth to create magic for others, has had a separate life in the concert hall and on solo CDs but is actually quite mediocre. The best and most melodious piece in the opera is actually Blanche's other act three aria "I can smell the sea air," during which she imagines how she'll die at sea. It's too bad Previn didn't compose more music like this undeniably lovely aria. Mitch's arioso in act two, "You know when it's the right thing," about the need to love, is also quite pretty and tender. On the other hand, the loud, brassy orchestral interlude between scenes 3 (the rape) and four in act three is virtually worthless, like background music for a Grade C action flick. *A Streetcar Named Desire* has been recorded and telecast, but it's unlikely to become a standard repertory piece. Williams' play, however, is truly timeless. Other adaptations of Williams' plays include Lee Hoiby's (born 1926) well-received *Summer and Smoke* (1971) and Bruce Saylor's *Orpheus Descending*, which premiered at Lyric Opera of Chicago in 1994. It has a libretto by J. D. McClatchy of *Emmaline* fame.

In contrast to Previn's mess, Mark Adamo's *Little Women*, a folk opera which also premiered in 1998 (and was also telecast), is, despite flaws, lovely, poignant and all together admirable. On occasion the music for *Little Women* may seem overwrought and melodramatic without reason (in the prologue for instance), and Adamo may seem too caught up musical theater concepts and devices, but he can also write music of great sensitivity, lyricism, and — yes — melody. The famous story, which takes place just after the Civil War, details the lives and loves of the March sisters, especially Jo, who has some trouble growing up. Highlights include Meg's aria, "Things change, Jo," in which she tries to explain to her sister that she still loves her and the family but is now a woman with other needs. Jo's suitor Bhaer is given an outstanding, somewhat Straussian aria in act two, with words by Goethe, "Kennst du das Land," as Bhaer demonstrates what, to him, is art. This beautiful piece, describing a dream of peace and paradise, is far and away the best thing in the opera, but it is so different in style from the rest (which at times sounds Coplandesque) that it almost seems to come out of nowhere. Other notable pieces include Alma and Gordon's act one duet "We stand together," as they "recite" their wedding vows for Meg and Brooke who wish to use them at their own wedding; this becomes a background quartet as the latter couple join in behind dialogue between the boy Laurie and Jo. Having Laurie turned down by Jo as the two couples sing wedding vows in counterpoint is a very effective and dramatic touch. The effect of Jo's Broadway-style act one aria, "We're perfect as we are," however, is blunted by inserting tiresome sections of her trying to come up with the right words as she writes a passage in her book, and her aria in the prologue, "That worked for the moment," doesn't benefit from its shuddering, jerking background music whatever its intention. The whole "truth or fabrication" sequence (this is a game the March sisters play) goes on far too long and has unattractive music. But the opera ends on a high note: Jo's "Let me look at you," as she realizes and accepts that nothing and no one stays the same forever, is a lovely closing number. The moving postscript has Bhaer show up in the attic to be permanently reunited with Jo, the woman he loves. Compared to other modern-day operas, *Little Women* is a little gem.

Another 1998 premiere was Henry Mollicone's folk opera *Coyote Tales*, with a libretto by Sheldon Harnick of Broadway fame, which debuted at Lyric Opera of Kansas City. A lonely coyote surrounded by nothing but water prays to the sun or Great Spirit to help him create other creatures to keep him company, which include foxes, witchy hags called "skookums," and the native Pavayoykyasi and the maiden he loves. The coyote falls in love with a star, but after singing a duet with it he falls to the ground. Which is why today coyotes bay at the sky at night — to chastise the star who let the father of them all drop down to earth. And so on. Mollicone's score is lyrical and generally well orchestrated, perfectly attractive and pleasant and sometimes even better than that, it just isn't especially distinctive. But just when you're apt to dismiss Mollicone, he comes up with something quite lovely, and his vocal writing is often first-rate even when the melody isn't. In general, *Coyote Tales* is nice if unspectacular. Mollicone's *Gabriel's Daughter* premiered in 2003 at the Central City Opera.

Touted as a pop opera of sorts, but not really warranting the attention this appellation gave it, *Marie Christine* (1999) had words and music by Michael John Lachiusa and a story that was an updating of the Medea legend transplanted to New Orleans. Although the premise was certainly interesting, it was not especially well developed. It's all handled musically in a way that reminds one of Andrew Lloyd Webber (especially *Jesus Christ Super-*

star) as the composer uses a variety of forms—pop, rock, soul, mostly—but while there are some very pleasant numbers, this is not a score of any great distinction even by pop opera standards. Some of the recitatives and numbers, such as a duet between Marie and her lover Dante entitled "I don't hear the ocean," have operatic pretensions. Marie's "Tell Me" has a dramatic flair à la Webber. Marie is also given a nice lullaby to sing in "I will love you," and her "I will give you my money," in which she promises everything for the sake of her love for Dante, is smoky, insinuating, and quite effective. Incredibly, the nadir of *Marie Christine* is yet another what-a-great-city-Chicago-is song, which is pretty poor compared to others.

John Harbison's *The Great Gatsby* was commissioned by the Metropolitan Opera to commemorate the 25th anniversary of the debut of conductor and artistic director James Levine. While Fitzgerald's novel is not a good choice for operatic treatment to begin with, it probably could have been turned into a better musical stage work than Harbison's opera, which at times is more like a travesty. A distressing amount of the music is unmemorable and unpleasant, and the characters remain utterly one-dimensional throughout. As *Gatsby* is set in the jazz age, there are some snappy jazz pastiches inserted into the score, but a better composer might have gotten across this jazzy "feel" by interpolating it within a classical tradition (as Korngold did in a scene in his *Die Katrin*, for instance). There is an attractive, dissonant, somehow old-fashioned overture (which would have been "modern" fifty or more years ago) which is a sinuous and well-orchestrated piece. In Myrtle's aria "I never said that!" Harbison desperately tries to keep the music interesting with a rather jangling, popping background but the vocal line is just hopeless. Later, Myrtle's literal wailing after Tom hits her is extremely non-euphonious to listen to. Nick meets Gatsby to the background of a tango, then a Charleston takes over as Gatsby briefly interacts with some others; this is all very flavorful, but hardly opera, and not very challenging, original, or impressive.

Gatsby is given a decent enough aria in "Everyone was here but the one who matters," but it's the orchestration that makes it work more than the melody. An interlude between scenes one and two is just a lot of noise. However, act two does end on a high note. Scene four, when Daisy and Gatsby meet at Nick's after five years, has the best sustained music in the opera, culminating in an informal love duet that, with its many pauses, suggests suspended, but mounting erotic attraction. If every scene had been handled with this lyricism and intelligence, *Gatsby* might have amounted to more than a time-passer. Act two has a couple of respectable minor pieces, but nothing that stands out. Having been mounted by the Met, *The Great Gatsby* might have a life span that it doesn't really deserve. Then again, lots of operas have been mounted for a season or two at the Met and never been heard from again.

Another opera that played the Met (although it originated elsewhere) is William Bolcom's *A View from the Bridge* (1999) from the play by Arthur Miller. Bolcom is a well-respected composer but, if *View* is any indication, he simply lacks the melodic impetus and orchestrative skills to compose a great opera. As in Previn's adaptation of *Streetcar* the only power that this opera has comes from Miller's original (if dated) stage play. The protagonist Eddie has a thing for his niece Catherine, and does everything he can to destroy the illegal immigrant, Rudolpho, that she's fallen in love with. He calls in the authorities to have Rudolpho deported, but with this deplorable act that turns the whole neighborhood against him only winds up destroying himself. In act one, the bit with the minor character Mike only saying "yeah" during the sequence which introduces him, Louis and Eddie smacks of musical comedy; this continues throughout the opera and becomes very tiresome. Just as audiences thought "at last — a melody" when they heard "Rock of Ages" in *Emmaline*, they do the same when the song "Paper Doll" (composed by Johnny S. Black) is sung by Rudolpho in scene five. Bolcom introduces his own song into scene seven when Rudolpho warbles a love poem to New York ("I love the beauty of the view at home").

Calling this minor aria "gorgeous," which one critic did, is a severe overstatement. The melody isn't bad but it's neither developed well nor particularly well-orchestrated, and doesn't even have a bravura finish. Audiences at Met performances cheered this piece, first, because it was an oasis in a desert, second, because it praises the great city in the wake of September 11th, and lastly, because it was sung quite well by the tenor (although it's certainly not a hard piece to sing). And it never quite escapes a certain "Broadway" aura. Marco's aria in scene five of act two ("To America I sailed on a ship called Hunger") is a total bust, proof positive that Bolcom has no real idea how to compose compelling opera. What should be a bitter, despairing, tragic outcry is just a forgettable, tuneless, poorly orchestrated bit of "blah." The famous kissing scene between Eddie and Rudolpho — the former wants to call the latter's "manhood" into question as one more attempt to drive a wedge between him and Catherine — actually calls into question the sexual orientation of both men. Modern-day audiences, who have lived through Gay Rights, Gay Marriages, and an attitude towards homosexuality that is much more honest and sophisticated than it was when Miller first wrote his play, will probably see Rudolpho as Eddie's true lust object, not Catherine; Eddie is the cliché of the closet queen whose inability to accept himself proves destructive to everyone around him and especially to himself. Presented so close to the twenty-first century, *View from the Bridge* comes off a bit as the product of people who are somewhat behind the times.

Tod Machover's opera *Resurrection* was commissioned by the Houston Grand Opera and premiered there in 1999. It is at least the third operatic version of Leo Tolstoy's novel. (The two previous versions were Alfano's *Risurrezione*— see chapter 3 — and Jan Cikker's *Vekriesenie*. Machover's version has the same basic plotline as Alfano's.) Machover had previously done what became known as "the first computer opera," a work entitled *VALIS*, which had its admirers. His *Brain Opera* encouraged participation from the live audience or over the internet. It is not in any way surprising that Houston Grand Opera commissioned a work from such a kitschmeister as Machover; what is surprising is that the result, *Resurrection*, turned out as good as it did. That is entirely because Machover, whatever his limitations as a composer, didn't forget what so many modern-day operatic composers such as Bolcom and Previn and many others do: that opera is about *singing*. Machover at least gives his characters something to actually sing that is often worth hearing.

Machover has a sure dramatic hand, but the electronic effects he employs tend to trivialize and undermine the score, although others feel differently. Anthony Brandt, Assistant Music Professor at Rice University claims that "In *Resurrection* the electronics are most often in the background, subtly enhancing important melodic lines and adding heft to the orchestral sonorities.... Machover makes a powerful statement about music's ability to capture the full range of our experience."[3] Most serious opera fans will feel that Machover should put away his tiresome computer and synthesizer and work with a real orchestra, if he's able to. The electronic effects, meant to "punch up," "clarify," and add "extra dimension" to the music and which are supposed to blend into the score, actually stick out like bright red boils on a baby's behind. Worse, they give the whole project a "rock opera" aura. Not so strangely, some of the music of this very modern piece — such as an act one duet for the Prince and Marlova ("Is this a dream") sounds like ersatz baroque music. The flashback scene with Katerina rushing to find the Prince on the train to tell him of the baby is quite effective, as it was in Alfano's version years earlier. So is Katerina's aria "He's gone! He's gone!" in which she sings of her despair over the situation she finds herself in. This piece too is rather baroque in nature, with an added passionate component. Katerina also has an excellent aria at the end of act one ("Look at me, look at me!") in which, reacting to the Prince's proposal, she tells him that it's all coming too late and she is no longer the woman who once loved him. The music in the marching-to-Siberia scene in act two is often tender and expressive, although the flogging scene (of "subversive" teacher Peter) is kitschy and unnecessary. The final duet ("Do for the World/We must live") in which Katerina and the Prince realize how their feelings for one another have changed them, is outstanding, although some listeners might think the piece a bit too "pop"; again, the electronics in the background don't help at all.

Other pieces in the score are much less successful. The Prince's aria "What have I done" (he is appalled at the sentencing of his former lover) is pretty dreadful, with an especially poor, jangling background that's meant to depict tormented emotions but only sounds idiotic. However, the discordant backgrounds as the Prince prepares to sell his possessions to the consternation of family members, again illustrating his desperate and unsettled mind, is not so unpleasant because the vocal writing here is good. *Resurrection* is hardly for all tastes — it isn't as good as Alfano's version — but who would have expected Machover's adaptation to "sing" as well as it does?

As the twentieth century began to evaporate and fade into the twenty-first, many of the operatic trends that had begun in the last hundred years — in the last decade, in fact — continued unabated. For instance, at one point during Michael Berkeley's (b. 1948) operatic version of *Jane Eyre* (2000), the mad Mrs. Rochester, according to stage directions in the libretto — and this is a sure sign of desperation — bares her breasts for the audience. Let's hope those are mighty impressive breasts, for there is little else to recommend about *Jane Eyre*, at least on the musical end.

David Malouf's libretto, which neatly compresses and encapsulates the story of the governess Jane and the tormented Rochester, is quite short (the whole opera takes up a little over seventy minutes in two acts), but certainly provides a talented composer with all that he or she might need to showcase their abilities. But Berkeley muffs virtually every opportunity at making something out of what Malouf has handed him. *Jane Eyre* can't even be classified as effective music theater because the score makes the whole thing so tedious; 72 minutes seems like three hours.

The opera begins with that typical "horror movie" music so common to modern operas. Quotes from Donizetti's *Lucia di Lammermoor* (which little Adele, Jane's charge, sings in one scene), only point up how almost comically awful Berkeley's music can be. The vocal writing is wretched. (Some singers prefer this kind of music. When they sing Puccini, they have to wonder how much of the applause is for them and how much for Puccini. With composers like Berkeley, the singers know they are getting all of the applause.) Berkeley's only "trick" is to use the same, admittedly effective background music for all of Rochester's arias. Jane and Rochester's duet, "I Will Marry You," in which they at last express their love for each other, is repetitive, utterly unromantic and trite. If the composer wanted to avoid the excesses of a typical love duet, he should have replaced it with something more memorable. He may well have felt that standard romantic music was inappropriate, seeing as how the wedding never takes place (Rochester already has a wife, the madwoman hidden in the manor), but couldn't the music have been in some way worthwhile? But then at the very end of the opera Berkeley, who has shown nothing but disdain for lyricism throughout the piece, resorts to it for the final reunion duet for Jane and Rochester ("Jane, Jane, is it really you?"), which is actually perfectly pleasant but much too little, too late. Berkeley is typical of composers who think if they finally resort to Dreaded Melody (one suspects Berkeley's melodic well does not run too deep) before the final curtain the audience will be fooled into thinking they've been sitting through *Il trovatore*. It never works. *Jane Eyre* is in its way as "well-done" a "modern," mostly non-melodious opera as any of its ilk, which, sadly, isn't saying much. *Jane Eyre* was commissioned by the Cheltenham International Festival of Music, where it premiered at the Music Theatre Wales in June of 2000. Berkeley is also the composer of *Baa Baa Black Sheep*.

Across the ocean, Jake Heggie's operatic version of *Dead Man Walking* premiered in 2001, and like most operas from living composers (and living librettists, in this case Terrence McNally) especially if they are tireless self-promoters, it received a lot of attention. Due to a scarcity of great music and memorable arias, *Dead Man Walking* emerges a skillfully done work of agitprob music theater but not great opera. A political opera like *Dead Man Walking*—and it is one of the most political of all operas—invites political commentary whether the composer wants it or not, but for our purposes we'll stick to the music, but not without first saying that it's hard to see *Dead Man Walking* as being objective on the subject of capital punishment when death penalty opponents held a torch light vigil across the street from San Francisco Opera on the night of its premiere in 2001. And is it either accurate or fair to equate the execution of—let's face it—scum like the lead character of this opera with the savage murder of innocent victims?

In the disturbing prologue, Joseph De Rocher (a composite character) and his brother attack, rape and kill a teenage couple. Sentenced to death, Joseph writes to Sister Helen and asks her to come to see him. He insists on his innocence and is hoping she can help him. Sister Helen is opposed to capital punishment but insists that Joseph must accept responsibility for his actions. The families of his victims are outraged that Sister Helen seems to show compassion for him and his family but not for them. Sister Helen, sharing the pain of Joseph's mother, believes that executing Joseph will only create "another victimized family." Under the nun's guidance, Joseph confesses his guilt and is led away to receive a lethal injection.

The opera begins with an attractive romantic prelude, bolstered by Heggie's rich orchestration. A derivative Sunday school hymn-pastiche sung by Sister Helen ("He will gather around us") is at least energetic and pleasant. There is a very effective and touching scene in act one with the Sister and the parents of the victims ("You don't know what it's like"), which becomes a sextet when De Rocher's mother also joins in. The music is just as "sympathetic" when it is announced that Joseph has been denied a pardon, equating the dead kids — who are never named, further dehumanizing them, which is perhaps the point — with their murderer. The very effective act one finale has everything and everyone closing in on Sister Helen in her mind in a tremendous, powerful rabble that ends, in contrast, as she quietly gets change for a soda.

There are some other pleasant pieces in act one, but the arias and duets and other "numbers" in act two — which are denoted in the libretto in the event you can't tell them from the recitatives — are undistinguished, with the exception of a dramatic ensemble as De Rocher is lead to the death chamber. The actual execution scene isn't totally silent (lethal injection, while unpleasant, is certainly more humane than what Joseph did to his victims); one can hear the noise of the machinery that sends the killer out of this world in a nicely theatrical touch. McNally's libretto tries hard to make you feel sorry for De Rocher as he dies; McNally hedges his bets by having De Rocher's last thoughts be of his victims and their families (but keep in mind that De Rocher is a fictional character). *Dead Man Walking* is more the story of Sister Helen Prejean than it is of "Joseph De Rocher" (and certainly his victims), therefore it is hopelessly limited by and to her rather superficial, muddle-headed, and illogical viewpoint. Within those limitations it has some memorable moments and music, even if the score is not one most opera fans would want to listen to repeatedly.

The same is undoubtedly true of Deborah Dratell's *Lilith*, which was given a stage premiere by New York City Opera in 2001. Dratell was also one of three composers who contributed to the collection of one- acts entitled *Central Park* in 2000, with librettos by well-known playwrights. (Wendy Wasserstein wrote the libretto for *The Festival of Regrets*, which was scored by Dratell.) *Lilith* looks at Adam's first wife, Lilith, and her conflict with his second, more submissive wife, Eve. The music for *Lilith* is not entirely terrible and has some interesting, attractive moments, but the main problem with the piece is that Dratell has written a perfectly nice ballet but not an opera. The libretto hasn't enough dramatic vitality, and there is absolutely no vocal writing of distinction, leaving the singers completely at sea. Talented soprano Lauren Flanigan, cast as Eve in the production, had to endure the indignity of fluttering around in an unflattering slip for most of the evening. Peter G. Davis wrote in *New York* that "the score ... comes off more as a collection of miscellaneous sound effects than a thought-out composition," which is, sadly, true of many other modern operas. Davis added that "To judge from the impoverished works that regularly reach the stage these days, music is no longer the major element of an opera, but just another ingredient."

But hope springs eternal. The days of Verdi, Wagner, Puccini, Mascagni, Strauss and so on may be over — except in the better opera houses — but somewhere out there even now there may be a man or woman with enough respect for, and knowledge of, the past to compose music that is fresh and new and original, but gloriously alive with singable, wonderful melody.

Chapter Notes

Chapter 1

1. Buzzini's *Turandot* premiered at La Scala and was given twelve performances before vanishing forever.
2. Claims have been made that the mad scene in Franchetti's *Cristoforo Columbo*, which debuted eight years before *Tosca*, has a five chord motif that is supposedly similar to Scarpia's motif in *Tosca*. It is unlikely, however, that Puccini stole any music from Franchetti — or would need to.
3. French composer André Messager wrote an opera based on the Pierre Lati novel "Madame Chrysanthéme," which probably influenced Belasco's play.
4. *Giacomo Puccini e l'opera internazionale.*
5. *Richard Strauss: Man, Musician, Enigma.* Michael Kennedy.
6. *Puccini: A Biography.* Mary Jane Phillips-Matz.

Chapter 2

1. In his write ups on Mascagni in at least two popular opera guides William Ashbrook can't seem to get past Mascagni's "opportunistic nature" and alleged fascist ties. While grudgingly admitting the value of some of his music, Ashbrook is clearly no admirer and has little appreciation of Mascagni's work and should have been the last person to be summing up the composer's career and achievements. Judging from his brief, often misleading, and occasionally inaccurate essays of Mascagni's works in the *Viking Opera Guide* it's as if he hardly bothered to listen to the operas more than once, if that. A lot of the negative blather about Mascagni has to be laid at his doorstep.
2. "The Two Wooden Shoes" had previ-

ously been turned into an opera by Franco Vittadini entitled *Anima Allegra.*
3. *Puccini: A Biography.* Mary Jane Phillips-Matz.
4. *Mascagni.* David Stivender.

Chapter 3

1. *A Prima Donna's Progress: An Autobiography of Joan Sutherland.*
2. *Puccini: A Biography.* Mary Jane Phillips-Matz.

Chapter 4

1. *Opera News.* July 1997.
2. "Seduced by Zarzuela." Steven Blier. *Opera News.* July 1997.

Chapter 5

1. *Massenet.* James Harding.
2. Ibid.
3. *Richard Strauss: Man, Musician, Enigma.* Michael Kennedy.
4. *Puccini: A Biography.* Mary Jane Phillips-Matz.
5. Some information on *Pénélope* gleaned from liner notes to LP.
6. *Aaron Copland: The Life and Work of an Uncommon Man.* Howard Pollack.
7. *Prokofiev: From Russia to the West.* David Nice.

Chapter 6

1. *Richard Strauss: Man, Musician, Enigma.* Michael Kennedy.

2. *Benjamin Britten: A Biography*. Humphrey Carpenter.
3. *Puccini: A Biography*. Mary Jane Phillips-Matz.

Chapter 7

1. *The Last Prodigy: A Biography of Erich Wolfgang Korngold."* Brendan G. Carroll.
2. Other examples include Messager's *Fortunio* and Wolf-Ferrari's *I gioielli della Madonna*.
3. Aaron Copland described atonalism thusly in his book, "What to Listen for in Music:" "(atonalists) write melodies that have no tonal center of any kind. Instead, they choose the twelve tones of the chromatic scale, giving equal rights to each one of the semitones. Self-imposed rules forbid the repetition of any one of the twelve tones until the other eleven have been sounded. This larger tone gamut, plus an increased use of wider and wider skips between single notes, has left many listeners confused, if not exasperated."
4. *Britten*. Carpenter.
5. *Puccini*. Phillips-Matz.
6. Liner notes to *Sly* by Herbert Rosendorfer.

Chapter 10

1. *Frederick Delius*. Sir Thomas Beecham.
2. Some information on Ethel Smyth gleaned from liner notes by Ronald Crichton.
3. Letter from Floyd to author.
4. Letter from Curtin to author. (Ms. Curtin's other twentieth century favorites include Floyd's *Susannah*, Blitzstein's *Regina*, and Lee Hoiby's *A Month in the Country*.)

Chapter 11

1. *Victor Herbert*. Edward Waters.
2. *ibid.*
3. Other African-American composers of this period included Harry Lawrence Freeman (1869–1954), who composed *Valdo* (1906) and others; Clarence Cameron White (1880–1960), composer of *Ovango* (1956); and William Grant Still (1895–1978), who came out with *Troubled Island* in 1937.
4. *The Complete Opera Book*; 1935 edition. Gustave Kobbé.

5. *Aaron Copland The Life and Work of an Uncommon Man*. Howard Pollack.
6. Ironically, Copland's own music was generally full of a great deal of deep feeling. Interestingly, at twelve he attempted his own version of *Cavalleria rusticana* and got as far as setting Turridu's first aria to music that somewhat resembled Mascagni's original.
7. All of this is lost, of course, in the fairly dreadful film version.
8. *Mark the Music: The Life and Times of Marc Blitzstein*. Eric A. Gordon.

Chapter 12

1. Although Andrea Bocelli has been called a modern-day Mario Lanza, the only similarity between the two is that both gained fame singing opera in venues other than opera houses. Lanza had a magnificent voice and great dramatic power, and it was a serious loss that he never sang outside movies except in concerts. By any standard Bocelli is not in Lanza's league.
2. *Mark the Music*. Gordon.
3. Letter from Floyd to author.

Chapter 13

1. As quoted in *New York* Magazine piece on "CNN operas."
2. Letter from Floyd to author.
3. *ibid.*
4. It is not known if either George W. or Laura Bush have themselves actually listened to any of Floyd's operas, but it is not likely.
5. Other twentieth century women composers of opera include Mary Carr Moore *(Narcissa* 1912); Amy Marcy Beach *(Cabildo* 1945); Meredith Monk *(Atlas* 1991); and Libby Larsen *(Frankenstein* 1990).
6. While Herrmann's *Vertigo* score could be — and has been — dismissed as warmed over *Tristan*, there is no denying that his exhilarating overture for *North by Northwest*, so unusually and vividly orchestrated, is a major piece for the composer.

Chapter 14

1. Assorted quotes on *Bomarzo* from liner notes to LP.
2. Letter from Bonynge to author.

3. Anthony Tommasini; September 30th, 2002.
4. Donald Westwood; February 8th, 1997.

Chapter 15

1. Letter from Bonynge to author.

Chapter 16

1. According to Peter G. Davis in *New York*: "Adams ... actually boasts about his ignorance of operatic tradition (see the September/October 1991 *Harvard* Magazine)."
2. Liner notes for *Caritas CD*.
3. Liner notes for *Resurrection* CD.

20th Century Arias, Duets, Intermezzos of Note

"Have you seen a child the color of wheat?" Quartet: *Amahl and the Night Visitors*. Menotti.

"Sir wir schonda." Act two duet for Ariadne and Bacchus: *Ariadne auf Naxos*. Strauss.

Ariane's scene three aria: *Ariane*. Martinu.

Andante/string sextet prelude: *Capriccio*. Strauss.

Coming of dawn orchestral interlude: act one of *Cunning Little Vixen*. Janáček.

"Gluck, mas mir verlieb." Act one duet: *Das Tote Stadt*. Korngold.

"Der Kaiser's Abschied." Aria: *Der Kaiser von Atlantis*. Ullmann.

"Orestes! Orestes! Orestes!" Elektra's aria: *Elektra*. Strauss.

"Fanny." Act one aria: *Fanny*. Rome.

"Non colombelle." Act one tenor aria: *Isabeau*. Mascagni.

Act two love quartet: *La rondine*. Puccini.

"Depuis le jour." Act two aria: *Louise*. Charpentier.

"Un bel dì;" Cio Cio San's act two aria: *Madama Butterfly*. Puccini.

Overture: *Makropulos Case*. Janáček.

"Rise up, my love, my fair one." Act two duet: *Merry Mount*. Hanson.

"Columbia! Bright Goddess of the Free!" Act two aria: *Natoma*. Herbert.

Orchestral music, act one, as Palestrina completes his mass: *Palestrina*, Pfitzner.

"Bene morro d'amore." Act two aria: *Parisina*. Mascagni.

"Bess, you is my woman." Act two duet: *Porgy and Bess*. Gershwin.

"Wanderer's Song." Act one chorus: *Sarlatan*. Haas.

"Old Man River." Aria: *Show Boat*. Kern.

"Senza mamma." Aria: *Suor Angelica*. Puccini.

"The promise of living." Act one quintet: *The Tender Land*. Copland.

"Vissi d'arte." Aria from act two: *Tosca*. Puccini.

"No! Mai nessun m'aura!" Act two aria: *Turandot*. Puccini.

"Reine Lieb, die ich suchte." Duet: *Violanta*. Korngold.

"A radiant spring sky." Scene one aria: *War and Peace*. Prokofiev.

Discography

Adriana Lecouvreur. Cilea. (**A**) C: Mario Rossi; Orchestra del Teatro San Carlo di Napoli. Magda Olivero (Adriana); Franco Corelli (Maurizio). Giuletta Simionato (Princess). 1959. (**B**) C: Franco Capuana; Orchestra dell'Academia di Santa Cecilia, Roma. Renata Tebaldi (Adriana); Mario Del Monaco (Maurizio); Giuletta Simionato (Princess). 1962. Both are excellent recordings with top singers. The latter is in stereo. Del Monaco holds the next to last note in his act three aria about defeating the Russian troops with bravura length and intensity.

Die ägyptische Helena. Strauss. C: Joseph Keilberth; Orchester der Bayerischen Staatsoper. Leonie Rysanek (Helena); Bernd Aldenhoff (Menelas); Annelies Kupper (Aithra); Hermann Uhde (Altair); Richard Holm (Da-ud). Orfeo. Live mono 1956 recording is excellent.

Albert Herring. Britten. C: Benjamim Britten; English Chamber Orchestra. With: Peter Pears; Sheila Rex; Sylvia Fisher. Pears' horrible voice almost ruins his otherwise good "performance" as Albert.

Alexandre bis. Martinů. C: František Jílek; Brno Janáček Opera Orchestra. Daniela Sounova (Armande); Rene Tuček (Alexandre). Supraphon. Acceptable recording of Martinů's one act opera buffa.

Amahl and the Night Visitors. Menotti. C: Schippers; NBC Television Orchestra. Chet Allen (Amahl); Rosemary Kulhmann (Mother). From the original TV production of the opera, this is excellent in all departments.

Amica. Mascagni. C: Pace; Hungarian Radio Orchestra. Katia Ricciarelli (Amica); Fabio Armiliato (Giorgio); Walter Donati (Rinaldo.) Well-conducted by Pace and superbly sung by Amiliato and Donati. Riccia-relli has trouble with the difficult tessitura, to put it mildly, but otherwise sings with passion and conviction.

L'amore dei tre re. Montemezzi. C: Nello Santi; London Symphony Orchestra. Anna Moffo (Fiora); Plácido Domingo (Avito); Pablo Elvira (Manfredo); Cesare Siepi (Archibaldo); Ryland Davies (Flaminio). With this cast you can't go wrong; Elvira's work is especially stunning.

Antigone. Honneger. C: Maurice Le Roux; Orchestre National.

Antony and Cleopatra. Barber. C: Christian Badea; Spoleto Festival Orchestra. Jeffrey Wells (Antony); Esther Hinds (Cleo); Robert Grayson (Caesar). New World. Live recording of the opera that opened the new Met.

Arabella. Strauss. C: Sir Georg Solti; Wiener Philharmoniker. With: Lisa Della Casa; Hilde Gueden; George London.

Arald. Bretan. C: Cristian Mandeal; Philharmonic Orchestra Moldavia, Iasi. Alexandru Agache (Seer); Ionel Voineag (Arald); Sanda Sandru (Maria). Nimbus. Very well done with excellent singers; baritone Agache is especially strong.

Ariadne auf Naxos. Strauss. C: Kurt Masur; Gewandhausorchester, Leipzig. With Jessye Norman; Dietrich Fischer-Dieskau.

Ariane et Barbe-bleue. Dukas. C: Armind Jordan; Nouvel Orchestre Philharmonique. Katherine Ciesinski (Ariane); Gabirel Bacquier (Barbe-bleue). Erato. Although Bacquier has little to sing as Barbebleue, Ciesinski makes a top-notch Ariane.

Arlechinno. Busoni. C: Kent Nagano; Orchestre de l'Opéra de Lyon. Ernest Theo Richter (Arlechinno); Suzanne Mentzer (Columbina). Virgin.

Assassinio nella cattedrale. Pizzetti. C: Gianandrea Gavazzeni; La Scala Orchestra. Nicola Rossi-Lemeni (Thomas Becket); Leyla Gencer (First Chorister); Aldo Bertocci (Herald). Allegro. Excellent live 1958 recording of Pizzetti's best-known opera.

Atlántida. De Falla. C: Edmon Colomer; Joven Orquesta Nacional de España. With Simon Estes; Maria Bayo; Teresa Berganza. Valois.

Ballad of Baby Doe. Moore. (A) C: Emerson Buckley; New York City Opera Orchestra. Beverly Sills (Baby Doe); Walter Cassel (Tabor); Frances Bible (Augusta); Beatrice Krebs (Mama McCourt). (B) Jan Grissom (Baby Doe); Brian Steele (Tabor); Dana Krueger (Augusta); Myrna Paris (Mama McCourt). Both versions are quite good; the first has an edge due to Sills' superlative singing and earnest portrayal of the lead character, but the second version is also well-sung by a talented cast.

Belfagor. Respighi. C: Lamberto Gardelli; Hungarian State Orchestra. Sylvia Sars (Candida); Giorgio Lamberti (Baldo); Lajos Miller (Balfagor). Hungaroton. First-rate, enthusiastically sung and conducted recording of this opera, with wonderful vocalizing by the leads.

Bethlehem. Boughton. C: Alan G. Melville; City of London Sinfonia. Helen Field (Virgin Mary); Richard Bryan (Gabriel); Roger Bryson (Joseph); Graeme Matheson-Bruce (Herod). Hyperion. Nice recording of this choral drama, with countertenor Richard Bryan a stand-out.

Betrothal in a Monastery. Prokofiev. C: Valery Gergiev; Orchestra St. Petersburg. Nikolai Gassiev (Don Jerome); Anna Netrebko (Louisa); Marianna Tarassova (Clara). Polygram. First-rate recording of Prokofiev's comedy.

Bluebeard's Castle. Bartók. C: Pierre Boulez; BBC Symphony Orchestra. Siegmund Nimsgern (Bluebeard); Tatiana Troyanos (Judith). Sony. Superb interpretation of Bartók's masterpiece features Boulez, Troyanos and Nimsgern working in top form.

Bomarzo. Ginastera. C: Julis Rudel: Opera Society of Washington Orchestra. Salvador Novoa (Duke); David Prather (Shepherd Boy); Isabel Penagos (Julia); Michael Devlin (Father). An exemplary cast, especially Novoa, who is superb.

Brigadoon. Loewe. (A) Original cast album. C: Franz Allers; with Marion Bell, Pamela Britten, David Brooks, Lee Sullivan. RCA. (B) C: John McGinn; London Sinfonietta. Brent Barrett (Tommy); Rebecca Luker (Fiona); Judy Kaye (Meg); John Mark Ainsley (Charlie). The original cast is well-sung but the second version is more complete. However, Barrett's voice is woefully inadequate for the operatic-like songs of Tommy.

Candide. Bernstein. (A) Original cast recording with Barbara Cook and Richard Rounseville. (B) 1989 recording conducted by Bernstein and featuring June Anderson and Jerry Hadley. Both recordings are recommended. The first has such delights as Rounseville's rendition of "Eldorado," while the second offers Jerry Hadley's expressive version of "Candide's Song (Nothing More than This)"; etc. The latter recording is also complete, while the former has only selections. Fans of *Candide* will feel that both recordings are essential.

Capriccio. Strauss. (A) C: Wolfgang Sawallisch; Philharmonia Orchestra. Elisabeth Schwarzkopf (Gräfin); Nicolia Gedda (Flamand); Dietrich Fischer-Dieskau (Olivier). (B) C: Ulf Schirmer; Wiener Philharmoniker. Kiri Te Kanawa (Gräfin); Uwe Heilmann (Flamand); Olaf Bár (Olivier). The first recording is a true classic, while the second stereo set is not without its virtues.

Carmina Burana. Orff. C: Gaetano Delogu; Prague Symphony Orchestra. With: Ivan Kusnjer (baritone); Vladimir Dolezal (tenor); Zdena Klaubová (soprano). Well-done recording of Orff's song cycle-oratorio.

Carousel. Rodgers. (A) Original Broadway Cast. With: John Raitt. (B) Movie Soundtrack. With: Gordon MacRae. (C) C: Paul Genignani; Royal Philharmonic Orchestra. Samuel Ramey (Billy); Barbara Cook (Julie); Sarah Brightman (Carrie); David Rendall (Enoch Snow). Ramey and Cook are hardly the perfect Billy and Julie at this point, but nonetheless they sing the roles very well. Rendall and Brightman are fine as Snow and Carrie.

Cecelia Valdes. Roig. Martha Perez (Cecelia); Aida Pujol (Isabel); Ruth Fernandez (Dolores); Francisco Natya (Leonardo). Mantilla. Nice recording of Gonzalo Roig's cuban zarzeula/operetta.

La cena della beffe. Giordano. C: Gian Paolo Sanzogno; Orchestra Sinfonica di Piacenza. Fabio Armiliato (Giannetto); Marco Chingari (Neri); Rita Lantieri (Ginevra). Live 1988 recording with good singers, especially Armiliato.

Cendrillon. Massenet. C: Julius Rudel; Philharmonia Orchestra. Frederica Von Stade (Cinderella); Nicolai Gedda (Le Prince Charmant); Jane Berbi (Madame de la Haltiere); Jules Bastin (Pandolfe); Ruth Welting (La Fee). CBS. Superb recording of Massenet's version of the Cinderella story with excellent conducting and a great cast headed by Von Stade and Gedda in top form.

Cherubin. Massenet. C: Pinchas Steinberg; Munich Radio Orchestra. Frederica von Stade (Cherubin); Samuel Ramey (Le Philosophe); June Anderson (L'Ensoleillad); Dawn Upshaw (Nina). BMG. Excellent on every level, with superb vocalizing from von Stade, Anderson and Ramey.

Cleopatra. Massenet. C: Patrick Fournillier; Nouvel Orchestre de Saint-Etienne. Kathryn Harries (Cleopatra); Didier Henry (Marc-Antoine); Jean-Luc Maurette (Spakos); Danielle Streiff (Octavie). Koch. The main singers all have quite good voices, but they lack the intensity and expressiveness that this material requires. The characters suffer, feel passion and rage — little of which is reflected by the cast.

Comedy on the Bridge/Veselohra na moste. Martinů. C: František Jílek; Brno Janáček Opera Orchestra. With: Rene Tuček; Richard Novak; Anna Borova. Excellent recording of the composer's radio opera.

Consul. Menotti. C: Richard Hickox; Spoleto Festival Orchestra. Susan Bollock (Magda); Louis Otey (John); Jacalyn Kreitzer (Mother). Chandos. Good recording of this uneven opera.

Coyote Tales. Mollicone. C: Russell Patterson; Kansas City Symphony Opera Orchestra. Michael Ballan (Coyote); Gregory Keil (Pavayoykyasi); Suzan Hanson (Maiden). Well done and well-sung by all.

Crucible. Ward. C: Emerson Buckley; New York City Opera Orchestra. Frances Bible (Elizabeth); Chester Ludgin (John); Patricia Brooks (Abigail); Norman Kelley (Reverend Parris); Naomi Farr (Sarah).

Cunning Little Vixen. Janáček. C: Bohu-mil Gegor; Orchestra of Prague National Theater. With: Helena Tattermuschova; Eva Zikmundova.

Cyrano de Bergerac. Alfano. C: Markus Frank; Kiel Philharmonic Orchestra. Roman Sadnik(Cyrano); Manuela Uhl (Roxane); Paul McNamara (Christian). BMG. First-rate recording, sung in French. Roman Sadnik is impressive as Cyrano; other roles also well sung.

Daphne. Strauss. C: Eugen Jochum; Bayerisches Staatsorchester. Annelies Kupper (Daphne); Hans Hopf (Leukippos); Lorenz Fehenberger (Apollo).

Dead Man Walking. Heggie. C: Patrick Summers; San Francisco Opera Orchestra. Susan Graham (Sister Prejean); John Packard (Joseph De Richer); Federica von Stade (Mrs. Patrick De Rocher). Well done on all levels, with superlative work by Graham, Packard, and von Stade.

Death in the Family. Mayer. C: David Gilbert; Manhattan School of Music Opera Theater Orchestra. Bert K.Johnson (Jay Follett); Jennifer Goode (Mary Follett); Ian Samplin (Rufus). Albany. Well-conducted and well-sung by all.

Death in Venice. Britten. C: Steuart Bedford; English Chamber Orchestra. With Peter Pears; John Shirley-Quirk. Pears gives a good "performance" despite the negative qualities of his voice, which almost seem suited to the role.

Death of Klinghoffer. Adams. C: Kent Nagano; Orchestra of the Opera De Lyon. Sanford Sylvan (Leon Klinghoffer); Sheila Nader (Marilyn Klinghoffer). Nonesuch.

Desire Under the Elms. Thomas. C: George Manahan; London Symphony Orchestra. James Morris (Cabot); Jerry Hadley (Peter); Victoria Livengood (Abbie). Naxos. Well-conducted if imperfect recording of Thomas' folk opera. Although he gets an "A" for effort, the role of Eben is not really a good fit for Hadley's voice. Morris is better, although at times he lacks enough expressiveness.

Doktor Faust. Busoni. C: Kent Nagano; Orchestre de l'Opéra National de Lyon. Dietrich Henschel (Doktor Faust); Dietrich Fischer-Dieskau (Poet); Kim Begley (Mephistopheles); Eva Jenis (Duchess). Erato. Complete with both Beaumont and Jarnach versions for comparison.

Don Quichotte. Massenet. C: Michel Plasson; Orchestre du Capitole de Toulouse. Teresa Berganza (Dulcinee); Jose, Van Dam (Don Quichotte); Alain Fondary (Sancho Panffia). EMI. Very good recording of this late Massenet opera.

Doña Francisquita. Vives. C: Miguel Roa; Orquesta Sinfónica de Sevilla. Aïnhoa Arteta (Fancisquita); Plácido Domingo (Fernando); Linda Mirabel (Aurora); Carlos Chausson (Don Matías); Mabel Perelstein (Doña Francisca). Fine recording of this zarzuela bolstered by presence of Domingo.

Edipo Re. Leoncavallo. C: Armando La Rosa Parodi; Orchestra del teatro San Carlo di Napoli. Giulio Fioravanti (Edipo); Luisa Malagrida (Giocasta); Luigi Infantino (Creonte). Good recording, but with quite a few cuts.

Elektra. Strauss. C: Sir Georg Solti; Vienna Philharmonic. With Regina Resnik; Birgit Nilsson; Marie Collier; Gerhard Stolze; Tom Krause.

Emmaline. Picker. C: George Manahan; Santa Fe Opera. With: Patricia Racette; Anne-Marie Owens; Curt Peterson. Live recording is good on all levels, with okay, mostly no-name cast. Racette is good but somehow not outstanding.

L'Enfant et les sortilèges. Ravel. C: Armin Jordan; Orchestra de la Suisse Romonde. Collette Alliot-Lucaz (L'Enfant); Elisabeth Vidal (le Feu); Audrey Michael (La Princesse). Erato. First-rate recording of Ravel's charming opera.

Face on the Barroom Floor. Mollicone. C: Henry Mollicone; Central City Opera Orchestra. Leanne McGiffin (Isabelle/Madeline); Barry McCauley (Larry/Matt); David Holloway (Tom/John). CRI. Conducted by the composer himself, this is sung by an appealing cast of fresh young voices.

La fanciulla del West. Puccini. C: Franco Capuana; Orchestra dell'Accademia di Santa Ceceilia, Roma. Renata Tabaldi (Minnie); Mario Del Monaco (Dick Johnson); Cornell Macneil (Jack Rance); Giorgio Tozzi (Jake Wallace); Piero di Palma (Nick). Splendid and powerful, all–Italian 1958 recording of Puccini's most under-valued masterpiece. The cast is first-rate and the leads incomparable, with Del Monaco singing his daunting arias with assurance and thrilling command.

Fanny. Rome. William Tabbert (Marius); Florence Henderson (Fanny); Ezio Pinza (Cesar); Walter Slezak (Panisse). Excellent original cast recording of this Broadway show/American opera. Pinza and Henderson are fine, and Tabbert's trademark high notes are ringing. Tabbert's rendition of the title song is a classic. Slezak acts the role of Panisse with panache, but his singing is rather painful to hear.

Fennimore and Gerda. Delius. C: Davies; Danish Radio Orchestra. With: Soderstrom, Tear, Rayner, Cook. HMV. Good singers do their best with perhaps Delius' least interesting opera.

Der ferne Klang. Schreker. C: Michael Halász; Hagen Philharmonic Orchestra. Elena Grigorescu (Greta); Thomas Harper (Fritz); Werner Hahn (the count). Naxos. First-rate recording of this opera.

Feuersnot. Strauss. C: Rudolf Kemper; Bayerisches Staatsorchester. With: Karl Ostertag; Max Proebstl. Arts. Fine recording of Strauss' second opera.

La fiamma. Respighi. C: Lamberto Gardelli; Hungarian State Orchestra. Ilona Tokody (Silvana); Peter Kelen (Donello); Sandor Solyom-Nagy (Basilio). Tokody is simply superb; Kelen, an acquired taste, sings with decided passion and expressivity.

Fiery Angel. Prokofiev. C; Valery Gergiev; Kirov Orchestra, St. Petersburg. Sergei Leiferkus (Ruprecht); Galina Gorchakova (Renata); Vladimir Goluzin (Agrippa). First-rate recording of this opera.

Fortunio. Messager. C: John Eliot Gardiner; Orchestre de l'Opera de Lyon. Thierry Dran (Fortunio); Colette Alliot-Lugaz (Jacqueline); Gille Cachemaille (Clavaroche); Michel Trempont (Andre). Erato. Fine recording of Messager's romantic comedy.

Four Saints in Three Acts. Thomson. C: Joel Thome; Orchestra of Our Time. Betty Allen (Commere); Benjamin Matthews (Compere); Arthur Thompson (St. Ignatius); Clamma Dale (St. Teresa I). Nonesuch.

Francesca da Rimini. Rachmaninov. C: Andrey Chistiakov. Marina Lapino (Francesca); Vitaly Tarastchenko (Paolo). Well-sung recording of Rachmaninov's version of the story.

Francesca da Rimini. Zandonai. C: Gianandrea Gavazzeni; Orchestra of La Scala,

1959. Magda Olivero (Francesca); Mario Del Monaco (Paolo). Despite being monaural and the annoying whispers of the prompters, this is an excellent recording, extremely well-sung by an intense Olivero (admittedly an acquired taste) and a spectacular Del Monaco, who can really sink his teeth into material like this. Very well conducted. There are at least two stereo versions, one with Domingo and conducted by Eve Queler, but while creditable, neither can compare to this version.

Die Frau ohne Schatten. C: Giuseppe Sinopoli; Staatskapelle Dresden. Deborha Voight (Die Kaiserin); Ben Heppner (Der Kaiser); Franz Grundheber (Barak); Sabine Hass (Sein Weib). Teldec. Voight is quite good as the empress, and Heppner has a beautiful voice. Not a perfect recording — a lot of cuts for one thing — but good.

From the House of the Dead. Janáček. C: Charles Mackerras; Weiner Philharmoniker. With: Jedlicka; Zidek; Zahradnicek. Decca. Excellent recording of final version of one of Janáček's greatest operas.

Gallantry. Moore. C: Stephen Rogers Radcliffe; New York Chamber Ensemble. Margaret Bishop (Lola); Richard Holmes (Dr. Gregg); Carl Halvarson (Donald); Julia Parks (Anna). Good, pleasantly sung recording of Moore's one act comic opera.

Gambler. Prokofiev. C; Valery Gergiev; Kirov Orchestra, St. Petersburg. Sergei Alexaskhin (General); Elena Obraztsova (Babulenka); Liubov Kazarnovskaya (Paulina); Vladimir Galuzin (Aleksey). Kirov. Quite good recording of this opera. Galuzin is not a perfect Aleksey, but he does sing with expressiveness.

El Gato Montés. Penella. C: Miguel Rosa; Orquesta Sinfónica de Madrid. Plácido Domingo (Rafael); Verónica Villarroel (Solea); El Gato/Juanillo (Juan Pons). Deutsche Grammophon. A superlative rendition of the zarzuela/opera, extremely well sung and conducted with verve. The only quibble: Pons sounds great but doesn't put forth enough emotion as the Wildcat.

Gianni Schicchi. Puccini. C: Lorin Maazel; London Symphony Orchestra. Tito Gobbi (Schicchi); Ileana Cotrubas (Lauretta); Plácido Domingo (Rinuccio). Excellent recording of the opera with a first-rate cast.

I gioiella della Madonna. Wolf-Ferrari. C: Alberto Erede; BBC Symphony Orchestra. Pauline Tinsely (Maliella); Andre Turp (Gennaro); Peter Glossop (Rafaele); Valerie Cockz (Carmela). 1976. BellaVoce. Turp's voice has the requisite sensitivity for Gennaro, and the others are also very good.

Golden Apple. Moross. Original cast. This CD only contains highlights but will give one a good taste of what the work was all about. Kay Ballard as Helen really scores with her big number "Lazy Afternoon" and the other singers range from adequate to excellent.

The Golden Cockerel. Rimsky-Korsakov. (A) C: Evgeny Svetlanov; Orchestra of the Bolshoi. Artur Eizen (Tsar Dodon); Oleg Biktimirov (astrologer); Elena Brileva (Queen). MCA. A robust live recording at the Bolshoi Theater. (B) C: Dimiter Manalov; Sofia National Opera Orchestra. Nikolai Stailov (Tsar Dodon); Lyubamir Dyakovski (astrologer); Elena Stoyanova (Queen). Capriccio. A first-class treatment. Others are available as well.

Golem. Bretan. C: Cristian Mandeal; Philharmonic Orchestra Moldavia, Iasi. Alexandru Agache (Golem); Tamas Daroczy (Rabbi Low); Sanda Sandru (Anna); Dan Zancu (Baruch). Very good recording with some splendid singers.

Good Soldier Schweik. Kurka. C: Alexander Platt; Chicago Opera Theater. Jason Collins (Schweik); Marc Embree (Lt. Lukash); Kelli Harrington (Mrs. Muller). Cedille. Good recording of this piece; Collins is first-rate as Schweik.

Goyescas. Granados. C: Antoni Ros Marbá; Orquesta Sinfónica de Madrid. Maria Bayo (Rosario); Ramón Vargas (Fernando); Enrique Baquerizo (Paquiro). Marbá conducts with gusto and Vargas and the other singers have wonderful voices. The only negative is that some of the singers, especially Bayo, aren't as expressive and intense as they need to be.

Griechische Passion. Martinů. C: Ulf Schirmer; Wiener Symphoniker. Christopher Ventris (Manolios); Nina Stemme (Katerina); Adrian Clarke (Kostandis); Anat Efraty (Lenio). Orf. Creditable but not quite first-rate recording of this opera. Ventris is excellent in the lead, however, and the other singers are fine.

Harvey Milk. Wallace. C: Donald Run-
nicles; San Francisco Opera Orchestra.
Robert Orth (Harvey Milk); Adam Jacobs
(Young Harvey); Raymond Very (Dan
White); Gidon Sakes (George Moscone).
Teldec. Enthusiastic recording of the pop
opera, with fine work from Orth, Jacobs,
and others.

Intermezzo. Strauss. C: Wolfgang Sawallisch; Sinfonie-Orchester der Bayerischen
Rundfunks. Dietrich Fischer-Dieskau
(Storch); Lucia Popp (Christine); Adolph
Dallapazza (Baron Lumer). Superb on all
levels: great cast; superior performances by
conductor and orchestra.

Into the Woods. Sondheim. C: Paul
Gemignani. With: Bernadette Peters; Joanna Gleason; Chip Zien; Tom Aldredge;
and others. Fine work by an excellent cast.
Peters' problematic voice is used appropriately in this show.

Irmelin. Delius. C: Norman Del Mar;
BBC Concert Orchestra. Eilene Hannan
(Irmelin); John Mitchinson (Nils). Taken
from BBC studio performance broadcast
this is beautifully conducted by Del Mar;
it's only flaw is that the at-times wobbly
tenor hardly sounds like a youth.

Isabeau. Mascagni. (**A**) C: Tullio Serafin;
Orchestra Sinfonia di San Remo. With
Marcella Pobbe; Pier Mirando Ferraro. (**B**)
C: Kees Bakels; Netherlands Radio Symphony Orchestra. Lynne Straw Piccolo (Isabeau); Adriaan Van Limpt (Folco); Henk
Smit (Raimondo). Bongiovanni. For a long
time the first version, a well-sung but murky
live recording, was the only recording available. (There were studio excerpts with the
same cast and conductor, also somewhat
murky). Serafin's conducting lacks the required intensity and pacing, and the orchestra sounds amatuerish at times. Pobbe is excellent, however, as is the stentorian Ferraro,
despite the peculiarities of his voice. The excellent Kees Bakels version, despite a few
quibbles, is now the *Isabeau* of choice. Piccolo and Van Limpt are excellent.

Jackie O. Daugherty. C: Christopher
Larkin; Houston Grand Opera Orchestra.
With: Nicole Heaston; Stephanie Novacek.

Jane Eyre. Berkeley. C: Michael Rafferty;
Music Theatre Wales Ensemble. Natasha
Marsh (Jane); Andrew Slater (Rochester);
Beverley Mills (Mrs. Fairfax). Chandos. As

good a recording of this opera as you're likely
to find.

Jenůfa. Janáček. C: Eve Queler; Opera
Orchestra of New York. Gabriela Benackova
(Jenůfa); Wieslaw Ochman (Laca); Peter Ka-
zaras (Steva); Leonie Rysanek (Kostelnicka);
Barbara Schramm (Grandmother). Live
1988 Carnegie Hall recording is first-rate.

Jonny spielt auf. Křenek. C: Lothar Za-
grosek; Gewandhausorcherster Leipzig.
Heinz Kruse (Max); Alessandra Marc
(Anita); Krister St. Hill (Jonny). London.
Excellent recording of Křenek's best-known
work serves the opera well and makes the
most of it.

Juha. C: Ulf Soderblom; Finnish National Opera Orchestra. With: Matti Lehti-
nen; Raili Kostia; Hendrik Krumm; Taru
Valjakka. Finlandia. Well done recording of
Merikanto's only opera.

Julian. Charpentier. 1935 recording,
conducted by the composer, of selections
from his Symphonie-Drame en 4 Actes.

Der Kaiser von Atlantis. Ullmann. C:
Lothar Jagrosek; Gewandhausorchester,
Leipzig. Michael Krauss (Kaiser Overall);
Martin Petzold (Ein Soldat); Christine
Oetze (Bubikopf); Walter Berry (Du Tod).
London.

Die Kathrin. C: Martyn Brabbins; BBC
Concert Orchestra. Melanie Diener (Kathrin); David Rendall (Francois); Robert Hay-
ward. (Malignac). CPO. Acceptable recording, although with problematical singers, and
perhaps not as rigorously conducted as
it might have been.

Katya Kabanová. Janáček. C: Charles
Mackerras; Vienna Philharmonic. Elisabeth
Soderstrom (Katerina); Petr Dvorsky (Boris);
Nadezda Kniplova (Marfu).

King Roger. Szymanowski. C: Sir Simon
Rattle. With: Elzbieta Szmytka; Thomas
Hampson; Philip Langridge; Rysard Mon-
kiewicz.

Koanga. Delius. C: Sir Charles S. Groves;
London Symphony Orchestra. Eugene
Holmes (Koanga); Claudia Lindsey (Palmyra); Gordon Wilock (Simon Perez); Jean
Allister (Clotilda). Intoglia. This recording
of Delius' best-known work is not as vigor-
ously conducted as it needs to be. Holmes
has a flavorful voice and sounds the part,
with nobility, but can't really handle the
high tessitura of the role.

Königskinder. Humperdinck. C: Fabio Luisi; Munchner Rundfunkorchester. Thomas Moser (King's son); Dagmar Schellenberger (Goose Girl); Dietrich Henschel (Fiddler); Marilyn Schmiege (Witch). Calig. Very well sung by all.

Lady Macbeth of Mtsensk District. Shostakovitch. C: Mstislav Rostropovich; London Philharmonic. Galina Vishnevskaya (Katerina); Nicolai Gedda (Sergei); Werner Krenn (Zinovy); Dimiter Petkov (Boris). Very good on all levels.

Die Liebe der Danae. Strauss. C: Loen Botstein; American Symphony Orchestra. Lauren Flanigan (Danae); Peter Coleman Wright (Jupiter); Hugh Smith (Midas). Telarc. Live Avery Fisher Hall recording is superb, virtually perfect on every possible level.

A Little Night Music. Sondheim. Original cast album has a couple of disappointing voices but is nevertheless recommended. Jonathan Tunick's orchestrations are excellent. With Len Cariou; Hermione Gingold; Patricia Elliott; Mark Lambert; Laurence Guittard; Victoria Mallory; Glynis Johns. D. Jamin-Bartlett makes the most of "The Miller's Son."

Little Women. Adamo. C: Patrick Summers; Houston Grand Opera Orchestra. Stephanie Novacek (Jo); Chad Shelton (Laurie); Margaret Lloyd (Amy); Stacey Tappen (Beth). Live 2000 recording of Adamo's opera is generally well-sung and well-conducted. Shelton is overwrought at times, but he's a talented singer with a nice voice.

Lodoletta. Mascagni. (A) C: Alberto Paoletti; Chorus of RAI; Milano, 1957. Giuliana Tavolaccini (Lodoletta); Giuseppe Campora (Flammen); Giulio Fioravanti (Giannetto). (B) Maria Spacagna (Lodoletta); Peter Kelan (Flammen). The first is the best overall recording with a fine soprano and a problematic but not bad tenor and is expertly conducted to bring out the sweep and passion of the music. The second is the best stereo recording, with the leads fine and persuasive. Two recordings done in Livorno are acceptable but not as good as these.

Louise. Charpentier. (A) C: Julius Rudel; Paris Opera Orchestra. Beverly Sills (Louise); Nicolai Gedda (Julien); Mignon Dunn

(Mother); Jose van Dam (Father). The best of the modern recordings, with Sills an excellent Louise and a fine supporting cast. Rigorously conducted with authentic French flair. A great introduction to this opera. (B) C: Georges Pretre; New Philharmonia Orchestra. Ileana Cotrubas (Louise); Plácido Domingo (Julien). Sony. Despite excellent singing from the leads and supporting cast, this heavy rendition sounds more German than French and completely misses many of the subtleties of the score. For Domingo purists primarily, but not without interest. (There is also a classic 1936 recording with Vallin and Thill.)

Love of Three Oranges. Prokofiev. C: Kent Nagano; Orchestre de l'Opéra de Lyon. Gabriel Bacquier (Le Roi); Jean-Luc Viala (Le Prince); Didier Henry (Pantalon); Michele LaGrange (Fata Morgana); Vincent Le Texier (Leandre). Virgin. Sung in French. Excellent on all counts.

Luisa Fernanda. Torroba. With: Juan Pons, Plácido Domingo, Veronica Villaroel. This eliminates the spoken dialoque sections, which are capsulized in the libretto. All three leads are in top form; Pons is much more expressive than he is on *El Gato Montés*. Excellent recording on all levels.

Lulu. Berg. C: Pierre Boulez; Orchestre de l'Opéra de Paris. Teresa Stratas (Lulu); Yvonne Minton (Geschwitz); Franz Mazura (Jack/Dr. Schon); Kenneth Riegel (Alwa).

Macbeth. Bloch. C; Friedemann Layer; Orchestre Philharmonique de Montpelier Languedoc-Roussillon. Jean-Philippe Lafont (Macbeth); Markella Hatzinao (Lady Macbeth); Jean-Philippe Marlière (Macduff); Jacque Trussel (Banquo); Christer Bladin (Duncan). First-rate recording of Bloch's only opera.

Madama Butterfly. (A) C: Sir John Barbirolli; Orchestra del Teatro dell'Opera di Roma. Renata Scotto (Cio Cio San); Carlo Bergonzi (Pinkerton); Rolando Panerai (Sharpless); Anna di Stasio (Suzuki). Scotto is fine; Bergonzi shows some strain but is otherwise quite good. (B) C: Charles Rosekrans; Hungarian State Opera House Orchestra. Maria Spacagna (Cio Cio San); Richard Di Renzi (Pinkerton); Erich Parce (Sharpless); Richard Markley (Goro); Sharon Graham (Suzuki). Vox. The original 1904 La Scala version, as well as all the revisions. Fine work from Spacagna and Di Renzi. **(C)** C: Herbert von Karajan; Weiner Philharmoniker. Mirella Freni (Cio Cio San); Luciano Pavorotti (Pinkerton). Freni is excellent, while Pavarotti, although eternally over-rated, really delivers on his third act aria. Very well conducted at the proper tempo.

Madame Sans-Gêne. Giordano. C: Stefano Ranzoni; Orchestra Sinfonica dell'Emilia Romagna. With Mirella Freni; Giorgio Merighi; Maura Buda.

Maddalena. Prokofiev. C: Gennadi Rozhdestvensky; U.S.S.R. Ministry of Culture Symphony Orchestra. E. Ivanova (Maddalena); A. Martynov (Genaro); S. Yakovenko (Stenio). Melodiya. First-rate recording of this little-heard example of Russian verismo.

Magdalena. Villa-Lobos. C: Evans Haile; Orchestra New England. With Judy Kaye; George Rose; Faith Esham; Kevin Gray; Jerry Hadley and others. Kevin Gray's Broadway-style voice isn't always up to the demands of the score; Hadley should have been assigned his role.

Magic Fountain. Delius. C; Norman Del Mar; BBC Concert Orchestra. John Mitchinson (Solano); Katherine Pring (Watawa). Taken from a 1977 BBC broadcast, this is a fine recording; even Mitchinson is in good form. There are many sound effects — bubbling fountains, storms, etc. — which may not have been necessary but have an undeniable impact.

Makropulos Case. Janáček. C: Bohumil Gregor; Prague National Orchestra. Libuse Prylová (Emilia); Ivo Zldek (Gregor); Viktor Kocl (Janek); Premysl Kocl (Prus). Supraphon. Outstanding interpretation of Janáček's great opera with a particularly excellent Prylová and heartfelt, rigorous conducting from Gregor.

Man of La Mancha. Leigh. **(A)** Original Broadway cast with Richard Kiley; Joan Diener; Richard Rounseville; Irving Jacobson; Ray Middleton. **(B)** C: Paul Gemignani; American Theatre Orchestra. With Plácido Domingo; Julia Migenes; Jerry Hadley; Mandy Patinkin; Samuel Ramey. The first version is impeccable, with superb work from the entire cast; further, Richard Rounseville's singing of "To Each His Dulcinea" is one of the prime joys of 20th century

Broadway. On the second version, the genuinely Spanish Domingo sounds more like Sancho Panza than Don Quixote at times but when he hits the high note on "Impossible Dream"...! Generally well-sung; Patinkin is okay as Sancho but won't make you forget Jacobson in the original.

Man Who Mistook His Wife for a Hat. Nyman. C: Michael Nyman; Institute of Contemporary Arts London. Emile Belcourt (Dr. S.); Sarah Leonard (Mrs. P.); Frederick Westcott (Dr. P.). CBS. Fine recording of this unusual opera.

Margot-la-Rouge. Delius. C: Norman Del Mar; BBC Concert Orchestra. Arabesque. Emphatically sung and conducted live radio performance of the opera.

Marie Christine. Lachiusa. Original cast album features excellent work from Audra McDonald in the title role along with other good singers.

Markheim. Floyd. C: Knud Anderson; New Orleans Opera Orchestra. Norman Treigle (Markheim); Alan Crofoot (Josiah Creach); Audrey Schuh (Tess); William Diard (Stranger). RAI. Treigle and Crofoot are excellent but Daird's voice isn't big or dramatic enough to handle the powerful singing required by the stranger/devil.

Marouf. Rabaud. C: Pierre-Michel Le-Conte; RTF Orchestra. Henri Legay (Marouf); Lina Dachary (Princess); Janine Capderou (Fatimah); Andre Vessieres (Sultan); Jean Mollieu (Fellah); Stanislaus Staskiewicz (Ali). Very well-sung recording of this opera, with Legay and Mollieu especially outstanding.

Maskerade. Nielsen. C: Ulf Schirmer; Danish National Radio Symphony Orchestra. Aage Haugland (Jeronimus); Gert-Henning Jensen (Leander); Henriette Bonde-Hansen (Leonora); Bo Skovhus (Henrik); Susanne Resmark (Magdeleone). Decca. A superb recording, conducted with great enthusiasm and skill by Ulf Schirmer. Jensen and Skovhus are especially notable, but others in the cast are also excellent.

Mathis der Maler. Hindemith. C: Rafael Kubelick; Symphonie Orchester des Bayerischen Rundfunks. Dietrich Fischer-Dieskau (Mathis); James King (Albrect); Urszula Koszut (Regina); Rose Wagemann (Ursula); William Cochran (Schwalb). EMI. Excellent, superbly-cast recording with

Fischer-Dieskau and King at the top of their form.

Medium. Menotti. C: Lawrence Rapchak; Ensemble of Chicago Opera Theater. Patrice Michaels Bedi (Monica); Joyce Castle (Baba). Cedille. Among several recordings of the opera, this version is well-sung and as good as any.

Midsummer Marriage. Tippett. C: Sir Colin Davis; Orchestra of Royal Opera House, Covent Garden. Alberto Remedios (Mark); Joan Carlyle (Jenifer); Elizabeth Harwood (Bella); Stuart Burrows (Jack); Helen Watts (Sosostris); Raimund Herincx (King Fisher). Lyrita. Very well-conducted and well-sung by entire cast, especially romantic leads Remedios and Carlyle, but all are excellent.

Miserly Knight. Rachmaninov. C: Andrey Chistiakov; Bolshoi Theatre Orchestra. Vladimir Kudriashov (Albert); Mikhail Krutikov (Baron); Vladislav Verestmikov (Duke). Excellent recording of this opera, with superlative work from Kudriashov and Krutikov.

Miss Julie. Rorem. C: David Gilbert; Manhattan School of Music Symphony Orchestra. Theodora Fried (Miss Julie); Philip Torre (PHilip); Heather Sarris (Christine). David Blackburn (Niels). Acceptable "amateur" recording of Rorem's opera, which not even seasoned professionals could rescue from mediocrity.

Mona Lisa. Schillings. C: Klauspeter Seibel; Keil Philharmonic Orchestra. Beate Bilandzija (Mona Lisa); Klaus Wellprecht (Francisco); Albert Bonnema (Giovanni). CPO. Some of the singers are not quite up to the demands of the score — not to mention "verismo" — and the tempo is rather slow.

Moses und Aron. Schoenberg. C: Sir George Solti; Chicago Symphony Orchestra. Franz Mazura (Moses); Philip Langridge (Aron); Aage Haugland (Priest). Langridge is especially excellent, singing with great conviction and persuasiveness. Solti conducts as if he truly believes in the score.

The Most Happy Fella. Loesser. C: Robert Weede (Tony); Jo Sullivan (Rosabella); Susan Johnson (Cleo); Art Lund (Joe). Sony. Original cast album contains the entire show, every bit of music, and even dialogue sequences. The one recording of this operatic musical to own.

Mother of Us All. Thomson. C: Raymond Leppard; Santa Fe Opera. With: Mignon Dunn; James Atherton; Philip Booth. New World. Acceptable recording of this opera, although the occasional, atypical shrillness of Dunn is no help.

Nerone. Boito. C: Eve Queler; Hungarian State Opera Orchestra. With: Ilona Tokody; Janos B. Nagy. Rigorous version of Boito's lost opera.

Nerone. Mascagni. C: Kees Bakel; Radio Symphony Orchestra di Hilversum. Georgi Tcholakov (Nerone); Lynne Strow Piccolo (Atte); Rosanna Didone (Egloge). Bongiovanni. Excellent recording with first-rate singers and conducting. Tcholakov tackles the role with just the right fervor and sings it with attractive conviction; Piccolo is suitably commanding; and Didone has a voice of an unusual quality.

Notre Dame. Schmidt. C: Christof Perick; Radio Symphony Orchester Berlin. Kurt Moll (Quasimodo); Gwyneth Jones (Esmerelda); James King (Phoebus). Capriccio. First-rate recording featuring an excellent Moll.

Oedipe. Enescu. C: Lawrence Foster; Orchestre Philharmonique de Monte-Carlo. Jose Van Dam (Oedipe); Gabriel Bacquier (Tiresias); Marvel Vanaud (Creon); Nicolai Gedda (Le Berger); Barbara Hendricks (Antigone). Excellent recording with a top cast and splendid conducting.

Oedipus Rex. Stravinsky. C; Neeme Jarvi; Orchestre de la Suisse Romande. Peter Svenson (Oedipus); Gabriele Schnaut (Jocasta); Franz Grundheber (Creon).

L'oracolo. Leoni. C; Richard Bonynge; National Philharmonic Orchestra. Joan Sutherland (Ah-Joe); Ryland Davies (San-Lui); Tito Gobbi (Cim-Fen); Richard Van Allen (Win-Shee). Superb 1977 recording. Sutherland handles the material very well; Davies is smooth and expressive; and the others also excel. Very well conducted by Bonynge.

Osud. Janáček. C; Sir Charles Mackerras; Welsh National Opera Orchestra. Helen Field (Mila); Philip Langridge (Zjuny); Kathryn Harries (Mila's Mother). EMI. Well-conducted and generally well-sung, although Langridge's overly dramatic, insensitive delivery is totally devoid of shading and subtlety.

El pajaro azul. Millán. C: Benito Lauret; Orquesta Sinfonica. With: Montserrat Caball,; Vincente Sardinero; Francisco Ortiz; Antonio Barras; Carmen DeCamp. Extremely well-sung recording of tuneful zarzuela.

Palestrina. Pfitzner. C: Otmar Suitner; Staatskapelle Berlin. Peter Schreier (Palestrina); Siegfried Lorenz (Borromeo); Hans-Joachin Ketelsen (Morone). Berlin Classics.

Parade. Brown. C: Eric Stern. Brent Carver (Leo Frank); Carolee Carmello (Lucille Frank); Kirk McDonald (Frankie Epps); Christy Carlson Romano (Mary Phagan); John Hickok (Governor Slaton); Ray Aranha (Newt Lee). This is an excellent original cast recording of the American pop opera despite Carmello's somewhat affected (but also effective) singing style; Carver is on the money, however.

Parisina. Mascagni. (A) C: Pierluigi Urbini; RAI orchestra, 1977. Emma Renzi (Parisina); Michele Molese (Ugo); Mirella Rarutto (Stella); Benito Di Gello (Nicolo). (B) C: Enrique Diemecke; Orchestre Philharmonique de Montpelier Languedoc-Roussillon. Denia Mazzola (Parisina); Vitali Taraschenko (Ugo). First recording features excellent conducting and passionate singers, has a few minor cuts, and includes music for act four. Second stereo recording has an excellent Parisina and is generally well-conducted. Act four is not included, and there are numerous regrettable cuts in act two.

Passion. Sondheim. Donna Murphy (Fosca); Jere Shea (Giorgio). Original cast recording. Excellent performances from Murphy, Shea, and the other cast members.

Penelope. Faure. C: Charles Dutoit; Orchestre Philharmonique de Monte-Carolo. Jessye Norman (Penelope); Alain Vanzo (Ulysses); Jose Van Dam (Eumee); Jean Dupouy. Erato. Fine cast with a particularly excellent Van Dam.

Peter Grimes. Britten. C: Sir Colin Davis; Orchestra of Royal Opera House Covent Garden. Jon Vickers (Grimes); Heather Harper (Ellen); Jonathan Summers (Balstrode). Philips. Vickers is superb as Grimes — better than his material, in fact — and this is an exemplary recording all around.

Il piccolo Marat. Mascagni. C: Kees Bakels. Daniel Galvez-Vallejo (Little Marat); Susan Neves (Mariella). 1992 Live concert. Bakels brings out all of the drama of the work although the pace sometimes flags. Neves and Galvez-Vallejo are outstanding. There are at least two other recordings of this opera but this one is easily the best. Avoid at all costs the version on Fone records, (distributed by Allegro) with tenor Umberto Borso.

Pilgrim's Progress. Vaughn Williams. C; Richard Hickox; Orchestra of Royal Opera House. Gerald Finley (Pilgrim); Jeremy White (Evangelist); Peter Coleman-Wright (John Bunyan). Chandos. More than acceptable recording of Vaughn Williams' most ambitious opera.

Pinotta. Mascagni. (A) C: Gennero D'Angelo. Maria Luisa Cioni (Pinotta); Giuseppi Veetechi (Baldo); Lina Puglisi (Andrea). (B) C: Dirk De Caluwe; Orchestra Festival di Bruxelles. Gloria Guida Borrelli (Pinotta); Antonio De Palma (Baldo); Thomas Murk (Andrea). The first, a radio recording, is preferred, with the correct tempo and emphasis, although the latter is creditable.

Piper of Hamelin. Flagello. C: Jonathan Strasser; Manhattan School of Music Prepatory Division. Brace Negron (Piper); Troy Doney (Mayor); Nicole McQuade (soloist). Newport. Pretty good for an amateur rendition of the children's opera with solid singing from the leads.

Porgy and Bess. C: Simon Rattle; London Philharmonic. Willard White (Porgy); Cynthia Haymon (Bess); Damon Evans (Sportin' Life); Gregg Baker (Crown). Recording of excellent 1989 Glyndebourne production is overall superior, well sung and conducted.

Postcard from Morocco. Argento. C: Philip Brunelle; Minnesota Opera. Sarita Roche (Lady with Hand Mirror); Barbara Brandt (Lady with Candy Box); Vern Sutton (Mr. Owen); Barry Busse (Man with Shoe Sample Kit). CRI. Nice recording of this opera with stand-out work by baritone Barry Busse.

Powder Her Face. Adès. C: Thomas Adès; Almeida Ensemble. Jill Gomez (Duchess); Valdine Anderson (Maid and Others); Naill Morris (Electrician and Others); Roger Bryson (Hotel Manager and

Others). EMI. Recording of the world premiere, conducted by the composer.

I quattro rusteghi. Wolf-Ferarri. C: Ettore Gracis; Orchestra di Teatro Communale di Torino. Nicola Rossi-Lemeni (Lunardo); Mariella Adani (Lucieta); Agostino Lazzari (Filipeto); Magda Olivero (Felice). Acceptable if somewhat murky-sounding live 1969 recording. Olivero adds some zest in the pivotal role of Felice.

A Quiet Place. Bernstein. C: Leonard Bernstein; Austrian Radio Symphony Orchestra. Chester Ludgin (Old Sam); Beverly Morgan (Dede): John Branstetter (Junior); Peter Kazaras (Francois); Edward Crafts (Young Sam); Wendy White (Dinah). Live 1986 recording makes clear what's wrong with Bernstein's ill-advised sequel to/expansion of *Trouble in Tahiti*. With the exception of the sections from *Tahiti* and other bits, Bernstein conducts better than he composes. There are separate recordings of *Trouble in Tahiti* which may be preferable to the listener, although not conducted by Bernstein.

Rake's Progress. Stravinsky. C: John Eliot Gardiner; London Symphony Orchestra. Ian Bostrige (Tom); Deborah York (Anne); Bryn Terfel (Shadow); Anne Sofie von Otter (Baba). Very well conducted recording with superlative work from York, Bostridge, Terfel and von Otter.

Rape of Lucretia. Britten. C: Benjamin Britten; English Chamber Orchestra. Janet Baker (Lucretia); John Shirley-Quirk (Collatinus); Benjamin Luxon (Tarquinius). Decca. Conducted by the composer, this is probably the best recording of the work you are likely to find. Peter Pears does minimal damage in the role of the "male chorus."

Un re in ascolto. Beria. C: Lorin Maazel; Wiener Philharmoniker. Theo Adam (Prospero); Heinz Zednick (Regista); Patricia Wise (Protagonista). Legno. Live recording from the Salzburg Festival.

Regina. Blitzstein. C: John Mauceri; Scottish Opera Orchestra. Katherine Ciesinski (Regina); Samuel Ramey (Horace); Sheri Greenawald (Birdie); Angelina Reaux (Alexandra). Excellent recording of this opera includes spoken dialoque sections. Ramey adds an extra touch of class as Horace.

Renard. Stravinsky. C: Robert Ziegler; Matrix Ensemble.

Resurrection. Machover. C: Patrick Summers; Houston Grand Opera Orchestra. Joyce DiDonato (Katerina); Scott Hendricks (Prince Dimitry); Katherine Ciesinski (Sofia). This recording of Machover's version of Tolstoy's novel, featuring further "electronic enhancement," is well-done and generally well-sung.

El Retablo de Maese Pedro. Falla. C: Robert Ziegler; Matrix Ensemble. Wellsung, especially by the boy soprano and Don Quixote.

Der Ring des Polykrates. Korngold. C: Klauspeter Serbel; Deutsches Symphony Orchestra. With: Endrik Wattrick; Beate Bilandzija. First-rate recording of Korngold's first opera.

Rise and Fall of the City of Mahagonny. Weill. C: Wilhelm Bruckner-Ruggeberg; North German Radio Orchestra. With Lotte Lenya; Heinz Sauerbaum; Gisela Litz. Lenya can put over some of the songs but hasn't much of a voice. "Jim's" non-operatic voice is the best on the recording.

Risurrezione. Alfano. C: Elio Boncampagni; RAI Turin Orchestra. Magda Olivero (Katiusha); Giuseppe Gismondo (Prince Dimitri); Fernanda Cadoni (Sofia). Gala. (Monoraul.) Spendid recording of Alfano's masterpiece with (imperfections aside) impassioned singing par excellence from Olivero and Gismondo.

La rondine. Puccini. C: Lorin Maazel; London Symphony Orchestra. Kiri Te Kanawa (Magda); Plácido Domingo (Ruggero); David Rendall (Prunier). Excellent 1983 recording would be perfect if not for the criminal exclusion of the aria "Parigi."

Der Rosenkavalier. Strauss. C: Leonard Bernstein; Vienna Philharmonic. Christa Ludwig (Feldmarschallin); Gwyneth Jones (Octavian); Walter Berry (Ochs); Lucia Popp (Sophie); Plácido Domingo (tenor). Interesting recording with Domingo a stand-out as the Italian tenor.

Rusalka. Dvořák. C: Václay Neumann; Czech Philharmonic. Gabriela Benackova-Capova (Rusalka); Vera Soukupova (Jezibaba); Wieslaw Ochman (Prince).

Saint François d'Assise. Messiaen. C: Seiji Ozawa. Chorus and Orchestra du Théâtre National de l'Opéra de Paris. Jos, Van Dam (St. François); Christiane Eda-Pierre (Angel); Kenneth Riegel (Leper);

Michel Philippe (Brother Leon); Georges Gautier (Brother Masseo). Cybela. There is little difference between this verison and the one conducted by Kent Nagano, which also stars Van Dam, who is excellent in both sets. Eda-Pierre has perhaps a richer voice as the Angel in the Ozawa version than Dawn Upshaw in the Nagano set. Georges Gautier is a stand-out in the Ozawa version. The performers in any case are vastly superior to the material.

Saint of Bleecker Street. Menotti. C: Richard Hickox; Spoleto Festival Orchestra. Julia Melinek (Annina); Timothy Richards (Michele); Pamela Helen Stephen (Desideria); John Marcus Bindel (Don Marco); Yvonne Howard (Assunta). Chandos. Okay recording of Menotti's "music drama" with a cast that is not always up to the demands of the verismo-like score.

Salome. Strauss. C: Christoph von Dahnanyi; Weiner Philharmoniker. Catherine Malfitano (Salome); Bryn Terfel (John the Baptist). Terfel is excellent; Malfitano's imperfect high notes are occasionally distracting.

Sapho. Massenet. C: Bernard Keefe; BBC Orchestra. Milla Andrew (Sapho/ Fanny); Alexander Oliver (Jean); George Macpherson (Cesaire). D'oro. Live London Performance; 1973. Excellent recording with a great cast.

Sarlatan. Haas. C: Isreal Yinan; Prague State Opera Orchestra. Vladmirir Chmelo (Pustrpalk); Anda-Louise Bogza (Rosina); Jitka Svobodova (Amaranta).

Savitri. Holst. C; Glen Barton Cortese; Manhattan School of Music Chamber Sinfonia. Jessica Miller (Savitri); Kyu Won Han (Death); Simon O'Neill (Satyavan). Phoenix. Well-done recording with good singers.

Schwanda the Bagpiper. Weinberger. C: Josef Schmidhuber; Munich Radio Orchestra. Hermann Prey (Schwanda); Lucia Popp (Dorotka); Siegfried Jerusalem (Babinsky).

Die schweigsame Frau. Strauss. C; Wolfgang Sawallisch; Bayerisches Staatsorchester. Kurt Böhme (Morosus); Donald Grobe (Henry); Reri Grist (Aminta). Orfeo. Live recording from Bayerische Staatsoper has cuts but is very well conducted and well sung by tenor Donald Grobe and others.

Second Hurricane. Copland. C: Leonard Bernstein; New York Philharmonic. Soloists and Chorus of the High School of Music and Art. Sony. Not bad for an amateur cast. Bernstein also supplies the narration.

Il segreto di Susanna. Wolf-Ferrari. C: John Pritchard; Philharmonia Orchestra. Renata Scotto (Countess); Renato Bruson (Count). Nice recording of this one-act comedy, with Scotto and Bruson in fine form.

Semyon Kotko. Prokofiev. C: Valery Gergiev; Kirov Opera Orchestra, St. Petersburg. Viktor Lutsiuk (Semyon); Tatiana Pavlovskaya (Sofya); Gennady Bezzubenkov (Tkachenko); Mikola (Evgeny Akimov). Philips. Excellent recording of this great opera, with fine work from the cast, especially Lutsiuk and Akimov.

Showboat. Kern. (A) Recording of 1951 MGM motion picture with Howard Keel, Kathryn Grayson, and William Warfield. (B) Conductor: McGlinn; London Sinfonietta. With Jerry Hadley, Frederica von Stade; Teresea Stratas. EMI. The second version is well-sung, especially by Stratas, but sounds as if it has an over-reliance on the synthesizer. The first version is also well-sung and features William Warfield's definitive recording of "Old Man River."

Sì. Mascagni. Margherita Vivian (Sì); Maura Nicoletti (Luciano); Antonio Comas (Cleo). Generally well sung and conducted recording.

Siberia. Giordano. C: Danilo Belardinelli; RAI Orchestra, Milan. Luisa Maragliano (Stephana); Amedea Zambon (Vassili); Walter Monachesi (Gleby). Allegro. Outstanding live radio recording of Giordano's opera. Maragliano and Zambon give impassioned performances and are in excellent vocal form.

1600 Pennsylvania Avenue. Bernstein. C: Kent Nagano; London Symphony Orchestra. Thomas Hampson (President); June Anderson (First Lady); Barbara Hendricks (Seena); Kenneth Tarver (Lud); Victor Acquah (Little Lud). Subtitled *A White House Cantata*, this is a superb recording of Bernstein/Alan Jay Lerner's sadly forgotten musical. Orchestrations are by Bernstein, Sid Ramin, and Hershy Kay. An excellent cast includes some well-known opera singers who appropriately tone themselves down (sometimes too much) for the material. Kenneth Tarver and Victor Acquah are also first-rate.

Die Soldaten. Zimmermann. C: Bernhard Kontarsky; Staatstheater Stuttgart. Nancy Shade (Marie); Michael Ebbecke (Stolzius); William Cochran (Despartes). Teldec.

Song of Norway. Grieg (Wright and Forrest). C: John Owen Edwards; Philharmonia Orchestra. Donald Maxwell (Grieg); David Rendall (Nordraak); Valerie Masterson (Nina); Diana Montague (Louisa). This includes all of the music from the operetta and is generally well done.

Story of a Real Man. Prokofiev. C: Mark Ermier; Orchestra of Bolshoi Theater. With: Glatirava Deomido. Chandos.

Street Scene. Weill. **(A)** C: Maurice Abravanel. Polyna Storka (Anna); Anne Jeffreys (Rose); Brian Sullivan (Sam); Hope Emerson (Emma). Highlights from the original Broadway cast recording of 1947. **(B)** C: John Mauceri; Scottish Opera Orchestra. Josephine Barstow (Anna); Samuel Ramey (Frank); Angelina Reaux (Rose); Jerry Hadley (Sam); Kurt Ollmann (Harry). London. Complete, well-sung version includes dialogue sequences as well.

Streetcar Named Desire. Previn. C: Andre Previn; San Francisco Opera Orchestra. Renee Fleming (Blanche); Rodney Gilfry (Stanley); Elizabeth Futral (Stella); Anthony Dean Griffey (Mitch). Deutsche Grammophon. Previn himself conducts this live recording of his opera, thus guaranteeing the composer's intentions are delivered for better or worse. Good cast doesn't hurt.

Sunday in the Park with George. Sondheim. Mandy Patinkin (George); Bernadette Peters (Dot). RCA. "Singers" like Patinkin and Peters do not much help this recording of one of Sondheim's weakest musicals.

Suor Angelica. Puccini. C: Lorin Maazel; Philharmonia Orchestra. Renata Scotto (Angelica); Marilyn Horne (Princess); Ileona Cotrubas (Genovieffo). Great cast and first-rate recording.

Susannah. Floyd. C: Kent Nagano; Orchestre de l'Opéra de Lyon. Cheryl Studer (Susannah); Samuel Ramey (Olin Blitch); Jerry Hadley (Sam Polk); Kenn Chester (Little Bat). Virgin. Good but somehow not quite top-notch recording of the opera; Studer and Ramey are fine. It's worth seeking out the original version with Phyllis Curtin as Susannah.

Sweeney Todd. Sondheim. C: Andrew Litton; New York Philharmonic. Patti Lupone (Mrs. Lovett); George Hearn (Sweeney Todd); Neil Patrick Harris (Toby); Audra McDonald (Old Woman). Excellent live concert version of Sondheim's best work has all the music from the show and is very well sung.

Sweet Bye and Bye. Beeson. C: Russell Patterson; Kansas City Lyric Theatre Orchestra. Noel Rogers (Sister Rose); Robert Owen Jones (Billy Wilcox); Carolyne James (Mother Rainey). Rather good recording of this opera, with a talented cast giving their all.

Il tabarro. Puccini. C: Lamberto Gardelli; Maggio Musicale Fiorentina. Renata Tebaldi (Georgetta); Mario Del Monaco (Michel); Robert Merrill (Luigi). A must-have for any fan of Puccini's verismo masterpiece.

The Telephone. Menotti. C: Stephen Rogers Radcliffe; New York Chamber Ensemble. Jeanne Ommerle (Lucy); Richard Holmes (Ben). Nice recording of Menotti's one-act comedy.

Tender Land. Copland. **(A)** C: Philip Brunelle; Orchestra of the Plymouth Music Series, MN. Elizabeth Corneaux (Laurie); Janis Hardy (Ma); LeRoy Lehr (Grandpa); Dan Dressen (Martin); James Bohn (Top). Virgin. **(B)** C: Murry Sidlin; Third Angle New Music Ensemble. Suzan Hanson (Laurie); Milagro Vargas (Ma); Richard Zeller (Grandpa); Robert MacNeil (Martin); Douglas Webster (Top). Koch. The first employs Copland's original orchestration and is superior to the second, an authorized "chamber" version of the opera which employs conductor Sidlin's reduced orchestra and arrangements. Both versions are very well sung, however.

Thérèse. Massenet. **(A)** C: Richard Bonynge; New Philharmonia Orchestra. Huguette Tourangeau (Thérèse); Ryland Davis (Armand); Louis Quilico (André). **(B)** C: Gerd Albrecht. Agnes Baltsa (Therese); Francisco Araiza (Armand). The first version is extrremely well-conducted, with a fine Tourangeau and a superb Davies. The second is also creditable, although the tempo is occasionally slow; on the plus side, Baltsa gives a little more than Tourangeau and makes the ending more moving.

Therese Raquin. Picker. C: Graeme Jenkins; Dallas Opera Orchestra. Diana Soviero (Lisette); Sara Fulgoni (Therese); Gordon Gietz (Camille); Richard Bernstein (Laurent). Chandos.

Tiefland. D'Albert. C: Marek Janowski; Münchner Rundfunkorchester. Eva Marton (Marta); Rene Kollo (Pedro); Kurt Moll (Sebastiano). Well-conducted and very well sung by all.

Titanic. Yeston. Original Broadway cast recording (Highlights). The mostly "pop" voices of the cast, while good and professional, take away from the often superior music.

Tosca. Puccini. C: Herbert von Karajan; Weiner Philharmoniker. Leontyne Price (Tosca); Giuseppe di Stefano (Cavaradossi); Giuseppe Taddei (Scarpia). Although Price may not be the perfect choice for a verismo piece, her voice is beautiful and she comes through quite expressively in the climactic scenes. Di Stefano shows some strain but is otherwise excellent. Taddei is on the money.

Die tote Stadt. Korngold. C: Erich Leindorfs; Munich Radio Orchestra. Rene Kollo (Paul); Carol Neblett (Marietta); Benjamin Luxon (Frank); Hermann Prey (Fritz). Neblett is superb and Kollo, although his voice is strained, sings with great feeling. Very well-conducted.

Treemonisha. Joplin. C: Gunther Schuller; Houston Grand Opera Orchestra. Carmen Balthrop (Treemonisha); Betty Allen (Monisha); Willard White (Ned); Curtis Rayam (Remus). Recording of Houston Grand Opera production; 1975. Joplin could not have been better served than by the cast of this recording. Schuller also arranged and orchestrated the music.

Troilus and Cressida. Walton. C: Richard Hickox; English Northern Philharmonia. Judith Howarth (Cressida); Arthur Davies (Troilus); Alan Opie (Diomede); Clive Bayles (Calkas); Nigel Robson (Pandorus); Yvonne Howard (Evadne). Chandos. Excellent recording with fine cast, especially Howarth and Davies.

Trouble in Tahiti. Bernstein. C: Arthur Winograd; MGM Orchestra. Beverly Wolff (Dinah); David Atkinson (Sam). Good recording of Bernstein's one-act opera in seven scenes before he incorporated it into *A Quiet Place.*

Turandot. Busoni. C: Kent Nagano; Orchestre de l'Opéra de Lyon. Mechthild Gessendorf (Turandot); Franz-Josef Selig (Altoum); Stefan Dahlberg (Kalaf). Virgin.

Turandot. Puccini. C: Leinsdorf. Birgit Nilsson (Turandot); Jussi Bjorling (Calaf); Renata Tebaldi (Lui); Giorgio Tozzi (Timur). Highly interesting recording of this opera. Tebaldi and Tozzi come off best, although Neilsen is certainly not bad. Bjorling is a little rough in spots — but what a voice!

Turn of the Screw. Britten. C: Steuart Bedford; Aldeburgh Festical Ensemble. Philip Longridge (Quint); Felicity Lott (Governess); Sam Pay (Miles); Eileen Hulse (Flora); Phyllis Connan (Mrs. Grose); Nadine Secunde (Miss Jessel). Collins. More than acceptable version of the opera; well-sung by all.

Vanessa. Barber. C: Dimitri Mitropoulos; Metropolitan Opera Orchestra. Eleanor Steber (Vanessa); Rosalind Elias (Erika); Regina Resnick (Old Baroness); Nicolai Gedda (Anatol); Giorgio Tozzi (Old Doctor).

View from the Bridge. Bolcom. C: Dennis Russell Davies; Lyric Opera of Chicago. Kim Josephson (Eddie); Catherine Malfitano (Beatrice); Gregory Turay (Rodolpho); Juliana Rambaldi (Catherine); Mark McCrary (Marco); Timothy Nolan (Alfieri). New World. Well-done and well-acted, for what it is.

La vida breve. Falla. C: Rafael Fruhbeck de Burgos; Orquesta Nacionale Espana. Victoria de los Angeles (Solud); Carlos Cossytta (Poca).

Village Romeo and Juliet. Delius. C: Klauspeter Seibel; Kiel Philharmonic Orchestra. Karsten Ruá (Sali); Eva-Christine Reimer (Vrenchen); Klaus Wallprecht (Dark Fiddler). Generally well-sung and well-done if perhaps too leisurely paced at times. Sung in German. There have been several other recordings although they may be hard to find.

Violanta. Korngold. C: Marek Janowski; Munich Radio Orchestra. Eva Marton (Violanta); Siegfried Jerusalem (Alfanso); Walter Berry (Simone). Excellent, very well-conducted recording with Marton and Jerusalem in top form.

Voss. Meale. C: Stuart Challender; Sydney Symphony Orchestra. Geoffrey Chard (Voss); Marilyn Richardson (Laura); Gregory Tomlinson (Harry); Robert Eddie (Judd). Philips. Excellent, beautifully sung recording of Meale's masterpiece.

War and Peace. Prokofiev. C: Mstislav Rostropovitch; Orchestre National de France. Lajos Miller (Prince Andrei); Galina Vichnievskaia (Natasha); Katherine Ciesinski (Sonia); Wieslaw Ochman (Pierre); Nicolai Gedda (Anatole); Eduard Tumagian (Napoleon). Erato. Excellent recording with especially fine work from Miller, Ochman, and Tumagian.

A Water Bird Talk. Argento. C: Richard Auldon Clark; Manhattan Chamber Orchestra. Vern Sutton (Lecturer). Newport. Excellent recording of Argento's short opera. Sutton does a fine job as the lecturer and has impeccable diction to boot.

Where the Wild Things Are. Knussen. C: Oliver Knussen; Glyndebourne Festival Orchestra. With: Rosemary Hardy; Mary King.

Wind Remains. Bowles. C: Jonathan Sheffer; Eos Ensemble. Carl Halvorson (tenor); Lucy Schaufer (mezzo). Catalyst. Recorded live at Alice Tully Hall and included on *The Music of Paul Bowles* CD. Well-sung and conducted.

Wozzeck. Berg. C: Claudio Abbado; Wiener Philharmoniker. Franz Grundheber (Wozzeck); Hildegard Behrens (Marie); Philip Langridge (Andres); Heinz Zednick (Captain). Live 1987 recording from Vienna State Opera with an excellent cast.

Wreckers. Smyth. C: Odaline de la Martinez; BBC Philharmonic. With Anne-Marie Owens; Justin Lavender; Peter Sid-

hom; David Wilson-Johnson. Conifer. Fine recording of Smyth's best-known opera.

Das Wunder der Heliane. Korngold. C: John Mauceri; RSO Berlin. Anna Tornova-Sintow (Heliane); Hartmut Welker (Der Herrscher); John David de Haan (Der Frernde). Sumptuous recording of Korngold's opera.

Wuthering Heights. Herrmann. C: Bernard Herrmann; Pro Arte Orchestra. Moraj Beaton (Cathy); Donald Bell (Heathcliff); John Kitchiner (Hindley); Pamela Bowden (Isabella); Joseph Ward (Edgar). Fine recording, conducted by the composer; sung with conviction by all.

X: The Life and Times of Malcolm X. Davis. C: William Henry Curry; Orchestra of St. Luke's. With: Eugene Perry; Thomas J. Young; Priscilla Baskerville.

Zaza. Leoncavallo. C: Tito Petralia; Orchestra Sinfonica di Milano della RAI. Clara Petrella (Zaza); Giuseppe Campora (Milio); Tito Turtura (Cascart). Live 1969 Turin recording. Petrella is excellent; Campora sings with expressiveness and has a flavorful voice although he strains painfully for high notes; Turtura is more on the mark as Cascart.

Note: Also consulted were private recordings and broadcasts of such operas as *Billy Budd*; *The Great Gatsby*; *Ghosts of Versailles*; *Christmas Carol*; *Legend of the Invisible City of Kitezh*; *Lizzie Borden*; *Mary, Queen of Scots*; *Paul Bunyan*; *Simon Bolivar*; *Sly*; *Voice of Ariadne*; *Wuthering Heights* (Floyd); and *Bilby's Doll*.

Bibliography

Books

Beecham, Sir Thomas. *Frederick Delius.* New York: Knopf, 1961.

Burton, Humphrey. *Leonard Bernstein.* New York: Doubleday, 1994.

Carpenter, Humphrey. *Benjamin Britten: A Biography.* New York: Scribners, 1992.

Carroll, Brendan G. *The Last Prodigy: A Biography of Erich Wolfgang Korngold.* Portland: Amadeus Press.

Copland, Aaron. *What to Listen for in Music.* New York: McGraw-Hill, 1939; 1957.

Cross, Milton. *Complete Stories of the Great Operas.* New York: Doubleday, 1957.

Dizikes, John. *Opera in America: A Cultural History.* New Haven: Yale University Press, 1993.

Flury, Roger. *Pietro Mascagni: A Bio-Bibliography.* Westport, Conn.: Greenwood Press; 2001.

Gordon, Eric A. *Mark the Music: The Life and Work of Marc Blitzstein.* New York: St. Martin's, 1989.

Greenfield, Howard. *Caruso.* New York: Putnam's, 1983.

Harding, James. *Massenet.* London: J.M. Dent and Sons, Ltd., 1970.

Holden, Amanda (editor). *The Viking Opera Guide.* New York: Viking, 1993.

Irvine, Demar. *Massenet.* Portland: Amadeus Press, 1994.

Jefferson, Alan. *Delius.* New York: Octagon Books, 1972.

Kennedy, Michael. *Richard Strauss: Man, Musician, Enigma.* Cambridge: Cambridge University Press, 1999.

Kirk, Elise. *American Opera.* Chicago: University of Illinois Press, 2001.

Kobbé, Gustave. *The Complete Opera Book.* New York: Putnam's, 1935. *Note:* More recent editions were also consulted.

Major, Norma. *Joan Sutherland.* Boston: Little, Brown, 1987.

Mallach, Alan. *Pietro Mascagni and His Operas.* Boston: Northeastern University Press, 2002.

McSpadden, J. Walker. *Operas and Musical Comedies.* New York: Crowell, 1946.

Nice, David. *Prokofiev: From Russia to the West; 1891–1935.* New Haven: Yale University Press, 2003.

Phillips-Matz, Mary Jane. *Puccini: A Biography.* Boston: Northeastern University Press, 2002.

Pollack, Howard. *Aaron Copland: The Life and Work of an Uncommon Man.* New York: Holt, 1999.

Schoell, William. *Heartbreaker: The Dorothy Dandridge Story.* Greensboro: Avisson Press, 2002.

Schonberg, Harold C. *The Lives of the Great Composers.* New York: W.W. Norton, 1970.

Secrest, Meryle. *Stephen Sondheim: A Life.* New York: Alfred A. Knopf, 1998.

Stivender, David. *Pietro Mascagni.* Pro Arte.

Sutherland, Joan. *Authobiography of Joan Sutherland: A Prima Donna's Progress.* Washington, D.C.: Regnery, 1997.

Vogel, Jaroslav. *Leoš Janáček.* New York: Norton, 1981.

Waters, Edward N. *Victor Herbert: A Life in Music.* New York: Macmillan, 1955.

Librettos

(Occasionally librettos other than the ones packaged with recordings were consulted. A list of these follows.)

Die ägyptische Helena. Strauss. Berlin: Adolph Fürstner, 1928. New York: Ricordi, 1928.

Arabella. Strauss. New York: Boosey & Hawkes, 1933.

Ariadne auf Naxos. Strauss. New York: Boosey & Hawkes, 1940.

Ballad of Baby Doe. Moore. New York: Program Pub. Co., 1956. Revised 1958.

Billy Budd. Britten. London: Boosey & Hawkes, 1951.

Bomarzo. Ginastera. New York: Boosey & Hawkes, 1967.

Brigadoon. Loewe. New York: Coward-McCann, 1947.

Candide. Bernstein. New York: Random House, 1957.

Carmina Burana. Orff. New York: Associated Music Publishers, 1953; Mainz: Schott, 1937.

Carousel. Rodgers. New York: Alfred A. Knopf, 1945.

Cendrillon. Massenet. New York: Souvenir Book Publishers.

Cleopatra. Massenet. New York: G. Schirmer, 1915.

Daphne. Strauss. London: Boosey & Hawkes, 1938; 1965.

Death in Venice. Britten. London: Faber Music, 1973.

Elegie für junge Liebende. Henze. Mainz: B. Schott, 1961.

L'Enfant et les sortilèges. Ravel. Bryn Maw, Pa.: Elkan-Vogel (Theodore Presser), 1925; 1932.

La fanciulla del West. Puccini. Milan: G. Ricordi, 1910; New York: Schirmer, 1910.

Fanny. Rome. New York: Random House, 1955.

Fiery Angel. Prokofiev. Booklet prepared for performance by Kirov Opera at the Met; July 1992.

Francesca da Rimini. Zandonia. New York: Schirmer, 1914. Met Opera Collection (G. Ricordi 1914).

Die Frau ohne Schatten. Strauss. Berlin: Fürstner, 1916; New York: Boosey & Hawkes, 1943.

From the House of the Dead. Janáček. Booklet commissioned by New York Philharmonic for first U.S. concert performance on March, 1983, Avery Fisher Hall, Lincoln Center, NYC.

Great Gatsby. Harbison. New York: G. Schirmer, 1999.

Intermezzo. Strauss. London: Boosey & Hawkes, 1924.

Königskinder. Humperdinck. New York: F. Rullman, 1910.

Louise. Charpentier. New York: Program Publishing Co., 1900.

Madame Sans-Gêne. Giordano. Milan: Sonzogno, 1914; New York: Schirmer, 1915.

Mathis der Maler. Hindemith. New York: B. Schott, 1935.

Mary, Queen of Scots. Musgrave. Kent: Novello, 1976.

Natoma. Herbert. New York: G. Schirmer, 1911.

Of Mice and Men. Floyd. New York: Belwin-Mills, 1971.

Peter Grimes. Britten. London: Hawkes & Son, 1945; 1961.

Rape of Lucretia. Britten. London: Boosey & Hawkes, 1946.

La rondine. New York: G. Ricordi, 1917.

Saint of Bleecker Street. Menotti. New York: G. Schirmer, 1954.

Salome. Strauss. Berlin: Adolf Fürstner, 1905; New York: Boosey & Hawkes, 1943.

Siberia. Giordano. New York: C.E. Burden: 1903.

Susannah. Floyd. New York: Boosey & Hawkes, 1956.

Il tabarro. Puccini. Melville, N.Y.: Belwin-Mills, 1956. (G. Ricordi 1918.)

Tiefland. D'Albert. New York: Boosey & Co., 1908.

Tosca. Puccini. New York: Fredd Rullman, Inc., 1900.

Die tote Stadt. Korngold. London: Schott; 1920 and Melville, N.Y.: Belwin-Mills, 1975.

Turandot. Puccini. New York: Souvenir Book Publishers, 1926.

Turn of the Screw. London: Boosey & Hawkes, 1955.

Village Romeo & Juliet. Delius. New York: Boosey & Hawkes, 1952.

Violanta. Korngold. New York: Ricordi, 1916.

Wozzeck. Berg. Berlin: Universal Editions, 1923.

Zaza. Leoncavallo. Milan: Sonzogno, 1900; New York: Schirmer, 1919.

Vocal Scores

Comedy on the Bridge. Martinů. New York: Boosey & Hawkes, 1951.

Face on the Barroom Floor. Mollicone. New York: Belwin-Mills, 1979.

I gioiella della Madonna. Wolf-Ferrari. New York: G. Schirmer, 1911.

Irmelin. Delius. London: Hawkes & Son, Ltd., 1953.

Maddalena. Prokofiev. London: Boosey & Hawkes, 1979.

Magic Fountain. Delius. London: Boosey & Hawkes, 1979.

Markheim. Floyd. New York: Boosey & Hawkes, 1966.

Merry Mount. Hanson. New York: Harms, Inc., 1934.

Moses und Aron. Schoenberg. New York: B. Schott, 1957.

Mother of Us All. Thomson. Chester, N.Y.: G. Schirmer, Inc., 1947.

Pilgrim's Progress. Vaughn Williams. London: Oxford University Press, 1951.

A Quiet Place (incorporating *Trouble in Tahiti*). Bernstein. New York: Jalni Publications, Boosey & Hawkes, 1984.

Rape of Lucretia. Britten. London: Boosey & Hawkes, 1946.

Regina. Blitzstein. New York: Chappell and Co., 1954

Riders to the Sea. Vaughn Williams. Oxford: Oxford University Press, 1936; 1964.

Sappho. Massenet. Paris: Heugel & Co., 1897; 1909.

Song of Norway. Grieg (Wright and Forrest). New York: Chappell and Co., 1944.

Street Scene. Weill. Milwaukee: Hal Leonard, 1948.

Titanic. Yeston. Port Charles, N.Y.: Cherry Lane Music, 1997.

Websites

www.amcoz.com.au
www.andante.com
www.boosey.com
www.cedillerecords.org
www.chester-novello.com
www.henrymollicone.com
www.highandlowny.tripod.com
www.mascagni.org.
www.musicassociatesofamerica.com
www.newyorkmetro.com
www.operaam.org/encore
www.operaamerica.org
www.schirmer.com
www.usoperaweb.com

Index